EURIPIDES

VI

LCL 495

EURIPIDES

BACCHAE
IPHIGENIA AT AULIS
RHESUS

EDITED AND TRANSLATED BY

DAVID KOVACS

HARVARD UNIVERSITY PRESS
CAMBRIDGE, MASSACHUSETTS
LONDON, ENGLAND
2002

First published 2002

LOEB CLASSICAL LIBRARY® is a registered trademark
of the President and Fellows of Harvard College

Library of Congress Control Number 2002068725
CIP data available from the Library of Congress

ISBN 978-0-674-99601-4

*Composed in ZephGreek and ZephText by
Technologies 'N Typography, Merrimac, Massachusetts.
Printed on acid-free paper and bound by
The Maple-Vail Book Manufacturing Group*

CONTENTS

PREFACE

This volume completes the edition of Euripides' extant plays. It has the same format as the others, and the Introduction to Volume One should be consulted for an explanation of my editorial policy. In a forthcoming book called *Euripidea Tertia* I explain some of my editorial choices and defend some of the translations adopted here.

I have several debts of gratitude to acknowledge. I began working on *Iphigenia in Aulis* in 1996–7 during a leave sponsored by the Division of Research of the National Endowment for the Humanities, but the main work on the volume and its predecessor was accomplished in 2000–1. I am extremely grateful both to my own university, which gave me a semester's leave, and to the Master and Fellows of Trinity College, Cambridge, who elected me to a visiting fellowship. Trinity's generosity and that of the Earhart Foundation allowed me to spend an entire year in Cambridge. Cambridge classicists are generous with their time, and I wish particularly to thank James Diggle, Roger Dawe, Eric Handley, and Pat Easterling for helpful discussion, as well as Charles Willink, who came up from London several times to discuss textual matters with me. *Iphigenia in Aulis* also benefited from an invitation from Martin West to join him in offering a seminar on the play in Oxford in 1997, when I was in residence there. My thanks to him and to the other participants. Margaretta Fulton's sharp eye and keen ear deserve credit for making these volumes more readable.

George Goold was an inspiring teacher of mine at Harvard, and his influence continued when as General Editor of the Loeb series he gave me, like so many of us doing Loeb volumes, the benefit of his immense learning, his keen sense of style, and his kindness and humanity. This volume is dedicated to his memory.

University of Virginia   David Kovacs

ABBREVIATIONS

BICS	*Bulletin of the Institute of Classical Studies, London*
CQ	*Classical Quarterly*
G&R	*Greece and Rome*
JHS	*Journal of Hellenic Studies*
QUCC	*Quaderni Urbinati di Cultura Classica*
YCS	*Yale Classical Studies*

BACCHAE

INTRODUCTION

In 408 B.C. Euripides went to live in Macedon as a guest of the Macedonian king Archelaus. In the spring of 406 news reached Athens that he had died, and Sophocles paid his respects to his great rival in the tragic art by dressing in black himself and bringing on his chorus in the opening ceremonies of the Dionysia without the customary garlands. Among Euripides' effects were three tragedies, *Bacchae*, *Iphigenia at Aulis*, and a third tragedy now lost, that were put on for the first time, probably in 405, by Euripides the Younger (his son or nephew) and crowned with a first prize.

In *Bacchae* the poet has dramatized one of several stories about the resistance offered to the worship of Dionysus when the god was first introduced into Greece. We know less than we would like about Dionysus in the classical period and before, but thanks to the Linear B tablets we can be sure that his worship goes back to the Bronze Age and the palace civilization of Mycenae and Pylos that produced the tablets. As portrayed in *Bacchae*, our earliest substantial witness, it was a religion of ecstasy, centered upon the experience of oneness with the god and with the *thiasos* (congregation or coven) of his worshipers. It seems to have provided, at stated times of the year, a release from conventional restraint, particularly for women, whose role in home and community was strictly circumscribed, allowing a brief period of truancy, not unlike Carnival, that paradoxically helped to maintain the usual order of things. Dionysus is credited with introducing viticulture and the liberating effect of wine. At Athens his two principal festivals, the City Dionysia in early spring and the Lenaea in late winter, became the venue for tragedy and comedy. Some scholars have seen a link between the liberation from restraint offered by Dionysus and the assumption of other roles and personalities that makes drama what it is, and the earliest evidence we have of enactment by impersonation (drama) is the Dionysiac festivals of the sixth century B.C.

In myth Dionysus' birthplace was Thebes, where his mother Semele was a princess, the daughter of Cadmus. Zeus became her lover, and Hera in jealousy played a deadly trick on her, persuading her to ask Zeus to promise her a favor, and when he had promised, to require the god to appear to her as he does to his immortal wife. Zeus could not refuse to honor his promise although he knew that the lightning that accompanies his divine presence would be fatal to his mortal beloved. But when Semele died, burnt to cinder by the thunderbolt, he rescued their child Dionysus and carried him to term in his own body, concealing him in his thigh. Dionysus came to birth a second time not in Greece but in Asia, and promptly went about winning over the population to his ecstatic worship.

At the beginning of the play the god has come back for the first time to Greece and to his native Thebes, bringing with him a band of Lydian worshipers, who make up the Chorus. But his mother's sisters will not receive the god, and they claim that the tale of Semele's divine lover was a lie told to cover ordinary unchastity, and that this was why Zeus blasted her with the thunderbolt. Dionysus makes short work of this opposition by driving the sisters in madness out of the city to Mount Cithaeron and with them all the women of Thebes. He departs to join them, his unwilling worshipers, and tells the Chorus of his willing worshipers to come and sing before the palace of Thebes, represented by the *skene*. The chorus sing a hymn of great beauty, telling of Dionysus' birth and praising the blessedness of his worship.

But the king of Thebes is young Pentheus, whose grandfather Cadmus has stepped down in his favor. He has heard while abroad of the departure of the women for the mountains, and believing that it is all an excuse for licentious behavior he storms into Thebes to put a stop to the work of the Lydian stranger (Dionysus in human form) who he hears is behind all this. When he finds his grandfather and the prophet Teiresias setting out to worship the god, a debate ensues in which Teiresias lauds the god's powers and Cadmus tells his grandson to respect the gods' laws but Pentheus refuses to listen. He sends servants off to capture the Lydian stranger. When the servant returns with his captive, Pentheus, with ill-concealed fascination, questions the disguised god about his rites and the blessedness they confer but is told that they are secret. The interview ends with Dionysus being escorted inside to be imprisoned at the palace.

Pentheus' attempts to imprison Dionysus are frustrated: the god shatters his prison with an earthquake and reappears, still in human disguise. He calmly tells the agitated king that someone is coming to tell him of events on the mountains. The bearer of news is a herdsman, and his report contradicts Pentheus' expectations in two respects. First, he reports that Pentheus' suspicions about licentiousness among the bacchants are unfounded. Second, the women are performing miraculous deeds, suckling wild animals and uncovering springs of water, wine, or milk by sticking their bacchic wands into the ground. The wonders continue when one of the other herdsman proposes that they capture Pentheus' mother Agave. This stings the bacchants into action, and they nearly kill the herdsmen before proceeding to dismember cattle and to vent their rage on the innocent inhabitants of nearby settlements, whose weapons they miraculously repel. The messenger draws the moral: best to come to terms with a god who can produce such miracles and is also giver of wine.

Pentheus, instead of being impressed, is enraged against the women and is on the point of launching a military expedition against them when a strange thing happens. At line 810—after an interjection I have translated "Stop!"—Dionysus makes, and Pentheus accepts, the suggestion that before attacking the women he should go and spy on them. The only way to do this, he is told, is to dress as a bacchant. After some hesitation the king makes the extraordinary decision to put himself in the hands of the Lydian stranger and be led by him to the mountains. After a choral ode Pentheus, now dazed and seeing double, is led forth by Dionysus. The Chorus call on the god to exact his vengeance.

A second messenger reports the result, how Pentheus tried to spy on the bacchants, how Dionysus set him atop a tall fir tree and called on his bacchants to take their revenge on him, and how the maenads, led by his mother

Agave, dislodged him from his perch and dismembered him in the deluded belief that he was lion.

Agave returns to Thebes, her son's head impaled on her bacchic wand, still under the delusion that it is the head of a lion. Then Cadmus arrives with the remains of his grandson's body, which he has collected from Cithaeron. Agave comes to her senses in conversation with him and realizes what a horrible crime she has committed. Our only copy of the play, a manuscript of the fourteenth century, is defective at the end of the play, having suffered extensive omissions at two points. But this much is plain, that Dionysus appears, upbraids Thebes for its unbelief, and prophesies that Cadmus and his wife must go into exile, become snakes, and lead a barbarian horde into Greece. The god justifies his cruel revenge by saying that the unbelief of his family had insulted him. The play ends with a lament, probably after the departure of Dionysus, between Cadmus and Agave and then some lines Euripides had used to end his *Alcestis, Andromache,* and *Helen*: "What heaven sends has many shapes, and many things the gods accomplish against our expectation. What men look for is not brought to pass, but a god finds a way to achieve the unexpected. Such was the outcome of this story."

When it was confidently believed in all scholarly quarters that Euripides was a skeptic and a mocker of religion, this tale of the spectacular punishment of impiety evoked various puzzled responses. The most extreme was that of A. W. Verrall, who supposed that beneath the ostensible action of a god wreaking his vengeance the cleverer members of the audience were supposed to pick up subtle clues that the supposed Dionysus was no god at all but only a human charlatan. Others maintained that the play was more complex than it seems, and that the audience were meant to be alienated or disquieted by the magnitude of Dionysus' revenge and thereby led to think of alternatives to the anthropomorphic religion of the Greeks. For others the conclusion seemed inescapable that Euripides had undergone some kind of conversion in the wilds of Macedonia, and that this play was his recantation. It is, however, no longer a universally accepted belief that Euripides was a skeptic, and we need not try so hard to construe the play as the work of one. On the view of Euripides set forth in the other introductions in this edition there is a basic continuity between his earlier and later plays: no one who takes seriously the theological dimension of *Medea* or *Hippolytus* or *Heracles* should be surprised by *Bacchae*.

Euripides took some pains to ensure that the applicability of this story is as wide as possible. In theory a story of resistance to a new god might be based around a simple opposition to what is new, a conservatism in clinging to the familiar. The resister might simply be ignorant that the new god he is opposing is really a god. The effect of such a play would be quite different from our *Bacchae*, and its implicit warning would extend only to those who were encountering new forms of religion and new divinities. But in the play we have, Euripides has gone to some trouble, and accepted some inconsistency, to make Pentheus an opponent not merely of new religion but of religion *tout court*. Both through the Chorus and through Cadmus and Teiresias he suggests that although Dionysus is a new divinity, his religion is old in itself. The Chorus in 71–2 say "I shall hymn Dionysus with the songs hallowed by use and wont." In the dialogue between Cadmus and Teiresias we find disparagement of "despising the gods, when one is a mortal," "playing the sophist where the gods are concerned," and ignoring "the traditions we have received from our fathers, old as time itself," traditions "no argument will overthrow, whatever subtleties have been invented by deep thinkers." The Chorus pointedly recommend keeping one's thoughts "far from men of excess," and accepting "what the simple folk believe and practice." The third stasimon, particularly 882–96, insists again that the worship of Dionysus be seen as merely one instance of age-old sanctities, coeval with time, grounded in nature, and deeper than human cleverness. (This perhaps explains why his worship is blended with that of the Mountain Mother and the Corybantes.) There is an obvious reason for Euripides to do this: Pentheus is to be an emblematic *theomachos* (fighter against gods), not merely someone who is opposed to a particular new divinity. His situation is generalized so that it fits more nearly the situation of Euripides' audience, and the young king's view of the origin of Dionysiac religion is parallel to the rationalistic strain of thought in the late fifth century, where belief in gods was explained as arising from natural causes. *Bacchae* is a fable for Euripides' own day.

Pentheus' relation to maenadism also requires comment. Particularly in need of explanation is the strange *volte-face* that he makes at line 810, abandoning his resolve to call out the army against the maenads and agreeing to go in disguise to spy them out. Certainly this is a highly irrational move: Pentheus puts himself in the power of someone he has hitherto considered his enemy, and the text gives few clues for understanding this decision. It has been suggested that Pentheus, believing that the women on the mountain are having sex with strangers, wants to watch them copulate, but there is no clear evidence of this in the text, and furthermore a Pentheus crippled by skopophilia would lack the representative quality we look for in a tragic hero. Rather, to understand Pentheus' change of heart here we must recall his earlier fascination (465–507) with the mystical bliss that Dionysus promises. Pentheus has a *secretorum spectandorum cupido*, a desire to witness what is secret; the secrets in question, though, are not those of sex but of a religion that Pentheus both rejects and cannot wholly disbelieve in.

SELECT BIBLIOGRAPHY

Editions

E. R. Dodds (Oxford, 1960²).
J. Roux (Paris, 1970–2).
E. C. Kopff (Leipzig, 1982).
R. Seaford (Warminster, 1996).

Literary Criticism

M. Arthur, "The Choral Odes of the *Bacchae* of Euripides," *YCS* 22 (1972), 145–79.
J. Gregory, "Some Aspects of Seeing in Euripides' *Bacchae*," *G&R* 32 (1985), 23–31.
V. Leinieks, *The City of Dionysus: A Study of Euripides' Bakchai* (Stuttgart and Leipzig, 1996).
J. R. March, "Euripides' *Bakchai*: a Reconsideration in the Light of Vase-Paintings," *BICS* 36 (1989), 33–65.
H. Oranje, *Euripides' Bacchae: The Play and Its Audience* (Leiden, 1984).

B. Seidensticker, "Sacrificial Ritual in the *Bacchae*," in G. W. Bowersock et al. edd., *Arktouros: Hellenic Studies Presented to Bernard Knox* (Berlin, 1979), pp. 181–90.

O. Taplin, *Greek Tragedy in Action* (Berkeley and Los Angeles, 1978), chs. 4–9.

Dramatis Personae

ΔΙΟΝΥΣΟΣ	DIONYSUS
ΧΟΡΟΣ	CHORUS of Asian bacchants
ΤΕΙΡΕΣΙΑΣ	TEIRESIAS, Theban prophet
ΚΑΔΜΟΣ	CADMUS, grandfather of Pentheus
ΠΕΝΘΕΥΣ	PENTHEUS, king of Thebes
ΘΕΡΑΠΩΝ	SERVANT of Pentheus
ΑΓΓΕΛΟΣ	MESSENGER, a herdsman
ΑΓΓΕΛΟΣ Β	SECOND MESSENGER, Pentheus' attendant
ΑΓΑΥΗ	AGAVE, mother of Pentheus

A Note on Staging

The *skene* represents the palace of Pentheus in Thebes. In front of it is the tomb of Semele, possibly represented by the altar that was a permanent part of the *orchestra*. Eisodos A leads to Theban locations such as Teiresias' house and place of augury, Eisodos B through the other side of the city (including the prison) to foreign parts and Mount Cithaeron.

ΒΑΚΧΑΙ

ΔΙΟΝΥΣΟΣ

Ἥκω Διὸς παῖς τήνδε Θηβαίαν χθόνα
Διόνυσος, ὃν τίκτει ποθ᾽ ἡ Κάδμου κόρη
Σεμέλη λοχευθεῖσ᾽ ἀστραπηφόρῳ πυρί·
μορφὴν δ᾽ ἀμείψας ἐκ θεοῦ βροτησίαν
5 πάρειμι Δίρκης νάμαθ᾽ Ἰσμηνοῦ θ᾽ ὕδωρ.
ὁρῶ δὲ μητρὸς μνῆμα τῆς κεραυνίας
τόδ᾽ ἐγγὺς οἴκων καὶ δόμων ἐρείπια
τυφόμενα Δίου πυρὸς ἔτι ζῶσαν φλόγα,
ἀθάνατον Ἥρας μητέρ᾽ εἰς ἐμὴν ὕβριν.
10 αἰνῶ δὲ Κάδμον, ἄβατον ὃς πέδον τόδε
τίθησι, θυγατρὸς σηκόν· ἀμπέλου δέ νιν
πέριξ ἐγὼ ᾽κάλυψα βοτρυώδει χλόῃ.
    λιπὼν δὲ Λυδῶν τοὺς πολυχρύσους γύας
Φρυγῶν τε, Περσῶν ἡλιοβλήτους πλάκας
15 Βάκτριά τε τείχη τήν τε δύσχιμον χθόνα
Μήδων ἐπελθὼν Ἀραβίαν τ᾽ εὐδαίμονα
Ἀσίαν τε πᾶσαν ἣ παρ᾽ ἁλμυρὰν ἅλα
κεῖται μιγάσιν Ἕλλησι βαρβάροις θ᾽ ὁμοῦ
πλήρεις ἔχουσα καλλιπυργώτους πόλεις,

---

14 Περσῶν Bothe: Π- θ᾽ C

BACCHAE

Enter by Eisodos A DIONYSUS.

DIONYSUS

To this land of Thebes I have come, I Dionysus, son of Zeus: Cadmus' daughter Semele, midwived by the lightning fire, once gave birth to me.[1] I have exchanged my divine form for a mortal one and have come to the waters of Dirce and Ismenus.[2] I see here by the palace the tomb of my lightning-slain mother and the ruins of her house, smouldering with the still-living flames of Zeus's fire: thus Hera's violence against my mother lives on forever. I praise Cadmus, who made this ground sacred and untrodden, a holy spot for his daughter. And I have covered it all around with the clustering growth of grapevines.

Leaving behind the gold-rich lands of the Lydians and Phrygians, I made my way to the sun-drenched plains of the Persians, the fortifications of Bactria, the harsh country of the Medes, prosperous Arabia, and all that part of Asia Minor that lies along the briny sea and possesses fine-towered cities full of Greeks and outlanders mingled

---

[1] Semele, daughter of Cadmus, was loved by Zeus. For the story see the Introduction.

[2] The two rivers of Thebes.

20 ἐς τήνδε πρῶτον ἦλθον Ἑλλήνων χθόνα,
τἀκεῖ χορεύσας καὶ καταστήσας ἐμὰς
τελετάς, ἵν' εἴην ἐμφανὴς δαίμων βροτοῖς.
πρώτας δὲ Θήβας τάσδε γῆς Ἑλληνίδος
ἀνωλόλυξα, νεβρίδ' ἐξάψας χροὸς

25 θύρσον τε δοὺς ἐς χεῖρα, κίσσινον βέλος·
ἐπεί μ' ἀδελφαὶ μητρός, ἃς ἥκιστ' ἐχρῆν,
Διόνυσον οὐκ ἔφασκον ἐκφῦναι Διός,
Σεμέλην δὲ νυμφευθεῖσαν ἐκ θνητοῦ τινος
ἐς Ζῆν' ἀναφέρειν τὴν ἁμαρτίαν λέχους,

30 Κάδμου σοφίσμαθ', ὧν νιν οὕνεκα κτανεῖν
Ζῆν' ἐξεκαυχῶνθ', ὅτι γάμους ἐψεύσατο.
   τοιγάρ νιν αὐτὸς ἐκ δόμων ᾤστρησ' ἐγὼ
μανίαις, ὄρος δ' οἰκοῦσι παράκοποι φρενῶν,
σκευήν τ' ἔχειν ἠνάγκασ' ὀργίων ἐμῶν.

35 καὶ πᾶν τὸ θῆλυ σπέρμα Καδμείων, ὅσαι
γυναῖκες ἦσαν, ἐξέμηνα δωμάτων·
ὁμοῦ δὲ Κάδμου παισὶν ἀναμεμειγμέναι
χλωραῖς ὑπ' ἐλάταις ἀνορόφους ἧνται πέτρας.
δεῖ γὰρ πόλιν τήνδ' ἐκμαθεῖν, κεἰ μὴ θέλει,

40 ἀτέλεστον οὖσαν τῶν ἐμῶν βακχευμάτων,
Σεμέλης τε μητρὸς ἀπολογήσασθαί μ' ὕπερ
φανέντα θνητοῖς δαίμον' ὃν τίκτει Διί.
   Κάδμος μὲν οὖν γέρας τε καὶ τυραννίδα
Πενθεῖ δίδωσι θυγατρὸς ἐκπεφυκότι,

45 ὃς θεομαχεῖ τὰ κατ' ἐμὲ καὶ σπονδῶν ἄπο
ὠθεῖ μ' ἐν εὐχαῖς τ' οὐδαμοῦ μνείαν ἔχει.
ὧν οὕνεκ' αὐτῷ θεὸς γεγὼς ἐνδείξομαι

14

together. I have now for the first time returned to Greece, having set everything in Asia a-dancing and having established my rites so that my divinity may be made manifest to mortals. And of Greek cities Thebes was the first I caused to ring with female cries: I clothed the women in fawnskin and put in their hands the thyrsus, that ivy-twined missile. For my mother's sisters, the last who should have done so, said that Dionysus was no son of Zeus but that she had been bedded by a mortal and then, by a clever invention of Cadmus, had ascribed her sexual misdeeds to Zeus. And that, they loudly proclaimed, is why Zeus killed her—for falsely claiming that he was her lover.

Because of this I myself have stung them in madness from their homes: they are out of their wits and live in the mountains, and I have forced them to wear the trappings of my rites. All the female seed of the Cadmeans, all the women there were, I have driven in madness from their houses. Mixed together with the daughters of Cadmus they sit upon the cliffs in the open air under the green fir trees. This city, though it is uninitiated in my bacchic rites, must learn them to the full, whether it wants to or no, and I must speak in my mother Semele's defense by appearing to mortals as the god she bore to Zeus.

Now Cadmus has given the kingship and its prerogatives to his daughter's son Pentheus. This man is a godfighter where my worship is concerned, forcibly excluding me from libations and making no mention of me in prayer. For this reason I will demonstrate to him and to all the

---

20 χθόνα t: πόλιν C   21 τἀκεῖ Wilamowitz: κἀκεῖ C
32 αὐτὸς Burges: -ὰς C   38 ἀνορόφους . . . πέτρας
Elmsley: -οις . . . -αις C   40 fort. τἄμ' ὅμως βακχεύματα

15

πᾶσίν τε Θηβαίοισιν. ἐς δ' ἄλλην χθόνα,
τἀνθένδε θέμενος εὖ, μεταστήσω πόδα,
50 δεικνὺς ἐμαυτόν· ἢν δὲ Θηβαίων πόλις
ὀργῇ σὺν ὅπλοις ἐξ ὄρους βάκχας ἄγειν
ζητῇ, ξυνάψω μαινάσι στρατηλατῶν.
ὧν οὕνεκ' εἶδος θνητὸν ἀλλάξας ἔχω
μορφήν τ' ἐμὴν μετέβαλον εἰς ἀνδρὸς φύσιν.
55 ἀλλ', ὦ λιποῦσαι Τμῶλον, ἔρυμα Λυδίας,
θίασος ἐμός, γυναῖκες ἃς ἐκ βαρβάρων
ἐκόμισα παρέδρους καὶ ξυνεμπόρους ἐμοί,
αἴρεσθε τἀπιχώρι' ἐν Φρυγῶν πόλει
τύπανα, Ῥέας τε μητρὸς ἐμά θ' εὑρήματα,
60 βασίλειά τ' ἀμφὶ δώματ' ἐλθοῦσαι τάδε
κτυπεῖτε Πενθέως, ὡς ὁρᾷ Κάδμου πόλις.
ἐγὼ δὲ βάκχαις, ἐς Κιθαιρῶνος πτυχὰς
ἐλθὼν ἵν' εἰσί, συμμετασχήσω χορῶν.

ΧΟΡΟΣ

Ἀσίας ἀπὸ γαίας
65 ἱερὸν Τμῶλον ἀμείψασα θοάζω
Βρομίῳ πόνον ἡδὺν
κάματόν τ' εὐκάματον, Βάκ-
χιον εὐαζομένα.
τίς ὁδῷ, τίς ὁδῷ; τίς
μελάθροις; ἔκτοπος ἔστω,
70 στόμα τ' εὔφημον ἅπας ἐξοσιούσθω·

53–4 del. Bernhardy
64 γαίας Bothe: γᾶς LP

16

Thebans that I am a god. And when I have set all here to rights, I shall journey on to another land and show myself there. But if the city of Thebes gets angry and tries to bring the bacchants from the mountain by force of arms, I will meet them in battle at the head of an army of maenads. That is why I have taken on mortal form and changed my appearance to that of a man.

(*calling toward Eisodos A*) So, my holy band, you women who have left Mount Tmolus, Lydia's bulwark, and whom I have brought from the outlands as my companions in rest and march, take up the drums that are native to Phrygia, drums invented by Mother Rhea and by me, come and stand about this royal palace of Pentheus and make a din so that Cadmus' city may see you! For my part I will go to the glens of Cithaeron, where the bacchants are, and take part with them in their dances.

Exit DIONYSUS *by Eisodos B. Enter by Eisodos A Dionysus' Asian followers as* CHORUS, *beating drums or tambourines.*

CHORUS

From the land of Asia,
leaving behind Tmolus the sacred mount, I have sped,
toiling for Bromios[3] a toil that is sweet
and a weariness that wearies happily,
making ecstatic cry to the bacchic god.
Who is in the road, who is in the road? Who
is in the palace? Let everyone come forth,
keeping their tongues mute in holy silence:

3 A cult title of Dionysus meaning "the Roaring God."

17

τὰ νομισθέντα γὰρ αἰεὶ
Διόνυσον ὑμνήσω.

στρ. α

ὦ μάκαρ, ὅστις εὐδαί-
μων τελετὰς θεῶν εἰ-
δὼς βιοτὰν ἁγιστεύει
75   καὶ θιασεύεται ψυ-
χὰν ἐν ὄρεσσι βακχεύ-
ων ὁσίοις καθαρμοῖσιν,
τά τε ματρὸς μεγάλας ὄρ-
για Κυβέλας θεμιτεύων
80   ἀνὰ θύρσον τε τινάσσων
κισσῷ τε στεφανωθεὶς
Διόνυσον θεραπεύει.
ἴτε βάκχαι, ἴτε βάκχαι,
Βρόμιον παῖδα θεὸν θεοῦ
85   Διόνυσον κατάγουσαι
Φρυγίων ἐξ ὀρέων Ἑλλάδος εἰς εὐ-
ρυχόρους ἀγυιάς, τὸν Βρόμιον·

ἀντ. α

ὅν ποτ᾽ ἔχουσ᾽ ἐν ὠδί-
νων λοχίαις ἀνάγκαι-
90   σι πταμένας Διὸς βροντᾶς
νηδύος ἔκβολον μά-
τηρ ἔτεκεν, λιποῦσ᾽ αἰ-
ῶνα κεραυνίῳ πλαγᾷ·
λοχίαις δ᾽ αὐτίκα νιν δέ-
95   ξατο θαλάμαις Κρονίδας Ζεύς,

18

I shall hymn Dionysus
with the songs hallowed by use and wont!

O blessed the man who,
happy in knowing the gods' rites,
makes his life pure
and joins his soul to the worshipful band,
performing bacchic rites upon the mountains,
with cleansings the gods approve:
he performs the sacred mysteries
of Mother Cybele of the mountains,
and shaking the bacchic wand up and down,
his head crowned with ivy,
he serves Dionysus.
On bacchants, on you bacchants!
Bring the roaring
son of a god, Dionysus,
from Phrygia's mountains to Hellas' streets,
broad for dancing! Bring Bromios!

His mother long ago
in forced pangs of labor,
after Zeus's thunderbolt had sped,
gave birth to him untimely
as she left her life behind
under the lightning's stroke.
Straightway Kronos' son Zeus
received him in birth's secret recesses

---

94 λοχίαις Dodds, praeeunte Jacobs: -οις LP
95 θαλάμαις Wecklein: -οις LP

κατὰ μηρῷ δὲ καλύψας
χρυσέαισιν συνερείδει
περόναις κρυπτὸν ἀφ᾽ Ἥρας.
ἔτεκεν δ᾽, ἀνίκα Μοῖραι
100 τέλεσαν, ταυρόκερων θεὸν
στεφάνωσέν τε δρακόντων
στεφάνοις, ἔνθεν ἄγραν θηρότροφον μαι-
νάδες ἀμφιβάλλονται πλοκάμοις.

στρ. β
105 ὦ Σεμέλας τροφοὶ Θῆ-
βαι, στεφανοῦσθε κισσῷ·
βρύετε βρύετε χλοήρει
μίλακι καλλικάρπῳ
καὶ καταβακχιοῦσθε δρυὸς
110 ἢ ἐλάτας κλάδοισι,
στικτῶν τ᾽ ἐνδυτὰ νεβρίδων
στέφετε λευκοτρίχων πλοκάμων
μαλλοῖς· ἀμφὶ δὲ νάρθηκας ὑβριστὰς
ὁσιοῦσθ᾽· αὐτίκα γᾶ πᾶσα χορεύσει,
115 Βρόμιος εὖτ᾽ ἂν ἄγῃ θιάσους
εἰς ὄρος εἰς ὄρος, ἔνθα μένει
θηλυγενὴς ὄχλος
ἀφ᾽ ἱστῶν παρὰ κερκίδων τ᾽
οἰστρηθεὶς Διονύσῳ.

ἀντ. β
120 ὦ θαλάμευμα Κουρή-

and concealed him in his thigh,
closing it up with golden pins
to keep him hid from Hera.
Then, when the Fates brought him to term,
he gave birth to the god with the horns of a bull
and crowned him with garlands of serpents:
that is why maenads catch beast-eating snakes
and drape their tresses with them.

O Thebes that nurtured Semele,
be crowned with ivy!
Abound, abound in the green
bryony with its lovely berries,
be consecrate as bacchant
with boughs of oak or fir,
and deck your dappled fawnskin garments
with white strands of wool!
Wrap the violent bacchic wand
in holiness![4] Forthwith the whole land shall dance,
when Bromios leads the worshipful bands
to the mountain, to the mountain, where there rests
the throng of women,
driven by Dionysus in madness
from their looms and shuttles.

O secret chamber of the Curetes,

[4] I. e. consecrate a fennel stalk as a thyrsus by twining ivy
about it.

102–3 θηρότροφον praeeunte Musgrave (-τρόφον) Allen:
-τρόφοι ‹L›P   115 εὖτ᾽ ἄν Elmsley: ὅτ᾽ L: ὅστις (et ἄγει) Tr

21

των ζάθεοί τε Κρήτας
Διογενέτορες έναυλοι,
ένθα τρικόρυθες άντροις
βυρσότονον κύκλωμα τόδε
125 μοι Κορύβαντες ηύρον·
βακχεία δ' άμα συντόνω
κέρασαν άδυβόα Φρυγίων
αυλών πνεύματι ματρός τε 'Ρέας ές
χέρα θήκαν, κτύπον ευάσμασι βακχάν·
130 παρά δέ μαινόμενοι Σάτυροι
ματέρος εξανύσαντο θεάς,
ές δέ χορεύματα
συνήψαν τριετηρίδων,
αίς χαίρει Διόνυσος.

επωδ.

135 ἡδὺς ἐν ὄρεσσιν, ὅταν
ἐκ θιάσων δρομαίων
πέσῃ πεδόσε, νεβρίδος ἔχων
ἱερὸν ἐνδυτόν, ἀγρεύων
αἷμα τραγοκτόνον, ὠμοφάγον χάριν,
140 ἱέμενος εἰς ὄρεα
Λύδι' ὅδ' ἔξαρχος Βρόμιος·
εὐοῖ.
ῥεῖ δὲ γάλακτι πέδον, ῥεῖ δ' οἴνῳ,
ῥεῖ δὲ μελισσᾶν νέκταρι.

---

[123] ἄντροις Musgrave: ἐν ἄν- LP   [126] βακχείᾳ δ' ἄμα
A. Y. Campbell (β- δ' ἀνὰ iam Dobree): ἀνὰ δὲ βακχεία LP

22

BACCHAE

O holy haunts of Crete
where Zeus was born!
There in the cave the thrice-helmed
Corybantes invented for me
this drum of tightened hide;
and in their intense ecstatic dance
they mingled it with the sweet-hallooing breath
of Phrygian pipes and put it into the hands of Mother
   Rhea,
to mark the measure for the bacchants' ecstatic dance.
And the maddened satyrs obtained it
from the Goddess Mother
and added it to the dances
of the second-year festivals
in which Dionysus delights.

Welcome is the god when on the mountains
he leaves the coursing covens
and falls to the ground,[5] his holy
garment of fawnskin about him, in pursuit
of the shed blood of the slain goat, the glad meal of raw
   flesh,
rushing to the mountains
of Lydia, this leader of ours, Bromios:
euhoi!
The ground runs with milk, runs with wine,
runs with the nectar of bees.

   5 Perhaps falling on the goat, his prey.

   141a Λύδι' Willink: Φρύγια Λύδι' LP

Συρίας δ᾿ ὡς λιβάνου κα-
145 πνὸν ὁ Βακχεὺς ἀνέχων
πυρσώδη φλόγα πεύκας
ἐκ νάρθηκος ἀίσσει
δρόμῳ καὶ χοροῖσιν
πλανάτας ἐρεθίζων
ἰαχαῖς τ᾿ ἀναπάλλων,
150 τρυφερόν βόστρυχον εἰς αἰθέρα ῥίπτων.
†ἅμα δ᾿ ἐπ᾿ εὐάσμασιν ἐπιβρέμει τοιάδ᾿·†
᾿Ω ἴτε βάκχαι,
ὦ ἴτε βάκχαι,
Τμώλου χρυσορόου χλιδά,
155 μέλπετε τὸν Διόνυσον
βαρυβρόμων ὑπὸ τυμπάνων,
εὔια τὸν εὔιον ἀγαλλόμεναι θεὸν
ἐν Φρυγίαισι βοαῖς ἐνοπαῖσί τε,
160 λωτὸς ὅταν εὐκέλαδος
ἱερὸς ἱερὰ παίγματα βρέμῃ σύνοχα
φοιτάσιν εἰς ὄρος εἰς ὄρος. ἡδομέ-
165 να δ᾿ ἄρα πῶλος ὅπως ἅμα ματέρι
φορβάδι κῶλον ἄγει ταχύπουν σκιρτήμασι βάκχα.

144–5 καπνὸν Wilamowitz: -ὸς LP
145 ἀνέχων Wilamowitz: δ᾿ ἔχων LP
148b π- ἐρεθίζων Wilamowitz: ἐ- π- LP
150 βόστρυχον Earle: πλόκαμον LP
151 fort. ἐπὶ δ᾿ εὐάσμασι τοιάδε βρέμει
169 βάκχα Musgrave: -χου LP

24

The bacchic god holds aloft,
fragrant as smoke from Syrian incense,
his flaming pine torch
lit from the fennel wand and rushes on,
now running, now dancing,
rebuking the stragglers,
spurring them on with joyous shouts,
and tossing his luxuriant locks to heaven.
And midst his ecstatic cries he calls,
"On bacchants,
on you bacchants,
pride of the River Tmolus that runs with gold:
sing Dionysus' praises
to the deep-roaring drums,
making ecstatic cries to the god of ecstasy
with Phrygian shouts and exclamations,
when the lovely pipe
shrills, all holy, its holy songs in concert
with those who go to the mountain, to the mountain!"
    Hence in joy,
like a colt with its grazing mother,
the bacchant leaps and gambols on nimble legs.

Enter by Eisodos A TEIRESIAS, *identifiable by his prophetic insignia but also wearing, somewhat incongruously, a garment of fawnskin and carrying a thyrsus. Since he is blind, he is led by a boy, who stands aside when he has delivered him to the palace.*

ΤΕΙΡΕΣΙΑΣ

170 τίς ἐν πύλαισι; Κάδμον ἐκκάλει δόμων,
Ἀγήνορος παῖδ᾽, ὃς πόλιν Σιδωνίαν
λιπὼν ἐπύργωσ᾽ ἄστυ Θηβαίων τόδε.
ἴτω τις, εἰσάγγελλε Τειρεσίας ὅτι
ζητεῖ νιν· οἶδε δ᾽ αὐτὸς ὧν ἥκω πέρι
175 ἅ τε ξυνεθέμην πρέσβυς ὢν γεραιτέρῳ,
θύρσους ἀνάπτειν καὶ νεβρῶν δορὰς ἔχειν
στεφανοῦν τε κρᾶτα κισσίνοις βλαστήμασιν.

ΚΑΔΜΟΣ

ὦ φίλταθ᾽, ὡς σὴν γῆρυν ᾐσθημεν κλύων
σοφὴν σοφοῦ παρ᾽ ἀνδρός, ἐν δόμοισιν ὤν.
180 ἥκω δ᾽ ἕτοιμος τήνδ᾽ ἔχων σκευὴν θεοῦ·
δεῖ γάρ νιν ὄντα παῖδα θυγατρὸς ἐξ ἐμῆς
[Διόνυσον ὃς πέφηνεν ἀνθρώποις θεὸς]
ὅσον καθ᾽ ἡμᾶς δυνατὸν αὔξεσθαι μέγαν.
ποῖ δεῖ χορεύειν, ποῖ καθιστάναι πόδα
185 καὶ κρᾶτα σεῖσαι πολιόν; ἐξηγοῦ σύ μοι
γέρων γέροντι, Τειρεσία· σὺ γὰρ σοφός.
ὡς οὐ κάμοιμ᾽ ἂν οὔτε νύκτ᾽ οὔθ᾽ ἡμέραν
θύρσῳ κροτῶν γῆν· ἐπιλελήσμεθ᾽ ἡδέως
γέροντες ὄντες.

ΤΕΙΡΕΣΙΑΣ

ταῦτ᾽ ἐμοὶ πάσχεις ἄρα·
190 κἀγὼ γὰρ ἡβῶ κἀπιχειρήσω χοροῖς.

---

178 ᾐσθημεν Elmsley (vide Bond ad HF 858): ᾐσθόμην LP
182 del. Dobree cl. 860

TEIRESIAS

Ho, gatekeeper! Call out of the house Cadmus, Agenor's son, who left Sidon and founded this citadel of Thebes! Let someone bring him the message that Teiresias wants to see him! He himself knows why I have come and the pact I made with him, one old man with another, to fasten together bacchic wands, wear fawnskin, and crown our heads with shoots of ivy.

Enter from the skene CADMUS, *wearing a garment of fawn-skin and carrying a thyrsus.*

CADMUS

Dearest friend, how glad I was, while still in the house, to hear your words, wise words coming from a wise man! And I have come in readiness, wearing the livery of the god: he is the son of my daughter, [Dionysus who stands revealed to men as a god,] and as far as in us lies he must be magnified. Where shall our dance steps take us, where shall we set our feet and shake our aged heads? You must give me guidance, Teiresias, grayhead to grayhead: you are wise. I will not grow weary day or night of beating the ground with my bacchic wand. How delightful it is that we forget our age!

TEIRESIAS

So your experience is the same as mine: I too am young and ready to try dancing.

ΚΑΔΜΟΣ

οὔκουν ὄχοισιν εἰς ὄρος περάσομεν.

ΤΕΙΡΕΣΙΑΣ

ἀλλ᾽ οὐχ ὁμοίως ἂν ὁ θεὸς τιμὴν ἔχοι.

ΚΑΔΜΟΣ

γέρων γέροντα παιδαγωγήσω σ᾽ ἐγώ.

ΤΕΙΡΕΣΙΑΣ

ὁ θεὸς ἀμοχθεὶ κεῖσε νῷν ἡγήσεται.

ΚΑΔΜΟΣ

195 μόνοι δὲ πόλεως Βακχίῳ χορεύσομεν.

ΤΕΙΡΕΣΙΑΣ

μόνοι γὰρ εὖ φρονοῦμεν, οἱ δ᾽ ἄλλοι κακῶς.

ΚΑΔΜΟΣ

μακρὸν τὸ μέλλειν· ἀλλ᾽ ἐμῆς ἔχου χερός.

ΤΕΙΡΕΣΙΑΣ

ἰδού, ξύναπτε καὶ ξυνωρίζου χέρα.

ΚΑΔΜΟΣ

οὐ καταφρονῶ ᾽γὼ τῶν θεῶν θνητὸς γεγώς.

200 οὐδ᾽ ἐνσοφιζόμεσθα τοῖσι δαίμοσιν.

ΤΕΙΡΕΣΙΑΣ

⟨οὐ γὰρ σοφοῦ πρὸς ἀνδρός ἐσθ᾽ ὑπερφρονεῖν⟩
πατρίους παραδοχάς, ἅς θ᾽ ὁμήλικας χρόνῳ
κεκτήμεθ᾽· οὐδεὶς αὐτὰ καταβαλεῖ λόγος,

200n Cadmo contin. Kovacs: Τε. LP

28

CADMUS

No chariot then will take us to the mountains.

TEIRESIAS

No, for then the god would be less honored.

CADMUS

I, an old man, shall lead an old man like a child.

TEIRESIAS

The god will bring us effortlessly there.

CADMUS

We alone shall dance in the god's honor.

TEIRESIAS

Yes, we alone have sense, the others none.

CADMUS

The wait is long. But take hold of my hand.

TEIRESIAS

There, clasp it, pair it with my own.

CADMUS

I do not despise the gods, mortal that I am, nor do I play the sophist where they are concerned.

TEIRESIAS

< No, it would not become a wise man to look down on > the traditions we have received from our fathers, old as time itself: no argument will overthrow them, whatever subtle-

---

οὐδ' εἰ δι' ἄκρων τὸ σοφὸν ηὕρηται φρενῶν.
ἐρεῖ τις ὡς τὸ γῆρας οὐκ αἰσχύνομαι,
205 μέλλων χορεύειν κρᾶτα κισσώσας ἐμόν;
οὐ γὰρ διήρηχ' ὁ θεός, οὔτε τὸν νέον
εἰ χρὴ χορεύειν οὔτε τὸν γεραίτερον,
ἀλλ' ἐξ ἁπάντων βούλεται τιμὰς ἔχειν
κοινάς, διαριθμῶν δ' οὐδέν' αὔξεσθαι θέλει.

ΚΑΔΜΟΣ

210 ἐπεὶ σὺ φέγγος, Τειρεσία, τόδ' οὐχ ὁρᾷς,
ἐγὼ προφήτης σοι λόγοις γενήσομαι·
Πενθεὺς πρὸς οἴκους ὅδε διὰ σπουδῆς περᾷ,
Ἐχίονος παῖς, ᾧ κράτος δίδωμι γῆς.
ὡς ἐπτόηται· τί ποτ' ἐρεῖ νεώτερον;

ΠΕΝΘΕΥΣ

215 ἔκδημος ὢν μὲν τῆσδ' ἐτύγχανον χθονός,
κλύω δὲ νεοχμὰ τήνδ' ἀνὰ πτόλιν κακά,
γυναῖκας ἡμῖν δώματ' ἐκλελοιπέναι
πλασταῖσι βακχείαισιν, ἐν δὲ δασκίοις
ὄρεσι θοάζειν, τὸν νεωστὶ δαίμονα
220 Διόνυσον, ὅστις ἔστι, τιμώσας χοροῖς,
πλήρεις δὲ θιάσοις ἐν μέσοισιν ἱστάναι
κρατῆρας, ἄλλην δ' ἄλλοσ' εἰς ἐρημίαν
πτώσσουσαν εὐναῖς ἀρσένων ὑπηρετεῖν,
πρόφασιν μὲν ὡς δὴ μαινάδας θυοσκόους,
225 τὴν δ' Ἀφροδίτην πρόσθ' ἄγειν τοῦ Βακχίου.
ὅσας μὲν οὖν εἴληφα, δεσμίους χέρας
σῴζουσι πανδήμοισι πρόσπολοι στέγαις·

30

ties have been invented by deep thinkers. Will someone say that in preparing to dance with my head crowned with ivy I show no respect for my old age? No, for the god has not distinguished old from young where dancing is concerned: he wants to receive joint honor from everyone and to be magnified by all without exception.

Enter by Eisodos B PENTHEUS *with retinue.*

CADMUS

Since you, Teiresias, cannot see the light, my words will interpret for you: Pentheus, Echion's son, to whom I have given the kingship, is now coming in haste toward the house. How upset he is! What surprising thing will he have to say?

PENTHEUS

(*to himself*) I happened to be out of the country, but I hear of strange mischief in this city, that the women have left our homes in fictitious ecstatic rites and flit about on the thick-shaded mountains, honoring the new god Dionysus, whoever he is, with their dancing. They set up full wine bowls in the middle of their assemblies and sneak off, one here, one there, to tryst in private with men. The pretext for all this is that they are maenads performing their rites, but they hold Aphrodite in higher regard than the bacchic god. All those I have caught are being kept in the public prison, their hands manacled, by my servants. All who are

---

206 οὔτε Matthiae: εἴτε LP   207 οὔτε Fix: εἴτε LP
211 λόγοις Tammaro: -ων LP
221 ἱστάναι Dawe: ἑστ- LP

ὅσαι δ' ἄπεισιν, ἐξ ὄρους θηράσομαι,
[Ἰνώ τ' Ἀγαυήν θ', ἥ μ' ἔτικτ' Ἐχίονι,
230 Ἀκταίονός τε μητέρ', Αὐτονόην λέγω,]
καί σφας σιδηραῖς ἁρμόσας ἐν ἄρκυσιν
παύσω κακούργου τῆσδε βακχείας τάχα.

λέγουσι δ' ὥς τις εἰσελήλυθε ξένος,
γόης ἐπῳδὸς Λυδίας ἀπὸ χθονός,
235 ξανθοῖσι βοστρύχοισιν εὔοσμος κόμην,
οἰνωπός, ὄσσοις χάριτας Ἀφροδίτης ἔχων,
ὃς ἡμέρας τε κεὐφρόνας συγγίγνεται
τελετὰς προτείνων εὐίους νεάνισιν.
εἰ δ' αὐτὸν εἴσω τῆσδε λήψομαι χθονός,
240 παύσω κτυποῦντα θύρσον ἀνασείοντά τε
κόμας, τράχηλον σώματος χωρὶς τεμών.
ἐκεῖνος εἶναί φησι Διόνυσον θεόν,
ἐκεῖνος ἐν μηρῷ ποτ' ἐρράφθαι Διός·
ὃς ἐκπυροῦται λαμπάσιν κεραυνίαις
245 σὺν μητρί, Δίους ὅτι γάμους ἐψεύσατο.
ταῦτ' οὐχὶ δεινὰ κἀγχόνης ἔστ' ἄξια,
⟨εἰ τόνδε χαίροντ' ἐς πόλιν παρήσομεν⟩
ὕβρεις ὑβρίζειν, ὅστις ἔστιν ὁ ξένος;

ἀτὰρ τόδ' ἄλλο θαῦμα· τὸν τερασκόπον
ἐν ποικίλαισι νεβρίσι Τειρεσίαν ὁρῶ
250 πατέρα τε μητρὸς τῆς ἐμῆς—πολὺν γέλων—
νάρθηκι βακχεύοντ'· ἀναίνομαι, πάτερ,
τὸ γῆρας ὑμῶν εἰσορῶν νοῦν οὐκ ἔχον.
οὐκ ἀποτινάξεις κισσόν; οὐκ ἐλευθέραν
θύρσου μεθήσεις χεῖρ', ἐμῆς μητρὸς πάτερ;

still missing I shall hunt out of the mountain, [Ino, Agave, who bore me to Echion, and Actaeon's mother, I mean Autonoe,] and when I have caught them fast in nets of iron, I will quickly put an end to this damnable reveling.

They say that a foreigner has arrived from Lydia, a wizard, an enchanter, his blond locks reeking of scent, with a face wine-colored and the charm of Aphrodite in his eyes. He consorts day and night with the young women, offering them ecstatic rites. If I catch him in this country, I'll stop him from beating his thyrsus on the ground and tossing his locks: I'll separate his head from his body! This is the man who claims Dionysus is a god, the man who says he was sewed up in the thigh of Zeus! In truth he was burnt up together with his mother in a gleam of lightning fire because she pretended she had lain with Zeus. Is it not dreadful and enough to make a man hang himself, ⟨if we are to allow this⟩ stranger, whoever he is, to commit such an outrage ⟨against the city with impunity⟩?

(catching sight of Cadmus and Teiresias) But here's another strange business: I see the diviner Teiresias dressed in dappled fawnskin, and my mother's father—a ridiculous sight—playing the bacchant with a wand. It pains me, old sir, to see your gray head acting so foolishly. Shake off that ivy, grandfather, and free your hand of that wand! This

---

229–30 del. Collmann
243 ἐρράφθαι Reiske: ἐρράφη fere LP
246 δεινὰ κἀγχόνης Mau: δεινῆς ἀγχόνης LP
247 ante h. v. lac. indic. Kovacs: v. del. Wilamowitz

255   σὺ ταῦτ' ἔπεισας, Τειρεσία· τόνδ' αὖ θέλεις
      τὸν δαίμον' ἀνθρώποισιν ἐσφέρων νέον
      σκοπεῖν πτερωτὰ κἀμπύρων μισθοὺς φέρειν.
      εἰ μή σε γῆρας πολιὸν ἐξερρύετο,
      καθῆσ' ἂν ἐν βάκχαισι δέσμιος μέσαις,
260   τελετὰς πονηρὰς εἰσάγων· γυναιξὶ γὰρ
      ὅπου βότρυος ἐν δαιτὶ γίγνεται γάνος,
      οὐχ ὑγιὲς οὐδὲν ἔτι λέγω τῶν ὀργίων.

ΧΟΡΟΣ

      τῆς δυσσεβείας. ὦ ξέν', οὐκ αἰδῇ θεούς;
265   Ἐχίονος δ' ὢν παῖς καταισχυνεῖς γένος
264   Κάδμον τε τὸν σπείραντα γηγενῆ στάχυν;

ΤΕΙΡΕΣΙΑΣ

      ὅταν λάβῃ τις τῶν λόγων ἀνὴρ σοφὸς
      καλὰς ἀφορμάς, οὐ μέγ' ἔργον εὖ λέγειν·
      σὺ δ' εὔτροχον μὲν γλῶσσαν ὡς φρονῶν ἔχεις,
      ἐν τοῖς λόγοισι δ' οὐκ ἔνεισί σοι φρένες.
270   [θράσει δὲ δυνατὸς καὶ λέγειν οἷός τ' ἀνὴρ
      κακὸς πολίτης γίγνεται νοῦν οὐκ ἔχων.]
      οὗτος δ' ὁ δαίμων ὁ νέος, ὃν σὺ διαγελᾷς,
      οὐκ ἂν δυναίμην μέγεθος ἐξειπεῖν ὅσος
      καθ' Ἑλλάδ' ἔσται. δύο γάρ, ὦ νεανία,
275   τὰ πρῶτ' ἐν ἀνθρώποισι· Δημήτηρ θεά—
      Γῆ δ' ἐστίν, ὄνομα δ' ὁπότερον βούλῃ κάλει·
      αὕτη μὲν ἐν ξηροῖσιν ἐκτρέφει βροτούς·

257 πτερωτὰ Herwerden: -τοὺς LP
263 δυσσεβείας Reiske: εὐσεβ- LP

34

is your doing, Teiresias: you want to introduce this new divinity to mankind and read his bird signs and entrails and take fees! If you weren't protected by your gray hair, you would be sitting in prison surrounded by bacchants for introducing these wicked rites. Wherever women get the gleaming grape to drink in their feasts, everything about their rites is diseased.

CHORUS LEADER

What impiety! Stranger, do you not reverence the gods? You are Echion's son: are you going to bring shame on your family and on Cadmus who sowed the crop of the Earth-born?[6]

TEIRESIAS

When a wise man has a good case to argue, eloquence is easy. As for you, though you think yourself clever and have a ready tongue, there is no intelligence in what you say. [A man whose power lies in brashness and who is a fluent speaker becomes a bad citizen if he lacks sense.]

This new divinity you are laughing to scorn—I could not fully express how great he will be in Greece. Two things are chief among mortals, young man: the goddess Demeter—she is Earth but call her either name you like—nourishes mortals with dry food. But he who came next,

---

6 Cadmus sowed the teeth of a dragon on the soil of Thebes. These sprouted as the Sown Men, fierce warriors who were the ancestors of the Theban nobility.

---

264 post 265 trai. Musgrave
270–1 del. Hartung
270 θράσει Bothe: θρασὺς LP

ὃς δ' ἦλθ' ἔπειτ', ἀντίπαλον ὁ Σεμέλης γόνος
βότρυος ὑγρὸν πῶμ' ηὗρε κἀσηνέγκατο
280 θνητοῖς, ὃ παύει τοὺς ταλαιπώρους βροτοὺς
λύπης, ὅταν πλησθῶσιν ἀμπέλου ῥοῆς,
ὕπνον τε λήθην τῶν καθ' ἡμέραν κακῶν
δίδωσιν, οὐδ' ἔστ' ἄλλο φάρμακον πόνων.
οὗτος θεοῖσι σπένδεται θεὸς γεγώς,
285 ὥστε διὰ τοῦτον τἀγάθ' ἀνθρώπους ἔχειν.

καὶ διαγελᾷς νιν, ὡς ἐνερράφη Διὸς
μηρῷ; διδάξω σ' ὡς καλῶς ἔχει τόδε.
ἐπεί νιν ἥρπασ' ἐκ πυρὸς κεραυνίου
Ζεύς, ἐς δ' Ὄλυμπον βρέφος ἀνήγαγεν νέον,
290 Ἥρα νιν ἤθελ' ἐκβαλεῖν ἀπ' οὐρανοῦ,
Ζεὺς δ' ἀντεμηχανήσαθ' οἷα δὴ θεός·
ῥήξας μέρος τι τοῦ χθόν' ἐγκυκλουμένου
αἰθέρος, ἔδωκε τόνδ' ὅμηρον ἐκτιθεὶς
Διόνυσον Ἥρας νεικέων· χρόνῳ δέ νιν
295 βροτοὶ ῥαφῆναί φασιν ἐν μηρῷ Διός,
ὄνομα μεταστήσαντες, ὅτι θεᾷ θεὸς
Ἥρᾳ ποθ' ὡμήρευσε †συνθέντες† λόγον.

μάντις δ' ὁ δαίμων ὅδε· τὸ γὰρ βακχεύσιμον
καὶ τὸ μανιῶδες μαντικὴν πολλὴν ἔχει·
300 ὅταν γὰρ ὁ θεὸς ἐς τὸ σῶμ' ἔλθῃ πολύς,
λέγειν τὸ μέλλον τοὺς μεμηνότας ποιεῖ.
Ἄρεώς τε μοῖραν μεταλαβὼν ἔχει τινά·

278 ὃς δ' Fix: ὅδ' LP   ἔπειτ', ἀντίπαλον Housman: ἐπὶ
τἀντίπαλον fere LP

the son of Semele, discovered as its counterpart the drink that flows from the grape cluster and introduced it to mortals. It is this that frees trouble-laden mortals from their pain—when they fill themselves with the juice of the vine—this that gives sleep to make one forget the day's troubles: there is no other treatment for misery. Himself a god, he is poured out in libations to the gods, and so it is because of him that men win blessings from them.

And do you ridicule him because he was sewn in the thigh of Zeus? I will show you that this story too makes sense. When Zeus had snatched him from the lightning-bolt's blaze and had brought him as a young babe to Olympus, Hera wanted to hurl him out of heaven. But Zeus, god that he is, made a scheme to answer Hera's: breaking off a part of the sky that surrounds the earth, he gave her this as a hostage and thereby rescued Dionysus from Hera's contentiousness. As time passed, mortals said that he was sewn up into the thigh of Zeus, altering the word because they failed to understand that as god to goddess he had served as Hera's hostage.[7]

The god is also a prophet: for the ecstatic and the manic have mantic powers in large measure. When the god enters someone in force, he causes him in madness to predict the future. He has also taken a share of Ares: often when an

---

[7] I.e. mishearing or misunderstanding that he was saved by "Zeus's hostage (*homēros*)" they began to say that "Zeus's thigh (*mēros*)" saved him.

289 νέον Aldina: θεόν LP
293 ἔδωκε . . . ἐκτιθεὶς Borthwick: ἔθηκε . . . ἐκδιδοὺς LP
297 fort. ὡμήρευσ' ἀσυνετοῦντες

στρατὸν γὰρ ἐν ὅπλοις ὄντα κἀπὶ τάξεσιν
φόβος διεπτόησε πρὶν λόγχης θιγεῖν
305 μανία τε· καὶ τοῦτ᾽ ἐστὶ Διονύσου πάρα.
ἔτ᾽ αὐτὸν ὄψῃ κἀπὶ Δελφίσιν πέτραις
πηδῶντα σὺν πεύκαισι δικόρυφον πλάκα,
πάλλοντα καὶ σείοντα βακχεῖον κλάδον,
μέγαν τ᾽ ἀν᾽ Ἑλλάδ᾽. ἀλλ᾽ ἐμοί, Πενθεῦ, πιθοῦ·
310 μὴ τὸ κράτος αὔχει δύναμιν ἀνθρώποις ἔχειν,
μηδ᾽, ἢν δοκῇς μέν, ἡ δὲ δόξα σου νοσῇ,
φρονεῖν δόκει τι· τὸν θεὸν δ᾽ ἐς γῆν δέχου
καὶ σπένδε καὶ βάκχευε καὶ στέφου κάρα.
⟨ἃ δ᾽ ἐς γυναῖκας εἶπες οὐ φροντιστέον·⟩
οὐχ ὁ Διόνυσος †σωφρονεῖν† ἀναγκάσει
315 γυναῖκας ἐς τὴν Κύπριν, ἀλλ᾽ ἐν τῇ φύσει
[τὸ σωφρονεῖν ἔνεστιν ἐς τὰ πάντ᾽ ἀεί]
τοῦτο· σκοπεῖν χρή· καὶ γὰρ ἐν βακχεύμασιν
οὖσ᾽ ἥ γε σώφρων οὐ διαφθαρήσεται.
ὁρᾷς; σὺ χαίρεις, ὅταν ἐφεστῶσιν πύλαις
320 πολλοί, τὸ Πενθέως δ᾽ ὄνομα μεγαλύνῃ πόλις·
κἀκεῖνος, οἶμαι, τέρπεται τιμώμενος.
ἐγὼ μὲν οὖν καὶ Κάδμος, ὃν σὺ διαγελᾷς,
κισσῷ τ᾽ ἐρεψόμεσθα καὶ χορεύσομεν,
πολιὰ ξυνωρίς, ἀλλ᾽ ὅμως χορευτέον,
325 κοὐ θεομαχήσω σῶν λόγων πεισθεὶς ὕπο.
μαίνῃ γὰρ ὡς ἄλγιστα, κοὔτε φαρμάκοις
ἄκη λάβοις ἂν οὔτ᾽ ἄνευ τούτων νοσεῖς.

army is under arms and drawn up for battle, it is seized by a
mad fear before it even begins battle: this too comes from
Dionysus. One day you will see him also on the cliffs of
Delphi, dancing with his pine torches on the upland be-
tween the twin peaks, shaking and brandishing his bac-
chic wand and greatly honored in Hellas. So do as I say,
Pentheus: don't think that kingly rule is the most powerful
force in human life, and if you have ideas but unsound
ones, you must not think you are wise. Receive the god into
the land, pour libations to him, join the ecstatic dance,
crown your head!

‹As to what you said about the women—give it no more
thought:› Dionysus will not compel women to act foolishly
where sex is concerned. Rather, such folly lies in their own
nature [that chastity dwells in them in all respects always].
Remember: even in ecstatic worship a chaste woman will
not be corrupted.

Don't you see? You enjoy it when crowds stand at your
gates and the city shouts aloud the name of Pentheus. The
god too, I think, takes pleasure in honor. I shall crown my
head with ivy and join the dance, and so will Cadmus,
whom you mock. We are a pair of grayheads, but still we
must dance. Your words will not persuade me to fight
against a god. You are mad and most painfully so: some
drug has caused it, and no drug can cure it.

---

305 τε Kovacs, nulla in fine prioris v. distinctione: δὲ LP

314 ante h. v. lac. indic. Wilamowitz   μὴ σωφρονεῖν P2 et t:
μὴ φρονεῖν Musgrave: fort. παραφρονεῖν

316 om. t, del. Kirchhoff cl. *Hip.* 80   317 v. dist. Kirchhoff

327 νοσεῖς] νόσου Dobree

EURIPIDES

ΧΟΡΟΣ

ὦ πρέσβυ, Φοῖβόν τ' οὐ καταισχύνεις λόγοις,
τιμῶν τε Βρόμιον σωφρονεῖς, μέγαν θεόν.

ΚΑΔΜΟΣ

330 ὦ παῖ, καλῶς σοι Τειρεσίας παρήνεσεν.
οἴκει μεθ' ἡμῶν, μὴ θύραζε τῶν νόμων·
νῦν γὰρ πέτῃ τε καὶ φρονῶν οὐδὲν φρονεῖς.
κεἰ μὴ γὰρ ἔστιν ὁ θεὸς οὗτος, ὡς σὺ φής,
παρὰ σοὶ λεγέσθω· καὶ καταψεύδου καλῶς
335 ὡς ἔστι, Σεμέλη θ' ἵνα δοκῇ θεὸν τεκεῖν,
ἡμῖν τε τιμὴ παντὶ τῷ γένει προσῇ.

ὁρᾷς τὸν Ἀκταίωνος ἄθλιον μόρον,
ὃν ὠμόσιτοι σκύλακες ἃς ἐθρέψατο
διεσπάσαντο, κρεῖσσον' ἐν κυναγίαις
340 Ἀρτέμιδος εἶναι κομπάσαντ' ἐν ὀργάσιν.
ὃ μὴ πάθῃς σύ· δεῦρό σου στέψω κάρα
κισσῷ· μεθ' ἡμῶν τῷ θεῷ τιμὴν δίδου.

ΠΕΝΘΕΥΣ

οὐ μὴ προσοίσεις χεῖρα, βακχεύσεις δ' ἰών,
μηδ' ἐξομόρξῃ μωρίαν τὴν σὴν ἐμοί;
345 τῆς σῆς ⟨δ'⟩ ἀνοίας τόνδε τὸν διδάσκαλον
δίκην μέτειμι. στειχέτω τις ὡς τάχος,
ἐλθὼν δὲ θάκους τοῦδ' ἵν' οἰωνοσκοπεῖ
μοχλοῖς τριαίνου κἀνάτρεψον ἔμπαλιν,
ἄνω κάτω τὰ πάντα συγχέας ὁμοῦ,
350 καὶ στέμματ' ἀνέμοις καὶ θυέλλαισιν μέθες·

335 Σεμέλη θ' Tyrwhitt: Σεμέλης LP   345 ⟨δ'⟩ Matthiae

CHORUS LEADER

Old sir, your words bring no disgrace on Phoebus, and you are sensible for honoring Bromios, a great god.

CADMUS

My lad, Teiresias has given you good advice: make your home with us, not beyond the bounds of established custom. At the moment you are all in the air: you are clever, but your cleverness amounts to nothing. Even if this god does not exist, as you maintain, you should say that he does and tell a wholesome lie: thus Semele will be thought to have given birth to a god and your whole family will win honor.

You can see the miserable death of Actaeon, torn to pieces by the flesh-devouring hounds he himself had raised: he boasted in the mountain glades that he was better in the hunt than Artemis. Let this not be your fate! Come here, let me garland your head with ivy: join us in giving honor to the god.

He tries to put an ivy crown on Pentheus' head. Pentheus rejects it with contempt.

PENTHEUS

Keep your hands to yourself, don't wipe your folly off on me! Go off and play the bacchant! <But> this man who taught you your madness—I shall punish him. (*to his retinue*) Go, someone, quickly, to this man's seat of prophecy, where he watches his birds, and pry it up, overturn it with a crowbar! Turn the whole place upside down and throw his

---

347 τοῦδ' Musgrave: τούσδ' LP

μάλιστα γάρ νιν δήξομαι δράσας τάδε.

οἱ δ' ἀνὰ πόλιν στείχοντες ἐξιχνεύσατε
τὸν θηλύμορφον ξένον, ὃς ἐσφέρει νόσον
καινὴν γυναιξὶ καὶ λέχη λυμαίνεται.
355 κἄνπερ λάβητε, δέσμιον πορεύσατε
δεῦρ' αὐτόν, ὡς ἂν λευσίμου δίκης τυχὼν
θάνῃ, πικρὰν βάκχευσιν ἐν Θήβαις ἰδών.

ΤΕΙΡΕΣΙΑΣ

ὦ σχέτλι', ὡς οὐκ οἶσθα ποῦ ποτ' εἶ λόγων.
μέμηνας ἤδη, καὶ πρὶν ἐξεστὼς φρενῶν.
360 στείχωμεν ἡμεῖς, Κάδμε, κἀξαιτώμεθα
ὑπέρ τε τούτου καίπερ ὄντος ἀγρίου
ὑπέρ τε πόλεως τὸν θεὸν μηδὲν νέον
δρᾶν. ἀλλ' ἕπου μοι κισσίνου βάκτρου μέτα,
πειρῶ δ' ἀνορθοῦν σῶμ' ἐμόν, κἀγὼ τὸ σόν·
365 γέροντε δ' αἰσχρὸν δύο πεσεῖν· ἴτω δ' ὅμως,
τῷ Βακχίῳ γὰρ τῷ Διὸς δουλευτέον.
Πενθεὺς δ' ὅπως μὴ πένθος εἰσοίσει δόμοις
τοῖς σοῖσι, Κάδμε· μαντικῇ μὲν οὐ λέγω,
τοῖς πράγμασιν δέ· μῶρα γὰρ μῶρος λέγει.

στρ. α

ΧΟΡΟΣ

370 Ὁσία πότνα θεῶν,

359 ἐξεστὼς Bothe: ἐξέστης LP

42

sacred fillets to the storm winds! That will hurt him most of all!

Exit servant by Eisodos A.

You others, go about the city and track down that effeminate stranger who is infecting the women with a new disease and playing havoc with their marriages. If you catch him, bring him here in chains so that he may die by stoning: he will find that his ecstatic dancing in Thebes has cost him dear!

Exit other servants by Eisodos B.

TEIRESIAS

Unhappy man, how little you know what you are saying! You are now quite deranged, though you have lost your head before now. Cadmus, let us go and pray for him, wild man though he is, and for the city, that the god may not harm us. Accompany me with your ivied staff and try to support me, as I will you: two old men falling down would be a disgrace. Still, if it happens, so be it: we must serve Zeus's son, the bacchic god. Take care that Pentheus does not bring sorrow[8] on your house, Cadmus. I do not say this by my prophetic art but by looking at the facts: his talk is folly and he's a fool.

Exit by Eisodos B CADMUS and TEIRESIAS, followed by the latter's guide. Pentheus remains in front of the palace.

CHORUS

Holiness, queen in heaven,

8 "Sorrow" here is *penthos*, making a play on Pentheus' name.

Ὁσία δ' ἃ κατὰ γᾶν
χρυσέᾳ πτέρυγι φέρῃ,
τάδε Πενθέως ἀίεις;
ἀίεις οὐχ ὁσίαν
375 ὕβριν ἐς τὸν Βρόμιον, τὸν
Σεμέλας, τὸν παρὰ καλλι-
στεφάνοις εὐφροσύναις δαί-
μονα πρῶτον μακάρων; ὃς τάδ' ἔχει,
θιασεύειν τε χοροῖς
380 μετά τ' αὐλοῦ γελάσαι
ἀποπαῦσαί τε μερίμνας,
ὁπόταν βότρυος ἔλθῃ
γάνος ἐν δαιτὶ θεῶν, κισ-
σοφόροις δ' ἐν θαλίαις ἀν-
385 δράσι κρατὴρ ὕπνον ἀμφιβάλλῃ.

ἀντ. α

ἀχαλίνων στομάτων
ἀνόμου τ' ἀφροσύνας
τὸ τέλος δυστυχία·
ὁ δὲ τᾶς ἡσυχίας
390 βίοτος καὶ τὸ φρονεῖν
ἀσάλευτόν τε μένει καὶ
συνέχει δώματα· πόρσω
γὰρ ὅμως αἰθέρα ναίον-
τες ὁρῶσιν τὰ βροτῶν οὐρανίδαι.
395 τὸ σοφὸν δ' οὐ σοφία
τό τε μὴ θνατὰ φρονεῖν.
βραχὺς αἰών· ἐπὶ τούτῳ

44

Holiness, you that pass over the earth
with golden wing,
do you hear of these deeds of Pentheus?
Do you hear of his impious
violence against Bromios,
Semele's son, the chief god invoked
amid the fair-garlanded
delights of the feast? These are his powers,
to blend us, by dance, with the worshipful band,
to laugh to the sound of piping,
and to vanquish care
when to the sacred meal
comes the gleam of the grape
and upon men in their ivy-decked feasts
the wine bowl casts a mantle of sleep.

Tongues that know no bridle
and folly that knows no law
end in misery.
But the peaceful life
and good sense—
no billows toss these:
these bind together men's houses.
For though they dwell far off in the sky
the gods of heaven look on mortal doings.
Cleverness is not wisdom,
nor is it wise to think thoughts not mortal.
Our life is short: this being so

---

372 χρυσέα πτέρυγι φέρῃ W. H. Thompson: χρυσέα πτέρυγα
φέρεις fere LP

δέ τις ἂν μεγάλα διώκων
τὰ παρόντ' οὐχὶ φέροι. μαι-
400   νομένων οἵδε τρόποι καὶ
κακοβούλων παρ' ἔμοιγε φωτῶν.

στρ. β

ἱκοίμαν ποτὶ Κύπρον,
νᾶσον τᾶς Ἀφροδίτας,
ἵν' οἱ θελξίφρονες νέμον-
405   ται θνατοῖσιν Ἔρωτες
Πάφον, τὰν ἑκατόστομοι
βαρβάρου ποταμοῦ ῥοαὶ
καρπίζουσιν ἄνομβροι,
οὗ θ' ἁ καλλιστευομένα
410   Πιερία, μούσειος ἕδρα,
σεμνὰ κλειτὺς Ὀλύμπου·
ἐκεῖσ' ἄγε μ', ⟨ὦ⟩ Βρόμιε Βρόμιε,
πρόβακχ' εὔιε δαῖμον.
415   ἐκεῖ Χάριτες, ἐκεῖ δὲ Πόθος, ἐκεῖ δὲ βάκ-
χαις θέμις ὀργιάζειν.

ἀντ. β

ὁ δαίμων ὁ Διὸς παῖς
χαίρει μὲν θαλίαισιν,
φιλεῖ δ' ὀλβοδότειραν Εἰ-

399 φέροι Tyrwhitt: -ει LP
402 Κύπρον Elmsley: τὰν K- LP
404 ἵν' οἱ Heath: ἵνα LP: ἐν ᾗ Nauck
406 τὰν Diggle: θ' ἂν LP
409 οὗ θ' Schoene: ὅπου δ' LP

a man who pursues great things
may miss what lies at hand. To live thus
is to be, in my judgment,
a madman and a fool.

May I wend my way to Cyprus,
Aphrodite's island,
where the Erotes[9] who charm mortal hearts
make their home
in Paphos, a place the hundred streams
of the barbarian river
make fertile without rain;[10]
and may I go to where stands fairest
Pieria, the Muses' haunt,
holy slope of Mount Olympus:
take me there, ⟨O⟩ Bromios, Bromios,
leader of my worship, god of ecstasy!
There live the Graces, there lives Desire, there may the
    bacchants
hold their joyous rites!

The god, Zeus's son,
rejoices in the feast,
he loves wealth-giving

[9] Deities of love who attend Aphrodite.
[10] The "barbarian river" is the Nile, which according to some
ancient sources, passed under the sea to reemerge and fertilize
the south coast of Cyprus. See *Helen* 151.

---

412 μ' ⟨$\hat{\omega}$⟩ Hartung: $\mu\epsilon$ LP
413 $\pi\rho\acute{o}\beta\alpha\kappa\chi$' $\epsilon\breve{v}\iota\epsilon$ Hermann: $\pi\rho\sigma\beta\alpha\kappa\chi\acute{\eta}\iota\epsilon$ LP

420 ῥήναν, κουροτρόφον θεάν.
 ἴσαν δ᾽ ἔς τε τὸν ὄλβιον
 τόν τε χείρονα δῶκ᾽ ἔχειν
 οἴνου τέρψιν ἄλυπον·
 μισεῖ δ᾽ ᾧ μὴ ταῦτα μέλει,
425 κατὰ φάος νύκτας τε φίλας
 εὐαίωνα διαζῆν,
 σοφὰν δ᾽ ἀπέχειν πραπίδα φρένα τε
 περισσῶν παρὰ φωτῶν·
430 τὸ πλῆθος ὅ τι τὸ φαυλότερον ἐνόμισε χρῆ-
 ταί τε, τόδ᾽ ἂν δεχοίμαν.

ΘΕΡΑΠΩΝ

 Πενθεῦ, πάρεσμεν τήνδ᾽ ἄγραν ἠγρευκότες
435 ἐφ᾽ ἣν ἔπεμψας, οὐδ᾽ ἄκρανθ᾽ ὡρμήσαμεν.
 ὁ θὴρ δ᾽ ὅδ᾽ ἡμῖν πρᾶος οὐδ᾽ ὑπέσπασεν
 φυγῇ πόδ᾽, ἀλλ᾽ ἔδωκεν οὐκ ἄκων χέρας,
 οὐκ ὠχρός, οὐδ᾽ ἤλλαξεν οἰνωπὸν γένυν,
 γελῶν δὲ καὶ δεῖν κἀπάγειν ἐφίετο
440 ἔμενέ τε, τοὐμὸν εὐτρεπὲς ποιούμενος.
 κἀγὼ δι᾽ αἰδοῦς εἶπον· Ὦ ξέν᾽, οὐχ ἑκὼν
 ἄγω σε, Πενθέως δ᾽ ὅς μ᾽ ἔπεμψ᾽ ἐπιστολαῖς.
   ἃς δ᾽ αὖ σὺ βάκχας εἶρξας, ἃς συνήρπασας
 κᾆδησας ἐν δεσμοῖσι πανδήμου στέγης,
445 φροῦδαί γ᾽ ἐκεῖναι λελυμέναι πρὸς ὀργάδας
 σκιρτῶσι Βρόμιον ἀνακαλούμεναι θεόν·

---

421 ἴσαν Tr: ἴσα LP   433 τε τόδ᾽ ἂν δεχοίμαν Kirchhoff
(δεχοίμαν iam Musgrave): τ᾽ ἐν τῷδε λεγοίμην ἂν LP

BACCHAE

Peace, the goddess who rears boys to manhood.
Equally both to the rich
and to the lowly he has given
the painless joy of wine.
He hates the man who does not make this his aim,
by day and through the sweetness of night
to live a life of bliss,
and to keep his heart and his thoughts wise,
far from men of excess.
What the simple folk believe and practice
that shall I accept.

Enter by Eisodos B a SERVANT *with others of Pentheus'
retinue leading* DIONYSUS *in chains.*

SERVANT

Pentheus, here we are with the prey you sent us to catch:
our errand was successful. This is a tame beast, we found:
he did not take to his heels in flight, nor did the hue of his
wine-colored cheeks turn ashen, but without objection he
held out his hands, waiting for me and telling me with a
laugh to tie him up and lead him away, which made my
task easier. I felt shame and said, "Stranger, it is not of my
own free will that I take you away but on the orders of
Pentheus, who sent me."

As for the bacchant women you have restrained, arrest-
ing and chaining them up in the public prison, they are
gone: free of their bonds they skipped off toward the
mountain glades, calling on the god Bromios. The chains

---

436 δ' del. Dawe
438 οὐκ Bothe: οὐδ' LP

49

αὐτόματα δ' αὐταῖς δεσμὰ διελύθη ποδῶν
κλῇδές τ' ἀνῆκαν θύρετρ' ἄνευ θνητῆς χερός.
πολλῶν δ' ὅδ' ἀνὴρ θαυμάτων ἥκει πλέως

450 ἐς τάσδε Θήβας. σοὶ δὲ τἆλλα χρὴ μέλειν.

ΠΕΝΘΕΥΣ

μέθεσθε χειρῶν τοῦδ'· ἐν ἄρκυσιν γὰρ ὢν
οὐκ ἔστιν οὕτως ὠκὺς ὥστε μ' ἐκφυγεῖν.
   ἀτὰρ τὸ μὲν σῶμ' οὐκ ἄμορφος εἶ, ξένε,
ὡς ἐς γυναῖκας, ἐφ' ὅπερ ἐς Θήβας πάρει·

455 πλόκαμός τε γάρ σου ταναὸς οὐ πάλης ὕπο,
γένυν παρ' αὐτὴν κεχυμένος, πόθου πλέως·
λευκὴν δὲ χροιὰν ἐκ παρασκευῆς ἔχεις,
οὐχ ἡλίου βολαῖσιν ἀλλ' ὑπὸ σκιᾶς
τὴν Ἀφροδίτην καλλονῇ θηρώμενος.

460   πρῶτον μὲν οὖν μοι λέξον ὅστις εἶ γένος.

ΔΙΟΝΥΣΟΣ

οὐκ ὄκνος οὐδείς· ῥᾴδιον δ' εἰπεῖν τόδε.
τὸν ἀνθεμώδη Τμῶλον οἶσθά που κλύων.

ΠΕΝΘΕΥΣ

οἶδ', ὃς τὸ Σάρδεων ἄστυ περιβάλλει κύκλῳ.

ΔΙΟΝΥΣΟΣ

ἐντεῦθέν εἰμι, Λυδία δέ μοι πατρίς.

ΠΕΝΘΕΥΣ

465 πόθεν δὲ τελετὰς τάσδ' ἄγεις ἐς Ἑλλάδα;

451 μέθεσθε Burges: μαίνεσθε LP
457 ἐκ παρασκευῆς Kirchhoff: εἰς παρασκευὴν LP

50

were loosed from their feet of their own accord, and keys opened doors with no mortal hand to turn them. Full of marvels has this man arrived in Thebes. But what follows must be your concern.

PENTHEUS

Release his hands! He is in the net and is not fast enough to escape from me. (*His servants remove the manacles from Dionysus.*)

Well, quite an attractive fellow you are, stranger—attractive to women, which is why you have come to Thebes. Your hair is long—no wrestler you—and it comes tumbling down all the way to your cheeks: how full of desire it is! And you deliberately keep your skin white: it is not in the sun's rays but in the shade that you hunt for love by means of your beauty.

But first tell me what your country is.

DIONYSUS

I feel no hesitation: the question is easy. I suppose you have heard of flowery Mount Tmolus.

PENTHEUS

Yes: it encircles the city of Sardis.

DIONYSUS

That is where I come from: Lydia is my country.

PENTHEUS

What is the source of these rites you bring to Greece?

---

461 οὐκ ὄκνος Wakefield: οὐ κόμπος LP

ΔΙΟΝΥΣΟΣ

Διόνυσος αὐτός μ' εἰσέβησ', ὁ τοῦ Διός.

ΠΕΝΘΕΥΣ

Ζεὺς δ' ἔστ' ἐκεῖ τις, ὃς νέους τίκτει θεούς;

ΔΙΟΝΥΣΟΣ

οὔκ, ἀλλ' ὁ Σεμέλην ἐνθάδε ζεύξας γάμοις.

ΠΕΝΘΕΥΣ

πότερα δὲ νύκτωρ σ' ἢ κατ' ὄμμ' ἠνάγκασεν;

ΔΙΟΝΥΣΟΣ

470   ὁρῶν ὁρῶντα, καὶ δίδωσιν ὄργια.

ΠΕΝΘΕΥΣ

τὰ δ' ὄργι' ἐστὶ τίν' ἰδέαν ἔχοντά σοι;

ΔΙΟΝΥΣΟΣ

ἄρρητ' ἀβακχεύτοισιν εἰδέναι βροτῶν.

ΠΕΝΘΕΥΣ

ἔχει δ' ὄνησιν τοῖσι θύουσιν τίνα;

ΔΙΟΝΥΣΟΣ

οὐ θέμις ἀκοῦσαί σ', ἔστι δ' ἄξι' εἰδέναι.

ΠΕΝΘΕΥΣ

475   εὖ τοῦτ' ἐκιβδήλευσας, ἵν' ἀκοῦσαι θέλω.

ΔΙΟΝΥΣΟΣ

ἀσέβειαν ἀσκοῦντ' ὄργι' ἐχθαίρει θεοῦ.

[466] αὐτός μ' Π: ἡμᾶς LP   εἰ[σέβησ' Π, coni. Abresch: εὐσέβησ' LP
[468] ἐνθάδε ζεύξας Musgrave: ἐνθάδ' ἔζευξεν LP

BACCHAE

DIONYSUS

Dionysus himself initiated me, Zeus's son.

PENTHEUS

Is there some Zeus there who fathers new gods?

DIONYSUS

No: I mean the one here who was Semele's lover.

PENTHEUS

And was it in a dream or in your waking sight that he con-
scripted you?

DIONYSUS

We could see one another: and he gave me rites.

PENTHEUS

These rites—what is their nature?

DIONYSUS

They may not be told to the uninitiated.

PENTHEUS

But those who perform them—what kind of benefit do
they get?

DIONYSUS

You are not allowed to hear—though the rites are well
worth knowing.

PENTHEUS

A clever counterfeit answer this, to pique my curiosity!

DIONYSUS

The god's rites are hostile to anyone who practices impiety.

ΠΕΝΘΕΥΣ

ὁ θεός, ὁρᾶν γὰρ φῂς σαφῶς, ποῖός τις ἦν;

ΔΙΟΝΥΣΟΣ

ὁποῖος ἤθελ'· οὐκ ἐγὼ 'τασσον τόδε.

ΠΕΝΘΕΥΣ

τοῦτ' αὖ παρωχέτευσας εὖ γ' οὐδὲν λέγων.

ΔΙΟΝΥΣΟΣ

480   δόξει τις ἀμαθεῖ σοφὰ λέγων οὐκ εὖ φρονεῖν.

ΠΕΝΘΕΥΣ

ἦλθες δὲ πρῶτα δεῦρ' ἄγων τὸν δαίμονα;

ΔΙΟΝΥΣΟΣ

πᾶς ἀναχορεύει βαρβάρων τάδ' ὄργια.

ΠΕΝΘΕΥΣ

φρονοῦσι γὰρ κάκιον Ἑλλήνων πολύ.

ΔΙΟΝΥΣΟΣ

τάδ' εὖ γε μᾶλλον· οἱ νόμοι δὲ διάφοροι.

ΠΕΝΘΕΥΣ

485   τὰ δ' ἱερὰ νύκτωρ ἢ μεθ' ἡμέραν τελεῖς;

ΔΙΟΝΥΣΟΣ

νύκτωρ τὰ πολλά· σεμνότητ' ἔχει σκότος.

ΠΕΝΘΕΥΣ

τοῦτ' ἐς γυναῖκας δόλιόν ἐστι καὶ σαθρόν.

ΔΙΟΝΥΣΟΣ

κἀν ἡμέρᾳ τό γ' αἰσχρὸν ἐξεύροι τις ἄν.

PENTHEUS

The god—what did he look like? You claim you saw him clearly.

DIONYSUS

He looked as he wished to look: I had no say in the matter.

PENTHEUS

Another evasive answer: you talk nonsense so cleverly.

DIONYSUS

Speak wisdom to a fool and he will think you foolish.

PENTHEUS

Is this the first place you brought the god?

DIONYSUS

No: all barbarians dance in observance of these rites.

PENTHEUS

Yes, they're much less clever than the Greeks.

DIONYSUS

In this case more so. But their customs are different.

PENTHEUS

Do you practice your rites at night or by day?

DIONYSUS

Mostly at night: darkness lends solemnity.

PENTHEUS

This is an immoral trick aimed at women.

DIONYSUS

Someone could engage in shameful deeds even by day.

---

477 ὁ θεός Brunck: τὸν θεὸν LP   ὁρᾶν γὰρ Musgrave: γὰρ ὁ- LP   479 γ᾽ οὐδὲν Burges: κοὐδὲν LP

ΠΕΝΘΕΥΣ

δίκην σε δοῦναι δεῖ σοφισμάτων κακῶν.

ΔΙΟΝΥΣΟΣ

490 σὲ δ᾽ ἀμαθίας γε κἀσεβοῦντ᾽ ἐς τὸν θεόν.

ΠΕΝΘΕΥΣ

ὡς θρασὺς ὁ βάκχος κοὐκ ἀγύμναστος λόγων.

ΔΙΟΝΥΣΟΣ

εἴφ᾽ ὅ τι παθεῖν δεῖ· τί με τὸ δεινὸν ἐργάσῃ;

ΠΕΝΘΕΥΣ

πρῶτον μὲν ἁβρὸν βόστρυχον τεμῶ σέθεν.

ΔΙΟΝΥΣΟΣ

ἱερὸς ὁ πλόκαμος· τῷ θεῷ δ᾽ αὐτὸν τρέφω.

ΠΕΝΘΕΥΣ

495 ἔπειτα θύρσον τόνδε παράδος ἐκ χεροῖν.

ΔΙΟΝΥΣΟΣ

αὐτός μ᾽ ἀφαιροῦ· τόνδε Διονύσῳ φορῶ.

ΠΕΝΘΕΥΣ

εἱρκταῖσί τ᾽ ἔνδον σῶμα σὸν φυλάξομεν.

ΔΙΟΝΥΣΟΣ

λύσει μ᾽ ὁ δαίμων αὐτός, ὅταν ἐγὼ θέλω.

ΠΕΝΘΕΥΣ

ὅταν γε καλέσῃς αὐτὸν ἐν βάκχαις σταθείς.

496 Διονύσῳ Collmann: -ου LP

PENTHEUS

You'll pay for your knavish cleverness.

DIONYSUS

And you for your obtuseness and impiety against the god.

PENTHEUS

How brash is this bacchant! What a practiced speaker!

DIONYSUS

Tell me what I must undergo: what is the terrible penalty you mean to inflict?

PENTHEUS

First I shall cut off your delicate locks.

DIONYSUS

My locks are sacred: I grow them long in the god's honor.

Pentheus cuts off some of Dionysus' hair.

PENTHEUS

Next, hand over that wand.

DIONYSUS

Take it from me yourself: I carry it, but it belongs to Dionysus.

Pentheus takes the thyrsus.

PENTHEUS

We will keep you penned up inside and under guard.

DIONYSUS

Dionysus himself will free me when I so desire.

PENTHEUS

Sure, when you stand surrounded by bacchants and call on him.

57

ΔΙΟΝΥΣΟΣ

500 καὶ νῦν ἃ πάσχω πλησίον παρὼν ὁρᾷ.

ΠΕΝΘΕΥΣ

καὶ ποῦ 'στιν; οὐ γὰρ φανερὸς ὄμμασίν γ' ἐμοῖς.

ΔΙΟΝΥΣΟΣ

παρ' ἐμοί· σὺ δ' ἀσεβὴς αὐτὸς ὢν οὐκ εἰσορᾷς.

ΠΕΝΘΕΥΣ

λάζυσθε· καταφρονεῖ με καὶ Θήβας ὅδε.

ΔΙΟΝΥΣΟΣ

αὐδῶ με μὴ δεῖν σωφρονῶν οὐ σώφροσιν.

ΠΕΝΘΕΥΣ

505 ἐγὼ δὲ δεῖν γε, κυριώτερος σέθεν.

ΔΙΟΝΥΣΟΣ

οὐκ οἶσθ' ὅ τι ζῇς, οὐδ' ὃ δρᾷς, οὐδ' ὅστις εἶ.

ΠΕΝΘΕΥΣ

Πενθεύς, Ἀγαυῆς παῖς, πατρὸς δ' Ἐχίονος.

ΔΙΟΝΥΣΟΣ

ἐνδυστυχῆσαι τοὔνομ' ἐπιτήδειος εἶ.

ΠΕΝΘΕΥΣ

χώρει· καθείρξατ' αὐτὸν ἱππικαῖς πέλας
510 φάτναισιν, ὡς ἂν σκότιον εἰσορᾷ κνέφας.
ἐκεῖ χόρευε· τάσδε δ' ἃς ἄγων πάρει
κακῶν συνεργοὺς ἢ διεμπολήσομεν
ἢ χεῖρα δούπου τοῦδε καὶ βύρσης κτύπου

---

506 ὅ τι ζῇς] ὃ βάζεις Cobet   ὃ δρᾷς Reiske: ὁρᾷς LP

DIONYSUS

Yes, even now he is near and sees what I am undergoing.

PENTHEUS

Where is he? To my eyes he is not in evidence.

DIONYSUS

He's with me: since you are a godless man you do not see him.

PENTHEUS

Seize him! He's treating me and Thebes with contempt!

DIONYSUS

And I forbid it: I am sane and you are not.

PENTHEUS

I say bind him, and I have more authority than you.

DIONYSUS

You do not know what your life is or what you are doing or who you are.

PENTHEUS

I am Pentheus, son of Agave and Echion.

DIONYSUS

Your name fits you well for misfortune.[11]

PENTHEUS

Off now! Shut him up near the horses' corncribs, so that his eyes get plenty of darkness. Do your dancing there! As for these women you have brought with you as your partners in mischief, either I shall sell them or, when I have stopped

11 See note on line 367 above.

παύσας ἐφ᾽ ἱστοῖς δμωίδας κεκτήσομαι.

ΔΙΟΝΥΣΟΣ

515 στείχοιμ᾽ ἄν· ὅ τι γὰρ μὴ χρεὼν οὔτοι χρεὼν
παθεῖν. ἀτάρ τοι τῶνδ᾽ ἄποιν᾽ ὑβρισμάτων
μέτεισι Διόνυσός σ᾽, ὃν οὐκ εἶναι λέγεις·
ἡμᾶς γὰρ ἀδικῶν κεῖνον ἐς δεσμοὺς ἄγεις.

ΧΟΡΟΣ

στρ.

Ἀχελῴου θύγατερ,
520 πότνι᾽ εὐπάρθενε Δίρκα,
σὺ γὰρ ἐν σαῖς ποτε παγαῖς
τὸ Διὸς βρέφος ἔλαβες,
ὅτε μηρῷ πυρὸς ἐξ ἀθανάτου Ζεὺς
525 ὁ τεκὼν ἥρπασέ νιν, τάδ᾽ ἀναβοάσας·
Ἴθι, Διθύραμβ᾽, ἐμὰν ἄρ-
σενα τάνδε βᾶθι νηδύν·
ἀναφαίνω σε τόδ᾽, ὦ Βάκ-
χιε, Θήβαις ὀνομάζειν.
530 σὺ δέ μ᾽, ὦ μάκαιρα Δίρκα,
στεφανηφόρους ἀπωθῇ
θιάσους ἔχουσαν ἐν σοί.
τί μ᾽ ἀναίνῃ; τί με φεύγεις;
ἔτι ναὶ τὰν βοτρυώδη
535 Διονύσου χάριν οἴνας,

528 ἀναφαίνω Hermann: -φανῶ LP

their clapping and drum beating, keep them as slaves to
tend my looms.

DIONYSUS

I'm ready to go: I shall not suffer anything I am not meant
to suffer. But Dionysus, you know, will punish you for this
highhandedness, Dionysus who you claim does not exist.
You wrong me, but it's him you're leading off to prison.

Exit into the skene DIONYSUS *and* PENTHEUS *with retinue,
including* SERVANT.

CHORUS

Daughter of Achelöus,
Lady Dirce, fair maiden,
on you I call, for in your streams
you once received Zeus's babe
when Zeus his father snatched him from the ever-blazing
   fire
and put him in his thigh and cried out,
"Come, Dithyrambus,[12] enter here
my male womb!
I proclaim to Thebes
that she should call you by this name."
But you, O Dirce blessed,
reject me though I have on your banks
sacred bands of worshipers adorned with wreaths.
Why reject me, why run from me?
One day yet—I swear it by the clustered
joy of Dionysus' vine—

[12] A name of Dionysus, connecting him with the choral songs
in his honor called dithyrambs.

ἔτι σοι τοῦ Βρομίου μελήσει.

ἀντ.

[οἴαν οἴαν ὀργὰν]
ἀναφαίνει χθόνιον
γένος ἐκφύς τε δράκοντός
540 ποτε Πενθεύς, ὃν Ἐχίων
ἐφύτευσε χθόνιος,
ἀγριωπὸν τέρας, οὐ φῶτα βρότειον,
φόνιον δ' ὥστε γίγαντ' ἀντίπαλον θεοῖς·
545 ὃς ἔμ' ἐν βρόχοισι τὰν τοῦ
Βρομίου τάχα ξυνάψει,
τὸν ἐμὸν δ' ἐντὸς ἔχει δώ-
ματος ἤδη θιασώταν
σκοτίαισι κρυπτὸν εἱρκταῖς.
550 ἐσορᾷς τάδ', ὦ Διὸς παῖ
Διόνυσε, σοὺς προφήτας
ἐν ἁμίλλαισιν ἀνάγκας;
μόλε, χρυσῶπα τινάσσων,
ἄνα, θύρσον κατ' Ὀλύμπου,
555 φονίου δ' ἀνδρὸς ὕβριν κατάσχες.

ἐπῳδ.

πόθι Νύσας ἄρα τᾶς θη-
ροτρόφου θυρσοφορεῖς
θιάσους, ὦ Διόνυσ'; ἢ
κορυφαῖς Κωρυκίαις;
560 τάχα δ' ἐν ταῖς πολυδένδροισιν Ὀλύμπου
θαλάμαις, ἔνθα ποτ' Ὀρφεὺς κιθαρίζων

one day yet Bromios shall be your care.

[What anger]
He shows his earthborn
origin, that he was born from a dragon,
does Pentheus, son
of earthborn Echion,
a monster with visage wild, no man of mortal frame
but one of the murderous Giants who opposed the gods.
And soon he will bind me,
Dionysus' servant, in the knotted ropes,
and he keeps within his palace
my fellow in the sacred band,
concealing him in a dark prison.
Do you mark, O Dionysus,
son of Zeus, that your spokesmen
are at grips with oppression?
Come down from Olympus, my lord,
shaking your gold-gleaming wand,
and check the violence of this man of blood!

Where then on the slopes of Nysa, nurse of wild beasts,
do you lead your sacred bands
with your holy wand, O Dionysus?
Or is it on Corycia's peaks?
Perhaps in the leafy coverts
of Olympus where Orpheus, playing his lyre,

---

537 del. Bothe
545 ἔμ' ἐν Dobree: με LP
549 σκοτίαισι κρυπτὸν Bothe: σκοτίαις κ- ἐν LP
554 Ὀλύμπου Kirchhoff: Ὄλυμπον LP

σύναγεν δένδρεα μούσαις,
σύναγεν θῆρας ἀγρώστας.
565 μάκαρ ὦ Πιερία,
σέβεταί σ' Εὔιος, ἥξει
τε χορεύσων ἅμα βακχεύ-
μασι, τόν τ' ὠκυρόαν
διαβὰς Ἀξιὸν εἱλισ-
570 σομένας μαινάδας ἄξει
Λυδίαν τε τὸν εὐδαιμονίας βροτοῖς
ὀλβοδόταν πατέρ', ὃν ἔκλυον
εὔιππον χώραν ὕδασιν
575 καλλίστοισι λιπαίνειν.

ΔΙΟΝΥΣΟΣ

ἰώ,
κλύετ' ἐμᾶς κλύετ' αὐδᾶς,
ἰὼ βάκχαι, ἰὼ βάκχαι.

ΧΟΡΟΣ

τίς ὅδε, τίς πόθεν ὁ κέλαδος
ἀνά μ' ἐκάλεσεν Εὐίου;

ΔΙΟΝΥΣΟΣ

580 ἰὼ ἰώ, πάλιν αὐδῶ,
ὁ Σεμέλας, ὁ Διὸς παῖς.

ΧΟΡΟΣ

ἰὼ ἰὼ δέσποτα δέσποτα,
μόλε νυν ἁμέτερον ἐς

565 μάκαρ Hermann: μάκαιρ' LP

64

once assembled the trees by his song,
assembled the beasts of the wild.
Happy Pieria,
Euhios[13] honors you,
and he will come to dance with his bacchants:
he will lead his whirling bacchants,
crossing the swift-running
current of the River Axius
and the Lydias, father of prosperity and giver
of wealth to mortals, which with its lovely waters
makes rich, so I have heard,
a land blessed with horses.

DIONYSUS

(*within*) Ho there,
hear my voice,
ho, bacchants, ho bacchants!

CHORUS

Who is it, what and whence the voice
of Euhios that calls my name?

DIONYSUS

Ho, I say once more,
I, Semele's and Zeus's son!

CHORUS

Hail, master, master,
come then to join our thiasos,

---

13 A cult title of Dionysus.

571–2 εὐδαιμονίας Burges: τᾶς εὐδ- LP
573 πατέρ᾽, ὃν Ferrari: πατέρα τε τὸν LP

θίασον, ὦ Βρόμιε Βρόμιε.

ΔΙΟΝΥΣΟΣ

585 ⟨σεῖε⟩ πέδον χθονός, Ἔννοσι πότνια.

ΧΟΡΟΣ

—ἆ ἆ,
τάχα τὰ Πενθέως μέλαθρα διατι-
νάξεται πεσήμασιν.
ὁ Διόνυσος ἀνὰ μέλαθρα·
590 σέβετέ νιν. —σέβομεν ὤ.
—ἴδετε λάιν᾿ ⟨ὦ⟩ ἔμβολα κίοσιν
τάδε διάδρομα· Βρόμιος ἀλαλάζεται
στέγας ⟨τᾶσδ᾿⟩ ἔσω.

ΔΙΟΝΥΣΟΣ

ἅπτε κεραύνιον αἴθοπα λαμπάδα,
595 σύμφλεγε σύμφλεγε δώματα Πενθέος.

ΧΟΡΟΣ

ἆ ἆ,
πῦρ οὐ λεύσσεις, οὐδ᾿ αὐγάζῃ,
Σεμέλας ἱερὸν ⟨τόνδ᾿⟩ ἀμφὶ τάφον,
ἅν ποτε κεραυνόβολος ἔλιπε
φλόγα Διὸς βροντά;
600 δίκετε πεδόσε δίκετε τρομερὰ
σώματα, μαινάδες·
ὁ γὰρ ἄναξ ἄνω κάτω τιθεὶς ἔπεισι

585 ⟨σεῖε⟩ Wilamowitz   591 λάιν᾿ ⟨ὦ⟩ Willink (τὰ iam
del. Dobree): τὰ λάινα LP   ἔμβολα κίοσιν Willink: κίοσιν ἔ-
LP   593 ⟨τᾶσδ᾿⟩ Willink

O Bromios, Bromios!

DIONYSUS

‹Shake› the level earth, O Goddess Earthquake!

CHORUS A

Ah, ah!
Soon the palace of Pentheus
will be shaken and fall!
Dionysus is in the house!
Worship him!

CHORUS B

We worship him, ah!

CHORUS A

See, here on the columns the stone lintels
are falling apart! Bromios is raising a shout
in the palace ‹here›.

DIONYSUS

Kindle the glowing blaze of lightning,
burn up, burn up the palace of Pentheus!

CHORUS

Ah, ah,
do you not see, not mark the fire
about Semele's holy tomb ‹here›,
the flame left behind
by Zeus's lightning?
Hurl to the ground your trembling bodies,
hurl them, maenads!
Our lord, Zeus's son is attacking this house,

---

597 ‹τόνδ'› Willink
599 Διὸς βροντά ed. Hervag.: Δίου βροντᾶς fere LP

μέλαθρα τάδε Διὸς γόνος.

ΔΙΟΝΥΣΟΣ

βάρβαροι γυναῖκες, οὕτως ἐκπεπληγμέναι φόβῳ
605 πρὸς πέδῳ πεπτώκατ'; ᾔσθεσθ', ὡς ἔοικε, Βακχίου
διατινάξαντος τὰ Πενθέως δώματ'· ἀλλ' ἀνίστατε
σῶμα καὶ θαρσεῖτε σαρκὸς ἐξαμείψασαι τρόμον.

ΧΟΡΟΣ

ὦ φάος μέγιστον ἡμῖν εὐίου βακχεύματος,
ὡς ἐσεῖδον ἀσμένη σε, μονάδ' ἔχουσ' ἐρημίαν.

ΔΙΟΝΥΣΟΣ

610 εἰς ἀθυμίαν ἀφίκεσθ', ἡνίκ' εἰσεπεμπόμην,
Πενθέως ὡς ἐς σκοτεινὰς ὁρκάνας πεσούμενος;

ΧΟΡΟΣ

πῶς γὰρ οὔ; τίς μοι φύλαξ ἦν, εἰ σὺ συμφορᾶς
    τύχοις;
ἀλλὰ πῶς ἠλευθερώθης ἀνδρὸς ἀνοσίου τυχών;

ΔΙΟΝΥΣΟΣ

αὐτὸς ἐξέσωσ' ἐμαυτὸν ῥᾳδίως ἄνευ πόνου.

ΧΟΡΟΣ

615 οὐδέ σου συνῆψε χεῖρας δεσμίοισιν ἐν βρόχοις;

ΔΙΟΝΥΣΟΣ

ταῦτα καὶ καθύβρισ' αὐτόν, ὅτι με δεσμεύειν δοκῶν

606 τὰ Πενθέως δώματ'· ἀλλ' ἀνίστατε Musgrave: δῶμα
Πενθέως· ἀλλ' ἐξανίστατε LP
    607 σαρκὸς Wasse: σάρκας LP
    613 τυχών] χερῶν F. W. Schmidt, φυγών Dodds

turning it topsy-turvy!

They prostrate themselves on the ground. Enter from the skene DIONYSUS.

DIONYSUS
Barbarian women, are you so frightened that you have fallen to the ground? It seems you have heard the bacchic god shaking Pentheus' palace. But stand on your feet, take heart, and stop quaking.

CHORUS LEADER
O supreme light of deliverance to all our ecstatic band, how glad I am to see you: I was alone and bereft!

DIONYSUS
Were you disheartened when I was taken inside, thinking I would be thrown into Pentheus' dark prison?

CHORUS LEADER
Of course: who was going to defend me if you met with disaster? But how did you get free after encountering this man of sin?

DIONYSUS
I rescued myself: it was easy and cost no trouble.

CHORUS LEADER
But did he not tie your hands together with a noose?

DIONYSUS
That was just it, the insult I paid him: he thought he was

---

615 χεῖρας Diggle: χεῖρα LP

οὔτ' ἔθιγεν οὔθ' ἥψαθ' ἡμῶν, ἐλπίσιν δ' ἐβόσκετο.
πρὸς φάτναις δὲ ταῦρον εὑρών, οὗ καθεῖρξ' ἡμᾶς
   ἄγων,
τῷδε περὶ βρόχους ἔβαλλε γόνασι καὶ χηλαῖς
   ποδῶν,
620 θυμὸν ἐκπνέων, ἱδρῶτα σώματος στάζων ἄπο,
χείλεσιν διδοὺς ὀδόντας· πλησίον δ' ἐγὼ παρὼν
ἥσυχος θάσσων ἔλευσσον. ἐν δὲ τῷδε τῷ χρόνῳ
ἀνετίναξ' ἐλθὼν ὁ Βάκχος δῶμα καὶ μητρὸς τάφῳ
πῦρ ἀνῆψ'· ὁ δ' ὡς ἐσεῖδε, δώματ' αἴθεσθαι δοκῶν
625 ᾖσσ' ἐκεῖσε κᾆτ' ἐκεῖσε, δμωσὶν Ἀχελῷον φέρειν
ἐννέπων, ἅπας δ' ἐν ἔργῳ δοῦλος ἦν, μάτην πονῶν.
   διαμεθεὶς δὲ τόνδε μόχθον, ὡς ἐμοῦ πεφευγότος,
ἵεται ξίφος κελαινὸν ἁρπάσας δόμων ἔσω.
κᾆθ' ὁ Βρόμιος, ὡς ἔμοιγε φαίνεται, δόξαν λέγω,
630 φάσμ' ἐποίησεν κατ' αὐλήν· ὁ δ' ἐπὶ τοῦθ'
   ὡρμημένος
ᾖσσε κἀκέντει φαεννὸν ⟨αἰθέρ'⟩, ὡς σφάζων ἐμέ.
πρὸς δὲ τοῖσδ' αὐτῷ τάδ' ἄλλα Βάκχιος λυμαίνεται·
δώματ' ἔρρηξεν χαμᾶζε· συντεθράνωται δ' ἅπαν
πικροτάτους ἰδόντι δεσμοὺς τοὺς ἐμούς· κόπου δ'
   ὕπο
635 διαμεθεὶς ξίφος παρεῖται· πρὸς θεὸν γὰρ ὢν ἀνὴρ
ἐς μάχην ἐλθεῖν ἐτόλμησ'. ἥσυχος δ' ἐκβὰς ἐγὼ
δωμάτων ἥκω πρὸς ὑμᾶς, Πενθέως οὐ φροντίσας.
   ὡς δέ μοι δοκεῖ (ψοφεῖ γοῦν ἀρβύλη δόμων ἔσω)
ἐς προνώπι' αὐτίχ' ἥξει. τί ποτ' ἄρ' ἐκ τούτων ἐρεῖ;
640 ῥᾳδίως γὰρ αὐτὸν οἴσω, κἂν πνέων ἔλθῃ μέγα·

tying me up, but he didn't lay a hand on me, it was an idle hope he fed on. Near the corncrib where he took me to lock me up he found a bull, and it was this animal's legs and hooves that he roped up. He was panting hard, his body was bathed in sweat, and he was chewing his lip. I sat nearby and looked on without a word. While this was going on, Bacchus came and shook the palace and made fire blaze up on his mother's tomb. Pentheus saw this, and thinking that his house was on fire he rushed here and there, ordering his servants to bring water (all his slaves fell to), but it was for nothing.

Then thinking that I had escaped he ceased from these efforts, snatched up a dark-gleaming sword, and rushed into the house. And then Bromios, I think—I'm telling you how it seemed to me—caused an apparition in the palace. Pentheus set off in pursuit of this and stabbed at ⟨the air⟩, thinking he was slaughtering me. And the bacchic god did him other injury beyond this. He razed his house to the ground, the whole thing is shattered: he has seen a bitter end to his imprisoning of me. He has dropped his sword and is exhausted: though a man he dared to fight against a god. As for me, I left the house quietly and came to you, unconcerned about Pentheus.

He will soon, I think, come out before the palace—at any rate, I hear the tread of boots inside the door. What will he say after all this? No matter: I will have no trouble enduring him even if he comes out huffing and puffing. It is a

---

630 φάσμ' Jacobs: φῶς LP
631 ⟨αἰθέρ'⟩ Canter
636 ἐκβὰς ἐγὼ Heinisch: ἐκ βάκχας ἄγων LP

πρὸς σοφοῦ γὰρ ἀνδρὸς ἀσκεῖν σώφρον᾽
εὐοργησίαν.

ΠΕΝΘΕΥΣ

πέπονθα δεινά· διαπέφευγέ μ᾽ ὁ ξένος,
ὃς ἄρτι δεσμοῖς ἦν κατηναγκασμένος.
ἔα ἔα·
645 ὅδ᾽ ἐστὶν ἀνήρ· τί τάδε; πῶς προνώπιος
φαίνῃ πρὸς οἴκοις τοῖς ἐμοῖς, ἔξω βεβώς;

ΔΙΟΝΥΣΟΣ

στῆσον πόδ᾽, ὀργῇ δ᾽ ὑπόθες ἥσυχον πόδα.

ΠΕΝΘΕΥΣ

πόθεν σὺ δεσμὰ διαφυγὼν ἔξω περᾷς;

ΔΙΟΝΥΣΟΣ

οὐκ εἶπον, ἢ οὐκ ἤκουσας, ὅτι λύσει μέ τις;

ΠΕΝΘΕΥΣ

650 τίς; τοὺς λόγους γὰρ ἐσφέρεις καινοὺς ἀεί.

ΔΙΟΝΥΣΟΣ

ὃς τὴν πολύβοτρυν ἄμπελον φύει βροτοῖς.

ΠΕΝΘΕΥΣ

ὠνείδισας δὴ τοῦτο Διονύσῳ καλόν.

⟨ΔΙΟΝΥΣΟΣ

καλῶν μὲν οὖν τήνδ᾽ ἦλθεν ἐς πόλιν πλέως.⟩

647 πόδα] βάσιν Blomfield
652 post h. v. lac. indic. Hermann, suppl. Wecklein

72

wise man's part to practice gentleness and self-control.

Enter from the skene PENTHEUS *with retinue.*

PENTHEUS

I have been monstrously treated: he's escaped me, the
stranger who was just now chained and under arrest!

But look! Here is the man! How can it be that you have
come outside and show yourself at the door of my palace?

DIONYSUS

Hold on! Calm your anger!

PENTHEUS

How is it that you have escaped your manacles and come
out?

DIONYSUS

Did I not say—or did you fail to hear it—that someone
would free me?

PENTHEUS

Who? Your talk is always strange.

DIONYSUS

He who grows the rich-clustered vine for mortals.

PENTHEUS

The fine deed you mention is in fact a reproach to Diony-
sus.

‹DIONYSUS

But Dionysus has come into this city full of such fine
deeds.›

ΠΕΝΘΕΥΣ

κλῄειν κελεύω πάντα πύργον ἐν κύκλῳ.

ΔΙΟΝΥΣΟΣ

τί δ'; οὐχ ὑπερβαίνουσι καὶ τείχη θεοί;

ΠΕΝΘΕΥΣ

655   σοφὸς σοφὸς σύ, πλὴν ἃ δεῖ σ' εἶναι σοφόν.

ΔΙΟΝΥΣΟΣ

ἃ δεῖ μάλιστα, ταῦτ' ἔγωγ' ἔφυν σοφός.
   κείνου δ' ἀκούσας πρῶτα τοὺς λόγους μάθε,
ὃς ἐξ ὄρους πάρεστιν ἀγγελῶν τί σοι·
ἡμεῖς δέ σοι μενοῦμεν, οὐ φευξούμεθα.

ΑΓΓΕΛΟΣ

660   Πενθεῦ κρατύνων τῆσδε Θηβαίας χθονός,
ἥκω Κιθαιρῶν' ἐκλιπών, ἵν' οὔποτε
λευκῆς χιόνος ἀνεῖσαν εὐαγεῖς βολαί.

ΠΕΝΘΕΥΣ

ἥκεις δὲ ποίαν προστιθεὶς σπουδὴν λόγου;

ΑΓΓΕΛΟΣ

βάκχας ποτνιάδας εἰσιδών, αἳ τῆσδε γῆς
665   οἴστροισι λευκὸν κῶλον ἐξηκόντισαν,
ἥκω φράσαι σοὶ καὶ πόλει χρῄζων, ἄναξ,
ὡς δεινὰ δρῶσι θαυμάτων τε κρείσσονα.
θέλω δ' ἀκοῦσαι πότερά σοι παρρησίᾳ

661 οὔτι πω Willink

PENTHEUS

Shut all the towered gates, all the way round the city!
Those are my orders!

Two of his retinue go down the two eisodoi to convey this order.

DIONYSUS

What's this? Do not gods leap over walls?

PENTHEUS

You are clever, clever, except where you ought to be clever.

DIONYSUS

Where cleverness is most needed, there I am clever.

Enter by Eisodos B a herdsman as MESSENGER.

But first listen to this man and learn what he has to say:
he has come from the mountains to bring you some news.
You will find me waiting here, I won't run away.

MESSENGER

Pentheus, king of this land of Thebes, I have come here
from Cithaeron, where glistening falls of white snow still
descend.

PENTHEUS

And what weighty message do you bring?

MESSENGER

I have seen the wild bacchant women, who ran from this
city in madness with their white feet in rapid motion, and I
have come to tell you and the city, my lord, that they are
doing strange deeds that outstrip wonder. But I want you
to tell me whether I should speak freely about what hap-

φράσω τὰ κεῖθεν ἢ λόγον στειλώμεθα·
670 τὸ γὰρ τάχος σου τῶν φρενῶν δέδοικ', ἄναξ,
καὶ τοὐξύθυμον καὶ τὸ βασιλικὸν λίαν.

ΠΕΝΘΕΥΣ

λέγ', ὡς ἀθῷος ἐξ ἐμοῦ πάντως ἔσῃ·
[τοῖς γὰρ δικαίοις οὐχὶ θυμοῦσθαι χρεών.]
ὅσῳ δ' ἂν εἴπῃς δεινότερα βακχῶν πέρι,
675 τοσῷδε μᾶλλον τὸν ὑποθέντα τὰς τέχνας
γυναιξὶ τόνδε τῇ δίκῃ προσθήσομεν.

ΑΓΓΕΛΟΣ

ἀγελαῖα μὲν βοσκήματ' ἄρτι πρὸς λέπας
μόσχων ὑπεξήκριζον, ἡνίχ' ἥλιος
ἀκτῖνας ἐξίησι θερμαίνων χθόνα.
680 ὁρῶ δὲ θιάσους τρεῖς γυναικείων χορῶν,
ὧν ἦρχ' ἑνὸς μὲν Αὐτονόη, τοῦ δευτέρου
μήτηρ Ἀγαυὴ σή, τρίτου δ' Ἰνὼ χοροῦ.
ηὗδον δὲ πᾶσαι σώμασιν παρειμέναι,
αἱ μὲν πρὸς ἐλάτης νῶτ' ἐρείσασαι φόβην,
685 αἱ δ' ἐν δρυὸς φύλλοισι πρὸς πέδῳ κάρα
εἰκῇ βαλοῦσαι σωφρόνως, οὐχ ὡς σὺ φὴς
ᾠνωμένας κρατῆρι καὶ λωτοῦ ψόφῳ
θηρᾶν καθ' ὕλην Κύπριν ἠρημωμένας.
ἡ σὴ δὲ μήτηρ ὠλόλυξεν ἐν μέσαις
690 σταθεῖσα βάκχαις ἐξ ὕπνου κινεῖν δέμας,
μυκήμαθ' ὡς ἤκουσε κεροφόρων βοῶν.
αἱ δ' ἀποβαλοῦσαι θαλερὸν ὀμμάτων ὕπνον
ἀνῇξαν ὀρθαί, θαῦμ' ἰδεῖν εὐκοσμίας,

pened there or be circumspect in my speech. I fear your mind's hastiness, my lord, its irascibility, and your all too royal temper.

Say on, for I will do nothing to hurt you: [one ought not to be angry with just men.] the stranger the things you report about the bacchants, the more harshly I shall punish this man, who has suggested these crafty ways to them.

It was the hour when the sun sheds its beams on the earth to warm it. Our grazing herds of cattle were just climbing to the uplands when I saw three covens, three choruses of women, one led by Autonoe, and a second by your mother Agave, while the third was led by Ino. They all lay sleeping, their bodies relaxed: some lay on their backs upon fir branches, others in no order rested their heads on the ground amid oak leaves, chastely. They were not, as you maintain, drunk with the wine bowl and the sound of the pipe, or going off separately in the green wood to find Aphrodite.

Your mother Agave, hearing the lowing of the horned cattle, stood up in the midst of the bacchants and gave a whoop, telling them to stir themselves from sleep. They rubbed the deep sleep from their eyes and stood upright, a marvel of ordered calm to look at, young women and

---

669 λόγῳ Dawe cl. *Or.* 607
673 del. Nauck cl. fr. 287.1

νέαι παλαιαὶ παρθένοι τ᾽ ἔτ᾽ ἄζυγες.
695 καὶ πρῶτα μὲν καθεῖσαν εἰς ὤμους κόμας
νεβρίδας τ᾽ ἀνεστείλανθ᾽ ὅσαισιν ἁμμάτων
σύνδεσμ᾽ ἐλέλυτο, καὶ καταστίκτους δορὰς
ὄφεσι κατεζώσαντο λιχμῶσιν γένυν.
αἱ δ᾽ ἀγκάλαισι δορκάδ᾽ ἢ σκύμνους λύκων
700 ἀγρίους ἔχουσαι λευκὸν ἐδίδοσαν γάλα,
ὅσαις νεοτόκοις μαστὸς ἦν σπαργῶν ἔτι
βρέφη λιπούσαις· ἐπὶ δ᾽ ἔθεντο κισσίνους
στεφάνους δρυός τε μίλακός τ᾽ ἀνθεσφόρου.
θύρσον δέ τις λαβοῦσ᾽ ἔπαισεν ἐς πέτραν,
705 ὅθεν δροσώδης ὕδατος ἐκπηδᾷ νοτίς·
ἄλλη δὲ νάρθηκ᾽ ἐς πέδον καθῆκε γῆς
καὶ τῇδε κρήνην ἐξανῆκ᾽ οἴνου θεός·
ὅσαις δὲ λευκοῦ πώματος πόθος παρῆν,
ἄκροισι δακτύλοισι διαμῶσαι χθόνα
710 γάλακτος ἑσμοὺς εἶχον· ἐκ δὲ κισσίνων
θύρσων γλυκεῖαι μέλιτος ἔσταζον ῥοαί.
ὥστ᾽, εἰ παρῆσθα, τὸν θεὸν τὸν νῦν ψέγεις
εὐχαῖσιν ἂν μετῆλθες εἰσιδὼν τάδε.
  ξυνήλθομεν δὲ βουκόλοι καὶ ποιμένες
715 κοινῶν λόγων δώσοντες ἀλλήλοις ἔριν
[ὡς δεινὰ δρῶσι θαυμάτων τ᾽ ἐπάξια].
καί τις πλάνης κατ᾽ ἄστυ καὶ τρίβων λόγων
ἔλεξεν εἰς ἅπαντας· Ὦ σεμνὰς πλάκας
ναίοντες ὀρέων, θέλετε θηρασώμεθα
720 Πενθέως Ἀγαυὴν μητέρ᾽ ἐκ βακχευμάτων
χάριν τ᾽ ἄνακτι θώμεθ᾽; εὖ δ᾽ ἡμῖν λέγειν

78

old and girls still unmarried. First they let their hair fall
to their shoulders, and those whose fastenings had come
undone adjusted their fawnskin garments, girdling the
dappled skins with snakes that licked their cheeks. New
mothers, their babies left behind and their breasts overfull
with milk, cradled gazelles or wolf cubs in their arms and
gave them to drink of their white milk. They decked them-
selves with crowns of ivy, oak, and flowering bryony. Some-
one took a thyrsus and struck it against a cliff, and out leapt
a dewy spring of water. Another sunk her fennel wand into
the ground, and the god at that spot put forth a fountain of
wine. All who desired a drink of milk dug with their finger-
tips in the ground and the white liquid bubbled up. From
their ivy-covered thyrsi dripped streams of honey. If you
had been there and seen this, you would have approached
in prayer the god you now disparage.

We cowherds and shepherds gathered together to talk
and dispute with one another [, that they are doing strange
deeds that outstrip wonder]. And one man, who spent time
in the city and was a clever speaker, said to us all, "Herds-
men, dwelling in these august mountain dells, shall we
capture Pentheus' mother Agave out of the bacchic band
and do our king a favor?" We thought this was a good idea

---

716 del. Dobree cl. 667

ἔδοξε, θάμνων δ' ἐλλοχίζομεν φόβαις
κρύψαντες αὑτούς· αἱ δὲ τὴν τεταγμένην
ὥραν ἐκίνουν θύρσον ἐς βακχεύματα,
725 Ἴακχον ἀθρόῳ στόματι τὸν Διὸς γόνον
Βρόμιον καλοῦσαι· πᾶν δὲ συνεβάκχευ' ὄρος
καὶ θῆρες, οὐδὲν δ' ἦν ἀκίνητον δρόμῳ.
κυρεῖ δ' Ἀγαυὴ πλησίον θρῴσκουσ' ἐμοῦ,
κἀγὼ 'ξεπήδησ' ὡς συναρπάσαι θέλων,
730 λόχμην κενώσας ἔνθ' ἐκρύπτομεν δέμας.
ἡ δ' ἀνεβόησεν· Ὦ δρομάδες ἐμαὶ κύνες,
θηρώμεθ' ἀνδρῶν τῶνδ' ὕπ'· ἀλλ' ἕπεσθέ μοι,
ἕπεσθε θύρσοις διὰ χερῶν ὡπλισμέναι.
ἡμεῖς μὲν οὖν φεύγοντες ἐξηλύξαμεν
735 βακχῶν σπαραγμόν, αἱ δὲ νεμομέναις χλόην
μόσχοις ἐπῆλθον χειρὸς ἀσιδήρου μέτα.
καὶ τὴν μὲν ἂν προσεῖδες εὔθηλον πόριν
μυκωμένην ἕλκουσαν ἐν χεροῖν δίχα,
ἄλλαι δὲ δαμάλας διεφόρουν σπαράγμασιν.
740 εἶδες δ' ἂν ἢ πλεύρ' ἢ δίχηλον ἔμβασιν
ῥιπτόμεν' ἄνω τε καὶ κάτω· κρεμαστὰ δὲ
ἔσταζ' ὑπ' ἐλάταις ἀναπεφυρμέν' αἵματι.
ταῦροι δ' ὑβρισταὶ κὰς κέρας θυμούμενοι
τὸ πρόσθεν ἐσφάλλοντο πρὸς γαῖαν δέμας,
745 μυριάσι χειρῶν ἀγόμενοι νεανίδων.
θᾶσσον δὲ διεφοροῦντο σαρκὸς ἐνδυτὰ
ἢ σὲ ξυνάψαι βλέφαρα βασιλείοις κόραις.
χωροῦσι δ' ὥστ' ὄρνιθες ἀρθεῖσαι δρόμῳ
πεδίων ὑποτάσεις, αἳ παρ' Ἀσωποῦ ῥοαῖς

and lay in ambush, hiding ourselves in the underbrush.
And the women at the appointed time of day began to
wave their thyrsoi and to worship Dionysus, calling on
Zeus's son Iacchus[14] with united voice as Bromios: the
whole mountain with its beasts was as possessed as they
were, and everything was set in rapid motion.

Agave's leaping happened to bring her near me, and I
left my hidingplace and jumped up to seize her. But she
cried out, "My coursing hounds, men are trying to hunt us
down! So follow me, follow me, your hands armed with
your bacchic wands!"

We ran away and thereby escaped being torn to pieces
by the bacchants. But they, with no iron weapons in their
hands, attacked some grazing cattle. You could have seen
one of the women tearing asunder a bellowing fatted calf
with her hands, while others tore heifers to pieces. You
could have seen their flanks and cloven hooves hurled this
way and that: pieces, drenched with blood, hung dripping
from the fir trees. Bulls that till then were violent, with
anger in their horns, were thrown to earth, dragged by
countless female hands: their covering of flesh was torn in
pieces faster than your majesty could blink your royal eyes.

They rose like birds and moved rapidly over the spread-
ing plains that near Asopus' waters produce abundant

---

[14] Iacchus, originally a separate divinity associated with the
Mysteries of Eleusis, became identified by the fifth century with
Dionysus.

---

738 ἕλκουσαν Reiske: ἕχουσαν LP

750 εὔκαρπον ἐκβάλλουσι Θηβαίοις στάχυν,
Ὑσιάς τ᾽ Ἐρυθράς θ᾽, αἳ Κιθαιρῶνος λέπας
νέρθεν κατῳκήκασιν, ὥστε πολέμιοι
ἐπεσπεσοῦσαι πάντ᾽ ἄνω τε καὶ κάτω
διέφερον· ἥρπαζον μὲν ἐκ δόμων τέκνα,
755 ὁπόσα δ᾽ ἐπ᾽ ὤμοις ἔθεσαν, οὐ δεσμῶν ὕπο
προσείχετ᾽ οὐδ᾽ ἔπιπτεν [ἐς μέλαν πέδον,
οὐ χαλκός, οὐ σίδηρος], ἐπὶ δὲ βοστρύχοις
πῦρ ἔφερον, οὐδ᾽ ἔκαιεν. οἱ δ᾽ ὀργῆς ὕπο
ἐς ὅπλ᾽ ἐχώρουν φερόμενοι βακχῶν ὕπο·
760 οὗπερ τὸ δεινὸν ἦν θέαμ᾽ ἰδεῖν, ἄναξ·
τοῖς μὲν γὰρ οὐχ ἥμασσε λογχωτὸν βέλος,
757a οὐ χαλκός, οὐ σίδηρος, ⟨ἔνθεον χρόα⟩,
κεῖναι δὲ θύρσους ἐξανεῖσαι χερῶν
ἐτραυμάτιζον κἀπενώτιζον φυγῇ
γυναῖκες ἄνδρας οὐκ ἄνευ θεῶν τινος.
765 πάλιν δ᾽ ἐχώρουν ὅθεν ἐκίνησαν πόδα
κρήνας ἐπ᾽ αὐτὰς ἃς ἀνῆκ᾽ αὐταῖς θεός,
νίψαντο δ᾽ αἷμα, σταγόνα δ᾽ ἐκ παρηίδων
γλώσσῃ δράκοντες ἐξεφαίδρυνον χροός.
    τὸν δαίμον᾽ οὖν τόνδ᾽, ὅστις ἔστ᾽, ὦ δέσποτα,
770 δέχου πόλει τῇδ᾽· ὡς τά τ᾽ ἄλλ᾽ ἐστὶν μέγας,
κἀκεῖνό φασιν αὐτόν, ὡς ἐγὼ κλύω,
τὴν παυσίλυπον ἄμπελον δοῦναι βροτοῖς.
οἴνου δὲ μηκέτ᾽ ὄντος οὐκ ἔστιν Κύπρις
οὐδ᾽ ἄλλο τερπνὸν οὐδὲν ἀνθρώποις ἔτι.

grain for the Thebans and hurled themselves like enemy troops upon Hysiae and Erythrae, which stand in the hill country of Cithaeron, in its lower reaches. There they turned everything upside down. They snatched children from houses, and all those they put upon their shoulders, though not held in place by any fastening, stayed without falling [onto the black earth, not bronze, not iron]. Upon the hair of their heads they carried fire, and it did not burn them. But the citizens, being plundered by the bacchants, rushed angrily to arms. And here occurred something dreadful to see: the men found that no weapon of theirs, whether bronze or iron, bloodied ‹the bacchants' god-possessed flesh›, whereas the women, fighting against men and hurling their thyrsoi at them, wounded them and put them to flight: some god was at work. They came back to the place from which they started, to the very springs the god had made gush up for them; they washed the blood off their hands, and the snakes with their tongues cleaned the drops from the skin of their cheeks.

So, master, receive this god into the city, whoever he is. For apart from his other greatness, they report this, I am told, that he gave to mortals the vine that puts an end to pain. If there is no wine, there is no Aphrodite or any other pleasure for mortals.

Exit MESSENGER *by Eisodos B.*

---

750 Θηβαίοις Brunck: -ων L: Θηβαῖον P
756b (=1065b) del. Jackson
757a post 761 trai. et suppl. Jackson

ΧΟΡΟΣ

775　ταρβῶ μὲν εἰπεῖν τοὺς λόγους ἐλευθέρους
πρὸς τὸν τύραννον, ἀλλ᾽ ὅμως εἰρήσεται·
Διόνυσος ἥσσων οὐδενὸς θεῶν ἔφυ.

ΠΕΝΘΕΥΣ

ἤδη τόδ᾽ ἐγγὺς ὥστε πῦρ ὑφάπτεται
ὕβρισμα βακχῶν, ψόγος ἐς Ἕλληνας μέγας.
780　ἀλλ᾽ οὐκ ὀκνεῖν δεῖ· στεῖχ᾽ ἐπ᾽ Ἠλέκτρας ἰὼν
πύλας· κέλευε πάντας ἀσπιδηφόρους
ἵππων τ᾽ ἀπαντᾶν ταχυπόδων ἐπεμβάτας
πέλτας θ᾽ ὅσοι πάλλουσι καὶ τόξων χερὶ
ψάλλουσι νευράς, ὡς ἐπιστρατεύσομεν
785　βάκχαισιν· οὐ γὰρ ἀλλ᾽ ὑπερβάλλει τάδε,
εἰ πρὸς γυναικῶν πεισόμεσθ᾽ ἃ πάσχομεν.

ΔΙΟΝΥΣΟΣ

πείθῃ μὲν οὐδέν, τῶν ἐμῶν λόγων κλύων,
Πενθεῦ· κακῶς δὲ πρὸς σέθεν πάσχων ὅμως
οὔ φημι χρῆναί σ᾽ ὅπλ᾽ ἐπαίρεσθαι θεῷ,
790　ἀλλ᾽ ἡσυχάζειν· Βρόμιος οὐκ ἀνέξεται
κινοῦντα βάκχας ⟨σ᾽⟩ εὐίων ὀρῶν ἄπο.

ΠΕΝΘΕΥΣ

οὐ μὴ φρενώσεις μ᾽, ἀλλὰ δέσμιος φυγὼν
σώσῃ τόδ᾽; ἢ σοὶ πάλιν ἀναστρέψω δίκην;

ΔΙΟΝΥΣΟΣ

θύοιμ᾽ ἂν αὐτῷ μᾶλλον ἢ θυμούμενος
795　πρὸς κέντρα λακτίζοιμι θνητὸς ὢν θεῷ.

BACCHAE

CHORUS LEADER

I hesitate to speak frankly to the ruler, but speak I shall:
there is no god greater than Dionysus.

PENTHEUS

The violence of these bacchants now blazes at our doors
like a fire: it shames us greatly in the eyes of Hellas. We
must not delay. (*to one of his retinue*) You, go to the Elec-
tran gate! Order a gathering of all hoplites, all riders of
swift-footed horses, brandishers of light shields and those
whose hands make the bowstring sing: we are going to war
with the bacchants! No, it's beyond all bearing if we endure
what these women are doing to us!

The servant departs by Eisodos B.

DIONYSUS

Listening to my words has not changed your mind at all,
Pentheus. Yet even though I have suffered bad treatment
from you, I advise you not to take up arms against a god but
to hold your peace. Bromios will not stand for it if you try to
rout the bacchants out of the mountains where they wor-
ship him.

PENTHEUS

No lectures from you! You have escaped your chains: see
that you don't lose that benefit. Or shall I punish you
again?

DIONYSUS

I would sacrifice to him rather than kick angrily against the
goad, man against god.

---

791 ⟨σ'⟩ Lenting

ΠΕΝΘΕΥΣ

θύσω, φόνον γε θῆλυν, ὥσπερ ἄξιαι,
πολὺν ταράξας ἐν Κιθαιρῶνος πτυχαῖς.

ΔΙΟΝΥΣΟΣ

φεύξεσθε πάντες· καὶ τόδ᾽ αἰσχρόν, ἀσπίδας
θύρσοισι βάκχας ἐκτρέπειν χαλκηλάτους.

ΠΕΝΘΕΥΣ

800 ἀπόρῳ γε τῷδε συμπεπλέγμεθα ξένῳ,
ὃς οὔτε πάσχων οὔτε δρῶν σιγήσεται.

ΔΙΟΝΥΣΟΣ

ὦ τᾶν, ἔτ᾽ ἔστιν εὖ καταστῆσαι τάδε.

ΠΕΝΘΕΥΣ

τί δρῶντα; δουλεύοντα δουλείαις ἐμαῖς;

ΔΙΟΝΥΣΟΣ

ἐγὼ γυναῖκας δεῦρ᾽ ὅπλων ἄξω δίχα.

ΠΕΝΘΕΥΣ

805 οἴμοι· τόδ᾽ ἤδη δόλιον ἐς ἐμὲ μηχανᾷ.

ΔΙΟΝΥΣΟΣ

ποῖόν τι, σῶσαί σ᾽ εἰ θέλω τέχναις ἐμαῖς;

ΠΕΝΘΕΥΣ

ξυνέθεσθε κοινῇ τάδ᾽, ἵνα βακχεύητ᾽ ἀεί.

ΔΙΟΝΥΣΟΣ

καὶ μὴν ξυνεθέμην τοῦτό γ᾽, ἴσθι, τῷ θεῷ.

799 βάκχας Wecklein: βακχῶν P
808 ἴσθι Musgrave: ἔστι P

PENTHEUS

I'll give him sacrifice: women's blood! That's what they deserve, and I shall shed lots of it in the glens of Cithaeron!

DIONYSUS

You'll all be put to flight. And it will be disgraceful if the bacchant women rout your bronze-backed shields with their thyrsoi.

PENTHEUS

What an impossible foreigner I'm grappling with here! Whether he's the doer or the sufferer, he won't keep quiet!

DIONYSUS

Friend, it is still possible to rescue this situation.

PENTHEUS

How? By taking orders from my own slaves?

DIONYSUS

I shall bring the women here without the use of arms.

PENTHEUS

Ah! This now is some trick you're trying to pull on me.

DIONYSUS

What trick? I'm offering to rescue you by my arts.

PENTHEUS

You've made a pact, you and they, so that you could keep dancing ecstatically forever!

DIONYSUS

You may be sure of that: this worship is our pact with the god.

ΠΕΝΘΕΥΣ

ἐκφέρετέ μοι δεῦρ' ὅπλα, σὺ δὲ παῦσαι λέγων.

ΔΙΟΝΥΣΟΣ

810 ἆ.

βούλῃ σφ' ἐν ὄρεσι συγκαθημένας ἰδεῖν;

ΠΕΝΘΕΥΣ

μάλιστα, μυρίον γε δοὺς χρυσοῦ σταθμόν.

ΔΙΟΝΥΣΟΣ

τί δ'; εἰς ἔρωτα τοῦδε πέπτωκας μέγαν;

ΠΕΝΘΕΥΣ

λυπρῶς νιν εἰσίδοιμ' ἂν ἐξῳνωμένας.

ΔΙΟΝΥΣΟΣ

815 ὅμως δ' ἴδοις ἂν ἡδέως ἅ σοι πικρά;

ΠΕΝΘΕΥΣ

σάφ' ἴσθι, σιγῇ δ' ὑπ' ἐλάταις καθημένας.

ΔΙΟΝΥΣΟΣ

ἀλλ' ἐξιχνεύσουσίν σε, κἂν ἔλθῃς λάθρᾳ.

ΠΕΝΘΕΥΣ

ἀλλ' ἐμφανῶς· καλῶς γὰρ ἐξεῖπας τάδε.

ΔΙΟΝΥΣΟΣ

ἄγωμεν οὖν σε κἀπιχειρήσεις ὁδῷ;

ΠΕΝΘΕΥΣ

820 ἄγ' ὡς τάχιστα, τοῦ χρόνου δέ σοι φθονῶ.

814 νιν] μὲν Bruhn   816 καθημένας J. S. Reid: -ήμενος P

PENTHEUS

Servants, my armor from the palace! And you, shut your mouth!

DIONYSUS

(*with imperious authority, countermanding Pentheus' orders*) Stop! Do you want to see them sitting together on the mountains?

PENTHEUS

(*as if under a spell*) Yes indeed: I'd give much gold to do so.

DIONYSUS

What? Have you conceived such a strong desire for this?

PENTHEUS

It would, of course, distress me to see them drunk.

DIONYSUS

And yet you would gladly see what pains you?

PENTHEUS

Yes, I would gladly see them, but sitting quietly under the fir trees.

DIONYSUS

But they will hunt you down, even if you go in secret.

PENTHEUS

Well I must go openly: that is good advice you give.

DIONYSUS

Shall I take you there? Will you attempt the journey?

PENTHEUS

Take me with all speed! I begrudge any delay!

---

820 σοι Nauck: σ' οὐ P

ΔΙΟΝΥΣΟΣ

στεῖλαί νυν ἀμφὶ χρωτὶ βυσσίνους πέπλους.

ΠΕΝΘΕΥΣ

τί δὴ τόδ'; ἐς γυναῖκας ἐξ ἀνδρὸς τελῶ;

ΔΙΟΝΥΣΟΣ

μή σε κτάνωσιν, ἢν ἀνὴρ ὀφθῇς ἐκεῖ.

ΠΕΝΘΕΥΣ

εὖ γ' εἶπας αὖ τόδ'· ὥς τις εἶ πάλαι σοφός.

ΔΙΟΝΥΣΟΣ

825   Διόνυσος ἡμᾶς ἐξεμούσωσεν τάδε.

ΠΕΝΘΕΥΣ

πῶς οὖν γένοιτ' ἂν ἃ σύ με νουθετεῖς καλῶς;

ΔΙΟΝΥΣΟΣ

ἐγὼ στελῶ σε δωμάτων ἔσω μολών.

ΠΕΝΘΕΥΣ

τίνα στολήν; ἢ θῆλυν; ἀλλ' αἰδώς μ' ἔχει.

ΔΙΟΝΥΣΟΣ

οὐκέτι θεατὴς μαινάδων πρόθυμος εἶ;

ΠΕΝΘΕΥΣ

830   στολὴν δὲ τίνα φῂς ἀμφὶ χρῶτ' ἐμὸν βαλεῖν;

ΔΙΟΝΥΣΟΣ

κόμην μὲν ἐπὶ σῷ κρατὶ ταναὸν ἐκτενῶ.

824 αὖ τόδ'· ὥς Wecklein: αὐτὸ καὶ P

DIONYSUS

Then dress yourself in a long linen robe.

PENTHEUS

Why that? Shall I become a woman instead of a man?

DIONYSUS

So that they won't kill you if you show yourself as a man there.

PENTHEUS

Good advice again! You were quite the clever fellow all along!

DIONYSUS

It is Dionysus who has given me this education.

PENTHEUS

How then can your advice be successfully put into effect?

DIONYSUS

I will go inside and dress you.

PENTHEUS

With what kind of clothes? A woman's? I feel shame.

DIONYSUS

Are you no longer an eager viewer of maenads?

PENTHEUS

But how did you say you would dress me?

DIONYSUS

First on your head I will cause your hair to grow long.[15]

15 Dionysus apparently means something miraculous: from 455–6 it would seem that Pentheus' hair is short, and from 1115–6 that Pentheus is not wearing a wig.

ΠΕΝΘΕΥΣ

τὸ δεύτερον δὲ σχῆμα τοῦ κόσμου τί μοι;

ΔΙΟΝΥΣΟΣ

πέπλοι ποδήρεις· ἐπὶ κάρᾳ δ᾽ ἔσται μίτρα.

ΠΕΝΘΕΥΣ

ἦ καί τι πρὸς τοῖσδ᾽ ἄλλο προσθήσεις ἐμοί;

ΔΙΟΝΥΣΟΣ

835   θύρσον γε χειρὶ καὶ νεβροῦ στικτὸν δέρος.

ΠΕΝΘΕΥΣ

οὐκ ἂν δυναίμην θῆλυν ἐνδῦναι στολήν.

ΔΙΟΝΥΣΟΣ

ἀλλ᾽ αἷμα θήσεις συμβαλὼν βάκχαις μάχην.

ΠΕΝΘΕΥΣ

ὀρθῶς· μολεῖν χρὴ πρῶτον ἐς κατασκοπήν.

ΔΙΟΝΥΣΟΣ

σοφώτερον γοῦν ἢ κακοῖς θηρᾶν κακά.

ΠΕΝΘΕΥΣ

840   καὶ πῶς δι᾽ ἄστεως εἶμι Καδμείους λαθών;

ΔΙΟΝΥΣΟΣ

ὁδοὺς ἐρήμους ἵμεν· ἐγὼ δ᾽ ἡγήσομαι.

ΠΕΝΘΕΥΣ

πᾶν κρεῖσσον ὥστε μὴ ᾽γγελᾶν βάκχας ἐμοί.

842 ᾽γγελᾶν Pierson: γελᾶν P

PENTHEUS

And what will be the second item of my costume?

DIONYSUS

A dress flowing down to your ankles; and on your head a
headdress.

PENTHEUS

Will you give me anything else in addition?

DIONYSUS

Yes, a dappled fawnskin and a thyrsus for your hand.

PENTHEUS

I could not bear to wear woman's clothing.

DIONYSUS

But you'll shed blood if you join battle with the bacchants.

PENTHEUS

You are right: best to go first and spy them out.

DIONYSUS

Well, that's a wiser course than chasing trouble with trou-
ble.

PENTHEUS

And how shall I get through the city without the Thebans'
seeing me?

DIONYSUS

We will go by deserted ways: I'll conduct you.

PENTHEUS

Well, any course is better than having the bacchants treat
me with contempt.

ΔΙΟΝΥΣΟΣ

843a ἐλθόντ᾽ ἐς οἴκους ⟨οἷα χρὴ στειλώμεθα⟩.

ΠΕΝΘΕΥΣ

843b ⟨ἐπίσχες· αὐτὸς⟩ ἂν δοκῇ βουλεύσομαι.

ΔΙΟΝΥΣΟΣ

ἔξεστι· πάντῃ τό γ᾽ ἐμὸν εὐτρεπὲς πάρα.

ΠΕΝΘΕΥΣ

845 στείχοιμ᾽ ἄν· ἢ γὰρ ὅπλ᾽ ἔχων πορεύσομαι
ἢ τοῖσι σοῖσι πείσομαι βουλεύμασιν.

ΔΙΟΝΥΣΟΣ

848 γυναῖκες, ἁνὴρ ἐς βόλον καθίσταται,
847 ἥξει δὲ βάκχας, οὗ θανὼν δώσει δίκην.
Διόνυσε, νῦν σὸν ἔργον· οὐ γὰρ εἶ πρόσω·
850 τεισώμεθ᾽ αὐτόν. πρῶτα δ᾽ ἔκστησον φρενῶν,
ἐνεὶς ἐλαφρὰν λύσσαν· ὡς φρονῶν μὲν εὖ
οὐ μὴ θελήσῃ θῆλυν ἐνδῦναι στολήν,
ἔξω δ᾽ ἐλαύνων τοῦ φρονεῖν ἐνδύσεται.
χρῄζω δέ νιν γέλωτα Θηβαίοις ὀφλεῖν
855 γυναικόμορφον ἀγόμενον δι᾽ ἄστεως
ἐκ τῶν ἀπειλῶν τῶν πρὶν αἷσι δεινὸς ἦν.
ἀλλ᾽ εἶμι κόσμον ὅνπερ εἰς Ἅιδου λαβὼν
ἄπεισι μητρὸς ἐκ χεροῖν κατασφαγεὶς
Πενθεῖ προσάψων· γνώσεται δὲ τὸν Διὸς
860 Διόνυσον, ὡς πέφυκεν ἐντελὴς θεός,
δεινότατος, ἀνθρώποισι δ᾽ ἠπιώτατος.

843 lac. indic. et suppl. Jackson

DIONYSUS

Let's go into the house ⟨and dress you properly⟩.

PENTHEUS

⟨Not so fast! I myself⟩ shall deliberate about what seems best.

DIONYSUS

You may do so: my services are completely at your disposal.

PENTHEUS

I shall go in. Either I shall set off in armor or I shall take your advice.

Exit PENTHEUS *with retinue into the* skene.

DIONYSUS

Women, the man is walking into the trap! He will go to join the bacchants, and there he will be punished with death!

Dionysus, it's now up to you (for you are not far away): let us punish him! First drive him from his senses, put giddy madness in his breast! If he is sane, he will never agree to put on woman's clothing, but if driven from his senses he will. I want the Thebans to laugh at him as he is led through the city in woman's dress, after all his earlier threats, which were so fierce. So, I am going now to dress Pentheus in the finery he will wear on his way to Hades, slain at the hands of his mother. He will learn that Dionysus is in the full sense a god, a god most dreadful to mortals—but also most gentle!

Exit DIONYSUS *into the* skene.

---

848 ante 847 trai. Musgrave   858 κάτεισι Wecklein
860 ὡς Jacobs: ὃς P   ἐντελὴς H. Hirtzel: ἐν τέλει P

ΧΟΡΟΣ

στρ.

    ἆρ' ἐν παννυχίοις χοροῖς
    θήσω ποτὲ λευκὸν
    πόδ' ἀναβακχεύουσα, δέραν
865 αἰθέρ' ἐς δροσερὸν ῥίπτους',
    ὡς νεβρὸς χλοεραῖς ἐμπαί-
    ζουσα λείμακος ἡδοναῖς,
    ἁνίκ' ἂν φοβερὰν φύγῃ
    θήραν ἔξω φυλακᾶς
870 εὐπλέκτων ὑπὲρ ἀρκύων,
    θωύσσων δὲ κυναγέτας
    συντείνῃ δράμημα κυνῶν,
    μόχθοις δ' ὠκυδρόμοις ἀελ-
    λὰς θρῴσκῃ πεδίον
    παραποτάμιον, ἡδομένα
875 βροτῶν ἐρημίαις σκιαρο-
    κόμοιό τ' ἔρνεσιν ὕλας;

    τί τὸ σοφόν; ἢ τι κάλλιον
    παρὰ θεῶν γέρας ἐν βροτοῖς
    ἢ χεῖρ' ὑπὲρ κορυφᾶς
880 τῶν ἐχθρῶν κρείσσω κατέχειν;
    ὅ τι καλὸν φίλον αἰεί.

ἀντ.

    ὁρμᾶται μόλις, ἀλλ' ὅμως
    πιστόν ⟨τι⟩ τὸ θεῖον
    σθένος· ἀπευθύνει δὲ βροτῶν

BACCHAE

CHORUS

Shall I ever in the nightlong dances
move my white feet
in ecstasy? Shall I toss
my head to the dewy heaven
like a fawn that plays
amid green meadow delights
when she has escaped the dread huntsmen,
eluding their guard
and leaping their fine-spun nets?
The houndsman with loud halloo
calls back his coursing dogs;
and she with swift-running zeal
leaps like a whirlwind over the plain
near the river, exulting
in her freedom from men and in the boscage
of the shadowy woodland.

What good is cleverness? Is there any god-given privilege
nobler in the sight of men
than to hold one's hand in triumph
over the heads of foes?
What is noble is always loved.

Slowly does heaven move, but still
its strength is ⟨something⟩ sure:
it brings to destruction those mortals

---

865 αἰθέρ' ἐς Musgrave: εἰς αἰθέρα P
873–4a ἀελλὰς Hermann: τ' ἀέλλαις P
875–6 σκιαροκόμοιο Nauck: -κόμου P
877 ἦ τι Willink olim: ἦ τί τὸ P   883 ⟨τι⟩ Nauck

885 τούς τ᾽ ἀγνωμοσύναν τιμῶν-
τας καὶ μὴ τὰ θεῶν αὔξον-
τας σὺν μαινομένᾳ δόξᾳ.
κρυπτεύουσι δὲ ποικίλως
δαρὸν χρόνου πόδα καὶ
890 θηρῶσιν τὸν ἄσεπτον. οὐ
γὰρ κρεῖσσόν ποτε τῶν νόμων
γιγνώσκειν χρὴ καὶ μελετᾶν.
κούφα γὰρ δαπάνα νομί-
ζειν ἰσχὺν τάδ᾽ ἔχειν,
ὅ τι ποτ᾽ ἄρα τὸ δαιμόνιον,
895 τό τ᾽ ἐν χρόνῳ μακρῷ νόμιμον
ἀεὶ φύσει τε πεφυκός.

τί τὸ σοφόν; ἢ τι κάλλιον
παρὰ θεῶν γέρας ἐν βροτοῖς
ἢ χεῖρ᾽ ὑπὲρ κορυφᾶς
900 τῶν ἐχθρῶν κρείσσω κατέχειν;
ὅ τι καλὸν φίλον αἰεί.

ἐπῳδ.

εὐδαίμων μὲν ὃς ἐκ θαλάσσας
ἔφυγε χεῖμα, λιμένα δ᾽ ἔκιχεν·
εὐδαίμων δ᾽ ὃς ὕπερθε μόχθων
905 ἐγένεθ᾽· ἕτερα δ᾽ ἕτερος ἕτερον
ὄλβῳ καὶ δυνάμει παρῆλθεν,
μυρίαι δ᾽ ἔτι μυρίοις
εἰσὶν ἐλπίδες· αἱ μὲν
τελευτῶσιν ἐν ὄλβῳ

98

who honor folly
and in the mad imagination of their hearts
do not reverence the gods.
The gods craftily conceal
the unhastening tread of time,
and they hunt down the impious man.
Never should a man's thought and practice
rise above the laws.
For it costs but little to believe
that these have sovereign power:
the might of heaven, whatever it be,
and what through long ages has ever been lawful
and upheld by nature.

What good is cleverness? Is there any god-given privilege
nobler in the sight of men
than to hold one's hand in triumph
over the heads of foes?
What is noble is always loved.

Blessed is he that out of the sea
escapes the storm and wins the harbor;
blessed he who triumphs over
trouble: one man surpasses another
in respect of wealth or power.
Furthermore, in countless hearts
there live countless hopes, some
ending in good fortune,

894a τάδ' Willink: τ' P: τόδ' Heath   897 vide ad 877
    905 ἕτερα Bothe: ἑτέρᾳ P   907 δ' ἔτι μυρίοις Paley:
μυρίοισιν ἔτ' P   909 ἀνόλβως Jackson

910 βροτοῖς, αἱ δ' ἀπέβασαν·
τὸ δὲ κατ' ἦμαρ ὅτῳ βίοτος
εὐδαίμων, μακαρίζω.

ΔΙΟΝΥΣΟΣ

σὲ τὸν πρόθυμον ὄνθ' ἃ μὴ χρεὼν ὁρᾶν
σπεύδοντά τ' ἀσπούδαστα, Πενθέα λέγω,
ἔξιθι πάροιθε δωμάτων, ὄφθητί μοι,
915 σκευὴν γυναικὸς μαινάδος βάκχης ἔχων,
μητρός τε τῆς σῆς καὶ λόχου κατάσκοπος.
πρέπεις δὲ Κάδμου θυγατέρων μορφὴν μιᾷ.

ΠΕΝΘΕΥΣ

καὶ μὴν ὁρᾶν μοι δύο μὲν ἡλίους δοκῶ,
δισσὰς δὲ Θήβας καὶ πόλισμ' ἑπτάστομον·
920 καὶ ταῦρος ἡμῖν πρόσθεν ἡγεῖσθαι δοκεῖς
καὶ σῷ κέρατα κρατὶ προσπεφυκέναι.
ἀλλ' ἦ ποτ' ἦσθα θήρ; τεταύρωσαι γὰρ οὖν.

ΔΙΟΝΥΣΟΣ

ὁ θεὸς ὁμαρτεῖ, πρόσθεν ὢν οὐκ εὐμενής,
ἔνσπονδος ἡμῖν· νῦν δ' ὁρᾷς ἃ χρή σ' ὁρᾶν.

ΠΕΝΘΕΥΣ

925 τί φαίνομαι δῆτ'; οὐχὶ τὴν Ἰνοῦς στάσιν
ἢ τὴν Ἀγαυῆς ἑστάναι, μητρός γ' ἐμῆς;

917 μορφὴν Musgrave: μορφῇ P

though some vanish away.
But the man whose life today is happy,
him I count blessed.

Enter DIONYSUS *from the* skene.

DIONYSUS
(*calling behind him into the palace*) You there, the one so keen to see what he shouldn't and eagerly trying what should not be tried, I mean Pentheus: come out before the house, show yourself to me, wearing the kit of a female bacchant, set to spy on your mother and on her band!

Enter PENTHEUS *from the* skene, *dressed as a woman and carrying a thyrsus. He is accompanied by a single attendant.*

    In looks you resemble exactly one of the daughters of Cadmus!

PENTHEUS
Look, I seem to see two suns in the sky! The seven-gated city of Thebes—I see two of them! And you seem to be going before me as a bull, and horns seem to have sprouted upon your head! Were you an animal before now? Certainly now you have been changed into a bull.

DIONYSUS
The god has made a truce and is with us now, though before he was our enemy. And now you see as you ought to see.

PENTHEUS
What do I look like? Do I not have the carriage of Ino or my mother Agave?

101

ΔΙΟΝΥΣΟΣ

αὐτὰς ἐκείνας εἰσορᾶν δοκῶ σ᾽ ὁρῶν.
ἀλλ᾽ ἐξ ἕδρας σοι πλόκαμος ἐξέστηχ᾽ ὅδε,
οὐχ ὡς ἐγώ νιν ὑπὸ μίτρᾳ καθήρμοσα.

ΠΕΝΘΕΥΣ

930   ἔνδον προσείων αὐτὸν ἀνασείων τ᾽ ἐγὼ
καὶ βακχιάζων ἐξ ἕδρας μεθώρμισα.

ΔΙΟΝΥΣΟΣ

ἀλλ᾽ αὐτὸν ἡμεῖς, οἷς σε θεραπεύειν μέλει,
πάλιν καταστελοῦμεν· ἀλλ᾽ ὄρθου κάρα.

ΠΕΝΘΕΥΣ

ἰδού, σὺ κόσμει· σοὶ γὰρ ἀνακείμεσθα δή.

ΔΙΟΝΥΣΟΣ

935   ζῶναί τέ σοι χαλῶσι κοὐχ ἑξῆς πέπλων
στολίδες ὑπὸ σφυροῖσι τείνουσιν σέθεν.

ΠΕΝΘΕΥΣ

κἀμοὶ δοκοῦσι παρά γε δεξιὸν πόδα·
τἀνθένδε δ᾽ ὀρθῶς παρὰ τένοντ᾽ ἔχει πέπλος.

ΔΙΟΝΥΣΟΣ

ἦ πού με τῶν σῶν πρῶτον ἡγήσῃ φίλων,
940   ὅταν παρὰ λόγον σώφρονας βάκχας ἴδῃς.

ΠΕΝΘΕΥΣ

πότερα δὲ θύρσον δεξιᾷ λαβὼν χερὶ
ἢ τῇδε βάκχῃ μᾶλλον εἰκασθήσομαι;

BACCHAE

DIONYSUS

When I look at you I think I see their very image. But a curl has come loose from its place beneath your headdress where I tucked it.

PENTHEUS

Inside the house I was shaking my locks this way and that in my bacchic ecstasy and dislodged it from its place.

DIONYSUS

Well, since it is my job to be your attendant, I will put it back: hold your head up straight.

PENTHEUS

There. You must be my hairdresser, for I am entirely given over to you.

He adjusts Pentheus' hair.

DIONYSUS

And your girdle is slack, and the pleats of your dress hang crooked below the ankle.

PENTHEUS

(*looking over his shoulder at his ankles*) That seems true of my right foot, though on this side the dress falls properly over the tendon.

DIONYSUS

I'm sure you'll think me your best friend when you see how surprisingly chaste the bacchants are.

PENTHEUS

If I want to look more like a bacchant, shall I hold the thyrsus in my right hand? Or like this?

ΔΙΟΝΥΣΟΣ

ἐν δεξιᾷ χρὴ χἅμα δεξιῷ ποδὶ
αἴρειν νιν· αἰνῶ δ' ὅτι μεθέστηκας φρενῶν.

ΠΕΝΘΕΥΣ

945 ἆρ' ἂν δυναίμην τὰς Κιθαιρῶνος πτυχὰς
αὐταῖσι βάκχαις τοῖς ἐμοῖς ὤμοις φέρειν;

ΔΙΟΝΥΣΟΣ

δύναι' ἄν, εἰ βούλοιο· τὰς δὲ πρὶν φρένας
οὐκ εἶχες ὑγιεῖς, νῦν δ' ἔχεις οἵας σε δεῖ.

ΠΕΝΘΕΥΣ

μοχλοὺς φέρωμεν ἢ χεροῖν ἀνασπάσω
950 κορυφαῖς ὑποβαλὼν ὦμον ἢ βραχίονα;

ΔΙΟΝΥΣΟΣ

μὴ σύ γε τὰ Νυμφῶν διολέσῃς ἱδρύματα
καὶ Πανὸς ἕδρας ἔνθ' ἔχει συρίγματα.

ΠΕΝΘΕΥΣ

καλῶς ἔλεξας· οὐ σθένει νικητέον
γυναῖκας· ἐλάταισιν δ' ἐμὸν κρύψω δέμας.

ΔΙΟΝΥΣΟΣ

955 κρύψῃ σὺ κρύψιν ἥν σε κρυφθῆναι χρεών,
ἐλθόντα δόλιον μαινάδων κατάσκοπον.

ΠΕΝΘΕΥΣ

καὶ μὴν δοκῶ σφας ἐν λόχμαις ὄρνιθας ὡς
λέκτρων ἔχεσθαι φιλτάτοις ἐν ἕρκεσιν.

ΔΙΟΝΥΣΟΣ

οὔκουν ἐπ' αὐτὸ τοῦτ' ἀποστέλλῃ φύλαξ;

DIONYSUS

In your right hand, and raise it as you raise your right foot. I commend your change of heart.

PENTHEUS

Might I be able to pick up the glens of Cithaeron on my shoulders, and the bacchants with them?

DIONYSUS

You might if you wanted: your previous mental state was not sound, but now you have the thoughts you ought to have.

PENTHEUS

Should we bring crowbars, or shall I tear them up with my fingers and put my shoulder or arm under the peaks?

DIONYSUS

No, don't destroy the haunts of the nymphs and the place where Pan plays his pipes!

PENTHEUS

Your advice is good: we should not conquer the women by force. I will hide myself in the fir trees.

DIONYSUS

You will find such hiding as a man should find who has gone to spy craftily on maenads.

PENTHEUS

Indeed, I imagine that like birds caught in bushes they are held fast in sweet enclosures of their beds.

DIONYSUS

Is it not just this that you are setting out to observe? You

960 λήψῃ δ᾽ ἴσως σφας, ἢν σὺ μὴ ληφθῇς πάρος.

ΠΕΝΘΕΥΣ

κόμιζε διὰ μέσης με Θηβαίας χθονός·
μόνος γὰρ αὐτῶν εἰμ᾽ ἀνὴρ τολμῶν τόδε.

ΔΙΟΝΥΣΟΣ

μόνος σὺ πόλεως τῆσδ᾽ ὑπερκάμνεις, μόνος·
τοιγάρ σ᾽ ἀγῶνες ἀναμένουσιν οὓς ἐχρῆν.
965 ἕπου δέ· πομπὸς εἰμ᾽ ἐγὼ σωτήριος,
κεῖθεν δ᾽ ἀπάξει σ᾽ ἄλλος . . .

ΠΕΝΘΕΥΣ

ἡ τεκοῦσά γε.

ΔΙΟΝΥΣΟΣ

. . . ἐπίσημον ὄντα πᾶσιν.

ΠΕΝΘΕΥΣ

ἐπὶ τόδ᾽ ἔρχομαι.

ΔΙΟΝΥΣΟΣ

φερόμενος ἥξεις . . .

ΠΕΝΘΕΥΣ

ἁβρότητ᾽ ἐμὴν λέγεις.

ΔΙΟΝΥΣΟΣ

. . . ἐν χερσὶ μητρός.

ΠΕΝΘΕΥΣ

καὶ τρυφᾶν μ᾽ ἀναγκάσεις.

ΔΙΟΝΥΣΟΣ

970 τρυφάς γε τοιάσδ᾽.

will catch them—unless you are caught first.

PENTHEUS

Take me through the middle of Thebes! Since I am brave
enough to do this, I am the only true man among them!

DIONYSUS

All alone you bear the burden for this city. And so struggles
lie ahead of you, the struggles that have been fated. So fol-
low me: I will guide you and keep you safe. But another
will bring you back . . .

PENTHEUS

Yes, my mother!

DIONYSUS

. . . conspicuous to everyone.

PENTHEUS

That is the goal of my journey!

DIONYSUS

You will arrive being carried . . .

PENTHEUS

What luxury you speak of!

DIONYSUS

. . . in your mother's arms.

PENTHEUS

You are determined actually to spoil me!

DIONYSUS

Yes, spoil you after my fashion.

---

962 αὐτῶν εἰμ' Elmsley: εἶμ' αὐτῶν P
965 πομπὸς Murray: π- δ' P

EURIPIDES

ἀξίων μὲν ἅπτομαι.

ΔΙΟΝΥΣΟΣ

δεινὸς σὺ δεινὸς κἀπὶ δείν' ἔρχη πάθη,
ὥστ' οὐρανῷ στηρίζον εὑρήσεις κλέος.
ἔκτειν', Ἀγαυή, χεῖρας αἵ θ' ὁμόσποροι
Κάδμου θυγατέρες· τὸν νεανίαν ἄγω
975 τόνδ' εἰς ἀγῶνα μέγαν, ὁ νικήσων δ' ἐγὼ
καὶ Βρόμιος ἔσται. τἄλλα δ' αὐτὸ σημανεῖ.

ΧΟΡΟΣ

στρ.

ἴτε θοαὶ Λύσσας κύνες, ἴτ' εἰς ὄρος,
θίασον ἔνθ' ἔχουσι Κάδμου κόραι,
ἀνοιστρήσατέ νιν
980 ἐπὶ τὸν ἐν γυναικομίμῳ στολᾷ
λυσσώδη κατάσκοπον μαινάδων.
μάτηρ πρῶτά νιν λευρᾶς ἀπὸ πέτρας
εὔσκοπος ὄψεται
δοκεύοντα, μαινάσιν δ' ἀπύσει·
985 Τίς ὅδ' ὀρειδρόμων μαστὴρ Καδμειᾶν
ἐς ὄρος ἐς ὄρος ἔμολ' ἔμολεν, ὦ βάκχαι;
τίς ἄρα νιν ἔτεκεν;
οὐ γὰρ ἐξ αἵματος
990 γυναικῶν ἔφυ, λεαίνας δέ τινος

983 εὔσκοπος Nauck: ἢ σκόλοπος L
985 ὀρειδρόμων μ- K- Nauck: K- μ- ὀριοδρόμων P
Καδμειᾶν Maas: -είων P

108

PENTHEUS

It's only what I deserve!

PENTHEUS proceeds slowly down Eisodos B.

DIONYSUS

Fearsome you are, fearsome, and fearsome are the sufferings to which you are headed: the fame you will win shall tower to heaven! Agave and the other daughters of Cadmus, stretch out your hands! I am bringing this young man to a great contest, where I shall be victorious, Bromios and I! The rest the event will make plain.

Exit DIONYSUS by Eisodos B following PENTHEUS.

CHORUS

On, you swift hounds of madness, on to the mountain,
where Cadmus' daughters keep their assembly!
Set them in frenzy
against him who in womanish dress
spies in madness upon the maenads!
His mother first from a sheer cliff
with keen eye shall catch sight of him,
as he plays the spy, and shall say to the maenads,
"Who is this has come, has come, to the mountain, the
    mountain
to search out the Theban mountain-treading women, O
    bacchants?
Who gave birth to him?
It was from no woman's blood
that he has sprung: he is the offspring

989–91 ἔφυ . . . ὅδ᾽ ἦ Hermann: ὅδ᾽ ἔφυ . . . ἦ P

109

ὅδ' ἢ Γοργόνων Λιβυσσᾶν γένος.

ἴτω δίκα φανερός, ἴτω
ξιφηφόρος φονεύου-
σα λαιμῶν διαμπὰξ
995 τὸν ἄθεον ἄνομον ἄδικον Ἐχίονος
τόκον γηγενῆ·

ἀντ.

ὃς ἀδίκῳ γνώμᾳ παρανόμῳ τ' ὀργᾷ
περὶ <σά,> Βάκχε, σᾶς τ' ὄργια ματέρος
μανείσᾳ πραπίδι
1000 παρακόπῳ τε λήματι στέλλεται,
τἀνίκατον ὡς κρατήσων βίᾳ.
γνωμᾶν σωφρόνισμα θάνατος· ἀόκνως <δ'>
ἐς τὰ θεῶν ἔφυ
βροτείως τ' ἔχειν ἄλυπος βίος.
1005 τὸ σοφὸν οὐ φθονῶ καιρῷ θηρεύου-
σι· τὰ δ' ἕτερα μεγάλα †φανερὰ τῶν ἀεὶ†
ἐπὶ τὰ καλὰ βίον,
ἦμαρ ἐς νύκτα τ' εὐ-
αγοῦντ' εὐσεβεῖν, τὰ δ' ἔξω νόμιμα
1010 δίκας ἐκβαλόντα τιμᾶν θεούς.

ἴτω δίκα φανερός, ἴτω

996 τόκον Elmsley e 1016: γόνον P   998 sic Murray
(<σά> iam Scaliger): περὶ βάκχι' ὄργια ματρός τε σᾶς P
1001 τἀνίκατον Wilamowitz: τὰν ἀνίκ- P

of some lioness or Libyan Gorgon."

Let justice proceed for all to see, let it proceed
with sword in hand, stabbing
through the throat
the man without god, law, or justice,
the earthborn son of Echion!

He with unjust purpose and lawless temper
toward your rites, Bacchus, and those of your mother
set out with maddened heart
and crazed wits,
thinking to master by force what cannot be mastered.
Death will be the chastener of his purposes: <but> to be
unhesitating toward the gods
and act as mortal should means a life without grief.
I feel no grudging resentment against those who pursue
   cleverness in due measure,
but it is other qualities, great and manifest, that lead the
   life
of mortals to success,
to practice purity and godliness
all the long day and into the night, honoring the gods
and banishing all customs that lie outside justice.

Let justice proceed for all to see, let it proceed

1002 σωφρόνισμα Dodds: σώφρονα P   ἀόκνως Kovacs:
ἀπροφάσιστος P   <δ'> Dodds   1004 βροτείως Murray:
-ῳ P   1005 φθονῶ καιρῷ θηρεύουσι post Heath (φθονῶ) et
Musgrave (κ- θ-) Diggle et Willink: φθόνῳ χαίρω θηρεύουσα P
   1006 φανέρ' ἄγει θνατῶν Willink

ξιφηφόρος φονεύου-
σα λαιμῶν διαμπὰξ
1015 τὸν ἄθεον ἄνομον ἄδικον Ἐχίονος
τόκον γηγενῆ.

ἐπῳδ.

φάνηθι ταῦρος ἢ πολύκρανος ἰδεῖν
δράκων ἢ πυριφλέγων
ὁρᾶσθαι λέων.
1020 ἴθ᾽, ὦ Βάκχε, θὴρ ἀγρευτᾷ βακχᾶν
προσώπῳ γελῶντι περίβαλε βρόχον
θανάσιμον ὑπ᾽ ἀγέλαν πεσόν-
τι τὰν μαινάδων.

ΑΓΓΕΛΟΣ Β

ὦ δῶμ᾽ ὃ πρίν ποτ᾽ ηὐτύχεις ἀν᾽ Ἑλλάδα
1025 [Σιδωνίου γέροντος, ὃς τὸ γηγενὲς
δράκοντος ἔσπειρ᾽ ὄφεος ἐν γαίᾳ θέρος],
ὥς σε στενάζω, δοῦλος ὢν μέν, ἀλλ᾽ ὅμως
[χρηστοῖσι δούλοις συμφορὰ τὰ δεσποτῶν].

ΧΟΡΟΣ

τί δ᾽ ἔστιν; ἐκ βακχῶν τι μηνύεις νέον;

ΑΓΓΕΛΟΣ Β

1030 Πενθεὺς ὄλωλε, παῖς Ἐχίονος πατρός.

1020 θὴρ ἀγρευτᾷ Kopff: θηραγρώτα P: θηραγρευτᾷ Dindorf
1021 προσώπῳ γελῶντι Murray: γ- π- P
1022 θανάσιμον ὑπ᾽ Bruhn: ἐπὶ θανάσιμον P
1025–6 del. Middendorf
1028 del. Dobree cl. Med. 54

with sword in hand, stabbing
through the throat
the man without god, law, or justice,
the earthborn son of Echion!

Show yourself as a bull in appearance or a many-headed
serpent or a lion
blazing like fire!
Go, Bacchus, and as beast, with smiling face,
cast the deadly noose upon the bacchants' hunter
as he falls
into the hands of the maenad band!

Enter by Eisodos B one of Pentheus' attendants as SECOND
MESSENGER.

SECOND MESSENGER
O house, which once prospered in the sight of Greece,
[house of the old man of Sidon, who sowed the earthborn
harvest of the dragon in the soil,] how I lament for you,
slave though I am! [To good slaves their masters' fortunes
are a calamity.][16]

CHORUS LEADER
What has happened? What news do you bring from the
bacchants?

SECOND MESSENGER
Pentheus, son of Echion, is dead!

16 This line is a quotation, truncated into nonsense, of *Medea*
54.

ΧΟΡΟΣ

ὦναξ Βρόμιε, θεὸς ⟨ὡς⟩ φαίνῃ μέγας.

ΑΓΓΕΛΟΣ Β

πῶς φῄς; τί τοῦτ᾽ ἔλεξας; ἦ ᾽πὶ τοῖς ἐμοῖς
χαίρεις κακῶς πράσσουσι δεσπόταις, γύναι;

ΧΟΡΟΣ

εὐάζω ξένα μέλεσι βαρβάροις·
1035   οὐκέτι γὰρ δεσμῶν ὑπὸ φόβῳ πτήσσω.

ΑΓΓΕΛΟΣ Β

Θήβας δ᾽ ἀνάνδρους, ⟨ὦ γύναι, τεθνηκότος
δοκεῖς ἄνακτος; ἐς ἀνίαρά σ᾽⟩ ὧδ᾽ ἄγεις.

ΧΟΡΟΣ

ὁ Διόνυσος ὁ Διὸς γόνος, οὐ Θῆβαι
κράτος ἔχουσ᾽ ἐμόν.

ΑΓΓΕΛΟΣ Β

συγγνωστὰ μέν σοι, πλὴν ἐπ᾽ ἐξειργασμένοις
1040   κακοῖσι χαίρειν, ὦ γυναῖκες, οὐ καλόν.

ΧΟΡΟΣ

ἔννεπέ μοι, φράσον, τίνι μόρῳ θνῄσκει
ἄδικος ἄδικά τ᾽ ἐκπορίζων ἀνήρ;

ΑΓΓΕΛΟΣ Β

ἐπεὶ θεράπνας τῆσδε Θηβαίας χθονὸς
λιπόντες ἐξέβημεν Ἀσωποῦ ῥοάς,

1031 ⟨ὡς⟩ Hense   1036 post ἀνάνδρους lac. quattuor
metrorum indic. Kovacs, post ἄγεις Seidler
  1037 Διὸς γόνος Dodds: Διόνυσος P

CHORUS

Bromios, my lord, ⟨how⟩ great a god you have proved!

SECOND MESSENGER

What do you mean? What is this you are saying? Do you take pleasure in the misfortunes of my master, woman?

CHORUS

I exult, foreigner that I am, in barbarian strain:
I no longer cower under the fear of prison!

SECOND MESSENGER

⟨Do you suppose, woman, that because our king is dead⟩ there are no men in Thebes? That is the way to bring ⟨trouble on yourself⟩.

CHORUS

It is Dionysus, Zeus's son, not Thebes,
who is my ruler!

SECOND MESSENGER

It is understandable in you, women, but still it is not a good thing to take pleasure in others' misfortunes.

CHORUS

Speak, tell me: how did he perish,
that wicked man, contriver of wickedness?

SECOND MESSENGER

Pentheus and I (for I was attending on my master) and the stranger who was our escort to the festival[17] had left behind the settlements of Thebes and had crossed the

---

17 There is an untranslatable ambiguity in *theoria*, which means both an official delegation to a religious festival and "viewing," a reference to Pentheus' design to spy on the bacchants.

1045 λέπας Κιθαιρώνειον εἰσεβάλλομεν
Πενθεύς τε κἀγώ (δεσπότῃ γὰρ εἱπόμην)
ξένος θ᾽ ὃς ἡμῖν πομπὸς ἦν θεωρίας.
   πρῶτον μὲν οὖν ποιηρὸν ἵζομεν νάπος,
τά τ᾽ ἐκ ποδῶν σιγηλὰ καὶ γλώσσης ἄπο
1050 σῴζοντες, ὡς ὁρῶμεν οὐχ ὁρώμενοι.
ἦν δ᾽ ἄγκος ἀμφίκρημνον, ὕδασι διάβροχον,
πεύκαισι συσκιάζον, ἔνθα μαινάδες
καθῆντ᾽ ἔχουσαι χεῖρας ἐν τερπνοῖς πόνοις.
αἱ μὲν γὰρ αὐτῶν θύρσον ἐκλελοιπότα
1055 κισσῷ κομήτην αὖθις ἐξανέστεφον,
αἱ δ᾽, ἐκλιποῦσαι ποικίλ᾽ ὡς πῶλοι ζυγά,
βακχεῖον ἀντέκλαζον ἀλλήλαις μέλος.
Πενθεὺς δ᾽ ὁ τλήμων θῆλυν οὐχ ὁρῶν ὄχλον
ἔλεξε τοιάδ᾽· Ὦ ξέν᾽, οὗ μὲν ἕσταμεν
1060 οὐκ ἐξικνοῦμαι μανιάδων ὄσσοις νόσων·
ὄχθων δ᾽ ἔπ᾽ ἀμβὰς ἐς ἐλάτην ὑψαύχενα
ἴδοιμ᾽ ἂν ὀρθῶς μαινάδων αἰσχρουργίαν.
   τοὐντεῦθεν ἤδη τοῦ ξένου θαυμάσθ᾽ ὁρῶ·
λαβὼν γὰρ ἐλάτης οὐράνιον ἄκρον κλάδον
1065 κατῆγεν ἦγεν ἦγεν ἐς μέλαν πέδον·
κυκλοῦτο δ᾽ ὥστε τόξον ἢ κυρτὸς τροχὸς
τόρνῳ γραφόμενος περιφορὰν ἑλικοδρόμον·
ὣς κλῶν᾽ ὄρειον ὁ ξένος χεροῖν ἄγων
ἔκαμπτεν ἐς γῆν, ἔργματ᾽ οὐχὶ θνητὰ δρῶν.
1070 Πενθέα δ᾽ ἱδρύσας ἐλατίνων ὄζων ἔπι,
ὄρθου μεθιεὶς διὰ χερῶν βλάστημ᾽ ἄνω
ἀτρέμα, φυλάσσων μὴ ἀναχαιτίσειέ νιν,

river Asopus and were striking into the rocky uplands of Cithaeron.

First we halted in a grassy dale, keeping our footsteps and our tongues silent so that we might see without being seen. There was a mountain glen with steep sides, with a stream flowing through it and pine trees to shade it, and there the maenads sat employing their hands in pleasant tasks. Some of them were restoring the mane of ivy to their tattered bacchic wands, while others, joyous as fillies escaped from their painted bridles, were singing bacchic songs to each other. Poor Pentheus, who could not see the crowd of women, said, "My foreign friend, from where I stand my eyes cannot make out their bacchic frenzy. But if I climbed that tall-necked fir tree overhanging the banks, I would see clearly the maenads' shameful behavior."

At this point I saw the stranger perform a miraculous deed. He took hold of the tip of a fir tree that rose toward heaven, and down he pulled, pulled, pulled it to the black earth. It began to curve like a bow or a rounded wheel when its shape is being traced by the peg-and-line with its spiraling rotation. So the stranger, drawing down with his hands the mountain tree, bent it to the ground, a deed no mortal could do. Then, having set Pentheus atop the fir branches, he set the tree straight again by letting the branches slip upwards through his hands—gently, taking

---

1056 post h. v. aliquid excidisse suspicatus est Wecklein

1060 μανιάδων . . . νόσων Jackson: μαινάδων . . . νόθων P
ὄσσοις Canter: ὅσοι P   1063 θαυμάσθ' Nauck: θαῦμ' P (τι
θαῦμ' P²)   1067 ἑλικοδρόμον Reiske: ἕλκει δρόμον P

1071 ὄρθου μεθιεὶς Kovacs (μεθιεις Π): ὀρθὸν μεθίει P

ὀρθὴ δ' ἐς ὀρθὸν αἰθέρ' ἐστηρίζετο,
ἔχουσα νώτοις δεσπότην ἐφήμενον.
1075 ὤφθη δὲ μᾶλλον ἢ κατεῖδε μαινάδας·
ὅσον γὰρ οὔπω δῆλος ἦν θάσσων ἄνω,
καὶ τὸν ξένον μὲν οὐκέτ' εἰσορᾶν παρῆν,
ἐκ δ' αἰθέρος φωνή τις, ὡς μὲν εἰκάσαι
Διόνυσος, ἀνεβόησεν· Ὦ νεάνιδες,
1080 ἄγω τὸν ὑμᾶς κἀμὲ τἀμά τ' ὄργια
γέλων τιθέμενον· ἀλλὰ τιμωρεῖσθέ νιν.
καὶ ταῦθ' ἅμ' ἠγόρευε καὶ πρὸς οὐρανὸν
καὶ γαῖαν ἐστήριζε φῶς σεμνοῦ πυρός.
σίγησε δ' αἰθήρ, σῖγα δ' ὕλιμος νάπη
1085 φύλλ' εἶχε, θηρῶν δ' οὐκ ἂν ἤκουσας βοήν.
αἱ δ' ὠσὶν ἠχὴν οὐ σαφῶς δεδεγμέναι
ἔστησαν ὀρθαὶ καὶ διήνεγκαν κόρας.
ὁ δ' αὖθις ἐπεκέλευσεν· ὡς δ' ἐγνώρισαν
σαφῆ κελευσμὸν Βακχίου Κάδμου κόραι,
1090 ᾖξαν πελείας ὠκύτητ' οὐχ ἥσσονες
[ποδῶν τρέχουσαι συντόνοις δραμήμασι,
μήτηρ Ἀγαυὴ σύγγονοί θ' ὁμόσποροι]
πᾶσαί τε βάκχαι· διὰ δὲ χειμάρρου νάπης
ἀγμῶν τ' ἐπήδων θεοῦ πνοαῖσιν ἐμμανεῖς.
1095 ὡς δ' εἶδον ἐλάτῃ δεσπότην ἐφήμενον,
πρῶτον μὲν αὐτοῦ χερμάδας κραταιβόλους
ἔρριπτον, ἀντίπυργον ἐπιβᾶσαι πέτραν,
ὄζοισί τ' ἐλατίνοισιν ἠκοντίζετο.
ἄλλαι δὲ θύρσους ἵεσαν δι' αἰθέρος
1100 Πενθέως, στόχον δύστηνον· ἀλλ' οὐκ ἤνυτον.

care not to unseat Pentheus—and sheer to sheer heaven it towered, with my master on its back. He now was seen by the maenads more than he saw them. He was just becoming visible sitting up there and the stranger was nowhere to be seen, when from the upper air a voice (I think it was Dionysus) shouted, "Young women, I bring you the man who is mocking you, me, and my rites: punish him!" And while he was still speaking, the light of a holy fire touched earth and heaven.

The upper air was still, the leaves of the wooded glade kept silence, and no sound of beast could be heard. The maenads had not taken in the shout with their ears, and they stood there erect, turning their gaze this way and that. The god a second time gave the order. When Cadmus' daughters had recognized the clear command of the bacchic god, they darted forward as swift as doves [running with intense effort of foot, mother Agave with her kindred sisters], and so did all the bacchant women: through the glen with its torrent and over boulders they leapt, maddened by the breath of the god.

When they saw my master perched on the fir tree, they first climbed a cliff that towered opposite him, hurled stones at him, and launched fir branches against him like javelins while others threw their wands through the air at him, and what a woeful sight was their aiming at him. But it

---

1091–2 om. II

κρεῖσσον γὰρ ὕψος τῆς προθυμίας ἔχων
καθῆσθ' ὁ τλήμων, ἀπορίᾳ λελημμένος.
τέλος δὲ δρυΐνοις συντριαινοῦσαι κλάδοις
ῥίζας ἀνεσπάρασσον ἀσιδήροις μοχλοῖς.
1105 ἐπεὶ δὲ μόχθων τέρματ' οὐκ ἐξήνυτον,
ἔλεξ' Ἀγαυή· Φέρε, περιστᾶσαι κύκλῳ
πτόρθου λάβεσθε, μαινάδες, τὸν ἀμβάτην
θῆρ' ὡς ἕλωμεν, μηδ' ἀπαγγείλῃ θεοῦ
χοροὺς κρυφαίους. αἱ δὲ μυρίαν χέρα
1110 προσέθεσαν ἐλάτῃ κἀξανέσπασαν χθονός.
ὑψοῦ δὲ θάσσων ὑψόθεν χαμαιριφὴς
πίπτει πρὸς οὖδας μυρίοις οἰμώγμασιν
Πενθεύς· κακοῦ γὰρ ἐγγὺς ὢν ἐμάνθανεν.

πρώτη δὲ μήτηρ ἦρξεν ἱερέα φόνου
1115 καὶ προσπίτνει νιν· ὁ δὲ μίτραν κόμης ἄπο
ἔρριψεν, ὥς νιν γνωρίσασα μὴ κτάνοι
τλήμων Ἀγαυή, καὶ λέγει παρηίδος
ψαύων· Ἐγώ τοι, μῆτερ, εἰμί, παῖς σέθεν
Πενθεύς, ὃν ἔτεκες ἐν δόμοις Ἐχίονος·
1120 οἴκτιρε δ' ὦ μῆτέρ με μηδὲ ταῖς ἐμαῖς
ἁμαρτίαισι παῖδα σὸν κατακτάνῃς.
ἡ δ' ἀφρὸν ἐξιεῖσα καὶ διαστρόφους
κόρας ἑλίσσουσ', οὐ φρονοῦσ' ἃ χρὴ φρονεῖν,
ἐκ Βακχίου κατείχετ', οὐδ' ἔπειθέ νιν.
1125 λαβοῦσα δ' ὠλέναισ' ἀριστερὰν χέρα,
πλευραῖσιν ἀντιβᾶσα τοῦ δυσδαίμονος
ἀπεσπάραξεν ὦμον, οὐχ ὑπὸ σθένους
ἀλλ' ὁ θεὸς εὐμάρειαν ἐπεδίδου χεροῖν·

was no use: he was too high for them to reach him, try as they might. Pentheus sat there trapped in helplessness. Finally they began to tear at the roots of the tree with crowbars not made of iron, trying to pry them up with branches of oak. When their efforts failed to reach their goal, Agave said, "Maenads, circle round and take hold of the tree so that we can catch the beast mounted on it: we don't want him to tell about our secret dances." They put their countless hands to the fir tree and pulled it out of the earth. Pentheus from his high perch fell to the ground with many a scream and moan: he knew that his end was near.

His mother was the priestess and began the killing, hurling herself upon him. He, however, wrenched his headdress from his hair so that poor Agave would recognize him and not kill him. He put his hand to her cheek and said, "It's me, mother, Pentheus, the son you bore in Echion's house! Have pity on me, mother! I have sinned, but do not kill your son!" But her mouth dripped foam and her eyes rolled: she was not in her right mind but possessed by the bacchic god, and his entreaty did not move her. Taking his right hand in her grip and planting her foot against the poor man's flank, she tore out his arm at the shoulder, using a strength not her own but put in her hands

---

1103 δρυΐνοις . . . κλάδοις Hartung: -ους . . . -ους ΠΡ
συντριαινοῦσαι Pierson: συγκεραυνοῦσαι ΠΡ

Ἰνὼ δὲ τἀπὶ θάτερ' ἐξηργάζετο,
1130 ῥηγνῦσα σάρκας, Αὐτονόη τ' ὄχλος τε πᾶς
ἐπεῖχε βακχῶν· ἦν δὲ πᾶσ' ὁμοῦ βοή,
ὁ μὲν στενάζων ὅσον ἐτύγχαν' ἐμπνέων,
αἱ δ' ὠλόλυζον. ἔφερε δ' ἡ μὲν ὠλένην,
ἡ δ' ἴχνος αὐταῖς ἀρβύλαις, γυμνοῦντο δὲ
1135 πλευραὶ σπαραγμοῖς· πᾶσα δ' ᾑματωμένη
χεῖρας διεσφαίριζε σάρκα Πενθέως.
κεῖται δὲ χωρὶς σῶμα, τὸ μὲν ὑπὸ στύφλοις
πέτραις, τὸ δ' ὕλης ἐν βαθυξύλῳ φόβῃ,
οὐ ῥᾴδιον ζήτημα· κρᾶτα δ' ἄθλιον,
1140 ὅπερ λαβοῦσα τυγχάνει μήτηρ χεροῖν,
πήξασ' ἐπ' ἄκρον θύρσον ὡς ὀρεστέρου
φέρει λέοντος διὰ Κιθαιρῶνος μέσου,
λιποῦσ' ἀδελφὰς ἐν χοροῖσι μαινάδων.
χωρεῖ δὲ θήρᾳ δυσπότμῳ γαυρουμένη
1145 τειχέων ἔσω τῶνδ', ἀνακαλοῦσα Βάκχιον
τὸν ξυγκύναγον, τὸν ξυνεργάτην ἄγρας,
τὸν καλλίνικον, ᾧ δάκρυα νικηφορεῖ.
ἐγὼ μὲν οὖν ‹τῇδ'› ἐκποδὼν τῇ ξυμφορᾷ
ἄπειμ', Ἀγαυὴν πρὶν μολεῖν πρὸς δώματα.
1150 τὸ σωφρονεῖν δὲ καὶ σέβειν τὰ τῶν θεῶν
κάλλιστον· οἶμαι δ' αὐτὸ καὶ σοφώτατον
θνητοῖσιν εἶναι κτῆμα τοῖσι χρωμένοις.

ΧΟΡΟΣ

ἀναχορεύσωμεν Βάκχιον,
ἀναβοάσωμεν ξυμφορὰν

by the god. Ino was destroying his other side, tearing his
flesh, and Autonoe and the rest of the bacchic throng at-
tacked him. The air was filled with cries: Pentheus moaned
with all the breath he had in him, and the women raised
the sacrificial shout. One woman was carrying an arm, an-
other a foot still in its boot, his flanks were stripped bare,
the flesh torn from them, and every woman, hands red
with blood, hurled Pentheus' flesh about like a ball. His
body lies scattered, some of it under the rough cliffs, other
parts in thick-growing woods, no easy thing to look for. As
for his luckless head, which his mother happened to take in
her hands, she has fixed it on the point of her bacchic wand
and is carrying it, as if it were the head of a mountain
lion, through the midst of Cithaeron, leaving her sisters
with the maenad companies. And now, exulting in this ill-
starred hunt, she has come within the walls, calling on the
bacchic god, her "fellow huntsman," her "companion in
the chase," "the glorious victor," by whose aid she has won
tears as victory prize. I, to be sure, am going away before
Agave comes to the palace, standing clear of ⟨this⟩ disas-
ter. The best thing of all is to practice moderation and wor-
ship the gods. That is also, I think, the wisest possession a
mortal can make use of.

Exit MESSENGER *by Eisodos A.*

CHORUS
Let us dance for joy in the bacchic god's honor,
Let us dance for joy at the calamity

1133 ὠλόλυζον Diggle: ἠλάλαζον P
1147 ᾧ Reiske: ἦ P   1148 ⟨τῆδ'⟩ Reiske

1155 τὰν τοῦ δράκοντος Πενθέος ἐκγενέτα,
    ὃς τὰν θηλυγενῆ
    στολὰν νάρθηκά τε πικρὸν Ἅιδα
    ἔλαβεν εὔθυρσον,
    ταῦρον προηγητῆρα συμφορᾶς ἔχων.
1160 βάκχαι Καδμεῖαι,
    τὸν καλλίνικον κλεινὸν ἐξεπράξατε
    ἐς γόον, ἐς δάκρυα·
    καλὸς ἀγὼν ἐν αἵματι στάζουσαν
    χέρα βαλεῖν τέκνου.

1165 ἀλλ', εἰσορῶ γὰρ ἐς δόμους ὁρμωμένην
    Πενθέως Ἀγαυὴν μητέρ' ἐν διαστρόφοις
    ὄσσοις, δέχεσθ' ἐς κῶμον εὐίου θεοῦ.

στρ.

ΑΓΑΥΗ

Ἀσιάδες βάκχαι . . .

ΧΟΡΟΣ
    τί με θροεῖς, γύναι;

ΑΓΑΥΗ

. . . φέρομεν ἐξ ὀρέων
1170 ἕλικα νεότομον ἐπὶ μέλαθρα,
    μακάριον θήραν.

1155 Πενθέος ἐκγενέτα Wilamowitz: ἐκ- Π- P
1157 τε πικρὸν Seidler: τε πιστὸν P: θ' ὁπλισμὸν Wilamowitz
1158 εὖ θαρσῶν Page
1164 βαλεῖν Kirchhoff: περιβαλεῖν P

of Pentheus, the dragon's offspring,
who took up the garb
of a woman and the bacchic wand in its beauty—
though 'twas bitter and deadly to him—
with a bull to lead him toward disaster.
You Theban bacchants,
famous is the song of victory you have won,
famous for lament, for tears!
A fine endeavor it is to drench
one's hand in the blood of a child!

Enter by Eisodos B AGAVE, *carrying a thyrsus with the
mask of Pentheus impaled on it.*

CHORUS LEADER
But look! I see Pentheus' mother Agave coming toward the
house, her eyes rolling in madness! Receive her into the
reveling band of the blissful god!

AGAVE
You bacchants of Asia . . .

CHORUS
What are you telling me, lady?

AGAVE
. . . we bring from the mountain
to the palace a sprig new-cut,
a fortunate catch!

1167 δέχεσθ' ἐς Verdenius: δέχεσθε P
1168 με θροεῖς Scaliger: με ὀρθεῖς P   γύναι Jackson: ὦ P

ΧΟΡΟΣ

ὁρῶ καί σε δέξομαι σύγκωμον.

ΑΓΑΥΗ

ἔμαρψα τόνδ' ἄνευ βρόχων
⟨λέοντος ἀγροτέρου⟩ νέον ἶνιν,
1175 ὡς ὁρᾶν πάρα.

ΧΟΡΟΣ

πόθεν ἐρημίας;

ΑΓΑΥΗ

Κιθαιρὼν . . .

ΧΟΡΟΣ

Κιθαιρών;

ΑΓΑΥΗ

. . . κατεφόνευσέ νιν.

ΧΟΡΟΣ

τίς ἁ βαλοῦσα;

ΑΓΑΥΗ

πρῶτον ἐμὸν τὸ γέρας.
1180 μάκαιρ' Ἀγαυὴ κλῃζόμεθ' ἐν θιάσοις.

ΧΟΡΟΣ

τίς ἄλλα;

ΑΓΑΥΗ

τὰ Κάδμου . . .

1174 lac. indic. Canter, suppl. Wecklein
1177 Κιθαιρών (alterum) Murray: τί K- P

126

CHORUS

I see it, and I accept you as my fellow reveler.

AGAVE

I captured without a noose
this young whelp <of a mountain lion>,
as you can see.

CHORUS

From what part of the wild?

AGAVE

Cithaeron . . .

CHORUS

Cithaeron?

AGAVE

. . . brought about his slaughter.

CHORUS

Who was she that struck him?

AGAVE

That honor belongs first to me.
I shall be called "Agave the blessed" among the god's wor-
shipers.

CHORUS

Who else struck?

AGAVE

Cadmus's . . .

ΧΟΡΟΣ

τί Κάδμου;

ΑΓΑΥΗ
. . . γένεθλα
μετ᾿ ἐμὲ μετ᾿ ἐμὲ τοῦδ᾿ ἔθιγε θηρός, εὐ-
τυχεῖς τᾷδ᾿ ἄγρᾳ.

<ΧΟΡΟΣ
εὐδαιμονίζω σ᾿, ὦ γύναι, καὶ συγγόνους,
ἄγρας τυχούσας τιμιωτάτης μακρῷ.>

ἀντ.

ΑΓΑΥΗ

μέτεχέ νυν θοίνας.

ΧΟΡΟΣ
τί μέτεχ᾿, ὦ τλᾶμον;

ΑΓΑΥΗ
1185   νέος ὁ μόσχος ἄρ-
τι γένυν ὑπὸ κόρυθ᾿ ἁπαλότριχα
κατάκομον θάλλει.

ΧΟΡΟΣ
πρέπει γ᾿ ὥστε θὴρ ἄγραυλος φόβᾳ.

ΑΓΑΥΗ
ὁ Βάκχιος κυναγέτας
1190   σοφὸς σοφῶς ἀνέπηλ᾿ ἐπὶ θῆρα
τόνδε μαινάδας.

[1183] post h. v. duo chori trimetros excidisse coni. Schoene

128

CHORUS

Cadmus's?

AGAVE

. . . daughters
second to me, second to me, wounded this beast: they were
    fortunate
in this hunt!

<CHORUS LEADER

How blessed you are in my eyes for your splendid catch,
my lady, and your sisters as well!>

AGAVE

Take part in the banquet, then!

CHORUS

What do you mean, take part, poor woman?

AGAVE

The calf is young,
his cheek just growing downy
under his crest of delicate hair.

CHORUS

Yes: its hair looks like a beast of the wild.

AGAVE

Dionysus the clever hunter
cleverly urged the maenads on
against this beast.

1188 γ' ὥστε θὴρ ἄγραυλος Kirchhoff: γὰρ ὥστε θηρὸς
ἀγραύλου P

ΧΟΡΟΣ

ὁ γὰρ ἄναξ ἀγρεύς.

ΑΓΑΥΗ

ἐπαινεῖς;

ΧΟΡΟΣ

ἐπαινῶ.

ΑΓΑΥΗ

τάχα δὲ Καδμεῖοι . . .

ΧΟΡΟΣ

1195   καὶ παῖς γε Πενθεύς.

ΑΓΑΥΗ

. . . ματέρ᾽ ἐπαινέσεται,
λαβοῦσαν ἄγραν τάνδε λεοντοφυᾶ.

ΧΟΡΟΣ

περισσάν.

ΑΓΑΥΗ

περισσῶς.

ΧΟΡΟΣ

ἀγάλλῃ;

ΑΓΑΥΗ

γέγηθα,
μεγάλα μεγάλα καὶ φανερὰ τᾷδ᾽ ἄγρᾳ
κατειργασμένα.

ΧΟΡΟΣ

1200   δεῖξόν νυν, ὦ τάλαινα, σὴν νικηφόρον

CHORUS

Yes, our lord is a hunter.

AGAVE

Do you praise me?

CHORUS

I praise you.

AGAVE

Soon the men of Thebes . . .

CHORUS

And also your son Pentheus.

AGAVE

. . . will praise the mother,
who has made the lion's whelp her catch.

CHORUS

Marvelous catch!

AGAVE

Marvelously done!

CHORUS

Are you joyous?

AGAVE

Exultant,
since with this catch I have accomplished
great deeds, great and plain to see!

CHORUS LEADER

So, poor woman, show the citizens the glorious prey you

ἀστοῖσιν ἄγραν ἣν φέρουσ᾽ ἐλήλυθας.

ΑΓΑΥΗ

ὦ καλλίπυργον ἄστυ Θηβαίας χθονὸς
ναίοντες, ἔλθεθ᾽ ὡς ἴδητε τήνδ᾽ ἄγραν,
Κάδμου θυγατέρες θηρὸς ἣν ἠγρεύσαμεν,
1205 οὐκ ἀγκυλωτοῖς Θεσσαλῶν στοχάσμασιν,
οὐ δικτύοισιν, ἀλλὰ λευκοπήχεσιν
χειρῶν ἀκμαῖσι. κᾆτ᾽ ἀκοντίζειν χρεὼν
καὶ λογχοποιῶν ὄργανα κτᾶσθαι μάτην;
ἡμεῖς δέ γ᾽ αὐτῇ χειρὶ τόνδε θ᾽ εἵλομεν
1210 χωρίς τε θηρὸς ἄρθρα διεφορήσαμεν.
ποῦ μοι πατὴρ ὁ πρέσβυς; ἐλθέτω πέλας.
Πενθεύς τ᾽ ἐμὸς παῖς ποῦ 'στιν; αἱρέσθω λαβὼν
πηκτῶν πρὸς οἴκους κλιμάκων προσαμβάσεις,
ὡς πασσαλεύσῃ κρᾶτα τριγλύφοις τόδε
1215 λέοντος ὃν πάρειμι θηράσασ᾽ ἐγώ.

ΚΑΔΜΟΣ

ἕπεσθέ μοι φέροντες ἄθλιον βάρος
Πενθέως, ἕπεσθε, πρόσπολοι, δόμων πάρος,
οὗ σῶμα μοχθῶν μυρίοις ζητήμασιν
φέρω τόδ᾽, εὑρὼν ἐν Κιθαιρῶνος πτυχαῖς
1220 διασπάρακτον κοὐδὲν ἐν ταὐτῷ πέδου
[λαβών, ἐν ὕλῃ κείμενον δυσευρέτῳ].
ἤκουσα γάρ του θυγατέρων τολμήματα,
ἤδη κατ᾽ ἄστυ τειχέων ἔσω βεβὼς
σὺν τῷ γέροντι Τειρεσίᾳ βακχῶν πάρα·
1225 πάλιν δὲ κάμψας εἰς ὄρος κομίζομαι

have brought with you.

AGAVE

Dwellers in fair-towered Thebes, come and see the catch,
the beast we daughters of Cadmus have snared! We caught
him not with the thong-hurled javelins the Thessalians use
or with nets but with the fingers of our pale-skinned hands.
After this, should one throw the javelin or get the weapons
armorers make? It is pointless. We caught the beast with
our bare hands and tore him limb from limb. Where is my
aged father? Let him come here. And where is my son
Pentheus? He should bring a ladder to the house so that
he can nail to the triglyphs the head of this lion I caught
before coming here.

Enter by Eisodos B CADMUS *with servants carrying a
draped stretcher.*

CADMUS

Follow me, servants, follow me, and carry the woeful bur-
den of Pentheus' body before the palace! I bring it after
endless labor of searching, having found it in the glades of
Cithaeron torn in pieces, no two parts in the same spot of
ground [having taken them up lying scattered in a wood
hard to search]. I heard from someone in the city about
my daughters' criminal deeds when I had returned from
the bacchants with old Teiresias and was already inside
the walls. I retraced my steps to the mountain and have

1207 κᾆτ᾽ ἀκοντίζειν Sandys: κᾆτα κομπάζειν P
1220 πέδου Jackson: -ῳ P
1221 del. Nauck
1224 πάρα Musgrave: πέρι P   v. del. Willink

τὸν κατθανόντα παῖδα μαινάδων ὕπο.
καὶ τὴν μὲν Ἀκταίων᾽ Ἀρισταίῳ ποτὲ
τεκοῦσαν εἶδον Αὐτονόην Ἰνώ θ᾽ ἅμα
ἔτ᾽ ἀμφὶ δρυμοὺς οἰστροπλῆγας ἀθλίας,
1230 τὴν δ᾽ εἶπέ τίς μοι δεῦρο βακχείῳ ποδὶ
στείχειν Ἀγαυήν, οὐδ᾽ ἄκραντ᾽ ἠκούσαμεν·
λεύσσω γὰρ αὐτήν, ὄψιν οὐκ εὐδαίμονα.

ΑΓΑΥΗ

πάτερ, μέγιστον κομπάσαι πάρεστί σοι,
πάντων ἀρίστας θυγατέρας σπεῖραι μακρῷ
1235 θνητῶν· ἁπάσας εἶπον, ἐξόχως δ᾽ ἐμέ,
ἣ τὰς παρ᾽ ἱστοῖς ἐκλιποῦσα κερκίδας
ἐς μεῖζον ἥκω, θῆρας ἀγρεύειν χεροῖν.
φέρω δ᾽ ἐν ὠλέναισιν, ὡς ὁρᾷς, τάδε
λαβοῦσα τἀριστεῖα, σοῖσι πρὸς δόμοις
1240 ὡς ἀγκρεμασθῇ· σὺ δέ, πάτερ, δέξαι χεροῖν·
γαυρούμενος δὲ τοῖς ἐμοῖς ἀγρεύμασιν
κάλει φίλους ἐς δαῖτα· μακάριος γὰρ εἶ,
μακάριος, ἡμῶν τοιάδ᾽ ἐξειργασμένων.

ΚΑΔΜΟΣ

ὦ πένθος οὐ μετρητόν, οὐχ οἷόν τ᾽ ἰδεῖν
⟨Πενθεὺς ἀνίας ὡς ἄρ᾽ ἦν ἐπώνυμος;
καλὴ μὲν ἄγρα, σοῦ τε συγγόνων τε σῶν⟩
1245 φόνον ταλαίναις χερσὶν ἐξειργασμένων.
καλὸν τὸ θῦμα καταβαλοῦσα δαίμοσιν
ἐπὶ δαῖτα Θήβας τάσδε κἀμὲ παρακαλεῖς.
οἴμοι κακῶν μὲν πρῶτα σῶν, ἔπειτ᾽ ἐμῶν·

brought back the son the maenads have killed. I saw
Autonoe, who bore Actaeon to Aristaeus, and Ino with her,
still in miserable madness amid the copses, but someone
said that Agave was coming here with maddened step—
and he was telling the truth: for I see her here, a sight
unblessed.

AGAVE

Father, you have the right to boast loudly that you begot
the world's bravest daughters: I said all of them, but espe-
cially me, since I have left my loom and shuttle and taken
on greater things, hunting beasts with bare hands. I grasp,
as you see, a prize of victory here so that it can be nailed up
on your house's walls. Father, take it in your hands. Exult in
my hunt and invite your friends to a feast: blessed, blessed
are you since we have accomplished this!

She offers him her thyrsus.

CADMUS

O grief past measure! Can one not see <that Pentheus was
named for sorrow?[18] A fine hunt it is for you and your sis-
ters> to accomplish bloodshed with your ill-starred hands,
and it is a fine sacrifice you have made to the gods and to
which you invite Thebes and me! O misery, yours first and

18 See above, note on line 367.

1244 οὐχ Kovacs: οὐδ' P
1245 ante h. v. lac. indic. Kovacs
1246 τὸ] fort. δὲ: sed cf. 243

ὡς ὁ θεὸς ἡμᾶς ἐνδίκως μὲν ἀλλ᾽ ἄγαν
1250 Βρόμιος ἄναξ ἀπώλεσ᾽ οἰκεῖος γεγώς.

ΑΓΑΥΗ

ὡς δύσκολον τὸ γῆρας ἀνθρώποις ἔφυ
ἔν τ᾽ ὄμμασι σκυθρωπόν. εἴθε παῖς ἐμὸς
εὔθηρος εἴη, μητρὸς εἰκασθεὶς τρόποις,
ὁπότε νεανίαισι Θηβαίοις ἅμα
1255 θηρῶν ὀριγνῷτ᾽· ἀλλὰ θεομαχεῖν μόνον
οἷός τ᾽ ἐκεῖνος. νουθετητέος, πάτερ,
σοῦστίν. τίς αὐτὸν δεῦρ᾽ ἂν ὄψιν εἰς ἐμὴν
καλέσειεν, ὡς ἴδῃ με τὴν εὐδαίμονα;

ΚΑΔΜΟΣ

φεῦ φεῦ· φρονήσασαι μὲν οἷ᾽ ἐδράσατε
1260 ἀλγήσετ᾽ ἄλγος δεινόν· εἰ δὲ διὰ τέλους
ἐν τῷδ᾽ ἀεὶ μενεῖτ᾽ ἐν ᾧ καθέστατε,
οὐκ εὐτυχοῦσαι δόξετ᾽ οὐχὶ δυστυχεῖν.

ΑΓΑΥΗ

τί δ᾽ οὐ καλῶς τῶνδ᾽ ἢ τί λυπηρῶς ἔχει;

ΚΑΔΜΟΣ

πρῶτον μὲν ἐς τόνδ᾽ αἰθέρ᾽ ὄμμα σὸν μέθες.

ΑΓΑΥΗ

1265 ἰδού· τί μοι τόνδ᾽ ἐξυπεῖπας εἰσορᾶν;

ΚΑΔΜΟΣ

ἔθ᾽ αὑτὸς ἤ σοι μεταβολὰς ἔχειν δοκεῖ;

ΑΓΑΥΗ

λαμπρότερος ἢ πρὶν καὶ διειπετέστερος.

then my own! How excessively our own lord Bromios has ruined us, however just it was!

AGAVE

How peevish old age is among mortals, how scowling its face! How I wish my son might be a good hunter, just like his mother, whenever he joined the young men in pursuit of beasts! But he's good only at fighting gods. You must speak to him, father. Someone call him here before me so that he can see me in my good fortune!

CADMUS

Ah, ah! If you all come to realize what you have done, you will suffer dreadfully! But if you remain throughout in your present state, though you will not be truly happy, you will at least not be thought miserable.

AGAVE

What part of this causes disgrace or pain?

CADMUS

First turn your eye to the heavens.

AGAVE

(*looking up*) There! What did you mean that I should look at?

CADMUS

Does it seem the same to you or altered?

AGAVE

It is brighter than before and clearer.

1254 ὁπότε Jackson: ὅτ᾽ ἐν P

ΚΑΔΜΟΣ

τὸ δὲ πτοηθὲν τόδ' ἔτι σῇ ψυχῇ πάρα;

ΑΓΑΥΗ

οὐκ οἶδα τοὖπος τοῦτο. γίγνομαι δέ πως
1270 ἔννους, μετασταθεῖσα τῶν πάρος φρενῶν.

ΚΑΔΜΟΣ

κλύοις ἂν οὖν τι κἀποκρίναι' ἂν σαφῶς;

ΑΓΑΥΗ

ὡς ἐκλέλησμαί γ' ἃ πάρος εἴπομεν, πάτερ.

ΚΑΔΜΟΣ

ἐς ποῖον ἦλθες οἶκον ὑμεναίων μέτα;

ΑΓΑΥΗ

Σπαρτῷ μ' ἔδωκας, ὡς λέγουσ', Ἐχίονι.

ΚΑΔΜΟΣ

1275 τίς οὖν ἐν οἴκοις παῖς ἐγένετο σῷ πόσει;

ΑΓΑΥΗ

Πενθεύς, ἐμῇ τε καὶ πατρὸς κοινωνίᾳ.

ΚΑΔΜΟΣ

τίνος πρόσωπον δῆτ' ἐν ἀγκάλαις ἔχεις;

ΑΓΑΥΗ

λέοντος, ὥς γ' ἔφασκον αἱ θηρώμεναι.

ΚΑΔΜΟΣ

σκέψαι νυν ὀρθῶς· βραχὺς ὁ μόχθος εἰσιδεῖν.

ΑΓΑΥΗ

1280 ἔα, τί λεύσσω; τί φέρομαι τόδ' ἐν χεροῖν;

CADMUS

Does your mind still feel giddy?

AGAVE

I don't know what you mean. But I am coming somehow to my senses and have abandoned my former frame of mind.

CADMUS

Will you hear me and answer truly?

AGAVE

Yes: I have forgotten what we said before, father.

CADMUS

To what household did you come at your marriage?

AGAVE

You married me to Echion, one of the Sown Men, they say.

CADMUS

Well, what son was born in that house to your husband?

AGAVE

Pentheus, his father's son and mine.

CADMUS

Whose head do you have in your hands then?

AGAVE

The hunters told me it is a lion's.

CADMUS

Look at it properly: the effort of doing so is slight.

AGAVE

Ah, what am I seeing? What is this that I carry in my hands?

1280 φέρομεν Elmsley

ΚΑΔΜΟΣ

ἄθρησον αὐτὸ καὶ σαφέστερον μάθε.

ΑΓΑΥΗ

ὁρῶ μέγιστον ἄλγος ἡ τάλαιν᾽ ἐγώ.

ΚΑΔΜΟΣ

μῶν σοι λέοντι φαίνεται προσεικέναι;

ΑΓΑΥΗ

οὔκ, ἀλλὰ Πενθέως ἡ τάλαιν᾽ ἔχω κάρα.

ΚΑΔΜΟΣ

1285 ὠμωγμένον γε πρόσθεν ἢ σὲ γνωρίσαι.

ΑΓΑΥΗ

τίς ἔκτανέν νιν; πῶς ἐμὰς ἦλθ᾽ ἐς χέρας;

ΚΑΔΜΟΣ

δύστην᾽ ἀλήθει᾽, ὡς ἐν οὐ καιρῷ πάρει.

ΑΓΑΥΗ

λέγ᾽, ὡς τὸ μέλλον καρδία πήδημ᾽ ἔχει.

ΚΑΔΜΟΣ

σύ νιν κατέκτας καὶ κασίγνηται σέθεν.

ΑΓΑΥΗ

1290 ποῦ δ᾽ ὤλετ᾽; ἦ κατ᾽ οἶκον, ἦ ποίοις τόποις;

ΚΑΔΜΟΣ

οὗπερ πρὶν Ἀκταίωνα διέλαχον κύνες.

ΑΓΑΥΗ

τί δ᾽ ἐς Κιθαιρῶν᾽ ἦλθε δυσδαίμων ὅδε;

CADMUS

Look at it, get surer knowledge.

AGAVE

Great woe is what I see, unhappy me!

CADMUS

Does it seem like a lion to you?

AGAVE

No: in my misery I hold Pentheus' head!

CADMUS

Yes, it was mourned before you even recognized it.

AGAVE

Who killed him? How did he come into my hands?

CADMUS

Unhappy truth, how untimely you have come!

AGAVE

Speak: my heart leaps at what is to come!

CADMUS

You killed him, you and your sisters.

AGAVE

Where did he perish? At home, or where?

CADMUS

In the place where Actaeon was torn apart by dogs.

AGAVE

Why did the poor man come to Cithaeron?

1281 αὐτὸ] αὖθις Reiske

ΚΑΔΜΟΣ

ἐκερτόμει θεὸν σάς τε βακχείας μολών.

ΑΓΑΥΗ

ἡμεῖς δ᾽ ἐκεῖσε τίνι τρόπῳ κατήραμεν;

ΚΑΔΜΟΣ

1295 ἐμάνητε, πᾶσά τ᾽ ἐξεβακχεύθη πόλις.

ΑΓΑΥΗ

Διόνυσος ἡμᾶς ὤλεσ᾽, ἄρτι μανθάνω.

ΚΑΔΜΟΣ

ὕβριν ⟨γ᾽⟩ ὑβρισθείς· θεὸν γὰρ οὐχ ἡγεῖσθέ νιν.

ΑΓΑΥΗ

τὸ φίλτατον δὲ σῶμα ποῦ παιδός, πάτερ;

ΚΑΔΜΟΣ

ἐγὼ μόλις τόδ᾽ ἐξερευνήσας φέρω.

ΑΓΑΥΗ

1300 ἦ πᾶν ἐν ἄρθροις συγκεκλημένον καλῶς;

. . . .

ΑΓΑΥΗ

Πενθεῖ δὲ τί μέρος ἀφροσύνης προσῆκ᾽ ἐμῆς;

ΚΑΔΜΟΣ

ὑμῖν ἐγένεθ᾽ ὅμοιος, οὐ σέβων θεόν.
τοιγὰρ συνῆψε πάντας ἐς μίαν βλάβην,

1297 ⟨γ᾽⟩ Heath   1298–1300 del. Wilamowitz (1300 iam
Nauck) ut ex eis superstites qui post 1329 perditi sunt
1300 post h. v. lac. indic. Victorius

142

CADMUS

He meant to mock the god and his rites by going there.

AGAVE

But how did *we* get there?

CADMUS

You were out of your wits, and the whole city was possessed by Bacchus.

AGAVE

Dionysus has destroyed us: now I realize this.

CADMUS

Yes, he had been deeply insulted: you did not consider him a god.

AGAVE

Where is the dear body of my son, father?

CADMUS

(*pointing to the stretcher*) Here: I bring it after a difficult search.

AGAVE

Has it been properly fitted together, limb with limb?

. . . .[19]

AGAVE

But what share did Pentheus have in my folly?

CADMUS

He was like you in not worshiping the god. And so the god joined you all, both my daughters and this man, in a single

[19] There is a lacuna here, possibly quite extensive. In it Agave may have joined Pentheus' head to his other remains.

143

ὑμᾶς τε τόνδε θ', ὥστε διολέσαι δόμους
1305 κἄμ', ὅστις ἄτεκνος ἀρσένων παίδων γεγὼς
τῆς σῆς τόδ' ἔρνος, ὦ τάλαινα, νηδύος
αἴσχιστα καὶ κάκιστα κατθανόνθ' ὁρῶ·
ᾧ δῶμ' ἀνέβλεφ', ὃς συνεῖχες, ὦ τέκνον,
τοὐμὸν μέλαθρον, παιδὸς ἐξ ἐμῆς γεγώς,
1310 πόλει τε τάρβος ἦσθα· τὸν γέροντα δὲ
οὐδεὶς ὑβρίζειν ἤθελ' εἰσορῶν τὸ σὸν
κάρα· δίκην γὰρ ἀξίαν ἐλάμβανες.
νῦν δ' ἐκ δόμων ἄτιμος ἐκβεβλήσομαι
ὁ Κάδμος ὁ μέγας, ὃς τὸ Θηβαίων γένος
1315 ἔσπειρα κἀξήμησα κάλλιστον θέρος.
   ὦ φίλτατ' ἀνδρῶν (καὶ γὰρ οὐκέτ' ὢν ὅμως
τῶν φιλτάτων ἔμοιγ' ἀριθμήσῃ, τέκνον),
οὐκέτι γενείου τοῦδε θιγγάνων χερὶ
τὸν μητρὸς αὐδῶν πατέρα προσπτύξῃ, τέκνον,
1320 λέγων· Τίς ἀδικεῖ, τίς σ' ἀτιμάζει, γέρον;
τίς σὴν ταράσσει καρδίαν λυπηρὸς ὤν;
λέγ', ὡς κολάζω τὸν ἀδικοῦντά σ', ὦ πάτερ.
νῦν δ' ἄθλιος μέν εἰμ' ἐγώ, τλήμων δὲ σύ,
οἰκτρὰ δὲ μήτηρ, τλήμονες δὲ σύγγονοι.
1325 εἰ δ' ἔστιν ὅστις δαιμόνων ὑπερφρονεῖ,
ἐς τοῦδ' ἀθρήσας θάνατον ἡγείσθω θεούς.

ΧΟΡΟΣ
τὸ μὲν σὸν ἀλγῶ, Κάδμε· σὸς δ' ἔχει δίκην
παῖς παιδὸς ἀξίαν μέν, ἀλγεινὴν δὲ σοί.

calamity, which has destroyed the house and me as well: I had no sons and then saw the offspring of your womb, poor woman, so shamefully and painfully killed. In him the house had found its sight again. O son, you were my daughter's child and were keeping my house from dissolution! You inspired fear in the city: no one, looking at you, dared to offer insult to me in my old age, for you were likely to exact a fitting penalty from him. But now I shall be an outcast from the house, unhonored, I, Cadmus the great, who sowed and reaped the lovely harvest that is the people of Thebes.[20]

O dearest of men (for even in death you are counted among those I love best, child), no more will you touch this beard of mine, my son, or embrace me, or call me grandfather, saying "Who is wronging you or showing you disrespect, sir? Who is troublesome and vexing your heart? Tell me, father, so that I can punish him who wrongs you." But now I am wretched, you are miserable, and your mother and her sisters pitiable in their suffering. If there is anyone who thinks nothing of heaven's power, let him look at this man's death and believe that the gods exist.

CHORUS LEADER
I feel grief at your misfortune, Cadmus. As for your grandson, he has received justice, however painful it is for you.

---

[20] See note on line 265 above.

1312 ἐλάμβανες Hermann: -εν P
1317 τέκνον Reiske: -ων P

ΑΓΑΥΗ

ὦ πάτερ, ὁρᾷς γὰρ τἄμ᾽ ὅσῳ μετεστράφη

. . . .

<ΔΙΟΝΥΣΟΣ>

. . . .

1330   δράκων γενήσῃ μεταβαλών, δάμαρ τε σὴ
ἐκθηριωθεῖσ᾽ ὄφεος ἀλλάξει τύπον,
ἣν Ἄρεος ἔσχες Ἁρμονίαν θνητὸς γεγώς.
ὄχον δὲ μόσχων, χρησμὸς ὡς λέγει Διός,
ἐλᾷς μετ᾽ ἀλόχου, βαρβάρων ἡγούμενος.
1335   πολλὰς δὲ πέρσεις ἀναρίθμῳ στρατεύματι
πόλεις· ὅταν δὲ Λοξίου χρηστήριον
διαρπάσωσι, νόστον ἄθλιον πάλιν
σχήσουσι· σὲ δ᾽ Ἄρης Ἁρμονίαν τε ῥύσεται
μακάρων τ᾽ ἐς αἶαν σὸν καθιδρύσει βίον.
1340   ταῦτ᾽ οὐχὶ θνητοῦ πατρὸς ἐκγεγὼς λέγω
Διόνυσος ἀλλὰ Ζηνός· εἰ δὲ σωφρονεῖν
ἔγνωθ᾽, ὅτ᾽ οὐκ ἠθέλετε, τὸν Διὸς γόνον
ηὐδαιμονεῖτ᾽ ἂν σύμμαχον κεκτημένοι.

ΚΑΔΜΟΣ

Διόνυσε, λισσόμεσθά σ᾽, ἠδικήκαμεν.

ΔΙΟΝΥΣΟΣ

1345   ὄψ᾽ ἐμάθεθ᾽ ἡμᾶς, ὅτε δὲ χρῆν οὐκ ᾔδετε.

---

¹³²⁹ post h. v. lac. indic. Tyrwhitt

BACCHAE

AGAVE

My father, since you see how changed my fortunes are,

. . . .[21]

Enter, by the mechane, DIONYSUS. *A change of costume or mask suggests that he is no longer in mortal disguise but a manifest god.*

‹DIONYSUS›

. . . . you will change your form and become a snake, and your wife, Ares' daughter Harmonia, whom you married though a mere mortal, will also take on the form of a serpent. Then at the head of a barbarian army you will drive an oxcart and will sack many cities with your innumerable host: that is what Zeus's prophecy says. And when they have plundered Apollo's oracle, they will have a miserable homecoming. But Ares will rescue you and Harmonia and settle you to live in the Land of the Blessed. It is I, Dionysus, who make this prediction, and my father is not a mortal but Zeus. If you all had known how to be moderate when you were refusing to, you would now have Dionysus as your ally and be enjoying blessedness.

CADMUS

Dionysus, we entreat your mercy: we have wronged you!

DIONYSUS

Late is your knowledge of me: you did not have it when you needed it.

---

21 There is another extensive lacuna here. The first part perhaps contained a lament by Agave over the body of Pentheus, the second the opening of Dionysus' speech.

ΚΑΔΜΟΣ

ἐγνώκαμεν ταῦτ'· ἀλλ' ἐπεξέρχῃ λίαν.

ΔΙΟΝΥΣΟΣ

καὶ γὰρ πρὸς ὑμῶν θεὸς γεγὼς ὑβριζόμην.

ΚΑΔΜΟΣ

ὀργὰς πρέπει θεοὺς οὐχ ὁμοιοῦσθαι βροτοῖς.

ΔΙΟΝΥΣΟΣ

πάλαι τάδε Ζεὺς οὑμὸς ἐπένευσεν πατήρ.

ΑΓΑΥΗ

1350   αἰαῖ, δέδοκται, πρέσβυ, τλήμονες φυγαί.

ΔΙΟΝΥΣΟΣ

τί δῆτα μέλλεθ' ἅπερ ἀναγκαίως ἔχει;

ΚΑΔΜΟΣ

ὦ τέκνον, ὡς ἐς δεινὸν ἤλθομεν κακὸν
⟨πάντες,⟩ σύ θ' ἡ τάλαινα σύγγονοί τε σαί,
ἐγώ θ' ὁ τλήμων· βαρβάρους ἀφίξομαι
1355   γέρων μέτοικος· ἔτι δέ μοὐστὶ θέσφατον
ἐς Ἑλλάδ' ἀγαγεῖν μιγάδα βαρβάρων στρατόν.
καὶ τὴν Ἄρεως παῖδ' Ἁρμονίαν, δάμαρτ' ἐμήν,
δράκων δρακαίνης ⟨σχῆμ'⟩ ἔχουσαν ἀγρίας
ἄξω 'πὶ βωμοὺς καὶ τάφους Ἑλληνικούς,
1360   ἡγούμενος λόγχαισιν· οὐδὲ παύσομαι
κακῶν ὁ τλήμων οὐδὲ τὸν καταιβάτην
Ἀχέροντα πλεύσας ἥσυχος γενήσομαι.

1353 ⟨πάντες⟩ Kirchhoff   1355 μοὐστὶ Haupt: μοι τὸ P
1356 βαρβάρων Burges: βάρβαρον P

148

CADMUS

We recognize this. But you chastize us too harshly.

DIONYSUS

Well, I was treated with contempt though a god.

CADMUS

Gods ought not to be like mortals in their tempers.

DIONYSUS

Long ago Zeus my father ordained this.

AGAVE

Ah ah, our miserable exile is firmly decreed, old sir!

DIONYSUS

Why then do you hesitate to carry out what is ordained?

Exit DIONYSUS *by the* mechane.

CADMUS

To what terrible misery we have come, daughter, ‹all of us,› you in your wretchedness and your sisters and I the unblest. I, an old man, must emigrate to the barbarians, and what is more, it is prophesied that I must lead against Greece an army of barbarians of many races. And my wife, Ares' daughter Harmonia—in the ‹form› of a fierce snake I must lead her, a serpent myself, against the altars and tombs of Greece, going before the spearmen. I shall have no surcease from misery, poor man that I am, and will not even sail the Acheron, that downward-flowing river, and find rest.

1358 ‹σχῆμ'› Nauck   ἀγρίας Lenting: -αν P

ΑΓΑΥΗ

ὦ πάτερ, ἐγὼ δὲ σοῦ στερεῖσα φεύξομαι.

ΚΑΔΜΟΣ

τί μ᾽ ἀμφιβάλλεις χερσίν, ὦ τάλαινα παῖ,
1365 ὄρνις ὅπως κηφῆνα πολιόχρων κύκνος;

ΑΓΑΥΗ

ποῖ γὰρ τράπωμαι πατρίδος ἐκβεβλημένη;

ΚΑΔΜΟΣ

οὐκ οἶδα, τέκνον· σμικρὸς ἐπίκουρος πατήρ.

ΑΓΑΥΗ

χαῖρ᾽, ὦ μέλαθρον, χαῖρ᾽, ὦ πατρία
πόλις· ἐκλείπω σ᾽ ἐπὶ δυστυχίᾳ
1370 φυγὰς ἐκ θαλάμων.

ΚΑΔΜΟΣ

στεῖχέ νυν, ⟨οὗ παῖδ᾽ ἴλη ᾽φθειρε
σκυλάκων,⟩ ὦ παῖ, τὸν Ἀρισταίου.

ΑΓΑΥΗ

στένομαί σε, πάτερ.

ΚΑΔΜΟΣ

κἀγὼ ⟨σέ⟩, τέκνον,
καὶ σὰς ἐδάκρυσα κασιγνήτας.

ΑΓΑΥΗ

δεινῶς γὰρ ⟨τοι⟩ τήνδ᾽ αἰκείαν
1375 Διόνυσος ἄναξ
τοὺς σούς, ⟨πάτερ,⟩ εἰς οἴκους ἔφερεν.

BACCHAE

AGAVE

But I, father, must go into exile deprived of you.

She embraces him.

CADMUS

Why do you put your arms about me, poor daughter, like a
swan embracing its white-haired and decrepit sire?

AGAVE

Where shall I turn, exiled from my country?

CADMUS

I do not know, child: your father is but small help.

AGAVE

Farewell, house! Farewell, ancestral city! Exiled from my
chamber I leave you in woe!

CADMUS

Go then, my daughter, ‹to where the hounds killed› the
son of Aristaeus.

AGAVE

I weep for you, father.

CADMUS

And I ‹for you,› my daughter, and for your sisters.

AGAVE

Yes: terrible is the ruin Lord Dionysus has brought on your
house, ‹father›.

1371 post ννν lac. indic. Kovacs, post Ἀρισταίου Hermann
1372 ‹σὲ› Barnes
1374 ‹τοι› Hermann
1375 ‹πάτερ› Hermann

ΚΑΔΜΟΣ

καὶ γὰρ ἔπασχεν δεινὰ πρὸς ἡμῶν,
ἀγέραστον ἔχων ὄνομ᾽ ἐν Θήβαις.

ΑΓΑΥΗ

χαῖρε, πάτερ, μοι.

ΚΑΔΜΟΣ

χαῖρ᾽, ὦ μελέα
1380 θύγατερ. χαλεπῶς ‹δ᾽› ἐς τόδ᾽ ἂν ἥκοις.

ΑΓΑΥΗ

ἄγετ᾽ ὦ πομποί με κασιγνήτας
ἵνα συμφυγάδας ληψόμεθ᾽ οἰκτράς.
ἔλθοιμι δ᾽ ὅπου
μήτε Κιθαιρὼν ‹ἔμ᾽ ἴδοι› μιαρὸς
1385 μήτε Κιθαιρῶν᾽ ὄσσοισιν ἐγώ,
μηδ᾽ ὅθι θύρσου μνῆμ᾽ ἀνάκειται·
βάκχαις δ᾽ ἄλλαισι μέλοιεν.

ΧΟΡΟΣ

πολλαὶ μορφαὶ τῶν δαιμονίων,
πολλὰ δ᾽ ἀέλπτως κραίνουσι θεοί·
1390 καὶ τὰ δοκηθέντ᾽ οὐκ ἐτελέσθη,
τῶν δ᾽ ἀδοκήτων πόρον ηὗρε θεός.
τοιόνδ᾽ ἀπέβη τόδε πρᾶγμα.

1377n Κα. Bothe: Δι. P   1377 ἔπασχεν Bothe, Hermann:
-ον P   ἡμῶν Kannicht: ὑμ- P   1380 ‹δ᾽› Reiske
        1384 ‹ἔμ᾽ ἴδοι› Kirchhoff
        1386 μηδ᾽ Wilamowitz: μήθ᾽ P

BACCHAE

CADMUS

Terrible was the treatment he had from us, since his name was unhonored in Thebes.

AGAVE

Farewell, father!

CADMUS

Farewell, poor daughter! Though you will scarcely manage to fare well.

AGAVE

Lead me, my escorts, to where I shall take my sisters as pitiable companions in exile! But let me come to a place where unclean Cithaeron shall never ‹see me› or my eyes see Cithaeron, and where I shall never be reminded of the dedicated thyrsus: let other bacchants have a care for them!

Exit by Eisodos B AGAVE *and* CADMUS *accompanied by Thebans.*

CHORUS LEADER

What heaven sends has many shapes, and many things the gods accomplish against our expectation. What men look for is not brought to pass, but a god finds a way to achieve the unexpected. Such was the outcome of this story.

Exit by Eisodos B the CHORUS.

IPHIGENIA AT AULIS

INTRODUCTION

In 408 B.C. Euripides left Athens to accept the hospitality of Archelaus of Macedon. In the winter of 407–6 he died in Macedon. *Iphigenia in Aulis* was among the plays first put on after his death, the others being *Bacchae* and the lost *Alcmaeon in Corinth*. The year is likely to have been 405: see England 1891, pp. xxxi–xxxii.

There is reason to believe that Euripides left *Iphigenia* unfinished at his death, and that the poet's literary executor, Euripides the Younger, who was either his son or his nephew, finished the incomplete draft. But more than one later hand has been at work to produce the text that we possess. The play was apparently revived in the fourth century, and additions and alterations were made by actors or producers to make it more appealing to a later audience. (See Page 1934.) In addition, at some point the end of the play suffered accidental damage, and someone quite incapable of imitating the language and meter of fifth-century tragedy tried to replace what had been lost. As a result of this history, the number of lines suspected by one scholar or another of being interpolated is far larger here than in any other Greek tragedy.

There are thus unusual problems for the editor. The present edition attempts to set out what the audience heard at its first performance, the joint product of Euripides and his literary executor. I enclose in square brackets everything that I judge to be later interpolation. Much of this later interpolation appears to have been done, as I will explain below, on a single occasion in the fourth century by an actor or producer (here called the Reviser) who altered the text substantially, cutting out as well as inserting material. Where I judge that lines belonging to the first production have been lost because of subsequent alterations, I mark such losses by a note to the English translation. The reader should also be warned that our only manuscript, L, exhibits more corruptions than usual, and it is necessary to emend more frequently both in genuine and in interpolated parts. To save space I have made my textual notes more selective, and James Diggle's edition (Oxford, 1994) should be consulted for a full account of the readings of L.

I describe here the plot as it appears in our manuscript. The scene is the tent of Agamemnon at Aulis on the Greek coast. The Greeks, gathered to make their expedition against Troy, have failed to get the proper winds, and the seer Calchas has declared that Artemis is angry and will be appeased only by the sacrifice of Iphigenia, Agamemnon's daughter. Agamemnon has sent a letter to his wife Clytaemestra telling her that Iphigenia must come to Aulis to marry Achilles. Only he and his inner circle (Menelaus, Odysseus, Calchas) know about this trick, and indeed only they know about the oracle of Calchas. But at the beginning of the play he has changed his mind and sends another letter countermanding his earlier message. Menelaus, whose wife Helen is the object of the expedition, intercepts the letter, and a quarrel of the brothers ensues. The quarrel is interrupted by the announcement that Iphigenia and her mother have arrived in Aulis. Agamemnon now sees that he has no choice but to go through with the sacrifice. The meeting between father and daughter is full of pathos, with Agamemnon's evasive and ambiguous answers to his daughter's naive questions making plain to the audience the anguish he feels.

Achilles, who has no idea what is going on, arrives by chance, and he and Clytaemestra meet in a scene of almost comic cross purposes—she speaking familiarly to the man she thinks her future son-in-law, he interpreting this as forwardness from his commander's wife. Once the misunderstanding is sorted out, both are angry at the deception. Achilles is willing to take up arms to defend the girl his name has helped to entrap, but he suggests that they first supplicate her father. The women confront Agamemnon, who confesses his designs but indicates his powerlessness and departs. Achilles enters once more and offers to defend the girl, but Iphigenia, realizing the hopelessness of the situation and abandoning her earlier fearfulness, resolves to offer herself willingly to the Greek cause. She is led off to sacrifice. A messenger describes the sequel, relating that at the last moment Artemis substituted a hind and spirited the girl away to safety.

There are several major problems, even before we reach the metrically impossible ending, that show the interference of a later hand, probably of the fourth century. It has been pointed out (see Willink 1971) that there is internal inconsistency on the question of who knows about the prophecy of Calchas. The idea of a secret prophecy made to Agamemnon's inner circle is implausible in itself (prophecies affecting an army are made to the army in epic and tragedy), and the view taken here and argued in greater detail elsewhere (see Kovacs 2003) is that in the production of 405 the prophecy was made to the entire army. The secret prophecy idea, introduced into the text by a man I call the Reviser, was intended to make possible scenes of touching irony, where anonymous characters, ignorant of the situation, ask naive questions about Iphigenia's presence in Aulis. Scenes where this motif is most prominent (the First Messenger scene, the entrance of Iphigenia) also contain highly suspicious features (the entrance of a character in mid line, the necessity for a fourth actor, language that is inelegantly repetitious) that suggest a later age. The Reviser had a taste for the spectacular and arranged the grand entrance of Clytaemestra and Iphigenia, with a chariot, horses, and a secondary chorus of Argive soldiers. He also apparently thought that pathos could be increased in several scenes by having the women bring along Iphigenia's baby brother Orestes, to be played by a doll or dummy (418–9, 621–6, 1241–52, etc.). The stylistic mannerisms of these interpolated passages are also to be detected in other parts of the play. We must remove his work to get at the original performance.

Unfortunately the Reviser did not merely add material but also took out lines belonging to the original production. His only truly substantial deletion is in the first episode (303–542), where there were probably clear indications in the original version that contradicted the Reviser's idea of a secret prophecy. The prologue and the entrance of Clytaemestra and Iphigenia have also been tampered with in ways that involved loss of genuine lines, though there the loss is slight. For the rest, we can recover substantially what the audience saw and heard in 405 by deleting the Reviser's work.

The end of the play poses further problems. The scene with the Second Messenger (1532–1629) contains lines (1578–1629) that appear to come from the very end of antiquity because neither classical vowel lengths nor the rules of tragic meter are observed. But even the part that does not violate metrical rules cannot, in the judgment of many scholars, have belonged to the first production. I agree and have bracketed the whole passage. There seems, however, to have been another version of the end of the play current in antiquity, and Aelian in his *On the Nature of Animals* quotes, as from Euripides' *Iphigenia*, two-and-a-half lines from what is apparently a speech by the goddess Artemis speaking from the *mechane*. (I print the fragment at the end of the play.) Since Euripides regularly ended his plays with the appearance of a *deus ex machina*, it would be attractive to think that this fragment is part of the genuine ending. But short as the fragment is, it contains two things ($a\dot{v}\chi\dot{\eta}\sigma ov\sigma\iota$ meaning "they will suppose" and $\chi\epsilon\rho\sigma\grave{\iota}v$ ... $\phi\acute{\iota}\lambda\alpha\iota\varsigma$, "*dear* hands") we may be sure Euripides did not write. They might be a supplement by Euripides the Younger and belonged to the first performance. On balance, though, it seems more likely that the first performance ended with line 1531. Like Heracles' daughter in *Children of Heracles*, Menoeceus in *Phoenician Women*, and Erechtheus' daughter in the lost *Erechtheus* Iphigenia has made a decision to give her life for her community, and the chances are good that like them she was not prevented by divine intervention from carrying out her decision.

What is this play, the last we have from Euripides' hand, really about? It would be a mistake to underestimate the importance of the motif of the Trojan War as pan-Hellenic campaign. Greece has suffered insult because of the theft of Helen, and it is a repeated theme, finding expression in the speeches of several characters, that the war is a necessary response. The soldiery are enthusiastic, and there is the repeated suggestion that the voice of the people is the voice of God, that the passion the Greeks feel for this enterprise has been put in their hearts by the will of heaven. This entails the death of Iphigenia. In the course of the action first Agamemnon, then Clytaemestra and Iphigenia, then Achilles attempt by cleverness, entreaty, or brute force to evade this heaven-ordained result, but in the end all except Clytaemestra come to see that it cannot be avoided. Iphigenia goes even further. In her great turnabout speech she turns her necessity into a free decision, sets her heart on the glory that will be hers, sees that her life belongs not only to her parents but also to the community, compares her sacrifice in point of necessity with that of the soldiers fighting in the war, resolves not to oppose the designs of Artemis, and ends with a ringing endorsement of Greek freedom, which can only be won by conquering the barbarians.

Reflection suggests that these sentiments are to be taken seriously and that they are in no sense "ironic" or "merely conventional." As noted above the theme of death by sacrifice of young persons in the cause of their community is one that Euripides dramatized several times throughout his career, and there is no indication that the death of Menoeceus or of Heracles' daughter was intended as anything but an effective remedy, calling forth wholehearted admiration, for a real problem. The whole structure of the play, which leads up to Iphigenia's change of heart, indicates a different conception of this sacrifice from that of Aeschylus, who depicts it as an unmitigated horror both for the daughter and for the father, the opening act in a war whose whole course is shown to be tainted by carelessness of Argive life as well as sacrilege against Trojan shrines. If there is any criticism of the Trojan War in our play, it is unemphatic nearly to the vanishing point. It would seem that Euripides has reshaped the story of the Greek fleet's departure from Aulis to express the way he thought such a war should be conducted. By the end of the play the whole community is playing its part: the Greek chieftains and their soldiers are eager to fight and risk their lives, Agamemnon, unlike Creon in *Phoenician Women*, sees the necessity of sacrifice, and Iphigenia is willing to offer her life for Greece. Only Clytaemestra holds out. We could speculate about why Euripides was led to depict the war of the Greek community against the barbarians in this way (was it his stay among the half-barbarian Macedonians, constantly under attack by their fully barbarian neighbors? was it the menace of Persian power, now intervening for one side or another in the last years of the Peloponnesian War?), but our inability to answer that question should not lead us to adopt a suspicious critical stance or deter us from reading the play in its plainest and most natural sense.

SELECT BIBLIOGRAPHY

Editions

E. B. England (London, 1891).
C. E. S. Headlam (Cambridge, 1896).
H. C. Günther (Leipzig, 1988).

W. Stockert (Vienna, 1992).

F. Turato (Venice, 2001).

Literary Criticism

J. Griffin, "Characterization in Euripides: *Hippolytos* and *Iphigenia in Aulis*," in C. B. R. Pelling, ed., *Characterization and Individuality in Greek Literature* (Oxford, 1990), pp. 128–49.

D. Kovacs, "Toward a Reconstruction of *Iphigenia Aulidensis*," *JHS* 123 (2003).

A. Lesky, *Greek Tragic Poetry* (New Haven, 1983), pp. 354–64.

M. McDonald, "Iphigenia's Philia: Motivation in Euripides' *Iphigenia at Aulis*," *QUCC* 63 (1990), 69–84.

G. Mellert-Hoffmann, *Untersuchungen zur 'Iphigenie in Aulis' des Euripides* (Heidelberg, 1969).

D. L. Page, *Actors' Interpolations in Greek Tragedy* (Oxford, 1934).

C. W. Willink, "The Prologue of *Iphigenia at Aulis*," *CQ* 21 (1971), 343–64.

Dramatis Personae

ΑΓΑΜΕΜΝΩΝ	AGAMEMNON, king of Argos
ΠΡΕΣΒΥΤΗΣ	OLD MAN, servant of Agamemnon
ΧΟΡΟΣ	CHORUS of women from Euboea
ΜΕΝΕΛΑΟΣ	MENELAUS, king of Sparta, brother of Agamemnon
ΑΓΓΕΛΟΣ	MESSENGER
ΚΛΥΤΑΙΜΗΣΤΡΑ	CLYTAEMESTRA, wife of Agamemnon
ΙΦΙΓΕΝΕΙΑ	IPHIGENIA, daughter of Agamemnon and Clytaemestra
ΑΧΙΛΛΕΥΣ	ACHILLES, leader of the Myrmidons
ΑΓΓΕΛΟΣ Β	SECOND MESSENGER

A Note on Staging

The central door of the *skene* represents the tent of Agamemnon in the Greek camp at Aulis. One of the side doors represents the quarters occupied by Agamemnon's servants. Eisodos A leads to Argos, Eisodos B to the seashore and the Greek ships.

165

ΙΦΙΓΕΝΕΙΑ Η ΕΝ ΑΥΛΙΔΙ

[ΑΓΑΜΕΜΝΩΝ
Ὦ πρέσβυ, δόμων τῶνδε πάροιθεν
στεῖχε.

ΠΡΕΣΒΥΤΗΣ
στείχω. τί δὲ καινουργεῖς,
Ἀγάμεμνον ἄναξ;

ΑΓΑΜΕΜΝΩΝ
σπεῦδε.

ΠΡΕΣΒΥΤΗΣ
σπεύδω.
μάλα τοι γῆρας τοὐμὸν ἄυπνον
5 καὶ ἐπ᾽ ὀφθαλμοῖς τοὐξὺ πάρεστιν.

1-48 interpolatori tribuo qui formam pristinam tragoediae,
qualem scaenae commiserat Euripides Minor, non leviter
mutavit, et quem in sequentibus Retractatorem nuncupabo (ab
Euripide abiud. Blomfield)
5 τοὐξὺ Wecklein: ὀξὺ L

---

1 Instead of the iambic monologue, addressed to the audience,
that begins all other extant plays of Euripides (except the proba-

166

IPHIGENIA AT AULIS

*The time is before dawn in the camp of the Greeks at Aulis.
From the* skene *enter* AGAMEMNON *carrying a letter*[1]

[AGAMEMNON

Old man, come out in front of the tent!

OLD MAN

(*within*) I'm coming! What strange business is this, lord
Agamemnon?

AGAMEMNON

Hurry!

Enter OLD MAN *from the* skene.

OLD MAN

I *am* hurrying! I have grown quite sleepless in my old age,
and my eyes have the sharp vision of wakefulness.

bly non-Euripidean *Rhesus*) we have an anapestic dialogue into
which is embedded (49–105) part of the expected opening mono-
logue. I have bracketed 1–48 and 106–62 as the work of the Re-
viser: they exhibit the secret prophecy theme (see Introduction)
and have other peculiarities. Lines 49–105 I regard as the remain-
der of the original prologue. Other scholars have taken a different
view.

167

ΑΓΑΜΕΜΝΩΝ

τίς ποτ' ἄρ' ἀστὴρ ὅδε πορθμεύει
σείριος ἐγγὺς τῆς ἑπταπόρου
Πλειάδος ᾄσσων ἔτι μεσσήρης;
οὔκουν φθόγγος γ' οὔτ' ὀρνίθων
10 οὔτε θαλάσσης· σιγαὶ δ' ἀνέμων
τόνδε κατ' Εὔριπον ἔχουσιν.

ΠΡΕΣΒΥΤΗΣ

τί δὲ σὺ σκηνῆς ἐκτὸς ἀίσσεις,
Ἀγάμεμνον ἄναξ;
ἔτι δ' ἡσυχία τήνδε κατ' Αὖλιν
15 καὶ ἀκίνητοι φυλακαὶ τειχέων.
στείχωμεν ἔσω.

ΑΓΑΜΕΜΝΩΝ

ζηλῶ σέ, γέρον,
ζηλῶ δ' ἀνδρῶν ὃς ἀκίνδυνον
βίον ἐξεπέρασ' ἀγνὼς ἀκλεής·
τοὺς δ' ἐν τιμαῖς ἧσσον ζηλῶ.

ΠΡΕΣΒΥΤΗΣ

20 καὶ μὴν τὸ καλόν γ' ἐνταῦθα βίου.

ΑΓΑΜΕΜΝΩΝ

τοῦτο δέ γ' ἐστὶν τὸ καλὸν σφαλερόν,
καὶ τὸ πρότιμον
γλυκὺ μέν, λυπεῖ δὲ προσιστάμενον.
τοτὲ μὲν τὰ θεῶν οὐκ ὀρθωθέντ'
25 ἀνέτρεψε βίον, τοτὲ δ' ἀνθρώπων

AGAMEMNON

What in the world is this baleful star that glides still high in the sky near the seven Pleiades?[2] No sound at any rate either from the birds or from the sea. A silence of winds holds sway along the Euripus[3] here.

OLD MAN

But you, lord Agamemnon, why do you dart out of the tent? All is still quiet here at Aulis, and the guards on the walls are not yet stirring. Let's go inside!

AGAMEMNON

I envy you, old man, envy any mortal who passes, unknown to fame, through a life without danger. I feel less envy for those in authority.

OLD MAN

But it is there we find all that is admired in life.

AGAMEMNON

This "what is admired" is a slippery thing: high honors, though sweet, cause pain when they light upon you. At times the gods do not grant success, and at others you

2 The baleful star (*seirios aster*) is probably not Sirius (Sirius is not near the Pleiades and it appears in mid heaven shortly before dawn in autumn) but either Aldebaran (Alpha Tauri) or a planet.

3 The narrow strait that flows between Euboea and the mainland of Greece.

---

22 πρότιμον Nauck: φιλότιμον L

γνῶμαι πολλαὶ
καὶ δυσάρεστοι διέκναισαν.

ΠΡΕΣΒΥΤΗΣ

οὐκ ἄγαμαι ταῦτ᾽ ἀνδρὸς ἀριστέως·
οὐκ ἐπὶ πᾶσίν σ᾽ ἐφύτευσ᾽ ἀγαθοῖς,
30 Ἀγάμεμνον, Ἀτρεύς. δεῖ δέ σε χαίρειν
καὶ λυπεῖσθαι· θνητὸς γὰρ ἔφυς.
κἂν μὴ σὺ θέλῃς, τὰ θεῶν οὕτω
βουλόμεν᾽ ἔσται. σὺ δὲ λαμπτῆρος
35 φάος ἀμπετάσας δέλτον τε γράφεις
τήνδ᾽ ἣν πρὸ χερῶν ἔτι βαστάζεις,
καὶ ταὐτὰ πάλιν γράμματα συγχεῖς
καὶ σφραγίζεις λύεις τ᾽ ὀπίσω
ῥίπτεις τε πέδῳ πεύκην, θαλερὸν
40 κατὰ δάκρυ χέων, κἀκ τῶν ἀπόρων
οὐδενὸς ἐνδεῖς μὴ οὐ μαίνεσθαι.
τί πονεῖς; τί νέον παρὰ σοί, βασιλεῦ;
φέρε κοίνωσον μῦθον ἐς ἡμᾶς.
45 πρὸς δ᾽ ἄνδρ᾽ ἀγαθὸν πιστόν τε φράσεις·
σῇ γάρ μ᾽ ἀλόχῳ ποτὲ Τυνδάρεως
πέμπει φερνὴν
συννυμφοκόμον τε δίκαιον.]

ΑΓΑΜΕΜΝΩΝ

Ἐγένοντο Λήδᾳ Θεστιάδι τρεῖς παρθένοι,
50 Φοίβη Κλυταιμήστρα τ᾽, ἐμὴ ξυνάορος,
Ἑλένη τε· ταύτης οἱ τὰ πρῶτ᾽ ὠλβισμένοι
μνηστῆρες ἦλθον Ἑλλάδος νεανίαι.

are crushed by the opinions of men, many and peevish as they are.

OLD MAN

I don't approve of such sentiments in a prince. Atreus did not beget you for a life of all blessings. You must feel pain as well as pleasure: you are a mortal. Though you do not like it, that is the will of the gods. But you are writing a letter by the gleam of lamplight, the letter you have in your hand. The words you have written you erase again, you seal the tablet and then break the seal, you throw the pine frame upon the ground, and weep copious tears. In your perplexity you are all but raving mad. What is this trouble of yours, what calamity has visited you, my king? Come, share the story with me. You will be speaking to a man good and true, for Tyndareus once gave me to your wife as dowry, a loyal attendant to the bride.]

AGAMEMNON

To Leda, daughter of Thestius, were born three daughters, Phoebe, my wife Clytaemestra, and Helen. For this last the most prosperous young men in Hellas came as suitors.

40–1 κἀκ Naber: καὶ L
43 παρὰ Porson: περὶ L

δειναὶ δ' ἀπειλαὶ καὶ κατ' ἀλλήλων φθόνος
ξυνίσταθ', ὅστις μὴ λάβοι τὴν παρθένον.
55 τὸ πρᾶγμα δ' ἀπόρως εἶχε Τυνδάρεῳ πατρί,
δοῦναί τε μὴ δοῦναί τε, τῆς τύχης ὅπως
ἅψαιτ' ἄθραυστα. καί νιν εἰσῆλθεν τάδε·
ὅρκους συνάψαι δεξιάς τε συμβαλεῖν
μνηστῆρας ἀλλήλοισι καὶ δι' ἐμπύρων
60 σπονδὰς καθεῖναι κἀπαράσασθαι τάδε·
ὅτου γυνὴ γένοιτο Τυνδαρὶς κόρη,
τούτῳ συναμυνεῖν, εἴ τις ἐκ δόμων λαβὼν
οἴχοιτο τόν τ' ἔχοντ' ἀπωθοίη λέχους,
κἀπιστρατεύσειν καὶ κατασκάψειν πόλιν
65 Ἕλλην' ὁμοίως βάρβαρόν θ' ὅπλων μέτα.
ἐπεὶ δ' ἐπιστώθησαν (εὖ δέ πως γέρων
ὑπῆλθεν αὐτοὺς Τυνδάρεως πυκνῇ φρενί),
δίδωσ' ἑλέσθαι θυγατρὶ μνηστήρων ἕνα,
ὅποι πνοαὶ φέροιεν Ἀφροδίτης φίλαι.
70 ἡ δ' εἵλεθ', ὅς σφε μήποτ' ὤφελεν λαβεῖν,
Μενέλαον. ἐλθὼν δ' ἐκ Φρυγῶν ὁ τὰς θεὰς
κρίνας ὅδ', ὡς ὁ μῦθος ἀνθρώπων ἔχει,
Λακεδαίμον', ἀνθηρὸς μὲν εἱμάτων στολῇ
χρυσῷ δὲ λαμπρός, βαρβάρῳ χλιδήματι,
75 ἐρῶν ἐρῶσαν ᾤχετ' ἐξαναρπάσας
Ἑλένην πρὸς Ἴδης βούσταθμ', ἔκδημον λαβὼν
Μενέλαον. ὁ δὲ καθ' Ἑλλάδ' οἰστρήσας ἔρῳ

53 φθόνος Markland: φόνος L
57 ἄθραυστα Nauck ex t: ἄριστα L

172

Terrible threats were about to be realized from the envy of her unsuccessful wooers. It was a dreadful quandary for Tyndareus her father, to give her in marriage or not: how could he deal with the situation and not come to ruin? An idea occurred to him: the suitors should take an oath to each other and join right hands on it—making their pact by means of a burnt sacrifice and swearing over the victim—that each would come to the defense of Helen's future husband if anyone robbed him of his wife and abducted her from home; they would make an expedition and overthrow the city by force of arms, whether it was Greek or barbarian. When they had sworn (for Tyndareus cleverly won them over to this), he allowed his daughter to choose one of the suitors, him to whom the sweet breezes of Aphrodite were carrying her. She chose Menelaus, and how I wish she had never chosen him! The man who judged the goddesses (so runs the story men tell) came from Phrygia[4] to Lacedaemon dressed in gaily colored clothing and gleaming with gold jewelry, the luxury of the barbarians. Helen fell in love with him and he with her, and since Menelaus was not at home, he carried her off to the cow pastures of Ida. But Menelaus, maddened with desire, invoked

---

[4] "Phrygia" and "Phrygian" are used in tragedy as synonyms for "Troy" and "Trojan." "The man who judged the goddesses" is Paris (Alexandros), who judged Hera, Athena, and Aphrodite in a beauty contest and awarded the prize to Aphrodite, who had bribed him with the offer of the most beautiful woman in the world.

---

69 ὅποι Lenting: ὅτου L
77 ἔρῳ (vel γ᾽ ἔρῳ) Willink: μόρῳ L: δρόμῳ Markland

ὅρκους παλαιοὺς Τυνδάρεω μαρτύρεται,
ὡς χρὴ βοηθεῖν τοῖσιν ἠδικημένοις.
80 τοὐντεῦθεν οὖν Ἕλληνες ἄξαντες δορί,
τεύχη λαβόντες στενόπορ᾽ Αὐλίδος βάθρα
ἥκουσι τῆσδε, ναυσὶν ἀσπίσιν θ᾽ ὁμοῦ
ἵπποις τε πολλοῖς ἅρμασίν τ᾽ ἠσκημένοι.
κἀμὲ στρατηγεῖν †κᾶτα† Μενέλεω χάριν
85 εἵλοντο, σύγγονόν γε· τἀξίωμα δὲ
ἄλλος τις ὤφελ᾽ ἀντ᾽ ἐμοῦ λαβεῖν τόδε.
ἠθροισμένου δὲ καὶ ξυνεστῶτος στρατοῦ
ἥμεσθ᾽ ἀπλοίᾳ χρώμενοι κατ᾽ Αὐλίδα.
Κάλχας δ᾽ ὁ μάντις ἀπορίᾳ κεχρημένοις
90 ἀνεῖλεν Ἰφιγένειαν ἣν ἔσπειρ᾽ ἐγὼ
Ἀρτέμιδι θῦσαι τῇ τόδ᾽ οἰκούσῃ πέδον,
καὶ πλοῦν τ᾽ ἔσεσθαι καὶ κατασκαφὰς Φρυγῶν
θύσασι, μὴ θύσασι δ᾽ οὐκ εἶναι τάδε.
κλυὼν δ᾽ ἐγὼ ταῦτ᾽ ὀρθίῳ κηρύγματι
95 Ταλθύβιον εἶπον πάντ᾽ ἀφιέναι στρατόν,
ὡς οὔποτ᾽ ἂν τλὰς θυγατέρα κτανεῖν ἐμήν.
οὗ δή μ᾽ ἀδελφὸς πάντα προσφέρων λόγον
ἔπεισε τλῆναι δεινά. κἀν δέλτου πτυχαῖς
γράψας ἔπεμψα πρὸς δάμαρτα τὴν ἐμὴν
100 πέμπειν Ἀχιλλεῖ θυγατέρ᾽ ὡς γαμουμένην,
τό τ᾽ ἀξίωμα τἀνδρὸς ἐκγαυρούμενος,
συμπλεῖν τ᾽ Ἀχαιοῖς οὕνεκ᾽ οὐ θέλοι λέγων,
εἰ μὴ παρ᾽ ἡμῶν εἶσιν ἐς Φθίαν λέχος·
πειθὼ γὰρ εἶχον τήνδε πρὸς δάμαρτ᾽ ἐμήν,

174

Tyndareus' oaths all throughout Greece and claimed that the suitors must help the injured party.

Thereafter the Greeks, rushing with martial ardor, took up their weapons and came here to Aulis, land of narrow crossing, equipped with great numbers of ships, shields, horses, and chariots. Me they chose as general, as a favor to Menelaus since I am his brother. How I wish someone else had received this honor instead of me! For when the army had mustered we were sitting at Aulis with unfavorable sailing weather, and to us in our perplexity Calchas the prophet foretold that we must sacrifice Iphigenia, my daughter, to Artemis who dwells in this region: if we sacrificed her we would be able to sail and overthrow the Phrygians, but otherwise not. When I heard this, I told Talthybius to proclaim in his high-pitched voice the dismissal of the entire army since I would never have the heart to kill my daughter. At this point my brother, making every sort of argument, persuaded me to bring myself to do a terrible thing. In a folded tablet I wrote a message and sent it to my wife, telling her that she should send our daughter to marry Achilles. I made much of the man's high position and said that he was not willing to sail with the Achaeans unless a daughter of mine came as bride to his house in Phthia. That was the way I persuaded my wife

---

80 δορί L: ποσίν t
84 κατ' ἴσα Willink, δῆτα Nauck, πᾶσι Reiske
87 δὲ] γὰρ Markland

105 ψευδῆ συνάψας ἀμφὶ παρθένου γάμον.
[μόνοι δ' Ἀχαιῶν ἴσμεν ὡς ἔχει τάδε
Κάλχας Ὀδυσσεὺς Μενέλεώς θ'. ἃ δ' οὐ καλῶς
ἔγνων τότ', αὖθις μεταγράφω καλῶς πάλιν
ἐς τήνδε δέλτον, ἣν κατ' εὐφρόνης ‹κνέφας›
110 λύοντα καὶ συνδοῦντά μ' εἰσεῖδες, γέρον.
ἀλλ' εἶα χώρει τάσδ' ἐπιστολὰς λαβὼν
πρὸς Ἄργος. ἃ δὲ κέκευθε δέλτος ἐν πτυχαῖς,
λόγῳ φράσω σοι πάντα τἀγγεγραμμένα·
114 πιστὸς γὰρ ἀλόχῳ τοῖς τ' ἐμοῖς δόμοισιν εἶ.

ΠΡΕΣΒΥΤΗΣ

117 λέγε καὶ σήμαιν', ἵνα καὶ γλώσσῃ
118 σύντονα τοῖς σοῖς γράμμασιν αὐδῶ.

ΑΓΑΜΕΜΝΩΝ

115 πέμπω σοι πρὸς ταῖς πρόσθεν
116 δέλτους, ὦ Λήδας ἔρνος,
119 μὴ στέλλειν τὰν σὰν ἶνιν πρὸς
120 τὰν κολπώδη πτέρυγ' Εὐβοίας
Αὖλιν ἀκλύσταν.
εἰς ἄλλας ὥρας γὰρ δὴ
παιδὸς δαίσομεν ὑμεναίους.

105 ἀμφὶ Markland: ἀντὶ L
106–63 Retractatori tribuo (106–14 ab Euripide abiud. Page, 115–63 Bremi)
107–8 Μενέλεως ‹ἐγώ› θ'. ἃ δ' οὐ / καλῶς τότ', αὖθις μεταγράφω Vitelli
109 ‹κνέφας› Barrett cl. Ph. 727: ‹σκιὰν› P²

176

by concocting a lie about the girl's marriage.[5] [The only Achaeans who know how these matters stand are Calchas, Odysseus, and Menelaus. The ignoble decisions I made at that time I have recast nobly in this letter, the letter which in <the dark> of night you saw me opening and closing, old man. But come now, take this letter and bear it to Argos. What this tablet contains in its double fold, everything written therein, I shall tell you in words. For you are faithful to my wife and to my house.

OLD MAN

Tell me, explain, so that what I say may agree with your writing.

AGAMEMNON

"I send you a letter in addition to my earlier one, O daughter of Leda: do not send your daughter to Aulis with its bays, protected from waves and jutting out toward Euboea. We will make the wedding feast for our daughter's marriage another time."

[5] The rest of the iambic monologue and the following anapaests, I argue elsewhere, are spurious, but the original will not have differed greatly in content. The remaining iambs would have gone on to relate that Agamemnon had changed his mind and was sending a second letter. This would have been followed by a scene in which the Old Man is called out and sent on his way, with Agamemnon retiring into the *skene,* as at 163 below.

117–8 ante 115 trai. Reiske
116 δέλτους Monk: -οις L

ΠΡΕΣΒΥΤΗΣ

καὶ πῶς Ἀχιλεὺς λέκτρων ἀπλακὼν

125 οὐ μέγα φυσῶν θυμὸν ἐπαρεῖ
σοὶ σῇ τ᾽ ἀλόχῳ; τόδε καὶ δεινόν·
σήμαιν᾽ ὅ τι φῄς.

ΑΓΑΜΕΜΝΩΝ

ὄνομ᾽, οὐκ ἔργον, παρέχων Ἀχιλεὺς
οὐκ οἶδε γάμους, οὐδ᾽ ὅ τι πράσσομεν,

130 οὐδέ τι κείνῳ παῖδ᾽ ἐπεφήμισα
νυμφείους εἰς ἀγκώνων
εὐνὰς ἐκδώσειν λέκτροις.

ΠΡΕΣΒΥΤΗΣ

δεινά γ᾽ ἐτόλμας, Ἀγάμεμνον ἄναξ,
ὃς τῷ τῆς θεᾶς σὴν παῖδ᾽ ἄλοχον

135 φατίσας ἦγες σφάγιον Δαναοῖς.

ΑΓΑΜΕΜΝΩΝ

οἴμοι, γνώμας ἐξέσταν,
αἰαῖ, πίπτω δ᾽ εἰς ἄταν.
ἀλλ᾽ ἴθ᾽ ἐρέσσων σὸν πόδα, γήρᾳ

140 μηδὲν ὑπείκων.

ΠΡΕΣΒΥΤΗΣ

σπεύδω, βασιλεῦ.

ΑΓΑΜΕΜΝΩΝ

μή νυν μήτ᾽ ἀλσώδεις ἵζου
κρήνας μήθ᾽ ὕπνῳ θελχθῇς.

OLD MAN

Won't Achilles, deprived of his bride, grow haughty and angry with you and your wife? This is a danger. Tell me what you say.

AGAMEMNON

Achilles is giving his name, not his actual self. He does not know about the wedding or what we are doing, and in no way have I said that my daughter is his bride for him to take to his arms and his bed.

OLD MAN

You brought yourself to do a terrible thing, lord Agamemnon! You claimed she was a bride for the goddess' son, but you meant to bring her as a victim for the Greeks!

AGAMEMNON

Ah me! I was out of my senses! Alas, I fell into madness! But go, move your feet swiftly and do not yield to old age!

OLD MAN

I hurry, my king!

AGAMEMNON

And do not sit by some spring in a grove or fall under the spell of sleep!

---

130 οὐδέ τι Willink: οὐδ᾽ ὅτι L

ΠΡΕΣΒΥΤΗΣ

εὔφημα θρόει.

ΑΓΑΜΕΜΝΩΝ

πάντῃ δὲ πόρον σχιστὸν ἀμείβων
145 λεῦσσε, φυλάσσων μή τίς σε λάθῃ
τροχαλοῖσιν ὄχοις παραμειψαμένη
παῖδα κομίζουσ' ἐνθάδ' ἀπήνη
Δαναῶν πρὸς ναῦς.

ΠΡΕΣΒΥΤΗΣ

ἔσται.

ΑΓΑΜΕΜΝΩΝ

κλήθρων δ' ἐξόρμοις
150 ἢν ἀντήσῃς πομπαῖσιν,
πάλιν ἐξόρμα, σεῖε χαλινούς,
ἐπὶ Κυκλώπων ἱεὶς θυμέλας.

ΠΡΕΣΒΥΤΗΣ

πιστὸς δὲ φράσας τάδε πῶς ἔσομαι,
λέγε, παιδὶ σέθεν τῇ σῇ τ' ἀλόχῳ;

ΑΓΑΜΕΜΝΩΝ

155 σφραγῖδα φύλασσ' ἣν ἐπὶ δέλτῳ
τῇδε κομίζεις. ἴθι. λευκαίνει
τόδε φῶς ἤδη λάμπουσ' ἠὼς
πῦρ τε τεθρίππων τῶν Ἀελίου·
160 σύλλαβε μόχθων. θνητῶν δ' ὄλβιος
ἐς τέλος οὐδεὶς οὐδ' εὐδαίμων·
οὔπω γὰρ ἔφυ τις ἄλυπος.]

OLD MAN

Don't say such a shocking thing!

AGAMEMNON

When you pass any fork in the road, look and take care that
no wagon with running wheels goes by you unnoticed,
bringing the girl here to the ships of the Greeks.

OLD MAN

It shall be done.

AGAMEMNON

If you come upon her escort already sped from her close-
barred chambers, send them back again, shake their reins,
speeding them to the temples the Cyclopes built!

OLD MAN

But tell me, if I say these things, how shall I seem trustwor-
thy to your daughter and your wife?

AGAMEMNON

Keep unbroken the seal on the letter you are carrying. Go!
See, the light-shedding dawn and the fire of Helios' chariot
are growing bright! Take up your task! No mortal is com-
pletely blessed or happy. No one has yet been born to a life
free of pain.]

Exit OLD MAN *by Eisodos A,* AGAMEMNON *into the* skene.
Enter by Eisodos B women of Euboea as CHORUS.

---

149 ἐξόρμοις Bothe: ἐξόρμα L
150 ἢν ἀντήσῃς πομπαῖσιν Günther: ἤν νιν πομπαῖς
ἀντήσῃς L
151 ἐξόρμα, σεῖε Blomfield: ἐξορμάσεις L

ΧΟΡΟΣ

στρ. α

    ἔμολον ἀμφὶ παρακτίαν
165 ψάμαθον Αὐλίδος ἐναλίας,
    Εὐρίπου διὰ χευμάτων
    κέλσασα στενοπόρθμων,
    Χαλκίδα πόλιν ἐμὰν προλιποῦσ᾽,
    ἀγχιάλων ὑδάτων τροφὸν
170 τᾶς κλεινᾶς Ἀρεθούσας,
    Ἀχαιῶν στρατιὰν ὡς ἐσιδοίμαν
    Ἀχαιῶν τε πλάτας ναυσιπόρους ἡ-
    μιθέων, οὓς ἐπὶ Τροίαν
    ἐλάταις χιλιόναυσιν
175 τὸν ξανθὸν Μενέλαόν ⟨θ᾽⟩
    ἁμέτεροι πόσεις
    ἐνέπουσ᾽ Ἀγαμέμνονά τ᾽ εὐπατρίδαν στέλλειν
    ἐπὶ τὰν Ἑλέναν, ἀπ᾽ Εὐ-
    ρώτα δονακοτρόφου
180 Πάρις ὁ βουκόλος ἂν ἔλαβε
    δῶρον τᾶς Ἀφροδίτας,
    ὅτ᾽ ἐπὶ κρηναίαισι δρόσοις
    Ἥρᾳ Παλλάδι τ᾽ ἔριν ἔριν
    μορφᾶς ἁ Κύπρις ἔσχεν.

ἀντ. α

185 πολύθυτον δὲ δι᾽ ἄλσος Ἀρ-
    τέμιδος ἤλυθον ὁρομένα,
    φοινίσσουσα παρῇδ᾽ ἐμὰν
    αἰσχύνᾳ νεοθαλεῖ,

CHORUS

I have arrived at the sandy shore
of Aulis by the sea,
coming to land across the narrow
currents of Euripus.
I have left my city of Chalcis,
nurse of the waters of glorious Arethusa
that runs near the sea,
to look upon the army of the Achaeans
and the Achaean seagoing ships of the demi-gods
whom, our husbands tell us,
Menelaus of the golden hair
and Agamemnon the nobly born
are putting forth
on a thousand barks
in quest of Helen, whom Paris the cowherd
took from the banks
of the reedy Eurotas,
a gift from Aphrodite received
when near the dewy spring
Cypris joined in strife, in strife
over beauty with Hera and Pallas.

I ran through the grove of Artemis,
full of sacrifice,
my cheeks reddening
with the blush of youthful modesty,

---

175 ⟨θ'⟩ Fritzsche
188 νεοθαλῆ Blaydes

ἀσπίδος ἔρυμα καὶ κλισίας
190 ὁπλοφόρους Δαναῶν θέλουσ᾽
ἵππων τ᾽ ὄχλον ἰδέσθαι.
κατεῖδον δὲ δύ᾽ Αἴαντε συνέδρω,
τὸν Οἰλέως Τελαμῶνός τε γόνον, τὸν
Σαλαμῖνος στέφανον, Πρω-
195 τεσίλαόν τ᾽ ἐπὶ θάκοις
πεσσῶν ἡδομένους μορ-
φαῖσι πολυπλόκοις
Παλαμήδεά θ᾽, ὃν τέκε παῖς ὁ Ποσειδῶνος,
Διομήδεά θ᾽ ἡδοναῖς
200 δίσκου κεχαρημένον,
παρὰ δὲ Μηριόνην, Ἄρεος
ὄζον, θαῦμα βροτοῖσιν,
τὸν ἀπὸ νησαίων τ᾽ ὀρέων
Λαέρτα τόκον, ἅμα δὲ Νι-
205 ρέα, κάλλιστον Ἀχαιῶν.
ἐπῳδ.

τὸν ἰσάνεμόν τε ποδοῖν
λαιψηροδρόμον Ἀχιλλέα,
τὸν ἁ Θέτις τέκε καὶ
Χείρων ἐξεπόνησεν,
210 ἴδον αἰγιαλοῖς παρά τε κροκάλαις
δρόμον ἔχοντα σὺν ὅπλοις·
ἅμιλλαν δ᾽ ἐπόνει ποδοῖν
πρὸς ἅρμα τέτρωρον
215 ἑλίσσων περὶ νίκας.
ὁ δὲ διφρηλάτας ἐβόα᾽

wishing to see the bulwark of shields
and the huts of the Greeks with armor upon them,
and the throng of their horses.
I saw the two Ajaxes sitting together,
the son of Oïleus and Telamon's son,
who is Salamis' crowning glory,
and Protesilaus and Palamedes,
whose father was Poseidon's son,
taking their delight
in draughts, with their pieces of intricate shape,
and Diomedes rejoicing in the pleasure
of throwing the discus,
and next to Meriones,
son of Ares and a wonder to mortals,
him from the rugged islands
the son of Laertes,[6] and along with them
Nireus, most handsome of the Achaeans.

And I saw him of the wind-swift feet,
Achilles the darting runner,
whom Thetis bore
and Chiron trained,
running in his armor
by the sand of the shore.
He was racing on foot
against a chariot and four
darting ahead to take the victory.
The driver, Eumelus,

6 Odysseus.

215 ἐρίζων Pikkolos

Εὔμηλος Φερητιάδας,
οὗ καλλίστους ἰδόμαν
χρυσοδαιδάλτοις στομίοις
220 πώλους κέντρῳ θεινομένους,
τοὺς μὲν μέσους ζυγίους
λευκοστίκτῳ τριχὶ βαλιούς,
τοὺς δ' ἔξω σειροφόρους
ἀντήρεις καμπαῖσι δρόμων
225 πυρσότριχας, μονόχαλα δ' ὑπὸ σφυρὰ
ποικιλοδέρμονας· οἷς παρεπάλλετο
Πηλεΐδας σὺν ὅπλοισι παρ' ἄντυγα
230 καὶ σύριγγας ἁρματείους.

στρ. β

ναῶν δ' εἰς ἀριθμὸν ἤλυθον
καὶ θέαν ἀθεσφάτων,
τὰν γυναικεῖον ὄψιν ὀμμάτων
ὡς πλήσαιμι λίχνον ἀδονᾶν.
235 καὶ κέρας μὲν ἦν
δεξιὸν πλάτας ἔχων
Φθιώτας ὁ Μυρμιδὼν Ἄρης
πεντήκοντα ναυσὶ θουρίαις.
χρυσέαις δ' εἰκόσιν κατ' ἄκρα Νη-
240 ρῇδες ἕστασαν θεαί,

218 οὗ Hermann: ὦ L
219 χρυσοδαιδάλτοις Tyrwhitt: -ους L   221–3 del. Willink
231–302 non ab Euripide profectos esse satis constat: utrum
Retractatori an Euripidi Minori tribuendi sint non liquet
232 ἀθεσφάτων Willink: -ον L

Pheres' grandson, was shouting,
and I saw his lovely steeds,
adorned with gold-wrought bridles,
being spurred on with a goad:
the midmost horses, bearing the yoke,
had manes dappled with gray,
while those outside, who bore the traces,
and faced the bends of the course,
had hair like fire and were spotted
below their solid-hoofed ankles. Beside them there leapt
the son of Peleus in his armor, keeping pace with the
    chariot's rail
and the hub of its wheels.[7]

I came to reckon and to behold
their wondrous ships,
to fill with pleasure
the greedy vision of my female eyes.
Holding the right flank
of the fleet
was the Myrmidon force from Phthia
with fifty swift ships.
In gilded images high upon their sterns
stood Nereids,

---

[7] Thus far the entrance song of the Chorus seems be the work of Euripides. The rest is by a later hand, though it might have been written by Euripides the Younger for the first performance.

---

233 γυναικεῖον Boeckh: -είαν L
234 λίχνον ἀδονᾶν Jackson: μείλινον ἀδονάν L
237 Μυρμιδὼν Hermann: -δόνων L

187

πρύμναις σῆμ' Ἀχιλλείου στρατοῦ.

ἀντ. β

Ἀργείων δὲ ταῖσδ' ἰσήρετμοι
νᾶες ἔστασαν πέλας·
ὧν ὁ Μηκιστέως στρατηλάτας
245 παῖς ἦν, Ταλαὸς ὃν τρέφει πατήρ,
Καπανέως τε παῖς
Σθένελος· Ἀτθίδας δ' ἄγων
ἑξήκοντα ναῦς ὁ Θησέως
παῖς ἑξῆς ἐναυλόχει, θεὰν
250 Παλλάδ' ἐν μωνύχοις ἔχων πτερω-
τοῖσιν ἅρμασιν θετόν,
εὔσημόν γε φάσμα ναυβάταις.

στρ. γ

Βοιωτῶν δ' ὅπλισμα πόντιον
πεντήκοντα νῆας εἰδόμαν
255 σημείοισιν ἐστολισμένας·
τοῖς δὲ Κάδμος ἦν
χρύσεον δράκοντ' ἔχων
ἀμφὶ ναῶν κόρυμβα·
Λήιτος δ' ὁ γηγενὴς
260 ἆρχε ναΐου στρατοῦ·
Φωκίδος δ' ἀπὸ χθονὸς
⟨ . . . .
 . . . . ⟩

²⁶¹ post h. v. lac. duorum vv. indic. L

the ensign of Achilles' fleet.

The Argives' ships in equal number
with these stood near.
Their commanders were the son of Mecisteus,[8]
raised by his grandfather Talaus,
and Sthenelus, son
of Capaneus. Next to them,
with sixty ships from Athens,
was encamped
Theseus' son,[9] who had the goddess Pallas
mounted on a chariot with winged steeds,
as the clear marker for his sailors.

The Boeotians' seagoing panoply,
fifty ships, I saw
blazoned with ensigns.
There was Cadmus
holding a golden serpent
aloft on the ships' high sterns.
Leïtus, one of the Sown Men,[10]
led this naval armament.
From the land of Phocis
⟨ . . . .
. . . . ⟩

8 Euryalus.
9 Either Demophon or Acamas could be meant here.
10 See note on *Bacchae* 264.

Λοκρὰς τε ταῖσδ᾽ ἴσας ἄγων
ναῦς ⟨ἦν⟩ Οἰλέως τόκος κλυτὰν
Θρονιάδ᾽ ἐκλιπὼν πόλιν.

ἀντ. γ

265 ἐκ Μυκήνας δὲ τᾶς Κυκλωπίας
παῖς Ἀτρέως ἔπεμπε ναυβάτας
ναῶν ἑκατὸν ἠθροϊσμένους·
σὺν δ᾽ ἀδελφὸς ἦν
ταγός, ὡς φίλος φίλῳ,
270 τᾶς φυγούσας μέλαθρα
βαρβάρων χάριν γάμων
πρᾶξιν Ἑλλὰς ὡς λάβοι.
ἐκ Πύλου δὲ Νέστορος
Γερηνίου κατειδόμαν
⟨ . . . .
. . . . ⟩
275 πρύμνας σῆμα ταυρόπουν ὁρᾶν,
τὸν πάροικον Ἀλφεόν.

ἐπῳδ.

Αἰνιάνων δὲ δωδεκάστολοι
νᾶες ἦσαν, ὧν ἄναξ
Γουνεὺς ἆρχε· τῶνδε δ᾽ αὖ πέλας
280 Ἤλιδος δυνάστορες,
οὓς Ἐπειοὺς ὠνόμαζε πᾶς λεώς·
Εὔρυτος δ᾽ ἄνασσε τῶνδε·
λευκήρετμον δ᾽ Ἄρη
Τάφιον †ἦγεν ὧν Μέγης ἄνασσε†,
285 Φυλέως λόχευμα,

190

and Locrian ships, equal in number with these,
were led by the son of Oïleus,
who left behind the famous city of Thronium.

From Mycenae, built by the Cyclopes,
the son of Atreus was escorting sailors
of a hundred ships mustered together,
and with him stood his brother
also commander, as kinsman with kinsman,
so that Hellas might exact requital
for her who fled his halls
to gain a barbarian marriage.
From Pylos I saw
of Gerenian Nestor
⟨ . . . .
. . . . ⟩
the ensign upon his stern, bull-footed in appearance,
the Alpheus River, his neighbor.

Of the Aenians twelve ships
there were, commanded
by lord Guneus. Next to them
were the lords of Elis,
whom the whole host called Epeians.
These were commanded by Eurytus
while the white-oared armament
of the Taphians was led by Meges,
son of Phyleus,

---

262 ταῖσδ' Markland: τοῖσδ' L   263 ⟨ἦν⟩ Hermann
268 ἀδελφὸς Markland: Ἄδραστος L
274 post h. v. lac. indic. Weil

τὰς Ἐχίνας λιπὼν
νήσους ναυβάταις ἀπροσφόρους.
Αἴας δ᾽ ὁ Σαλαμῖνος ἔντροφος
†δεξιὸν κέρας
290 πρὸς τὸ λαιὸν ξύναγε,
τῶν ἆσσον ὥρμει πλάταισιν†
ἐσχάταισι συμπλέκων
δώδεκ᾽ εὐστροφωτάταισι ναυσίν. ὡς
ἄιον καὶ ναυβάταν
295 εἰδόμαν λεών·
ᾧ τις εἰ προσαρμόσει
βαρβάρους βάριδας,
νόστον οὐκ ἀποίσεται,
ἐνθάδ᾽ οἷον εἰδόμαν
300 νάιον πόρευμα,
τὰ δὲ κατ᾽ οἴκους κλύουσα συγκλήτου
μνήμην σώζομαι στρατεύματος.

ΠΡΕΣΒΥΤΗΣ

Μενέλαε, τολμᾷς δείν᾽, ἅ σ᾽ οὐ τολμᾶν χρεών.

ΜΕΝΕΛΑΟΣ

ἄπελθε· λίαν δεσπόταισι πιστὸς εἶ.

ΠΡΕΣΒΥΤΗΣ

305 καλόν γέ μοι τοὔνειδος ἐξωνείδισας.

ΜΕΝΕΛΑΟΣ

κλαίοις ἄν, εἰ πράσσοις ἃ μὴ πράσσειν σε δεῖ.

299 οἷον Hermann: ἄιον L

who left the Echinae isles
inhospitable to sailors.
Ajax, nursling of Salamis,
made the right flank bend round
toward the left,
near which he anchored, mingling
with the ships on the end,
twelve most nimble vessels:
that is what I heard,
and I also saw the crew.
If anyone sets
barbarian barks against these,
no homecoming will he win,
such is the armada
I saw here and what I remember,
from what I heard at home,
of the assembled army.

Enter by Eisodos A MENELAUS, *carrying the letter, pursued by the* OLD MAN.

OLD MAN

Menelaus, it is a shocking thing you are daring to do! You should not be doing it!

MENELAUS

Go away! You are too loyal to your master!

OLD MAN

The reproach you make brings credit on me.

MENELAUS

You'll be sorry if you do what you shouldn't!

ΠΡΕΣΒΥΤΗΣ

οὐ χρῆν σε λῦσαι δέλτον, ἣν ἐγὼ 'φερον.

ΜΕΝΕΛΑΟΣ

οὐδέ γε φέρειν σὲ πᾶσιν Ἕλλησιν κακά.

ΠΡΕΣΒΥΤΗΣ

ἄλλοις ἁμιλλῶ ταῦτ'· ἄφες δὲ τήνδ' ἐμοί.

ΜΕΝΕΛΑΟΣ

310 οὐκ ἂν μεθείμην.

ΠΡΕΣΒΥΤΗΣ

οὐδ' ἔγωγ' ἀφήσομαι.

ΜΕΝΕΛΑΟΣ

σκήπτρῳ τάχ' ἆρα σὸν καθαιμάξω κάρα.

ΠΡΕΣΒΥΤΗΣ

ἀλλ' εὐκλεές τοι δεσποτῶν θνῄσκειν ὕπερ.

ΜΕΝΕΛΑΟΣ

μέθες· μακροὺς δὲ δοῦλος ὢν λέγεις λόγους.

ΠΡΕΣΒΥΤΗΣ

ὦ δέσποτ', ἀδικούμεσθα· σὰς δ' ἐπιστολὰς
315 ἐξαρπάσας ὅδ' ἐκ χερῶν ἐμῶν βίᾳ,
Ἀγάμεμνον, οὐδὲν τῇ δίκῃ χρῆσθαι θέλει.

OLD MAN

You shouldn't have opened the tablet I was carrying!

MENELAUS

And you shouldn't have been bringing mischief on all the Greeks!

OLD MAN

Argue this point with others. But give me the tablet.

He takes hold of it and each tries to wrest it from the other.

MENELAUS

I won't let go.

OLD MAN

Neither shall I.

MENELAUS

Then I will soon bloody your head with my scepter.

OLD MAN

Well, it is a glorious thing to be killed for one's master.

MENELAUS

Let go! You talk too much for a slave.

He wrests the tablet from him.

OLD MAN

(*in a loud voice*) Agamemnon, master, I am being wronged! This man has taken your letter from my hands by force and refuses to act justly!

Enter from the skene *AGAMEMNON.*

EURIPIDES

ΑΓΑΜΕΜΝΩΝ

ἔα·
τίς ποτ' ἐν πύλαισι θόρυβος καὶ λόγων ἀκοσμία;

ΜΕΝΕΛΑΟΣ

οὑμὸς οὐχ ὁ τοῦδε μῦθος κυριώτερος λέγειν.

ΑΓΑΜΕΜΝΩΝ

σὺ δὲ τί τῷδ' ἐς ἔριν ἀφῖξαι, Μενέλεως, βίᾳ τ'
ἄγεις;

ΜΕΝΕΛΑΟΣ

320 βλέψον εἰς ἡμᾶς, ἵν' ἀρχὰς τῶν λόγων ταύτας
λάβω.

ΑΓΑΜΕΜΝΩΝ

μῶν τρέσας οὐκ ἀνακαλύψω βλέφαρον, Ἀτρέως
γεγώς;

ΜΕΝΕΛΑΟΣ

τήνδ' ὁρᾷς δέλτον, κακίστων γραμμάτων ὑπηρέτιν;

ΑΓΑΜΕΜΝΩΝ

εἰσορῶ· καὶ πρῶτα ταύτην σῶν ἀπάλλαξον χερῶν.

ΜΕΝΕΛΑΟΣ

οὔ, πρὶν ἂν δείξω γε Δαναοῖς πᾶσι τἀγγεγραμμένα.

ΑΓΑΜΕΜΝΩΝ

325 ἦ γὰρ οἶσθ' ἃ μή σε καιρὸς εἰδέναι σήμαντρ' ἀνείς;

ΜΕΝΕΛΑΟΣ

ὥστε σ' ἀλγῦναί γ', ἀνοίξας ἃ σὺ κάκ' ἠργάσω
λάθρᾳ.

AGAMEMNON

Ah, ah! What's this confusion, these unseemly words, at my gates?

MENELAUS

I have more right to speak than he does.

AGAMEMNON

Why have you started a quarrel with this man, Menelaus? Why are you using force?

MENELAUS

Look at me: I want this as the starting point for my words.

AGAMEMNON

Shall I, a son of Atreus, be unable to raise my glance from fear?[11]

MENELAUS

Do you see this tablet, bearer of a vile message?

AGAMEMNON

I see it. And first you must let it out of your grasp.

MENELAUS

No, not until I show its contents to all the Greeks.

AGAMEMNON

What? Do you know what you should not know, having broken the seal?

MENELAUS

Yes, to your great chagrin I have exposed the mischief you were secretly doing.

---

11 There is a pun on "Atreus," as if it meant "fearless" (from *a-* "not" and *treo* "fear").

ΑΓΑΜΕΜΝΩΝ

πού δὲ κἄλαβές νιν; ὦ θεοί, σῆς ἀναισχύντου
φρενός.

ΜΕΝΕΛΑΟΣ

προσδοκῶν σὴν παῖδ᾽ ἀπ᾽ Ἄργους, εἰ στράτευμ᾽
ἀφίξεται.

ΑΓΑΜΕΜΝΩΝ

τί δέ σε τἀμὰ δεῖ φυλάσσειν; οὐκ ἀναισχύντου
τόδε;

ΜΕΝΕΛΑΟΣ

330 ὅτι τὸ βούλεσθαί μ᾽ ἔκνιζε· σὸς δὲ δοῦλος οὐκ ἔφυν.

ΑΓΑΜΕΜΝΩΝ

οὐχὶ δεινά; τὸν ἐμὸν οἰκεῖν οἶκον οὐκ ἐάσομαι;

ΜΕΝΕΛΑΟΣ

πλάγια γὰρ φρονεῖς, τὰ μὲν νῦν, τὰ δὲ πάλαι, τὰ δ᾽
αὐτίκα.

ΑΓΑΜΕΜΝΩΝ

εὖ κεκόμψευσαι πονηρά· γλῶσσ᾽ ἐπίφθονον σοφή.

ΜΕΝΕΛΑΟΣ

νοῦς δέ γ᾽ οὐ βέβαιος ἄδικον κτῆμα κοὐ σαφὲς
φίλοις.

335 [βούλομαι δέ σ᾽ ἐξελέγξαι, καὶ σὺ μήτ᾽ ὀργῆς
ὕπο

335–441 Retractatori tribuo (alios alii del. edd.): num genuini vv.
hic illic superstites sint (e.g. 370–2) incertum

AGAMEMNON

Ye gods, what shamelessness! How did you get your hands on it?

MENELAUS

I was waiting to see whether your daughter would come from Argos to the army.

AGAMEMNON

What business had you keeping watch over my affairs? Is that not shameless behavior?

MENELAUS

Because desire pricked me to it. And I am not your slave.

AGAMEMNON

This is monstrous! Shall I not be allowed to manage my own house?

MENELAUS

No, for your thoughts—present, past, and future—are devious.

AGAMEMNON

How cleverly you dress up wickedness! A ready tongue is a hateful thing.

MENELAUS

And an unsteady mind is an unjust thing: friends cannot rely on it.[12]

[But I want to show you up. Do not get angry and try

---

12 The rest of the episode, I argue elsewhere, has been considerably altered by the Reviser, who cut as well as added material. The plot requires only that Agamemnon resign himself to sacrificing his daughter and learn of her arrival in Aulis. Lines 442–53, 460–4, 467–8, and 538–42 might well come from his final speech.

ἀποτρέπου τἀληθὲς οὔτ' αὖ κατατενῶ λίαν ἐγώ.
οἶσθ', ὅτ' ἐσπούδαζες ἄρχειν Δαναΐδαις πρὸς Ἴλιον,
τῷ δοκεῖν μὲν οὐχὶ χρῄζων, τῷ δὲ βούλεσθαι
    θέλων,
ὡς ταπεινὸς ἦσθα, πάσης δεξιᾶς προσθιγγάνων
340 καὶ θύρας ἔχων ἀκλῄστους τῷ θέλοντι δημοτῶν
καὶ διδοὺς πρόσρησιν ἑξῆς πᾶσι, κεἰ μή τις θέλοι,
τοῖς τρόποις ζητῶν πρίασθαι τὸ φιλότιμον ἐκ
    μέσου;
κᾆτ', ἐπεὶ κατέσχες ἀρχάς, μεταβαλὼν ἄλλους
    τρόπους
τοῖς φίλοισιν οὐκέτ' ἦσθα τοῖς πρὶν ὡς πρόσθεν
    φίλος,
345 δυσπρόσιτος ἔσω τε κλῄθρων σπάνιος. ἄνδρα δ' οὐ
    χρεὼν
τὸν ἀγαθὸν πράσσοντα μεγάλα τοὺς τρόπους
    μεθιστάναι,
ἀλλὰ καὶ βέβαιον εἶναι τότε μάλιστα τοῖς φίλοις,
ἡνίκ' ὠφελεῖν μάλιστα δυνατός ἐστιν εὐτυχῶν.
    ταῦτα μέν σε πρῶτ' ἐπῆλθον, ἵνα σε πρῶθ' ηὗρον
    κακόν.
350 ὡς δ' ἐς Αὖλιν ἦλθες αὖθις χὠ Πανελλήνων
    στρατός,
οὐδὲν ἦσθ', ἀλλ' ἐξεπλήσσου τῇ τύχῃ τῇ τῶν θεῶν,
οὐρίας πομπῆς σπανίζων· Δαναΐδαι δ' ἀφιέναι
ναῦς διήγγελλον, μάτην δὲ μὴ πονεῖν ἐν Αὐλίδι.
ὡς ἄνολβον εἶχες ὄμμα σύγχυσίν τ', εἰ μὴ νεῶν
355 χιλίων ἄρχων τὸ Πριάμου πεδίον ἐμπλήσεις δορός.

to deflect the truth, and I for my part will not press my
charges too far. When you were eager to be the leader of
the Greeks to Ilium—not overtly wanting it but it was your
heart's desire—do you remember how humble you were,
clasping every man's hand, keeping your door unlocked to
any commoner who wished to enter, and opening yourself
to conversation with all and sundry even when they didn't
seek it? You sought by your demeanor to buy advancement
from the multitude. Then when you had won office, you
changed your manner and were no longer as friendly to
your former friends as before: you were hard to approach
and kept yourself scarce within doors. The good man ought
not to change his character when he fares well. That is
when he ought to be the most reliable to his friends, when
in his prosperity he can do them some good.

That is my first criticism, the first point on which I
found you base. But when you came to Aulis and the army
of the Greeks with you, you were reduced to nothing, be-
ing stunned by the fortune sent from the gods: you lacked
a favoring wind. The Greeks gave the order to dismiss
the ships and waste no more time in Aulis. How unhappy
your face was, what distress you showed at the fact that
you were not going to command a thousand ships and fill

---

336 οὔτ' αὖ Blomfield: οὔτοι L   κατατενῶ λίαν Boeckh:
καταινῶ λίαν σ' L
349 ηὗρον Reiske: εὔρω L
350 αὖθις] αὐτὸς Monk
354 τ', εἰ Musgrave: τε L
355 ἐμπλήσεις Musgrave: -σας L

κἀμὲ παρεκάλεις· Τί δράσω; τίνα δὲ πόρον εὕρω
  πόθεν;
ὥστε μὴ στερέντα σ᾽ ἀρχῆς ἀπολέσαι καλὸν κλέος.
κᾆτ᾽, ἐπεὶ Κάλχας ἐν ἱεροῖς εἶπε σὴν θῦσαι κόρην
Ἀρτέμιδι, καὶ πλοῦν ἔσεσθαι Δαναΐδαις, ἡσθεὶς
  φρένας
360 ἄσμενος θύσειν ὑπέστης παῖδα· καὶ πέμπεις ἑκών,
οὐ βίᾳ—μὴ τοῦτο λέξῃς—σῇ δάμαρτι, παῖδα σὴν
δεῦρ᾽ ἀποστέλλειν, Ἀχιλλεῖ πρόφασιν ὡς
  γαμουμένην.
κᾆθ᾽ ὑποστρέψας λέληψαι μεταβαλὼν ἄλλας
  γραφάς,
ὡς φονεὺς οὐκέτι θυγατρὸς σῆς ἔσῃ; μάλιστά γε.
365 οὗτος αὐτός ἐστιν αἰθὴρ ὃς τάδ᾽ ἤκουσεν σέθεν.
  μυρίοι δέ τοι πεπόνθασ᾽ αὐτό· πρὸς τὰ πράγματα
ἐκπονοῦσ᾽ ἔχοντες, εἶτα δ᾽ ἐξεχώρησαν κακῶς,
τὰ μὲν ὑπὸ γνώμης πολιτῶν ἀσυνέτου, τὰ δ᾽
  ἐνδίκως,
ἀδύνατοι γεγῶτες αὐτοὶ διαφυλάξασθαι πόλιν.
370 Ἑλλάδος μάλιστ᾽ ἔγωγε τῆς ταλαιπώρου στένω,
ἥ, θέλουσα δρᾶν τι κεδνόν, βαρβάρους τοὺς
  οὐδένας
καταγελῶντας ἐξανήσει διὰ σὲ καὶ τὴν σὴν κόρην.
μηδέν᾽ ἀνδρείας ἕκατι προστάτην θείμην χθονὸς
μηδ᾽ ὅπλων ἄρχοντα· νοῦν χρὴ τὸν στρατηλάτην
  ἔχειν
375 πόλεος· ὡς ἀρκῶν ἀνὴρ πᾶς, ξύνεσιν ἢν ἔχων τύχῃ.

Priam's land with soldiery! You asked my advice: "What shall I do? What help can I find and from what quarter?" so that you might not be deprived of your command and lose your chance for high renown. Then, when Calchas prophesied that if you sacrificed your daughter to Artemis the Greeks would be able to sail, your heart was gladdened and you cheerfully promised to sacrifice her. You sent a message willingly, not under duress (do not claim that!), that your wife should send your daughter here on the pretext that she was going to marry Achilles. And have you now been found out sending an altered message on the ground that you will no more be your daughter's slayer? Indeed you have. This same heaven is witness to your words.

Countless men have had this experience: they constantly struggle against events and then they meet with failure, some because of a foolish decision by the citizens, others deservedly, because they themselves cannot keep their cities safe. I lament most for poor Hellas! Though she wanted to accomplish something good, now, because of you and your daughter she will let the worthless barbarians go, barbarians who are mocking us. I wouldn't set anyone in charge of a city or an army because of his bravery. A city's general must have intelligence. Any man will be adequate provided he has sense.

---

364 ἔσῃ] fort. γένῃ
367 ἐγκονοῦσ' Wecklein   ἑκόντες Canter
373 ἀνδρείας Pantazidis: ἂν χρείους L
375 ἀρκῶν Weil: ἄρχων L

ΧΟΡΟΣ

δεινὸν κασιγνήτοισι γίγνεσθαι ψόγους
μάχας θ', ὅταν ποτ' ἐμπέσωσιν εἰς ἔριν.

ΑΓΑΜΕΜΝΩΝ

βούλομαί σ' εἰπεῖν κακῶς αὖ βραχέα, μὴ λίαν ἄνω
βλέφαρα πρὸς τἀναιδὲς ἀνάγων, ἀλλὰ
σωφρονεστέρως,

380 ὡς ἀδελφὸν ὄντ'· ἀνὴρ γὰρ χρηστὸς αἰδεῖσθαι
φιλεῖ.

εἰπέ μοι, τί δεινὰ φυσᾷς αἱματηρὸν ὄμμ' ἔχων;
τίς ἀδικεῖ σε; τοῦ κέχρησαι; χρηστὰ λέκτρ' ἐρᾷς
λαβεῖν;

οὐκ ἔχοιμ' ἄν σοι παρασχεῖν· ὧν γὰρ ἐκτήσω,
κακῶς

ἦρχες. εἶτ' ἐγὼ δίκην δῶ σῶν κακῶν, ὁ μὴ σφαλείς;

385 οὐ δάκνει σε τὸ φιλότιμον τοὐμόν, ἀλλ' ἐν ἀγκάλαις
εὐπρεπῆ γυναῖκα χρῄζεις, τὸ λελογισμένον παρεὶς
καὶ τὸ καλόν, ἔχειν. πονηροῦ φωτὸς ἡδοναὶ κακαί.
εἰ δ' ἐγώ, γνοὺς πρόσθεν οὐκ εὖ, μετεθέμην
εὐβουλίαν,

μαίνομαι; σὺ μᾶλλον, ὅστις ἀπολέσας κακὸν λέχος

390 ἀναλαβεῖν θέλεις, θεοῦ σοι τὴν τύχην διδόντος εὖ.
ὤμοσαν τὸν Τυνδάρειον ὅρκον οἱ κακόφρονες
φιλόγαμοι μνηστῆρες—ἡ δέ γ' Ἐλπίς, οἶμαι μέν,
θεός,

κἀξέπραξεν αὐτὸ μᾶλλον ἢ σὺ καὶ τὸ σὸν σθένος—
οὓς λαβὼν στράτευ'· ἕτοιμοι δ' εἰσὶ μωρίᾳ φρενῶν.

IPHIGENIA AT AULIS

CHORUS LEADER

It is a terrible thing when brothers have fights and recrimi-
nations and fall to quarreling.

AGAMEMNON

I want in my turn to say a few words of criticism to you, not
shamelessly raising my glance too high but in a more mod-
est style, as one ought to address a brother: a good man
usually feels inhibition. Tell me, why do you huff and puff
so terribly, and why is your face so red? Who is wronging
you? What do you lack? Do you long to get a good wife? I
cannot give you one. You did a bad job of controlling the
one you had. Am I then to pay the penalty for your fault
when it was not my mistake? It is not my ambition that
bothers you. Rather, you want to have a beautiful wife in
your arms, and you lay aside reason and decorum. Evil
men have evil pleasures. But if I, having made a wrong de-
cision earlier, now adopt good sense, am I mad? You are
more so. You lost a bad wife and yet you want to get her
back, even though heaven has done you a good turn. The
foolish suitors, eager for marriage, swore Tyndareus' oath:
Expectation, I think, is a goddess, and it was she, more
than you and your power, who gave you this opportunity.
Take these suitors and make your expedition. It is the folly
of their minds that has made them willing. Heaven is not so

---

376 ψόγους Musgrave: λόγους L
379 ἀνάγων Naber: ἀγαγών L
385 οὐ Murray: ἢ L
388 μετεθέμην εὐβουλίαν Monk cl. *Or.* 254: μετετέθην
εὐβουλίᾳ L

394a οὐ γὰρ ἀσύνετον τὸ θεῖον, ἀλλ' ἔχει συνιέναι
395 τοὺς κακῶς παγέντας ὅρκους καὶ
    κατηναγκασμένους.
τἀμὰ δ' οὐκ ἀποκτενῶ 'γὼ τέκνα· κοὐ τὸ σὸν μὲν εὖ
παρὰ δίκην ἔσται κακίστης εὐνιδος τιμωρίᾳ,
ἐμὲ δὲ συντήξουσι νύκτες ἡμέραι τε δακρύοις,
ἄνομα δρῶντα κοὐ δίκαια παῖδας οὓς ἐγεινάμην.
400   ταῦτά σοι βραχέα λέλεκται καὶ σαφῆ καὶ ῥᾴδια·
εἰ δὲ μὴ βούλῃ φρονεῖν εὖ, τἄμ' ἐγὼ θήσω καλῶς.

ΧΟΡΟΣ

οἵδ' αὖ διάφοροι τῶν πάρος λελεγμένων
μύθων, καλῶς δ' ἔχουσι, φείδεσθαι τέκνων.

ΜΕΝΕΛΑΟΣ

αἰαῖ, φίλους ἄρ' οὐκ ἐκεκτήμην τάλας.

ΑΓΑΜΕΜΝΩΝ

405 εἰ τοὺς φίλους γε μὴ θέλεις ἀπολλύναι.

ΜΕΝΕΛΑΟΣ

δείξεις δὲ ποῦ μοι πατρὸς ἐκ ταὐτοῦ γεγώς;

ΑΓΑΜΕΜΝΩΝ

συσσωφρονεῖν σοι βούλομ', ἀλλ' οὐ συννοσεῖν.

ΜΕΝΕΛΑΟΣ

ἐς κοινὸν ἀλγεῖν τοῖς φίλοισι χρὴ φίλους.

ΑΓΑΜΕΜΝΩΝ

εὖ δρῶν παρακάλει μ', ἀλλὰ μὴ λυπῶν ἐμέ.

senseless that it cannot tell when an oath is taken wrong-
fully and under compulsion. But I will not kill my children.
It shall never be that you enjoy undeserved happiness
because you have punished your wicked wife while I am
worn away by nights and days in tears because of lawless
and wicked acts against my own children.

That is my message to you—brief, clear, and easy to
understand. If you refuse to be sensible, I shall settle my
own affairs well.

CHORUS LEADER

This speech is different from the earlier one and a fine sen-
timent it is, to spare one's children.

MENELAUS

Ah ah, it seems I have no friends, poor man that I am!

AGAMEMNON

Yes you have, unless you mean to destroy them.

MENELAUS

How will you show me that you are my brother born?

AGAMEMNON

I want to share with you in good sense, not in mad folly.

MENELAUS

Kinsmen ought to have their griefs in common.

AGAMEMNON

Ask for my help by doing good to me, not by causing me
pain.

394a habent tt, om. L   396 κοὐ Lenting: καὶ L
407 βούλομαι κοὐ Nauck, βουλόμεσθ', οὐ Fix, βουλόμενος,
οὐ Vitelli

ΜΕΝΕΛΑΟΣ

410 οὐκ ἄρα δοκεῖ σοι τάδε πονεῖν σὺν Ἑλλάδι;

ΑΓΑΜΕΜΝΩΝ

Ἑλλὰς δὲ σὺν σοὶ κατὰ θεὸν νοσεῖ τινα.

ΜΕΝΕΛΑΟΣ

σκήπτρῳ νυν αὔχει, σὸν κασίγνητον προδούς.
ἐγὼ δ' ἐπ' ἄλλας εἶμι μηχανάς τινας
φίλους τ' ἐπ' ἄλλους.

ΑΓΓΕΛΟΣ
ὦ Πανελλήνων ἄναξ,
415 Ἀγάμεμνον, ἥκω παῖδά σοι τὴν σὴν ἄγων,
ἣν Ἰφιγένειαν ὠνόμαζες ἐν δόμοις.
μήτηρ δ' ὁμαρτεῖ, σῆς Κλυταιμήστρας δέμας,
καὶ παῖς Ὀρέστης, ὥς σφε τερφθείης ἰδών,
χρόνον παλαιὸν δωμάτων ἔκδημος ὤν.
420 ἀλλ' ὡς μακρὰν ἔτεινον, εὔρυτον παρὰ
κρήνην ἀναψύχουσι θηλύπουν βάσιν,
αὐταί τε πῶλοί τ'· ἐς δὲ λειμώνων χλόην
καθεῖμεν αὐτάς, ὡς βορᾶς γευσαίατο.
ἐγὼ δὲ πρόδρομος σῆς παρασκευῆς χάριν
425 ἥκω· πέπυσται γὰρ στρατός—ταχεῖα γὰρ
διῇξε φήμη—παῖδα σὴν ἀφιγμένην.
πᾶς δ' ἐς θέαν ὅμιλος ἔρχεται δρόμῳ,
σὴν παῖδ' ὅπως ἴδωσιν· οἱ δ' εὐδαίμονες
ἐν πᾶσι κλεινοὶ καὶ περίβλεπτοι βροτοῖς.
430 λέγουσι δ'· Ὑμέναιός τις ἢ τί πράσσεται;
ἢ πόθον ἔχων θυγατρὸς Ἀγαμέμνων ἄναξ

MENELAUS

So you have decided not to endure this labor in aid of Hellas?

AGAMEMNON

Hellas along with you is suffering from some divinely sent disease.

MENELAUS

Feel pride in your scepter, then, when you have betrayed your brother! I shall turn to other means and to other friends.

Enter by Eisodos A a MESSENGER.

MESSENGER

Lord of all the Greeks, Agamemnon, I have come bringing your daughter to you, the one you named Iphigenia in your halls. Her mother comes with her, your wife Clytaemestra, and also your son Orestes so that you may have the pleasure of seeing him: you have been a long time away from home. But since they have had a long journey, they are refreshing their female feet, both they and their mares. We have sent the mares into the green meadows to be foddered. I have come on ahead so that you may prepare. For swift rumor has run through the army, and they have learned that your daughter has arrived. The whole throng came running to see her: the fortunate are famous and the object of every mortal gaze. They are saying "Is a marriage taking place, or what is going on? Has lord Agamemnon brought his daughter here because he missed her?" From

---

412 αὔχει Tyrwhitt: αὐχεῖς L
418 ὥς σφε Vater: ὥστε L

ἐκόμισε παῖδα; τῶν δ' ἂν ἤκουσας τάδε·
Ἀρτέμιδι προτελίζουσι τὴν νεάνιδα,
Αὐλίδος ἀνάσσῃ. τίς νιν ἄξεταί ποτε;
435   ἀλλ' εἶα, τἀπὶ τοισίδ' ἐξάρχου κανᾶ,
στεφανοῦσθε κρᾶτα, καὶ σύ, Μενέλεως ἄναξ,
ὑμέναιον εὐτρέπιζε, καὶ κατὰ στέγας
λωτὸς βοάσθω καὶ ποδῶν ἔστω κτύπος·
φῶς γὰρ τόδ' ἥκει μακάριον τῇ παρθένῳ.]

ΑΓΑΜΕΜΝΩΝ

440   [ἐπῄνεσ'· ἀλλὰ στεῖχε δωμάτων ἔσω·
τὰ δ' ἄλλ' ἰούσης τῆς τύχης ἔσται καλῶς.]
    οἴμοι, τί φῶ δύστηνος; ἄρξωμαι πόθεν;
ἐς οἷ' ἀνάγκης ζεύγματ' ἐμπεπτώκαμεν·
ὑπῆλθε δαίμων, ὥστε τῶν σοφισμάτων
445   πολλῷ γενέσθαι τῶν ἐμῶν σοφώτερος.
    ἡ δυσγένεια δ' ὡς ἔχει τι χρήσιμον.
καὶ γὰρ δακρῦσαι ῥᾳδίως αὐτοῖς ἔχει,
ἅπαντά τ' εἰπεῖν. τῷ δὲ γενναίῳ φύσιν
ἄνολβα πάντα· προστάτην δὲ τοῦ βίου
450   τὸν ὄγκον ἔχομεν τῷ τ' ὄχλῳ δουλεύομεν.
ἐγὼ γὰρ ἐκβαλεῖν μὲν αἰδοῦμαι δάκρυ,
τὸ μὴ δακρῦσαι δ' αὖθις αἰδοῦμαι τάλας,
ἐς τὰς μεγίστας συμφορὰς ἀφιγμένος.
    [εἶέν· τί φήσω πρὸς δάμαρτα τὴν ἐμήν;
455   πῶς δέξομαί νιν; ποῖον ὄμμα συμβαλῶ;
καὶ γάρ μ' ἀπώλεσ' ἐπὶ κακοῖς ἅ μοι πάρα

448-9 ἅπαντά . . . ἄνολβα Musgrave: ἄνολβά . . . ἅπαντα L

210

others you would hear this: "They are performing the maiden's consecration to Artemis, mistress of Aulis. Who is going to make her his wife?"

But come now, in view of these things prepare the basket, garland your heads, and you, lord Menelaus, get ready the Hymen song! Let the pipe sound in the tents and let there be the sound of dancing feet! This day is a blessed one for the girl!]

AGAMEMNON
[I thank you. But go inside the tent. The rest will turn out well as our fate unfolds.

Exit MESSENGER *into the* skene.]

Ah me, what shall I say in my misery? Where shall I make a beginning? What a yoke of necessity have I fallen under! The god has attacked me stealthily and proved far craftier than my craftiness.

Low birth—what a good thing that is! Such people may weep without hesitation and say anything they like! But to a man of high birth all is misery. The prestige of our position controls our lives, and we are slaves to the masses. I shrink from weeping, shrink likewise, wretched man that I am, from not weeping since I have come into the worst of disasters.

[Come, what shall I tell my wife? How shall I receive her? With what expression shall I meet hers? In fact her arriving here uninvited is my undoing, coming on top of

---

449 πάντα Diggle: ταῦτα L
454-9 Retractatori tribuo (del. England)

ἐλθοῦσ᾽ ἄκλητος. εἰκότως δ᾽ ἅμ᾽ ἕσπετο
θυγατρὶ νυμφεύσουσα καὶ τὰ φίλτατα
δώσουσ᾽, ἵν᾽ ἡμᾶς ὄντας εὑρήσει κακούς.]

460   τὴν δ᾽ αὖ τάλαιναν παρθένον—τί παρθένον;
Ἅιδης νιν, ὡς ἔοικε, νυμφεύσει τάχα—
ὡς ᾤκτισ᾽· οἶμαι γάρ νιν ἱκετεύσειν τάδε·
Ὦ πάτερ, ἀποκτενεῖς με; τοιούτους γάμους
γήμειας αὐτὸς χὤστις ἐστί σοι φίλος.

465   [παρὼν δ᾽ Ὀρέστης ἐγγὺς ἀναβοήσεται
οὐ συνετὰ συνετῶς· ἔτι γάρ ἐστι νήπιος.]
αἰαῖ, τὸν Ἑλένης ὥς μ᾽ ἀπώλεσεν γάμον
γήμας ὁ Πριάμου Πάρις, ὃς εἴργασται τάδε.

[ΧΟΡΟΣ
κἀγὼ κατῴκτιρ᾽, ὡς γυναῖκα δεῖ ξένην
470   ὑπὲρ τυράννων συμφορᾶς καταστένειν.

ΜΕΝΕΛΑΟΣ
ἀδελφέ, δός μοι δεξιᾶς τῆς σῆς θιγεῖν.

ΑΓΑΜΕΜΝΩΝ
δίδωμι· σὸν γὰρ τὸ κράτος, ἄθλιος δ᾽ ἐγώ.

ΜΕΝΕΛΑΟΣ
Πέλοπα κατόμνυμ᾽, ὃς πατὴρ τοὐμοῦ πατρὸς
τοῦ σοῦ τ᾽ ἐκλήθη, τὸν τεκόντα τ᾽ Ἀτρέα,
475   ἦ μὴν ἐρεῖν σοι τἀπὸ καρδίας σαφῶς
καὶ μὴ 'πίτηδες μηδέν, ἀλλ᾽ ὅσον φρονῶ.
ἐγώ σ᾽ ἀπ᾽ ὄσσων ἐκβαλόντ᾽ ἰδὼν δάκρυ
ᾤκτιρα καὐτὸς ἀνταφῆκά σοι πάλιν
καὶ τῶν παλαιῶν ἐξαφίσταμαι λόγων,

the troubles I was suffering. But it is quite reasonable that she accompanied our daughter here to make her a bride and to give away her darling. And here she will find me disloyal.]

The poor maiden—yet why do I call her that when Hades, it seems will soon make her his bride?—how I pity her! I think that she will supplicate me with these words: "Father, do you mean to kill me? May you make a marriage like this, you and whoever is friend to you!" [Orestes will be there and will cry out—words that make no sense but are all too sensible: he is still a babe.] Ah, ah, what destruction was wrought upon me by Priam's son Paris when he married Helen! It is he who has done this.

[CHORUS LEADER
I too feel pity, in the way a foreign woman ought to lament for the misfortunes of a royal house.

MENELAUS
Brother, give me your hand to grasp.

Agamemnon gives his hand to Menelaus.

AGAMEMNON
I give it to you. You are the master, I am in misery.

MENELAUS
I swear by Pelops, who is called the father of my father and yours, I swear by Atreus our father, that I shall say plainly what is in my heart, no word in craftiness but only what I think. When I saw you weeping, I myself felt pity and shed tears in my turn for you: I step back from my former words,

---

465–6 Retractori tribuo (465 del. Conington, 466 Dindorf)
469–537 Retractatori tribuo (alios alii del. edd.)

480 οὐκ ἐς σὲ δεινός· εἰμὶ δ' οὕπερ εἶ σὺ νῦν.
  καί σοι παραινῶ μήτ' ἀποκτείνειν τέκνον
  μήτ' ἀνθελέσθαι τοὐμόν. οὐ γὰρ ἔνδικον
  σὲ μὲν στενάζειν, τἀμὰ δ' ἡδέως ἔχειν,
  θνήσκειν τε τοὺς σούς, τοὺς δ' ἐμοὺς ὁρᾶν φάος.

485 τί βούλομαι γάρ; οὐ γάμους ἐξαιρέτους
  ἄλλους λάβοιμ' ἄν, εἰ γάμων ἱμείρομαι;
  ἀλλ' ἀπολέσας ἀδελφόν, ὅν μ' ἥκιστα χρῆν,
  Ἑλένην ἕλωμαι, τὸ κακὸν ἀντὶ τἀγαθοῦ;
  ἄφρων νέος τ' ἦ, πρὶν τὰ πράγματ' ἐγγύθεν

490 σκοπῶν ἐσεῖδον οἷον ἦν κτείνειν τέκνα.
  ἄλλως τέ μ' ἔλεος τῆς ταλαιπώρου κόρης
  ἐσῆλθε, συγγένειαν ἐννοουμένῳ,
  ἣ τῶν ἐμῶν ἕκατι θύεσθαι γάμων
  μέλλει. τί δ' Ἑλένης παρθένῳ τῇ σῇ μέτα;

495 ἴτω στρατεία διαλυθεῖσ' ἐξ Αὐλίδος,
  σὺ δ' ὄμμα παῦσαι δακρύοις τέγγων τὸ σόν,
  ἀδελφέ, κἀμὲ παρακαλῶν ἐς δάκρυα.
  εἰ δέ τι κόρης σῆς θεσφάτων μέτεστι σοί,
  μὴ 'μοὶ μετέστω· σοὶ νέμω τοὐμὸν μέρος.

500 ἀλλ' ἐς μεταβολὰς ἦλθον ἀπὸ δεινῶν λόγων;
  εἰκὸς πέπονθα· τὸν ὁμόθεν πεφυκότα
  στέργων μετέπεσον. ἀνδρὸς οὐ κακοῦ τρόποι
  τοιοίδε, χρῆσθαι τοῖσι βελτίστοις ἀεί.

ΧΟΡΟΣ

  γενναῖ' ἔλεξας Ταντάλῳ τε τῷ Διὸς
505 πρέποντα· προγόνους οὐ καταισχύνεις σέθεν.

no longer threatening you. I stand now where you stand. I advise you not to kill your children, nor to take mine in their stead. For it is not right that you should grieve while my life is pleasant, or that your children should die while mine look on the light.

What is my aim? If I want to marry, can I not make another excellent marriage? Shall I destroy a brother, the last person I ought to destroy, and choose Helen, taking evil in exchange for good? I was young and foolish before I examined the matter from close at hand and saw what a thing it was to kill a child. Besides, pity for the poor girl entered my heart when I considered that she is my kinswoman and is about to be sacrificed for the sake of my marriage. What does your daughter have to do with Helen? Let the expedition be disbanded and leave Aulis! Stop wetting your face with tears, my brother, and calling upon me to weep. If you have any part in the oracles concerning your daughter, let me not have any part: I make my share over to you. Well, have I changed and left dread speech behind? What has happened to me is only natural. I have changed and begun to love a brother born from the same parents. A decent man acts in the best fashion always.

CHORUS LEADER
What you have said is noble and worthy of Tantalus, the son of Zeus: you do not bring disgrace upon your ancestors.

EURIPIDES

ΑΓΑΜΕΜΝΩΝ

αἰνῶ σε, Μενέλα᾽, ὅτι παρὰ γνώμην ἐμὴν
ὑπέθηκας ὀρθῶς τοὺς λόγους σοῦ τ᾽ ἀξίως.
ταραχὴ δ᾽ ἀδελφῶν διά τ᾽ ἔρωτα γίγνεται
πλεονεξίαν τε δωμάτων· ἀπέπτυσα
510 τοιάνδε συγγένειαν ἀλλήλοιν πικράν.
ἀλλ᾽ ἥκομεν γὰρ εἰς ἀναγκαίας τύχας,
θυγατρὸς αἱματηρὸν ἐκπρᾶξαι φόνον.

ΜΕΝΕΛΑΟΣ

πῶς; τίς δ᾽ ἀναγκάσει σε τήν γε σὴν κτανεῖν;

ΑΓΑΜΕΜΝΩΝ

ἅπας Ἀχαιῶν σύλλογος στρατεύματος.

ΜΕΝΕΛΑΟΣ

515 οὔκ, ἤν νιν εἰς Ἄργος γ᾽ ἀποστείλῃς πάλιν.

ΑΓΑΜΕΜΝΩΝ

λάθοιμι τοῦτ᾽ ἄν. ἀλλ᾽ ἐκεῖν᾽ οὐ λήσομεν.

ΜΕΝΕΛΑΟΣ

τὸ ποῖον; οὔτοι χρὴ λίαν ταρβεῖν ὄχλον.

ΑΓΑΜΕΜΝΩΝ

Κάλχας ἐρεῖ μαντεύματ᾽ Ἀργείων στρατῷ.

ΜΕΝΕΛΑΟΣ

οὔκ, ἢν θάνῃ γε πρόσθε· τοῦτο δ᾽ εὐμαρές.

ΑΓΑΜΕΜΝΩΝ

520 τὸ μαντικὸν πᾶν σπέρμα φιλότιμον κακόν.

216

AGAMEMNON

I thank you, Menelaus: contrary to my expectation you
have spoken rightly and in a manner worthy of yourself.
Estrangement of brothers happens because of rivalry in
love or greed to inherit a house. I hate the kind of blood
kinship that causes mutual pain. But we have reached the
point where we are forced to commit the bloody murder of
my daughter.

MENELAUS

How so? Who will force you to kill your own child?

AGAMEMNON

The entire assembled Greek army.

MENELAUS

No, not if you send her back to Argos.

AGAMEMNON

That I could manage to keep secret, but secrecy in this
other thing is beyond me.

MENELAUS

What is that? You ought not to be overly afraid of the
crowd.

AGAMEMNON

Calchas will tell the oracles to the Greek army.

MENELAUS

Not if he is killed first! That is easily done.

AGAMEMNON

The whole race of prophets is an ambitious bane.

---

510 ἀλλήλοιν Markland: -ων L

EURIPIDES

ΜΕΝΕΛΑΟΣ
οὗ δεῖ γ' ἄχρηστον, οὗ δὲ χρήσιμον πικρόν.

ΑΓΑΜΕΜΝΩΝ
ἐκεῖνο δ' οὐ δέδοικας οὔμ' ἐσέρχεται;

ΜΕΝΕΛΑΟΣ
ὃν μὴ σὺ φράζεις, πῶς ὑπολάβοιμ' ἂν λόγον;

ΑΓΑΜΕΜΝΩΝ
τὸ Σισύφειον σπέρμα πάντ' οἶδεν τάδε.

ΜΕΝΕΛΑΟΣ
525   οὐκ ἔστ' Ὀδυσσεὺς ὅ τι σὲ κἀμὲ πημανεῖ.

ΑΓΑΜΕΜΝΩΝ
ποικίλος ἀεὶ πέφυκε τοῦ τ' ὄχλου μέτα.

ΜΕΝΕΛΑΟΣ
φιλοτιμίᾳ μὲν ἐνέχεται, δεινῷ κακῷ.

ΑΓΑΜΕΜΝΩΝ
οὔκουν δοκεῖς νιν στάντ' ἐν Ἀργείοις μέσοις
λέξειν ἃ Κάλχας θέσφατ' ἐξηγήσατο,
530   κἄμ' ὡς ὑπέστην θῦμα, κᾆτ' ἐψευδόμην,
Ἀρτέμιδι θύσειν; οὐ ξυναρπάσας στρατόν,
σὲ κἄμ' ἀποκτείναντας Ἀργείους κόρην
σφάξαι κελεύσει; κἂν πρὸς Ἄργος ἐκφύγω,
ἐλθόντες αὐτοῖς τείχεσιν Κυκλωπίοις
535   συναρπάσουσι καὶ κατασκάψουσι γῆν.
τοιαῦτα τἀμὰ πήματ'· ὦ τάλας ἐγώ,

521 sic Murray: κοὐδὲν γ' ἄχρηστον οὐδὲ χρήσιμον παρόν L

218

MENELAUS

Yes, they are useless where they are needed, and where
they are useful, they bring grief.

AGAMEMNON

But are you not afraid of what I have in mind?

MENELAUS

How can I understand a consideration if you do not tell it
to me?

AGAMEMNON

The son of Sisyphus knows everything we have been dis-
cussing.

MENELAUS

Odysseus will cause no pain to you and me.

AGAMEMNON

He is always unreliable and sides with the rabble.

MENELAUS

To be sure, he is affected by ambition, a dread mischief.

AGAMEMNON

Don't you think that he will stand in the midst of the
Greeks and mention the omens Calchas interpreted and
say how I promised to make a sacrifice to Artemis and then
went back on my word? Will he not grab the Greek army
and order them to kill you and me and then slaughter the
girl? If I run to Argos, they will come and plunder and dig
up the land, Cylcopean walls and all! These are my trou-

---

530 κᾆτ' ἐψευδόμην Murray: κᾆτα ψεύδομαι L
531 οὐ Reiske: ὅς L

ὡς ἠπόρημαι πρὸς θεῶν τὰ νῦν τάδε.]

ἔν μοι φύλαξον, Μενέλεως, ἀνὰ στρατὸν
ἐλθών, ὅπως ἂν μὴ Κλυταιμήστρα τάδε
540 μάθῃ, πρὶν Ἅιδῃ παῖδ' ἐμὴν προσθῶ λαβών,
ὡς ἐπ' ἐλαχίστοις δακρύοις πράσσω κακῶς.
ὑμεῖς δὲ σιγήν, ὦ ξέναι, φυλάσσετε.

ΧΟΡΟΣ

στρ.

μάκαρες οἳ μετρίας θεοῦ
μετά τε σωφροσύνας μετέ-
545 σχον λέκτρων Ἀφροδίτας,
γαλανείᾳ χρησάμενοι
μανιάδων οἴστρων· ὅθι δὴ
δίδυμ' Ἔρως ὁ χρυσοκόμας
τόξ' ἐντείνεται χαρίτων,
550 τὸ μὲν ἐπ' εὐαίωνι πότμῳ,
τὸ δ' ἐπὶ συγχύσει βιοτᾶς.
ἀπενέπω νιν ἁμετέρων,
ὦ Κύπρι καλλίστα, θαλάμων.
εἴη δέ μοι μετρία
555 μὲν χάρις, πόθοι δ' ὅσιοι,
καὶ μετέχοιμι τᾶς Ἀφροδί-
τας, πολλὰν δ' ἀποθείμαν.

ἀντ

διάφοροι δὲ φύσεις βροτῶν,

538 φύλαξαι Headlam
542 δὲ Günther: τε L

bles. O unhappy me, how helpless the gods have now made
me!]

Take care of this one thing, Menelaus: go through the
army and make sure that Clytaemestra does not learn this
until I take my daughter and consign her to the under-
world. That way I shed the fewest tears in my misfortune.
And you, foreign ladies, say nothing.

Exit MENELAUS *by Eisodos B,* AGAMEMNON *and* OLD MAN
into the skene.

CHORUS
Blessed are they who with moderation
and self-control where the goddess is concerned
share in the couch of Aphrodite,
experiencing the calm absence
of mad passion's sting. In love
twofold are the arrows of pleasure
golden-haired Eros sets on his bowstring,
the one to give us a blessed fate,
the other to confound our life.
I forbid him, O Cypris most lovely,
to come to my bedchamber!
May my joy be moderate,
my desires godly,
may I have a share in Aphrodite
but send her away when she is excessive!

Various are the natures of mortals,

---

545 θέλκτρων Nauck
547 μανιάδων Wecklein: μαινόμεν' L

διάφοροι δὲ τρόποι· τὸ δ' ὀρ-
560 θῶς ἐσθλὸν σαφὲς αἰεί·
τροφαί δ' αἱ παιδευομένων
μέγα φέρουσ' ἐς τὰν ἀρετάν·
τό τε γὰρ αἰδεῖσθαι σοφία,
τάν τ' ἐξαλλάσσουσαν ἔχει
565 χάριν ὑπὸ γνώμας ἐσορᾶν
τὸ δέον· ἔνθα δόξα φέρει
κλέος ἀγήρατον βιοτᾷ.
μέγα τι θηρεύειν ἀρετάν,
γυναιξὶ μὲν κατὰ †Κύ-
570 πριν κρυπτάν†, ἐν ἀνδράσι δ' αὖ
κόσμος ἐνὼν ὁ μυριοπλη-
θὴς μείζω πόλιν αὔξει.

ἐπῳδ.

†ἔμολες†, ὦ Πάρις, ᾇτε σύ γε
βουκόλος ἀργενναῖς ἐτράφης
575 Ἰδαίαις παρὰ μόσχοις,
βάρβαρα συρίζων, Φρυγίων
αὐλῶν Οὐλύμπου καλάμοις
μιμήματ' ἀναπύων,
εὔθηλοι δ' ἐτρέφοντο βόες·
580 ὅθι κρίσις σ' ἔμενεν θεᾶν,
ἅ σ' ἐς Ἑλλάδα πέμπει·

559 διάφοροι Höpfner: διάτροποι L
559–60 τὸ δ' ὀρθῶς Musgrave: ὁ δ' ὀρθὸς L
561 αἱ] εὖ Nauck   παιδευομένων Monk: -όμεναι L
569–70 Κύπριν] μοῖραν Willink

various their characters. But what is truly
good is always manifest.
The nurture of the well educated
contributes much to goodness.
For a sense of shame is wisdom,
and it brings with it the surpassing
grace of seeing and knowing
the thing that is needful. Then what men think of you
shall bring to your life a fame that does not grow old.
To seek after goodness is something great:
for women it is in the hidden sphere
of love, while among men
when good order in its fullness is present,
it makes the city greater.

I have been told, Paris,
how you were raised as cowherd among the white
Idaean calves,
playing Asian melodies upon the syrinx,
imitating upon your reed pipe
the Phrygian aulos of Olympus[13]
while cows with full udders were grazing.
There the judgment of the goddesses awaited you,
a judgment that sent you to Hellas.

[13] An early singer, said to have been the inventor of the aulos,
an instrument something like an oboe.

---

571 ἐνὼν Markland: ἔνδον L
573 fort. ἔμαθον vel ἔκλυον: ἔμαθες Willink, tum 576 συρίζειν
578 μιμηματ[α αναπ]νων Π (suppl. Günther): μ- πνέων L
580 ὅθι (Bothe) κρίσις σ᾽ ἔμενεν Diggle: ὅτι σε κρίσις ἔμενε L

ἐλεφαντοδέτων πάροι-
θεν θρόνων ὃς στὰς Ἑλένας
ἐν ἀντωποῖς βλεφάροις
585 ἔρωτά τ᾽ ἔδωκας ἔρωτι τ᾽
αὐτὸς ἐπτοήθης.
ὅθεν ἔριν ἔριν
Ἑλλάδα σὺν δορὶ ναυσί τ᾽ ἄγεις
ἐς πέργαμα Τροίας.

[ΧΟΡΟΣ ⟨ΑΡΓΕΙΩΝ⟩

590 ἰὼ ἰώ· μεγάλαι μεγάλων
εὐδαιμονίαι· τὴν τοῦ βασιλέως
ἴδετ᾽ Ἰφιγένειαν, ἄνασσαν ἐμήν,
τὴν Τυνδάρεω τε Κλυταιμήστραν,
ὡς ἐκ μεγάλων ἐβλαστήκασ᾽
595 ἐπί τ᾽ εὐμήκεις ἥκουσι τύχας.
θεοί γ᾽ οἱ κρείσσους οἵ τ᾽ ὀλβοφόροι
τοῖς οὐκ εὐδαίμοσι θνητῶν.

ΧΟΡΟΣ
στῶμεν, Χαλκίδος ἔκγονα θρέμματα,

583 θρόνων Hermann: δόμων L   στὰς Jouan: τᾶς L
588 ἄγεις Page: -ει L
589 πέργαμα Τροίας Blomfield: Τ- π- L
590–630 Retractatori tribuo (590–7 ab Euripide abiud. G.
Dindorf, 598–606 L. Dindorf, 607–30 post alios Page)
590n ⟨Ἀργείων⟩ Murray

Before the ivory-inlaid
seat of Helen you stood,
and with your gaze turned to hers
you inspired love and with love
yourself were set aflutter.
Hence in strife, in strife
you are bringing Greece with spears and ships
to the citadel of Troy.

[*Enter by Eisodos A* IPHIGENIA *and* CLYTAEMESTRA *on a
chariot. They are accompanied by men or women of Argos,
who form a* SECOND CHORUS.

LEADER OF SECOND CHORUS[14]

Hail, hail! Great is the happiness of the great! See the
king's daughter, Iphigenia, our princess, and Tyndareus'
daughter Clytaemestra! They are descended from great
forebears, and broad are the fortunes into which they have
come! In the eyes of mortals who are lowly their betters,
the prosperous ones, are gods!

CHORUS LEADER

Let us take our stand, offspring of Chalcis, and receive the

14 I assign lines 590–630 to the Reviser. This passage aims at
an impressive spectacle: chariot entry with large entourage, bride
gifts brought into the tent, elaborate descent by Clytaemestra and
Iphigenia from the chariot, even a sleeping baby Orestes. The
opening lines must belong to a second chorus of men or women of
Argos: the women of Calchis would not address Iphigenia as "our
princess," nor could they have delivered 590–97, since they know
what is in store for Iphigenia and have no reason to indulge in
cruel irony. I have marked a lacuna before 631 and tried to guess
how the entrance of mother and daughter was originally arranged.

EURIPIDES

τὴν βασίλειαν δεξώμεθ' ὄχων
600 ἄπο μὴ σφαλερῶς ἐπὶ γαῖαν,
ἀγανῶς δὲ χεροῖν, μαλακῇ γνώμῃ,
μὴ ταρβήσῃ νεωστί μοι μολὸν
κλεινὸν τέκνον Ἀγαμέμνονος,
μηδὲ θόρυβον μηδ' ἔκπληξιν
605 ταῖς Ἀργείαις
ξεῖναι ξείναις παρέχωμεν.

ΚΛΥΤΑΙΜΗΣΤΡΑ

ὄρνιθα μὲν τόνδ' αἴσιον ποιούμεθα,
τὸ σόν τε χρηστὸν καὶ λόγων εὐφημίαν·
ἐλπίδα δ' ἔχω τιν' ὡς ἐπ' ἐσθλοῖσιν γάμοις
610 πάρειμι νυμφαγωγός. ἀλλ' ὀχημάτων
ἔξω πορεύεθ' ἃς φέρω φερνὰς κόρῃ
καὶ πέμπετ' ἐς μέλαθρον εὐλαβούμενοι.
σὺ δ', ὦ τέκνον μοι, λεῖπε πωλικοὺς ὄχους,
ἁβρὸν τιθεῖσα κῶλον ἀσφαλῶς χαμαί.
615 ὑμεῖς δὲ νεάνιδές νιν ἀγκάλαις ἔπι
δέξασθε καὶ πορεύσατ' ἐξ ὀχημάτων.
κἀμοὶ χερός τις ἐνδότω στηρίγματα,
θάκους ἀπήνης ὡς ἂν ἐκλίπω καλῶς.
αἱ δ' ἐς τὸ πρόσθεν στῆτε πωλικῶν ζυγῶν·
620 φοβερὸν γὰρ ἀπαράμυθον ὄμμα πωλικόν.
καὶ παῖδα τόνδε, τὸν Ἀγαμέμνονος γόνον,
λάζυσθ', Ὀρέστην· ἔτι γάρ ἐστι νήπιος.
τέκνον, καθεύδεις πωλικῷ δαμεὶς ὄχῳ;
ἔγειρ' ἀδελφῆς ἐφ' ὑμέναιον εὐτυχῶς·

226

queen from her chariot safely onto the ground: let us hold her softly and gently with our hands lest the glorious daughter of Agamemnon, so lately arrived, take fright. Let us not, as strangers to strangers, cause distress or dismay to the women of Argos.

CLYTAEMESTRA

I consider your kindness and fair words to be a good omen. I have some hope that it is for a good marriage that I have come to escort the bride. But take from my chariot the bride gifts I am bringing for the girl and carry them carefully into the tent. And you, my daughter, leave the chariot, putting your dainty foot safely upon the ground. You young women, receive her in your arms and convey her from the chariot. And let someone give me the support of a hand so that I can leave the chariot's seat in dignified fashion. The rest of you stand in front of the horses: if you don't comfort a horse, you can see panic in its eyes. And take this child Orestes here, the son of Agamemnon: he is still a babe. Are you sleeping, my son, lulled by the chariot? Wake then in happiness to your sister's marriage! Nobleman that you

---

602 τὸ νεωστὶ μολὸν Hermann
603 τέκνον] γέννημ᾽ Stadtmüller   Ἀγαμεμνόνιον Markland
604 μηδὲ] καὶ μὴ Hermann
614 ἀσφαλῶς χαμαί Hermann: ἀσθενές θ᾽ ἅμα L
615 νεάνιδές νιν Pierson: νεανίδαισιν L
619 οἱ δ᾽ Höpfner

625 ἀνδρὸς γὰρ ἀγαθοῦ κῆδος αὐτὸς ἐσθλὸς ὢν
λήψῃ, κόρης Νηρῇδος ἰσοθέου γένους.
ἑξῆς καθίστω δεῦρό μου ποδός, τέκνον·
πρὸς μητέρ᾽, Ἰφιγένεια, μακαρίαν δέ με
ξέναισι ταῖσδε πλησία σταθεῖσα θές,
630 καὶ δεῦρο δὴ πατέρα πρόσειπε σὸν φίλον.]

<ΚΛΥΤΑΙΜΗΣΤΡΑ
γυναῖκες, ἢ γιγνώσκετ᾽ εἰ δόμων ἔσω
ἢ φροῦδός ἐστιν οὑμὸς Ἀγαμέμνων πόσις;

ΧΟΡΟΣ
πάρεστι· καὶ μὴν αὐτὸς ἐκ δόμων περᾷ.>

ΙΦΙΓΕΝΕΙΑ
ὦ μῆτερ, ὑποδραμοῦσά σ᾽—ὀργισθῇς δὲ μή—
πρὸς στέρνα πατρὸς στέρνα τἀμὰ προσβαλῶ.

[ΚΛΥΤΑΙΜΗΣΤΡΑ
ὦ σέβας ἐμοὶ μέγιστον, Ἀγαμέμνων ἄναξ,
ἥκομεν, ἐφετμαῖς οὐκ ἀπιστοῦσαι σέθεν.

ΙΦΙΓΕΝΕΙΑ
635 ἐγὼ δὲ βούλομαι τὰ σὰ στέρν᾽, ὦ πάτερ,
ὑποδραμοῦσα προσβαλεῖν διὰ χρόνου·
ποθῶ γὰρ ὄμμα <δὴ> σόν· ὀργισθῇς δὲ μή.]

626 κόρης Νηρῇδος Murray: τὸ Νηρηῖδος L   ἰσοθέου
γένους Diggle: ἰσόθεον γένος L
627 καθίστω Markland: κάθησο L
628 fort. τῆς μητρός, levius post 627 distincto
629 θές Camper: δός L
631 ante h. v. lac. indic. Kovacs

228

are yourself you will get a nobleman for a brother-in-law, the godlike son of the Nereid. Come to your mother, Iphigenia, stand near me and make me blessed in the eyes of these foreign ladies. Come here and speak to your dear father.]

Enter by Eisodos A IPHIGENIA *and* CLYTAEMESTRA.

⟨CLYTAEMESTRA
Ladies, can you tell me whether my husband Agamemnon is within? Or is he away?

CHORUS LEADER
He is here. Look, he himself is coming out of his tent.⟩

Enter AGAMEMNON *from the* skene.

IPHIGENIA
(*running to embrace her father*) O mother, I shall run ahead of you—do not be angry with me—and press my breast against the breast of my father!

[CLYTAEMESTRA
O most honored in my eyes, lord Agamemnon, we have come in obedience to your command.

IPHIGENIA
I want to run and fling myself at your breast, father, after so long a time. I greatly desire to see your face. Do not be angry.]

633–7 del. Bremi (635–7 iam Porson)
637 ⟨δὴ⟩ Tr³

ΚΛΥΤΑΙΜΗΣΤΡΑ

ἀλλ᾽, ὦ τέκνον, χρή· φιλοπάτωρ δ᾽ ἀεί ποτ᾽ εἶ
μάλιστα παίδων τῷδ᾽ ὅσους ἐγὼ ᾽τεκον.

[ΙΦΙΓΕΝΕΙΑ

640 ὦ πάτερ, ἐσεῖδόν σ᾽ ἀσμένη πολλῷ χρόνῳ.

ΑΓΑΜΕΜΝΩΝ

καὶ γὰρ πατὴρ σέ· τόδ᾽ ἴσον ὑπὲρ ἀμφοῖν λέγεις.]

ΙΦΙΓΕΝΕΙΑ

χαῖρ᾽· εὖ δέ μ᾽ ἀγαγὼν πρὸς σ᾽ ἐποίησας, πάτερ.

ΑΓΑΜΕΜΝΩΝ

οὐκ οἶδ᾽ ὅπως φῶ τοῦτο καὶ μὴ φῶ, τέκνον.

ΙΦΙΓΕΝΕΙΑ

ἔα·
ὡς οὐ βλέπεις ἕκηλον ἄσμενός μ᾽ ἰδών.

ΑΓΑΜΕΜΝΩΝ

645 πόλλ᾽ ἀνδρὶ βασιλεῖ καὶ στρατηλάτῃ μέλει.

ΙΦΙΓΕΝΕΙΑ

παρ᾽ ἐμοὶ γενοῦ νῦν, μὴ ᾽πὶ φροντίδας τρέπου.

ΑΓΑΜΕΜΝΩΝ

ἀλλ᾽ εἰμὶ παρὰ σοὶ νῦν ἅπας κοὐκ ἄλλοθι.

ΙΦΙΓΕΝΕΙΑ

μέθες νυν ὀφρὺν ὄμμα τ᾽ ἔκτεινον φίλον.

ΑΓΑΜΕΜΝΩΝ

ἰδού, γέγηθά σ᾽ ὡς γέγηθ᾽ ὁρῶν, τέκνον.

CLYTAEMESTRA

Well, daughter, that is quite right. Of all the children I bore
your father you have always loved him the most.

[IPHIGENIA

O father, how glad I am to see you! It has been a long time!

AGAMEMNON

And your father is glad to see you. You speak for us both.]

IPHIGENIA

Hello, father. It was good that you brought me here to see
you.

AGAMEMNON

I do not know how I can accept your words or deny them.

IPHIGENIA

But what is this? You look distressed: you were glad to see
me before.

AGAMEMNON

A king and commander has many things on his mind.

IPHIGENIA

Spend time now with me, not with your worries.

AGAMEMNON

I am wholly with you now, not elsewhere.

IPHIGENIA

Unfurrow your brow, then, and smooth the face I love.

AGAMEMNON

There! (*darkly*) You cannot guess how glad I am to see you.

---

639 τῷδ᾽ Bothe: τῶνδ᾽ L   640–1 del. Kovacs
644 ἔκηλον Blomfield: εὔκηλον L

EURIPIDES

ΙΦΙΓΕΝΕΙΑ

650 κᾆπειτα λείβεις δάκρυ' ἀπ' ὀμμάτων σέθεν;

ΑΓΑΜΕΜΝΩΝ

μακρὰ γὰρ ἡμῖν ἡ 'πιοῦσ' ἀπουσία.

ΙΦΙΓΕΝΕΙΑ

652 [οὐκ οἶδ' ὅ τι φῄς, οὐκ οἶδα, φίλτατ' ἐμοὶ πάτερ.]
662 ποῦ τοὺς Φρύγας λέγουσιν ᾠκίσθαι, πάτερ;

ΑΓΑΜΕΜΝΩΝ

663 οὗ μήποτ' οἰκεῖν ὤφελ' ὁ Πριάμου Πάρις.

ΙΦΙΓΕΝΕΙΑ

664 μακρὰν ἀπαίρεις, ὦ πάτερ, λιπὼν ἐμέ.

ΑΓΑΜΕΜΝΩΝ

665 [εἰς ταὐτόν, ὦ θύγατερ, ἥκεις σῷ πατρί.]
653 συνετὰ λέγουσα μᾶλλον εἰς οἶκτόν μ' ἄγεις.

ΙΦΙΓΕΝΕΙΑ

ἀσύνετά νυν ἐροῦμεν, εἰ σέ γ' εὐφρανῶ.

ΑΓΑΜΕΜΝΩΝ

655 παπαῖ. τὸ σιγᾶν οὐ σθένω· σὲ δ' ᾔνεσα.

ΙΦΙΓΕΝΕΙΑ

μέν', ὦ πάτερ, κατ' οἶκον ἐπὶ τέκνοις σέθεν.

ΑΓΑΜΕΜΝΩΝ

θέλω γε· τοῦτο δ' οὐκ ἔχων ἀλγύνομαι.

662–5 post 652 trai. Jackson deletis post alios 652 et 665
657 τοῦτο Günther: τὸ θέλειν L

232

IPHIGENIA

Can your eyes be filled with tears, then?

AGAMEMNON

Yes, for our coming separation is a long one.

IPHIGENIA

[I do not know, not know, what you mean, dearest father.]
Where do they say the Phrygians live, father?

AGAMEMNON

Where I wish Priam's son Paris had never dwelt!

IPHIGENIA

You set off on a long journey, leaving me behind.

AGAMEMNON

[You have come to the same point, daughter, as your
father.] By speaking intelligently you cause me to feel
more pity.

IPHIGENIA

Then I will speak foolishly if it will cheer you up.

AGAMEMNON

(to himself) Ah me, how hard to hold my tongue! (aloud) I
thank you, daughter.

IPHIGENIA

Stay at home, father, near your children!

AGAMEMNON

I want to, and since I cannot I feel pain.

ΙΦΙΓΕΝΕΙΑ

ὄλοιντο λόγχαι καὶ τὰ Μενέλεω κακά.

ΑΓΑΜΕΜΝΩΝ

ἄλλους ὀλεῖ πρόσθ' ἁμὲ διολέσαντ' ἔχει.

ΙΦΙΓΕΝΕΙΑ

660 ὡς πολὺν ἀπῆσθα χρόνον ἐν Αὐλίδος μυχοῖς.

ΑΓΑΜΕΜΝΩΝ

661 καὶ νῦν γέ μ' ἴσχει δή τι μὴ στέλλειν στρατόν.

ΙΦΙΓΕΝΕΙΑ

666 φεῦ·
εἴθ' ἦν καλόν σοι κἄμ' ἄγειν σύμπλουν ὁμοῦ.

ΑΓΑΜΕΜΝΩΝ

ἔτ' ἔστι καὶ σοὶ πλοῦς, ἵν' ⟨οὐ⟩ μνήσῃ πατρός.

ΙΦΙΓΕΝΕΙΑ

σὺν μητρὶ πλεύσασ' ἢ μόνη πορεύσομαι;

ΑΓΑΜΕΜΝΩΝ

μόνη, μονωθεῖσ' ἀπὸ πατρὸς καὶ μητέρος.

ΙΦΙΓΕΝΕΙΑ

670 οὔ πού μ' ἐς ἄλλα δώματ' οἰκίζεις, πάτερ;

ΑΓΑΜΕΜΝΩΝ

ἐατέ· οὐ χρὴ τοιάδ' εἰδέναι κόρας.

666 σοι κἄμ' . . . ὁμοῦ Diggle: μοι σοί τ' . . . ἐμέ L
667 ἔτ' ἔστι Porson: αἰτεῖς τι; L   ⟨οὐ⟩ Musgrave
671 ἐατέ Stadtmüller: ἔα γε L

234

IPHIGENIA

War spears and Menelaus' woes—destruction take them!

AGAMEMNON

(*darkly*) Others ere then shall be destroyed by what has destroyed me!

IPHIGENIA

What a long time you have been gone in Aulis!

AGAMEMNON

Yes, and even now something prevents me from launching the expedition.

IPHIGENIA

Ah! How I wish it were proper for you to take me with you as a shipmate!

AGAMEMNON

You too have a voyage still to make, to a place where you will forget your father.

IPHIGENIA

Will I sail with my mother or alone?

AGAMEMNON

Alone, separated from mother and father.

IPHIGENIA

Can it be that you are settling me in another house, father?

AGAMEMNON

No more of this! Maidens should know nothing of such matters!

ΙΦΙΓΕΝΕΙΑ

σπεῦδ' ἐκ Φρυγῶν μοι, θέμενος εὖ τἀκεῖ, πάτερ.

ΑΓΑΜΕΜΝΩΝ

θῦσαί με θυσίαν πρῶτα δεῖ τιν' ἐνθάδε.

ΙΦΙΓΕΝΕΙΑ

ποίοισιν ἱεροῖς χρὴ τό γ' εὐσεβὲς σκοπεῖν;

ΑΓΑΜΕΜΝΩΝ

675   εἴσῃ σύ· χερνίβων γὰρ ἑστήξῃ πέλας.

ΙΦΙΓΕΝΕΙΑ

στήσομεν ἄρ' ἀμφὶ βωμόν, ὦ πάτερ, χορούς;

ΑΓΑΜΕΜΝΩΝ

ζηλῶ σὲ μᾶλλον ἢ 'μὲ τοῦ μηδὲν φρονεῖν.
  χώρει δὲ μελάθρων ἐντός—ὀφθῆναι κόραις
  πικρόν—φίλημα δοῦσα δεξιάν τέ μοι,
680   μέλλουσα δαρὸν πατρὸς ἀποικήσειν χρόνον.
  [ὦ στέρνα καὶ παρῇδες, ὦ ξανθαὶ κόμαι,
  ὡς ἄχθος ἡμῖν ἐγένεθ' ἡ Φρυγῶν πόλις
  Ἑλένη τε. παύω τοὺς λόγους· ταχεῖα γὰρ
  νοτὶς διώκει μ' ὀμμάτων ψαύσαντά σου.
685   ἴθ' ἐς μέλαθρα. σὲ δὲ παραιτοῦμαι τάδε,
  Λήδας γένεθλον, εἰ κατῳκτίσθην ἄγαν,
  μέλλων Ἀχιλλεῖ θυγατέρ' ἐκδώσειν ἐμήν.
  ἀποστολαὶ γὰρ μακάριαι μέν, ἀλλ' ὅμως
  δάκνουσι τοὺς τεκόντας, ὅταν ἄλλοις δόμοις
690   παῖδας παραδιδῷ πολλὰ μοχθήσας πατήρ.]

674 ποίοισιν Rauchenstein: ἀλλὰ ξὺν L

IPHIGENIA

Please hurry back from Phrygia, father, when you have
settled things there.

AGAMEMNON

I must make a certain sacrifice here first.

IPHIGENIA

With what rites must you determine what the gods re-
quire?

AGAMEMNON

You'll see: you will be standing near the lustral basin.

IPHIGENIA

Shall we then set up choruses about the altar, father?

AGAMEMNON

How I wish I knew as little as you do!

But go into the tent—maidens don't enjoy being looked
at—first giving me a kiss and your hand: you are going to
dwell for a long time far from your father.

He embraces her, and she exits into the skene.

[O breast and cheeks, O golden hair, what a burden the city
of the Phrygians and Helen have proved to us! I say no
more: the tears come quickly to my eyes as I hold you. Go
into the house. And I beg your forgiveness, daughter of
Leda, if I have lamented too much when about to give my
daughter in marriage to Achilles. Such a sending away is
blessed, to be sure, but it stings the hearts of parents when
the father who has worked so hard hands his daughters
over to another house.]

681–94 in susp. voc. Diggle (alios alii del. edd.)

ΚΛΥΤΑΙΜΗΣΤΡΑ

[οὐχ ὧδ' ἀσύνετός εἰμι, πείσεσθαι δέ με
καὐτὴν δόκει τάδ', ὥστε μή σε νουθετεῖν,
ὅταν σὺν ὑμεναίοισιν ἐξάγω κόρην·
ἀλλ' ὁ νόμος αὐτὰ τῷ χρόνῳ συνισχνανεῖ.]

695   τοὔνομα μὲν οὖν παῖδ' οἶδ' ὅτῳ κατήνεσας,
γένους δὲ ποίου χὠπόθεν μαθεῖν θέλω.

ΑΓΑΜΕΜΝΩΝ

Αἴγινα θυγάτηρ ἐγένετ' Ἀσωποῦ πατρός.

ΚΛΥΤΑΙΜΗΣΤΡΑ

ταύτην δὲ θνητῶν ἢ θεῶν ἔζευξε τίς;

ΑΓΑΜΕΜΝΩΝ

Ζεύς· Αἰακὸν δ' ἔφυσεν, Οἰνώνης πρόμον.

ΚΛΥΤΑΙΜΗΣΤΡΑ

700   τὰ δ' Αἰακοῦ παῖς τίς κατέσχε δώματα;

ΑΓΑΜΕΜΝΩΝ

Πηλεύς· ὁ Πηλεὺς δ' ἔσχε Νηρέως κόρην.

ΚΛΥΤΑΙΜΗΣΤΡΑ

θεοῦ διδόντος ἢ βίᾳ θεῶν λαβών;

ΑΓΑΜΕΜΝΩΝ

Ζεὺς ἠγγύησε καὶ δίδωσ' ὁ κύριος.

ΚΛΥΤΑΙΜΗΣΤΡΑ

γαμεῖ δὲ ποῦ νιν; ἢ κατ' οἶδμα πόντιον;

692 μή] fort. δεῖ vel χρή
700 τὰ Elmsley: τοῦ L

CLYTAEMESTRA

[No need to tell me this: I am not unfeeling, and you must suppose that I too shall be similarly affected when I send my daughter forth with wedding songs. But custom, in league with time, shall cause this to abate.]

Well, I know the name of the man to whom you promised our daughter, yet I would like to know what family and what region he comes from.

AGAMEMNON

Aegina was the daughter of Asopus.[15]

CLYTAEMESTRA

And was it god or mortal married her?

AGAMEMNON

Zeus. He sired Aeacus, Oenone's lord.[16]

CLYTAEMESTRA

Who claimed as heir the house of Aeacus?

AGAMEMNON

Peleus. And Peleus married Nereus' daughter.[17]

CLYTAEMESTRA

With a god's blessing or despite the gods?

AGAMEMNON

It was Zeus who gave her, Zeus who was her lord.

CLYTAEMESTRA

Where did he marry her? Was it in the sea?

[15] A river god.
[16] Oenone is another name for the island of Aegina.
[17] Thetis.

ΑΓΑΜΕΜΝΩΝ

705 Χείρων ἵν᾿ οἰκεῖ σεμνὰ Πηλίου βάθρα.

ΚΛΥΤΑΙΜΗΣΤΡΑ

οὗ φασι Κενταύρειον ᾠκίσθαι γένος;

ΑΓΑΜΕΜΝΩΝ

ἐνταῦθ᾿ ἔδαισαν Πηλέως γάμους θεοί.

ΚΛΥΤΑΙΜΗΣΤΡΑ

Θέτις δ᾿ ἔθρεψεν ἢ πατὴρ Ἀχιλλέα;

ΑΓΑΜΕΜΝΩΝ

Χείρων, ἵν᾿ ἤθη μὴ μάθοι κακῶν βροτῶν.

ΚΛΥΤΑΙΜΗΣΤΡΑ

710 φεῦ·
σοφός γ᾿ ὁ θρέψας χὠ διδοὺς σοφώτερος.

ΑΓΑΜΕΜΝΩΝ

τοιόσδε παιδὸς σῆς ἀνὴρ ἔσται πόσις.

ΚΛΥΤΑΙΜΗΣΤΡΑ

οὐ μεμπτός. οἰκεῖ δ᾿ ἄστυ ποῖον Ἑλλάδος;

ΑΓΑΜΕΜΝΩΝ

Ἀπιδανὸν ἀμφὶ ποταμὸν ἐν Φθίας ὅροις.

ΚΛΥΤΑΙΜΗΣΤΡΑ

ἐκεῖσ᾿ ἀπάξεις σὴν ἐμήν τε παρθένον;

ΑΓΑΜΕΜΝΩΝ

715 κείνῳ μελήσει ταῦτα τῷ κεκτημένῳ.

ΚΛΥΤΑΙΜΗΣΤΡΑ

ἀλλ᾿ εὐτυχοίτην. τίνι δ᾿ ἐν ἡμέρᾳ γαμεῖ;

AGAMEMNON

In Pelion's holy glens, where Chiron dwells.

CLYTAEMESTRA

Where, as men say, the Centaurs make their home?

AGAMEMNON

'Twas there the gods made Peleus' wedding feast.

CLYTAEMESTRA

Did Thetis raise Achilles, or his father?

AGAMEMNON

It was Chiron, lest he learn the ways of knaves.

CLYTAEMESTRA

Ah, wise the tutor, the entruster wiser still!

AGAMEMNON

The husband of your daughter—such is he.

CLYTAEMESTRA

I find no fault. In Greece where does he dwell?

AGAMEMNON

In Phthia near the banks of Apidanus.

CLYTAEMESTRA

Your girl and mine—is that then where you'll take her?

AGAMEMNON

That will be his concern, the one who weds her.

CLYTAEMESTRA

May they be happy! When's the wedding day?

---

714 ἀπάξεις Dobree: -ει L

EURIPIDES

ΑΓΑΜΕΜΝΩΝ
ὅταν σελήνης ἐντελὴς ἔλθῃ κύκλος.

ΚΛΥΤΑΙΜΗΣΤΡΑ
προτέλεια δ' ἤδη παιδὸς ἔσφαξας θεᾷ;

ΑΓΑΜΕΜΝΩΝ
μέλλω· 'πὶ ταύτῃ καὶ καθέσταμεν τύχῃ.

ΚΛΥΤΑΙΜΗΣΤΡΑ
720   κᾆτα δαίσεις τοὺς γάμους ἐς ὕστερον;

[ΑΓΑΜΕΜΝΩΝ
θύσας γε θύμαθ' ἁμὲ χρὴ θῦσαι θεοῖς.

ΚΛΥΤΑΙΜΗΣΤΡΑ
ἡμεῖς δὲ θοίνην ποῦ γυναιξὶ θήσομεν;

ΑΓΑΜΕΜΝΩΝ
ἐνθάδε παρ' εὐπρύμνοισιν Ἀργείων πλάταις.

ΚΛΥΤΑΙΜΗΣΤΡΑ
κακῶς ἀναξίως τε· συνενέγκαι δ' ὅμως.

ΑΓΑΜΕΜΝΩΝ
725   οἶσθ' οὖν ὃ δρᾶσον, ὦ γύναι· πιθοῦ δέ μοι.

ΚΛΥΤΑΙΜΗΣΤΡΑ
τί χρῆμα; πείθεσθαι γὰρ εἴθισμαι σέθεν.]

ΑΓΑΜΕΜΝΩΝ
ἡμεῖς μὲν ἐνθάδ', οὗπέρ ἐσθ' ὁ νυμφίος . . .

717 ἐντελὴς Musgrave: εὐτυχὴς L
721–6 del. Kovacs (720–6 in susp. voc. Diggle, 720–1 del.
Harberton, 723–4 Günther)

AGAMEMNON

When the moon's orb appears once more in fullness.

CLYTAEMESTRA

Have you made the early offering to the goddess?

AGAMEMNON

I shall. That is the business I'm upon.

CLYTAEMESTRA

You'll have the wedding banquet somewhat later?

[AGAMEMNON

Yes, when I've made the sacrifice I must.

CLYTAEMESTRA

Where shall we celebrate the women's feast?

AGAMEMNON

Here by the Argive vessels with fair prows.

CLYTAEMESTRA

She deserves better! Still may it be for good!

AGAMEMNON

What you must do is this: obey my words.

CLYTAEMESTRA

In what? My custom is to be obedient.]

AGAMEMNON

We, for our part, here where the bridegroom is . . .

---

724 κακῶς ἀναξίως Heath, Musgrave: καλῶς ἀναγκαίως L
726 εἰθίσμεσθά σοι Hermann

ΚΛΥΤΑΙΜΗΣΤΡΑ

μητρὸς τί χωρὶς δράσεθ', ἁμὲ δρᾶν χρεών;

ΑΓΑΜΕΜΝΩΝ

. . . ἐκδώσομεν σὴν παῖδα Δαναϊδῶν μέτα.

ΚΛΥΤΑΙΜΗΣΤΡΑ

730   ἡμᾶς δὲ ποῦ χρὴ τηνικαῦτα τυγχάνειν;

ΑΓΑΜΕΜΝΩΝ

χώρει πρὸς Ἄργος παρθένους τε τημέλει.

ΚΛΥΤΑΙΜΗΣΤΡΑ

λιποῦσα παῖδα; τίς δ' ἀνασχήσει φλόγα;

ΑΓΑΜΕΜΝΩΝ

ἐγὼ παρέξω φῶς ὃ νυμφίοις πρέπει.

ΚΛΥΤΑΙΜΗΣΤΡΑ

οὐχ ὁ νόμος οὗτος οὐδὲ φαῦλ' ἡγητέα.

ΑΓΑΜΕΜΝΩΝ

735   οὐ καλὸν ἐν ὄχλῳ σ' ἐξομιλεῖσθαι στρατοῦ.

ΚΛΥΤΑΙΜΗΣΤΡΑ

καλὸν τεκοῦσαν τἀμά μ' ἐκδοῦναι τέκνα.

ΑΓΑΜΕΜΝΩΝ

καὶ τάς γ' ἐν οἴκῳ μὴ μόνας εἶναι κόρας.

ΚΛΥΤΑΙΜΗΣΤΡΑ

ὀχυροῖσι παρθενῶσι φρουροῦνται καλῶς.

734 οὐδὲ . . . ἡγητέα Tucker: σὺ δὲ . . . ἡγῇ τάδε L
733–4 fort. delendi
735 ἐξομιλῆσαι England

CLYTAEMESTRA

What mother's office will you do without me?

AGAMEMNON

. . . will marry her amid the sons of Danaus.

CLYTAEMESTRA

While this is happening where must I be found?

AGAMEMNON

Return to Argos, take care of our daughters.

CLYTAEMESTRA

Leaving my girl? Who then shall raise the torch?[18]

AGAMEMNON

I shall provide the light the groom requires.

CLYTAEMESTRA

That is not right: one should not be so lax.

AGAMEMNON

It's not right you should dwell amidst the army.

CLYTAEMESTRA

It's right that I should give my girl in marriage.

AGAMEMNON

Right too your daughters not be left alone.

CLYTAEMESTRA

They're well secured within their maiden chambers.

18 It was the custom for the mother of the bride to hold a torch to provide light.

ΑΓΑΜΕΜΝΩΝ

πιθοῦ.

ΚΛΥΤΑΙΜΗΣΤΡΑ

μὰ τὴν ἄνασσαν Ἀργείαν θεάν.
740 ἐλθὼν δὲ τάξω πρᾶσσε, τὰν δόμοις δ᾽ ἐγώ·
ἃ χρὴ παρεῖναι νυμφίοισι πορσυνῶ.

ΑΓΑΜΕΜΝΩΝ

οἴμοι· μάτην ᾖξ᾽, ἐλπίδος δ᾽ ἀπεσφάλην,
ἐξ ὀμμάτων δάμαρτ᾽ ἀποστεῖλαι θέλων.
σοφίζομαι δὲ κἀπὶ τοῖσι φιλτάτοις
745 τέχνας πορίζω, πανταχῇ νικώμενος.
ὅμως δὲ σὺν Κάλχαντι τῷ θυηπόλῳ
κοινῇ τὸ τῇ θεῷ φίλον, ἐμοὶ δ᾽ οὐκ εὐτυχές,
ἐξευπορήσων εἶμι, μόχθον Ἑλλάδος.
[χρὴ δ᾽ ἐν δόμοισιν ἄνδρα τὸν σοφὸν τρέφειν
750 γυναῖκα χρηστὴν κἀγαθήν, ἢ μὴ γαμεῖν.]
στρ.

ΧΟΡΟΣ

ἥξει δὴ Σιμόεντα καὶ
δίνας ἀργυροειδεῖς
ἄγυρις Ἑλλάνων στρατιᾶς
ἀνά τε ναυσὶν καὶ σὺν ὅπλοις
755 Ἰλίου ἐς πετραίας
Φοιβήιον δάπεδον,

741 πορσυνῶ Jackson: παρθένοις L
747 τῇ θεῷ Rauchenstein: τῆς θεοῦ L
749–50 del. Hartung   750 γαμεῖν Hermann: τρέφειν L

AGAMEMNON

Be ruled by me!

CLYTAEMESTRA

No, by the goddess who rules Argos![19] You go and manage things outside the house, but I shall manage matters within. I shall provide what the bridal pair require.

Exit CLYTAEMESTRA *into the* skene.

AGAMEMNON

Ah, me! My eagerness has been for nothing! I tried to send my wife away but failed to reach my goal. I engage in subtlety and use craft on those closest to me, but I am defeated at every turn. Still, working together with Calchas the priest I shall go and provide what the goddess wants and what spells my unhappiness for me and toil for Hellas' hands. [A man who is wise must keep in his house a wife who is good and true—or he should not marry.]

Exit AGAMEMNON *by Eisodos B.*

CHORUS

They will come to the Simois
and its silvery eddies,
the whole assemblage of the Greek army,
and on their ships with spear in hand
they will reach the Phoebus-built land
of rocky Ilium.

19 Hera, who is also patron of marriage.

---

755 Ἰλίου ἐς πετραίας Willink: Ἴλιον ἐς τὸ Τροίας L

τὰν Κασσάνδραν ἵν' ἀκού-
ω ῥίπτειν ξανθοὺς πλοκάμους
χλωροκόμῳ στεφάνῳ δάφνας
760 κοσμηθεῖσαν, ὅταν θεοῦ
μαντόσυνοι πνεύσωσ' ἀνάγκαι.

ἀντ

στάσονται δ' ἐπὶ περγάμων
Τροίας ἀμφί τε τείχη
Τρῶες, ὅταν χάλκασπις Ἄρης
765 πόντιος εὐπρῴροιο πλάτας
εἰρεσίᾳ πελάζῃ
Σιμουντίοις ὀχετοῖς,
τὰν τῶν ἐν αἰθέρι δισ-
σῶν Διοσκούρων Ἑλέναν
770 ἐκ Πριάμου κομίσαι θέλων
γᾶς εἰς Ἑλλάδα δοριπόνων
ἀσπίσι καὶ λόγχαις Ἀχαιῶν.

ἐπῳδ.

[Πέργαμον δὲ Φρυγῶν πόλιν
λαΐνους περὶ πύργους
775 κυκλώσας Ἄρει φονίῳ,
λαιμοτόμους σπάσας κεφαλάς,
πέρσας πόλισμα κατ' ἄκρας,
θήσει κόρας πολυκλαύ-
780 τους δάμαρτά τε Πριάμου.

There, I am told, Cassandra
tosses her yellow hair,
adorned with the green crown
of myrtle when she is controlled
by the god's prophetic inspiration.

The Trojans will stand upon the citadel
of Troy and about its walls
when Ares with his shield of bronze
approaches the rivulets of Simois,
borne over the waves by an argosy
of broad-prowed ships,
trying to fetch Helen, the sister
of the two heavenly Dioscuri,
from Priam's land back to Greece
by the shields and lances
of the toil-laden Achaeans.

[Encircling Pergamum the Phrygian city
about its walls of stone
with deadly war
he shall take away severed heads,
sack the city utterly,
and make the maidens weep
and also Priam's wife.

---

769 Διοσκούρων] κάσιν Κούρων Willink
771 γᾶς εἰς Willink: ἐς γᾶν L   δοριπόνων Kirchhoff: -οις L
773–83 del. Hartung
776 σπάσας κεφαλάς Weil: κ- σ- L
777 πέρσας πόλισμα κατ᾽ ἄκρας Weil: πόλισμα Τροίας
πέρσας κατ᾽ ἄκρας πόλιν L

ἁ δὲ Διὸς Ἑλένα κόρα
πολύκλαυτος εἴσεται
πόσιν προλιποῦσα.]
785 μήτ᾽ ἐμοὶ μήτ᾽ ἐμοῖσι τέκνων τέκνοις
ἐλπὶς ἅδε ποτ᾽ ἔλθοι,
οἵαν αἱ πολύχρυσοι
Λυδαὶ καὶ Φρυγῶν ἄλοχοι
σχήσουσι, παρ᾽ ἱστοῖς
790 μυθεῦσαι τάδ᾽ ἐς ἀλλήλας·
Τίς ἄρα μ᾽ εὐπλοκάμου κόμας
ῥῦμα δακρυόεν τανύσας
πατρίδος ὀλλυμένας ἀπολωτιεῖ;
διὰ σέ, τὰν κύκνου δολιχαύχενος γόνον,
795 εἰ δὴ φάτις ἔτυμος ὥς
σ᾽ ἔτεκεν ὄρνιθι πταμένῳ ⟨Λήδα⟩
Διὸς ὅτ᾽ ἠλλάχθη δέμας, εἴτ᾽
ἐν δέλτοις Πιερίσιν
μῦθοι τάδ᾽ ἐς ἀνθρώπους
800 ἤνεγκαν παρὰ καιρὸν ἄλλως.

ΑΧΙΛΛΕΥΣ

ποῦ τῶν Ἀχαιῶν ἐνθάδ᾽ ὁ στρατηλάτης;
τίς ἂν φράσειε προσπόλων τὸν Πηλέως
ζητοῦντά νιν παῖδ᾽ ἐν πύλαις Ἀχιλλέα;
οὐκ ἐξ ἴσου γὰρ μένομεν Εὐρίπου πέλας;
805 οἱ μὲν γὰρ ἡμῶν, ὄντες ἄζυγες γάμων,

---

782 εἴσεται Willink: ἐσεῖται L
789 σχήσουσι Tyrwhitt: στή- L

But Zeus's daughter Helen
shall learn that it was to her cost
that she left her husband.]
May no foreboding
ever come to me or to my children's children
like that to be felt by the gilded Lydian women
and the wives of the Phrygians
as by their looms
they say to one another,
"What man, then, tightening his grasp
on my luxuriant hair to make me weep,
shall pluck me from my perished fatherland?"
And all on account of you, child of the long-necked swan,
if the tale is true that ⟨Leda⟩
bore you to a winged bird,
Zeus in altered shape—or it may be
that on the tablets of the Pierian Muses
these tales are borne to men
falsely and to no purpose.

Enter ACHILLES *by Eisodos B.*

ACHILLES

Where in this place is the Achaean general to be found?
One of his servants, tell him that the son of Peleus is look-
ing for him here at his gates! Are we not, all of us equally,
waiting idly near the Euripus? Some of us, being unmar-

---

790 μυθεύουσαι Matthiae   792 ῥῦμα Hermann: ἔρυμα L
796 σ᾽ ἔτεκεν Hermann: ἔτυχε Λήδα L   ⟨Λήδα⟩ (vel
⟨μάτηρ⟩) Willink
804 interrogationis nota dist. Hermann

οἴκους ἐρήμους ἐκλιπόντες, ἐνθάδε
θάσσουσ' ἐπ' ἀκταῖς, οἱ δ' ἔχοντες εὔνιδας
καὶ παῖδας· οὕτω δεινὸς ἐπτέρωκ' ἔρως
τῆσδε στρατείας Ἑλλάδ' οὐκ ἄνευ θεῶν.
810   τοὐμὸν μὲν οὖν δίκαιον ἐμὲ λέγειν χρέος,
ἄλλος δὲ χρῄζων αὐτὸς ὑπὲρ αὑτοῦ φράσει.
γῆν γὰρ λιπὼν Φάρσαλον ἠδὲ Πηλέα
μένω 'πὶ λεπταῖς ταισίδ' Εὐρίπου ῥοαῖς,
Μυρμιδόνας ἴσχων· οἱ δ' ἀεὶ προσκείμενοι
815   λέγουσ'· Ἀχιλλεῦ, τί μένομεν; πόσον χρόνον
ἔτ' ἐκμετρῆσαι χρὴ πρὸς Ἰλίου στόλον;
δρᾶ <δ'>, εἴ τι δράσεις, ἢ ἄπαγ' οἴκαδε στρατόν,
τὰ τῶν Ἀτρειδῶν μὴ μένων μελλήματα.

ΚΛΥΤΑΙΜΗΣΤΡΑ

ὦ παῖ θεᾶς Νηρῇδος, ἔνδοθεν λόγων
820   τῶν σῶν ἀκούσασ' ἐξέβην πρὸ δωμάτων.

ΑΧΙΛΛΕΥΣ

ὦ πότνι' Αἰδώς, τήνδε τίνα λεύσσω ποτὲ
γυναῖκα, μορφὴν εὐπρεπῆ κεκτημένην;

ΚΛΥΤΑΙΜΗΣΤΡΑ

οὐ θαῦμά σ' ἡμᾶς ἀγνοεῖν, οἷς μὴ πάρος
προσῆκες· αἰνῶ δ' ὅτι σέβεις τὸ σωφρονεῖν.

---

808 καὶ παῖδας Musgrave: ἄπαιδες L
808 ἐπτέρωκ' Jackson: ἐμπέπτωκ' L, quo servato πᾶσιν pro
Ἑλλάδ' 809 Hartung   810 χρέος Hennig: χρεών L
811 δὲ Kirchhoff: δ' ὁ L
813 ῥοαῖς Markland: πνοαῖς L

ried, have left our houses untended and sit here upon the
shore, while those who have them have left wives and chil-
dren. So great is the passion for this expedition that made
Hellas all astir by the will of the gods.

It is right for me to describe my own case. Someone
else who wants to can speak for himself. I have left Phar-
salus and Peleus behind and now wait beside the gentle
currents of the Euripus, keeping my Myrmidons in check.
But they, always pressing me, say, "Achilles, why are we
waiting? How much more time must we measure out on
this expedition against Troy? If you mean to do something,
do it—or take the army back home and do not wait around
for the laggard sons of Atreus!"

Enter from the skene CLYTAEMESTRA.

CLYTAEMESTRA

Son of the Nereid, I heard your words within and have
come out in front of the house.

ACHILLES

Lady Modesty, who is this woman I see here, one so lovely
to behold?

CLYTAEMESTRA

It is not surprising that you do not know me: we had no
connection before now. I am glad that you honor modesty.

---

814 δ' Monk: μ' L
815 πόσον Monk: ποῖον L
816 ἐκμετρεῖν χρὴ τὸν πρὸς Ἴλιον Wecklein
817 ⟨δ'⟩ Fix   823 οἷς Nauck: οὓς L
824 προσῆκες Nauck: προσέβης L

ΑΧΙΛΛΕΥΣ

825 τίς δ' εἶ; τί δ' ἦλθες Δαναϊδῶν ἐς σύλλογον,
γυνὴ πρὸς ἄνδρας ἀσπίσιν πεφαργμένους;

ΚΛΥΤΑΙΜΗΣΤΡΑ

Λήδας μέν εἰμι παῖς, Κλυταιμήστρα δέ μοι
ὄνομα, πόσις δέ μοὔστιν Ἀγαμέμνων ἄναξ.

ΑΧΙΛΛΕΥΣ

καλῶς ἔλεξας ἐν βραχεῖ τὰ καίρια.
830 αἰσχρὸν δέ μοι γυναιξὶ συμβάλλειν λόγους.

ΚΛΥΤΑΙΜΗΣΤΡΑ

μεῖνον—τί φεύγεις;—δεξιάν τ' ἐμῇ χερὶ
σύναψον, ἀρχὴν μακαρίων νυμφευμάτων.

ΑΧΙΛΛΕΥΣ

τί φῄς; ἐγώ σοι δεξιάν; αἰδοίμεθ' ἂν
Ἀγαμέμνον', εἰ ψαύοιμεν ὧν μή μοι θέμις.

ΚΛΥΤΑΙΜΗΣΤΡΑ

835 θέμις μάλιστα, τὴν ἐμὴν ἐπεὶ γαμεῖς
παῖδ', ὦ θεᾶς παῖ ποντίας Νηρηίδος.

ΑΧΙΛΛΕΥΣ

ποίους γάμους φῄς; ἀφασία μ' ἔχει, γύναι,
εἰ μή τι παρανοοῦσα καινουργεῖς λόγον.

ΚΛΥΤΑΙΜΗΣΤΡΑ

πᾶσιν τόδ' ἐμπέφυκεν, αἰδεῖσθαι φίλους
840 καινοὺς ὁρῶσι καὶ γάμου μεμνημένους.

<hr>

832 μακαρίων Markland: -ίαν L

ACHILLES

But who are you? Why have you, a woman, come to the mustering place of the Greeks, to men armored with shields?

CLYTAEMESTRA

I am the daughter of Leda, my name is Clytaemestra, and my husband is Agamemnon.

ACHILLES

How well you tell me the essentials in brief compass! But it is disgraceful for me to be speaking to a woman. (*He begins to leave.*)

CLYTAEMESTRA

Stay: why are you running away? Join your right hand with mine, to mark the beginning of blessed nuptials!

ACHILLES

What do you mean? Take your hand? I? I would feel shame before Agamemnon if I touched what I had no right to.

CLYTAEMESTRA

You have every right, son of the Nereid: you are marrying my daughter!

ACHILLES

What marriage are you talking about? I am struck speechless and wonder whether these strange words you say come from madness.

CLYTAEMESTRA

It is natural for anyone to feel inhibition when they see relatives who are new to them and are speaking of marriage.

EURIPIDES

ΑΧΙΛΛΕΥΣ

οὐπώποτ' ἐμνήστευσα παῖδα σήν, γύναι,
οὐδ' ἐξ Ἀτρειδῶν ἦλθέ μοι λόγος γάμων.

ΚΛΥΤΑΙΜΗΣΤΡΑ

τί δῆτ' ἂν εἴη; σὺ πάλιν αὖ λόγοις ἐμοῖς
εἴκαζ'· ἐμοὶ γὰρ θαύματ' ἐστὶ τὰ παρὰ σοῦ.

ΑΧΙΛΛΕΥΣ

845 θαύμαζε· κοινὸν <δ'> ἐστιν εἰκάζειν τάδε·
ἄμφω γὰρ ἐψευδόμεθα τοῖς λόγοις ἴσως.

ΚΛΥΤΑΙΜΗΣΤΡΑ

ἀλλ' ἦ πέπονθα δεινά; μαστεύω γάμους
οὐκ ὄντας, ὡς εἴξασιν· αἰδοῦμαι τάδε.

ΑΧΙΛΛΕΥΣ

ἴσως ἐκερτόμησε κἀμὲ καὶ σέ τις.
850 ἀλλ' ἀμελίᾳ δὸς αὐτὰ καὶ φαύλως φέρε.

ΚΛΥΤΑΙΜΗΣΤΡΑ

χαῖρ'· οὐ γὰρ ὀρθοῖς ὄμμασίν σ' ἔτ' εἰσορῶ,
ψευδὴς γενομένη καὶ παθοῦσ' ἀνάξια.

ΑΧΙΛΛΕΥΣ

καὶ σοὶ τόδ' ἐστὶν ἐξ ἐμοῦ· πόσιν δὲ σὸν
στείχω ματεύσων τῶνδε δωμάτων ἔσω.

843 λόγοις ἐμοῖς Diggle: -ους -οὺς L
844–5 εἴκαζ' . . . θαύμαζε Jackson: θαύμαζ' . . . εἴκαζε L
845 <δ'> Jackson
847 μαστεύω Nauck: μνηστεύω L

ACHILLES

I was never a suitor for your daughter's hand, lady, nor have the sons of Atreus said anything to me about a marriage.

CLYTAEMESTRA

What can be happening? Try again to guess on the basis of what I have told you. What you say amazes me.

ACHILLES

You may well feel amazement. But we can guess at these things in common. Perhaps we are both being tripped up by words.

CLYTAEMESTRA

Can it be that I have been terribly treated? I am eager for a nonexistent marriage, as it seems. I am abashed.

ACHILLES

Perhaps someone has fooled both you and me. But pay it no attention and treat it as nothing.

CLYTAEMESTRA

Farewell! I can no longer look you in the eye since I have spoken what is not so and received undeserved treatment!

ACHILLES

I feel the same toward you. But I am going to look for your husband inside the tent.

He starts to go toward the central door of the skene. *From one of the side doors the* OLD MAN *appears, speaking through the half-opened door.*

ΠΡΕΣΒΥΤΗΣ

855 ὦ ξέν’, Αἰακοῦ γένεθλον, μεῖνον· ὦ, σέ τοι λέγω,
τὸν θεᾶς γεγῶτα παῖδα, καὶ σέ, τὴν Λήδας κόρην.

ΑΧΙΛΛΕΥΣ

τίς ὁ καλῶν πύλας παροίξας; ὡς τεταρβηκὸς καλεῖ.

ΠΡΕΣΒΥΤΗΣ

δοῦλος, οὐχ ἁβρύνομαι τῷδ’· ἡ τύχη γὰρ οὐκ ἐᾷ.

ΑΧΙΛΛΕΥΣ

τίνος; ἐμὸς μὲν οὐχί· χωρὶς τἀμὰ κἀγαμέμνονος.

ΠΡΕΣΒΥΤΗΣ

860 τῆσδε τῆς πάροιθεν οἴκων, Τυνδάρεω δόντος
πατρός.

ΑΧΙΛΛΕΥΣ

ἕσταμεν· φράζ’, εἴ τι χρῄζεις, ὧν μ’ ἐπέσχες
οὕνεκα.

ΠΡΕΣΒΥΤΗΣ

ἦ μόνω παρόντε δῆτα ταῖσδ’ ἐφέστατον πύλαις;

ΑΧΙΛΛΕΥΣ

ὡς μόνοιν λέγοις ἄν, ἔξω δ’ ἐλθὲ βασιλείων δόμων.

ΠΡΕΣΒΥΤΗΣ

ὦ Τύχη πρόνοιά θ’ ἡμή, σώσαθ’ οὓς ἐγὼ θέλω.

---

857 τεταρβηκὸς England cl. *Alc.* 773: -κὼς L
862 παρόντε Porson: πάροιθεν L
863 μόνοιν Markland: -οις L

OLD MAN

Stranger, descendant of Aeacus, wait! I mean you, son of
the goddess! And you, daughter of Leda!

ACHILLES

Who is calling me from the half-opened door? What a
frightened call he makes!

OLD MAN

A slave. I do not plume myself on this: my fate does not
allow me to.

ACHILLES

Whose slave? Not at any rate one of mine, for my posses-
sions and Agamemnon's are separate.

OLD MAN

This woman's, who is in front of the tent, a gift of her father
Tyndareus.

ACHILLES

I stand and wait. Tell me what you want and why you have
stopped me.

OLD MAN

Is it only the two of you who are here standing at the gate?

ACHILLES

You may speak in the knowledge that we are alone. Come
out of the king's tent.

He emerges from the skene.

OLD MAN

O Fortune and my foresight, save those I have in mind!

ΑΧΙΛΛΕΥΣ

865 ὁ λόγος ἐς μέλλοντα σῶσαι χρόνον· ἔχει δ' ὄκνον
τινά.

⟨ΠΡΕΣΒΥΤΗΣ

δεξίαν, ἄνασσα, σύμβαλ' ἔκλυσίν τ' αἴνει κακῶν.⟩

ΚΛΥΤΑΙΜΗΣΤΡΑ

δεξιᾶς ἕκατι μὴ μέλλ', εἴ τί μοι χρῄζεις λέγειν.

ΠΡΕΣΒΥΤΗΣ

οἶσθα δῆτά μ', ὅστις ὢν σοὶ καὶ τέκνοις εὔνους
ἔφυν;

ΚΛΥΤΑΙΜΗΣΤΡΑ

οἶδά σ' ὄντ' ἐγὼ παλαιὸν δωμάτων ἐμῶν λάτριν.

ΠΡΕΣΒΥΤΗΣ

χὤτι μ' ἐν ταῖς σαῖσι φερναῖς ἔλαβεν Ἀγαμέμνων
ἄναξ;

ΚΛΥΤΑΙΜΗΣΤΡΑ

870 ἦλθες εἰς Ἄργος μεθ' ἡμῶν κἀμὸς ἦσθ' ἀεί ποτε.

ΠΡΕΣΒΥΤΗΣ

ὧδ' ἔχει. καὶ σοὶ μὲν εὔνους εἰμί, σῷ δ' ἧσσον
πόσει.

ΚΛΥΤΑΙΜΗΣΤΡΑ

ἐκκάλυπτε νῦν ποθ' ἡμῖν οὕστινας στέγεις λόγους.

---

865 μέλλοντα σῶσαι Schwabl: μέλλοντ' ἂν ὤσῃ L   ὄκνον
Hermann: ὄγκον L   post h. v. versum lac. indic. Walter
867 δῆτά μ' Porson: δῆθ' L

ACHILLES

May your tale bring us life hereafter! But it's slow in coming.

‹OLD MAN

Give me your right hand, lady, and promise to defend me from disaster!›

CLYTAEMESTRA

(*giving him her hand*) If you have anything to tell me, do not hesitate for want of a right hand.

OLD MAN

Do you know me, who I am and how loyal I have been to you and your children?

CLYTAEMESTRA

I know that you are an old servant of my house.

OLD MAN

And that lord Agamemnon received me with your father's dowry?

CLYTAEMESTRA

You came to Argos with me and have always been my servant.

OLD MAN

That is right. And I am loyal to you, but less so to your husband.

CLYTAEMESTRA

Reveal to me now the story you are concealing.

---

872 στέγεις F. W. Schmidt: λέγ- L

EURIPIDES

ΠΡΕΣΒΥΤΗΣ

παῖδα σὴν πατὴρ ὁ φύσας αὐτόχειρ μέλλει κτανεῖν
. . .

ΚΛΥΤΑΙΜΗΣΤΡΑ

πῶς; ἀπέπτυσ᾽, ὦ γεραιέ, μῦθον· οὐ γὰρ εὖ φρονεῖς.

ΠΡΕΣΒΥΤΗΣ

875 . . . φασγάνῳ λευκὴν φονεύων τῆς ταλαιπώρου
δέρην.

ΚΛΥΤΑΙΜΗΣΤΡΑ

ὦ τάλαιν᾽ ἐγώ. μεμηνὼς ἆρα τυγχάνει πόσις;

ΠΡΕΣΒΥΤΗΣ

ἀρτίφρων, πλὴν ἐς σὲ καὶ σὴν παῖδα· τοῦτο δ᾽ οὐ
φρονεῖ.

ΚΛΥΤΑΙΜΗΣΤΡΑ

ἐκ τίνος λόγου; τίς αὐτὸν οὑπάγων ἀλαστόρων;

ΠΡΕΣΒΥΤΗΣ

θέσφαθ᾽, ὥς γέ φησι Κάλχας, ἵνα πορεύηται
στρατὸς . . .

ΚΛΥΤΑΙΜΗΣΤΡΑ

880 ποῖ; τάλαιν᾽ ἐγώ, τάλαινα δ᾽ ἣν πατὴρ μέλλει
κτανεῖν.

ΠΡΕΣΒΥΤΗΣ

. . . Δαρδάνου πρὸς δώμαθ᾽, Ἑλένην Μενέλεως
ὅπως λάβῃ.

OLD MAN

Your daughter—the father who begot her is going to kill
her . . .

CLYTAEMESTRA

What? I reject the story with contempt! You are mad!

OLD MAN

. . . bloodying the poor girl's white neck with his sword!

CLYTAEMESTRA

O woe is me! Is my husband crazy?

OLD MAN

He is sane except where you and your daughter are con-
cerned. There he is mad.

CLYTAEMESTRA

For what reason? What is the spirit of vengeance that has
attacked him?

OLD MAN

Calchas says this is divinely decreed if the army is to go . . .

CLYTAEMESTRA

Where? Unhappy me, unhappy the girl her father is about
to kill!

OLD MAN

. . . to the house of Dardanus, so that Menelaus can get
Helen.

ΚΛΥΤΑΙΜΗΣΤΡΑ

εἰς ἄρ' Ἰφιγένειαν Ἑλένης νόστος ἦν πεπρωμένος;

ΠΡΕΣΒΥΤΗΣ

πάντ' ἔχεις· Ἀρτέμιδι θύσειν παῖδα σὴν μέλλει
πατήρ.

ΚΛΥΤΑΙΜΗΣΤΡΑ

ὁ δὲ γάμος τίν' εἶχε πρόφασιν, ᾧ μ' ἐκόμισεν ἐκ
δόμων;

ΠΡΕΣΒΥΤΗΣ

885 ἵν' ἀγάγοις χαίρουσ' Ἀχιλλεῖ παῖδα νυμφεύσουσα
σήν.

ΚΛΥΤΑΙΜΗΣΤΡΑ

ὦ θύγατερ, ἥκεις ἐπ' ὀλέθρῳ καὶ σὺ καὶ μήτηρ
σέθεν.

ΠΡΕΣΒΥΤΗΣ

οἰκτρὰ πάσχετον δύ' οὖσαι· δεινὰ δ' Ἀγαμέμνων
ἔτλη.

ΚΛΥΤΑΙΜΗΣΤΡΑ

οἴχομαι τάλαινα· δακρύων νάματ' οὐκέτι στέγω.

ΠΡΕΣΒΥΤΗΣ

εἴπερ ἀλγεινόν τὸ τέκνων στερόμενον, δακρυρρόει.

ΚΛΥΤΑΙΜΗΣΤΡΑ

890 σὺ δὲ τάδ', ὦ γέρον, πόθεν φῂς εἰδέναι πεπυσμένος;

884 ᾧ Musgrave: ἤ L
888 νάματ' Hense: τ' ὄμματ' L

CLYTAEMESTRA

So Helen's journey was fated to cause Iphigenia's ruin!

OLD MAN

You have the whole story. Her father is about to sacrifice your daughter to Artemis.

CLYTAEMESTRA

But the marriage for which he brought me from home, what was the reason for that?

OLD MAN

It was so that you would gladly bring your daughter, in order to marry her to Achilles.

CLYTAEMESTRA

My daughter, you have come here to your undoing, both you and your mother!

OLD MAN

Pitiable are your sufferings, you two. Dreadful is the deed Agamemnon has brought himself to do.

CLYTAEMESTRA

I am done for, poor woman that I am! I no longer refrain from weeping!

OLD MAN

Yes, weep: it is pitiful to be deprived of one's children!

CLYTAEMESTRA

But you, old man, where is it you say you heard these things?

---

889 στερόμενον, δακρυρρόει Weil: στερομένην δακρυρροεῖν

L

265

ΠΡΕΣΒΥΤΗΣ

δέλτον ᾠχόμην φέρων σοι πρὸς τὰ πρὶν
γεγραμμένα.

ΚΛΥΤΑΙΜΗΣΤΡΑ

οὐκ ἐῶν ἢ ξυγκελεύων παῖδ' ἄγειν θανουμένην;

ΠΡΕΣΒΥΤΗΣ

μὴ μὲν οὖν ἄγειν· φρονῶν γὰρ ἔτυχε σὸς πόσις τότ'
εὖ.

ΚΛΥΤΑΙΜΗΣΤΡΑ

κᾆτα πῶς φέρων γε δέλτον οὐκ ἐμοὶ δίδως λαβεῖν;

ΠΡΕΣΒΥΤΗΣ

895   Μενέλεως ἀφείλεθ' ἡμᾶς, ὃς κακῶν τῶνδ' αἴτιος.

ΚΛΥΤΑΙΜΗΣΤΡΑ

ὦ τέκνον Νηρῇδος, ὦ παῖ Πηλέως, κλύεις τάδε;

ΑΧΙΛΛΕΥΣ

ἔκλυον οὖσαν ἀθλίαν σε, τὸ δ' ἐμὸν οὐ φαύλως
φέρω.

ΚΛΥΤΑΙΜΗΣΤΡΑ

παῖδά μου κατακτενοῦσι σοῖς δολώσαντες γάμοις.

ΑΧΙΛΛΕΥΣ

μέμφομαι κἀγὼ πόσει σῷ, κοὐχ ἁπλῶς οὕτω φέρω.

ΚΛΥΤΑΙΜΗΣΤΡΑ

900   οὐκ ἐπαιδεσθήσομαι 'γὼ προσπεσεῖν τὸ σὸν γόνυ
θνητὸς ἐκ θεᾶς γεγῶτος· τί γὰρ ἐγὼ σεμνύνομαι;

OLD MAN

I had gone to bring a letter to you in regard to the earlier message.

CLYTAEMESTRA

Forbidding or urging me to bring my daughter to be killed?

OLD MAN

Forbidding it: at that time your husband was sane.

CLYTAEMESTRA

If you were carrying a tablet, why didn't you give it to me?

OLD MAN

Menelaus took it from me. He is the cause of these woes.

CLYTAEMESTRA

Son of the Nereid, offspring of Peleus, do you hear these things?

ACHILLES

I hear that you are miserable. My own situation I do not take lightly.

CLYTAEMESTRA

They are going to kill my daughter, having tricked her by marriage with you.

ACHILLES

I too am angry with your husband: I do not accept this without protest.

CLYTAEMESTRA

(*kneeling before Achilles*) I shall not be prevented by a sense of shame from falling at your knees. I am a mortal and you are a goddess' son: why should I give myself airs?

ἢ τινος σπουδαστέον μοι μᾶλλον ἢ τέκνου πέρι;
ἀλλ' ἄμυνον, ὦ θεᾶς παῖ, τῇ τ' ἐμῇ δυσπραξίᾳ
τῇ τε λεχθείσῃ δάμαρτι σῇ μάτην μέν, ἀλλ' ὅμως.

905   σοὶ καταστέψασ' ἐγώ νιν ἦγον ὡς γαμουμένην,
νῦν δ' ἐπὶ σφαγὰς κομίζω· σοὶ δ' ὄνειδος ἵξεται,
ὅστις οὐκ ἤμυνας· εἰ γὰρ μὴ γάμοισιν ἐζύγης,
ἀλλ' ἐκλήθης γοῦν ταλαίνης παρθένου φίλος πόσις.
πρὸς γενειάδος ⟨σε⟩, πρός σε δεξιᾶς, πρὸς
   μητέρος—

910   ὄνομα γὰρ τὸ σόν μ' ἀπώλεσ', ᾧ σ' ἀμυναθεῖν
   χρεών—
οὐκ ἔχω βωμὸν καταφυγεῖν ἄλλον ἢ τὸ σὸν γόνυ,
οὐδὲ φίλος οὐδεὶς πέλας μοι· τὰ δ' Ἀγαμέμνονος
   κλύεις,
ὠμὰ καὶ πάντολμ'· ἀφῖγμαι δ', ὥσπερ εἰσορᾷς,
   γυνὴ
ναυτικὸν στράτευμ' ἄναρχον [κἀπὶ τοῖς κακοῖς
   θρασύ,
915   χρήσιμον δ', ὅταν θέλωσιν]. ἢν δὲ τολμήσῃς σύ
   μου
χεῖρ' ὑπερτεῖναι, σεσώμεθ'· εἰ δὲ μή, οὐ σεσώμεθα.

ΧΟΡΟΣ

δεινὸν τὸ τίκτειν καὶ φέρει φίλτρον μέγα
πᾶσίν τε κοινόν ἐσθ' ὑπερκάμνειν τέκνων.

ΑΧΙΛΛΕΥΣ

[ὑψηλόφρων μοι θυμὸς αἴρεται πρόσω·

Is there anything for which I ought to be more in earnest
than my daughter? But help me in my misfortune, son of
the goddess, help her who was called, even if falsely, your
wife. It was for you that I decked her out and brought her
to be married, but now I'm bringing her to be slaughtered.
It will be a reproach to you if you do not help her. For even
if you were not married to her, you were at least called the
poor maiden's beloved husband. I entreat you by your
chin, by your right hand, by your mother (for it was your
name that destroyed me, and you must come to its de-
fense): I have no other altar to flee to except your knees,
and no friend stands near me. Agamemnon's deeds you
know: they are savage and unbridled. And I have come, as
you see, a woman to face a navy, an undisciplined rabble
[bold for mischief, though they can be good if they so
choose]. If you bring yourself to hold your hand over me in
protection, I am saved. Otherwise, I am lost.

CHORUS LEADER

Being a mother is strangely powerful, and it exercises a
great charm on the heart. To toil on behalf of one's children
is a trait everyone shares.

ACHILLES[20]

[My proud spirit has been stirred. Yet I know how to be

---

20 I have bracketed the first part of Achilles' speech as the
work of the Reviser, who may have deleted genuine lines.

---

902 ἢ τινος Diggle: ἐπὶ τίνος L   909 ⟨σε⟩ Markland
914–5 verba κἀπὶ . . . θέλωσι del. England
918 ἐσθ' Reiske: ὥσθ' L   919–43 Retractatori tribuo (919
del. Paley, 920–3 Hartung, 924–31 Paley, 932–41 Connington,
942–3 una cum 944–72 Dindorf)

920 ἐπίσταμαι δὲ τοῖς κακοῖσί τ' ἀσχαλᾶν
μετρίως τε χαίρειν τοῖσιν ἐξωγκωμένοις.
λελογισμένοι γὰρ οἱ τοιοίδ' εἰσὶν βροτῶν
ὀρθῶς διαζῆν τὸν βίον γνώμης μέτα.
ἔστιν μὲν οὖν ἵν' ἡδὺ μὴ λίαν φρονεῖν,
925 ἔστιν δὲ χὤπου χρήσιμον γνώμην ἔχειν.
ἐγὼ δ', ἐν ἀνδρὸς εὐσεβεστάτου τραφεὶς
Χείρωνος, ἔμαθον τοὺς τρόπους ἁπλοῦς ἔχειν.
καὶ τοῖς Ἀτρείδαις, ἢν μὲν ἡγῶνται καλῶς,
πεισόμεθ', ὅταν δὲ μὴ καλῶς, οὐ πείσομαι.
930 ἀλλ' ἐνθάδ' ἐν Τροίᾳ τ' ἐλευθέραν φύσιν
παρέχων, Ἄρη τὸ κατ' ἐμὲ κοσμήσω δορί.
   σὲ δ', ὦ σχέτλια παθοῦσα πρὸς τῶν φιλτάτων,
ἃ δὴ κατ' ἄνδρα γίγνεται νεανίαν,
τοσοῦτον οἴκτῳ περιβαλὼν καταστένω,
935 κοὔποτε κόρη σὴ πρὸς πατρὸς σφαγήσεται,
ἐμὴ φατισθεῖσ'· οὐ γὰρ ἐμπλέκειν πλοκὰς
ἐγὼ παρέξω σῷ πόσει τοὐμὸν δέμας.
τοὔνομα γάρ, εἰ καὶ μὴ σίδηρον ἤρατο,
τοὐμὸν φονεύσει παῖδα σήν. τὸ δ' αἴτιον
940 πόσις σός. ἁγνὸν δ' οὐκέτ' ἐστὶ σῶμ' ἐμόν,
εἰ δι' ἔμ' ὀλεῖται διά τε τοὺς ἐμοὺς γάμους
ἡ δεινὰ τλᾶσα κοὐκ ἀνεκτὰ παρθένος.
θαυμαστὰ δ' ὡς ἀνάξι' ἠτιμασμένη.]
   ἐγὼ κάκιστος ἦν ἄρ' Ἀργείων ἀνήρ,
945 ἐγὼ τὸ μηδέν, Μενέλεως δ' ἐν ἀνδράσιν,
[ὡς οὐχὶ Πηλέως, ἀλλ' ἀλάστορος γεγώς,]
εἴπερ φονεύει τοὐμὸν ὄνομα σῷ πόσει.

moderate in grieving at misfortune or rejoicing in lofty successes. Mortals like that have a reasoned hope of living their whole lives through intelligently. To be sure, there are times when it is pleasant not to be too wise, but also times when it is useful to have intelligence. I, who was raised in the house of the pious Chiron, have learned how to be straightforward in my ways. I will obey the sons of Atreus if they lead well, but if they don't I shall not. Keeping my nature frank and free both here and in Troy I shall glorify Ares with my spear so far as in me lies.

But you, so terribly treated by your near and dear, I shall envelop you with my pity and weep for you, as far as a young man may do so. Your daughter shall never be slaughtered by her father since she was called mine: I shall never lend myself to your husband so that he may weave his wiles. It is my name, though it has not taken up the sword, that will slay your daughter, and your husband is to blame. My person would be no longer pure if because of me and my marriage this maiden is put to death, a girl who has suffered terrible, insupportable treatment and been astonishingly dishonored.]

It seems that all along I have been the meanest of the Greeks, a nobody, a Menelaus among men,[21] [no son of Peleus but of an avenging spirit,] seeing that my name is committing murder for your husband. By Nereus, who was

21 Menelaus is often regarded as a poor fighter.

---

920 ἐπίσταμαι Musgrave: -ται L   934 οἴκτῳ Stockert:
οἶκτον L   καταστένω Matthiae: καταστελῶ L
938 ἠράμην Nauck, Paley
946 del. Stockert

μὰ τὸν δι᾽ ὑγρῶν κυμάτων τεθραμμένον
Νηρέα, φυτουργὸν Θέτιδος ἥ μ᾽ ἐγείνατο,
950 οὐχ ἅψεται σῆς θυγατρὸς Ἀγαμέμνων ἄναξ,
οὐδ᾽ εἰς ἄκραν χεῖρ᾽, ὥστε προσβαλεῖν πέπλοις·
ἢ Σίπυλος ἔσται πολύς, ἔρεισμα βαρβάρων,
ὅθεν πεφύκασ᾽ οἱ στρατηλάται γένος,
Φθίας δὲ τοὔνομ᾽ οὐδαμοῦ κεκλήσεται.
955 [πικροὺς δὲ προχύτας χέρνιβάς τ᾽ ἐνάρξεται
Κάλχας ὁ μάντις. τίς δὲ μάντις ἔστ᾽ ἀνήρ,
ὃς ὀλίγ᾽ ἀληθῆ, πολλὰ δὲ ψευδῆ λέγει
τυχών, ὅταν δὲ μὴ τύχῃ, διοίχεται;
οὐ τῶν γάμων ἕκατι—μυρίαι κόραι
960 θηρῶσι λέκτρον τοὐμόν—εἴρηται τόδε·
ἀλλ᾽ ὕβριν ἐς ἡμᾶς ὕβρισ᾽ Ἀγαμέμνων ἄναξ.
χρῆν δ᾽ αὐτὸν αἰτεῖν τοὐμὸν ὄνομ᾽ ἐμοῦ πάρα,
θήραμα παιδός· ἡ Κλυταιμήστρα δ᾽ ἐμοὶ
μάλιστ᾽ ἐπείσθη θυγατέρ᾽ ἐκδοῦναι πόσει.
965 ἔδωκά τἂν Ἕλλησιν, εἰ πρὸς Ἴλιον
ἐν τῷδ᾽ ἔκαμνε νόστος· οὐκ ἠρνούμεθ᾽ ἂν
τὸ κοινὸν αὔξειν ὧν μέτ᾽ ἐστρατευόμην.
νῦν δ᾽ οὐδέν εἰμι, παρὰ δὲ τοῖς στρατηλάταις
ἐν εὐμαρεῖ με δρᾶν τε καὶ μὴ δρᾶν κακῶς.]
970 τάχ᾽ εἴσεται σίδηρος, ὃν πρὶν ἐς Φρύγας
ἐλθεῖν φόνου κηλῖσι βαρβάρου χρανῶ,
εἴ τίς με τὴν σὴν θυγατέρ᾽ ἐξαιρήσεται.

---

952 πολύς Musgrave: πόλις L   ἔρεισμα Hartung: ὅρισμα
L   954 Φθίας δὲ τοὔνομ᾽ Jacobs: Φθία δὲ τοὐμόν τ᾽ L

raised in the sea waves, the father of my mother Thetis, King Agamemnon shall not touch your daughter, no, not lay his fingertip on her robes. Otherwise Mount Sipylus, the barbarians' bulwark, from whence our generals derive their lineage,[22] will be great, and the name of Phthia will be nowhere spoken. [To his cost will Calchas ply his sacrificial barley and holy water! And what is a prophet? A man who, if lucky, prophesies truly once in a while and falsely most of the time, while if he is unlucky, he's nowhere to be found! It is not from a desire for marriage that I have said this: countless girls want to marry me! Rather Agamemnon has treated me highhandedly. He ought to have asked me for the use of my name to snare his daughter. And Clytaemestra was most persuaded to give her daughter to me as a husband. I would have granted this to the Greeks if our journey to Ilium had been in trouble for want of it. I would not have refused to serve the common interest of my fellow soldiers. But now I am nothing, and in the eyes of the generals it doesn't matter whether they treat me well or ill.]

This sword will bear me witness: even before I get to Phrygia I shall stain it with barbarian blood[23] if someone

---

[22] Mount Sipylus in Asia Minor was the region from which Agamemnon's ancestor Tantalus came.

[23] I. e. the blood of the sons of Atreus, whose family origins near Mount Sipylus have just been noted.

955–69 Retractatori tribuo (omnes 942–72 ab Euripide abiud. Dindorf)   955 ἐνάρξεται Musgrave: ἀνάξ- L
959 οὐ Lenting: ἦ L   969 κακῶς Kirchhoff: καλῶς L
971 βαρβάρου Jackson: αἵματι L: Ἕλληνος Piccolomini

273

[ἀλλ' ἡσύχαζε· θεὸς ἐγὼ πέφηνά σοι
μέγιστος, οὐκ ὤν· ἀλλ' ὅμως γενήσομαι.

ΧΟΡΟΣ

975 ἔλεξας, ὦ παῖ Πηλέως, σοῦ τ' ἄξια
καὶ τῆς ἐναλίας δαίμονος, σεμνῆς θεοῦ.

ΚΛΥΤΑΙΜΗΣΤΡΑ

φεῦ·
πῶς ἄν σ' ἐπαινέσαιμι μὴ λίαν λόγοις,
μηδ' ἐνδεὴς τοῦδ' ἀπολέσαιμι τὴν χάριν;
αἰνούμενοι γὰρ ἀγαθοὶ τρόπον τινὰ
980 μισοῦσι τοὺς αἰνοῦντας, ἢν αἰνῶσ' ἄγαν.
    αἰσχύνομαι δὲ παραφέρουσ' οἰκτροὺς λόγους,
ἰδίᾳ νοσοῦσα· σὺ δ' ἄνοσος κακῶν ἐμῶν.
ἀλλ' οὖν ἔχει τι σχῆμα, κἂν ἄπωθεν ᾖ
ἀνὴρ ὁ χρηστός, δυστυχοῦντας ὠφελεῖν.
985 οἴκτιρε δ' ἡμᾶς· οἰκτρὰ γὰρ πεπόνθαμεν·
ἣ πρῶτα μέν σε γαμβρὸν οἰηθεῖσ' ἔχειν
κενὴν κατέσχον ἐλπίδ'· εἶτά σοι τάχα
ὄρνις γένοιτ' ἂν τοῖσι μέλλουσιν γάμοις
θανοῦσ' ἐμὴ παῖς, ὅ σε φυλάξασθαι χρεών.
990 ἀλλ' εὖ μὲν ἀρχὰς εἶπας, εὖ δὲ καὶ τέλη·
σοῦ γὰρ θέλοντος παῖς ἐμὴ σωθήσεται.
βούλῃ νιν ἱκέτιν σὸν περιπτύξαι γόνυ;
ἀπαρθένευτα μὲν τάδ'· εἰ δέ σοι δοκεῖ,
ἔξεισιν αἰδοῦς ὄμμ' ἔχουσ' ἐλεύθερον.
995 εἰ δ' οὐ παρούσης ταῦτα τεύξομαι σέθεν,
μενέτω κατ' οἴκους· σεμνὰ γὰρ σεμνύνεται.

robs me of your daughter. [So be calm: I have shown my-
self to you as a great god, and though I am no god, yet I
shall become one.

CHORUS LEADER

Son of Peleus, what you have said is worthy of you and of
the sea goddess, that august divinity.

CLYTAEMESTRA

Ah, ah! How can my words avoid praising you excessively?
How can I avoid falling short and losing your favor? For
when the good are praised, in some fashion they hate their
praisers if they praise to excess.

I feel shame at the piteous story I tell since the misfor-
tune is my own and you have no part in my trouble. Yet it is
creditable for a good man to help those in distress, even if
he is far removed from them. Have pity on us: our suffer-
ings deserve pity. In the first place in thinking I had you
for a son-in-law I was nurturing a vain hope. Secondly, it
would be a bad omen for your future marriage if my daugh-
ter is killed: you must avoid this. The beginning of your
speech was good, and the end likewise. If you are willing,
my daughter's life will be saved. Do you want her to grasp
your knees as a suppliant? That is not maidenly behavior,
but if you think it right, she will lay her modesty aside and
come out. But if I can win my request without her pres-
ence here, let her remain in the tent: those who show self-
respect are respected. Still, one should feel modesty only

973–4 del. Hartung
975–1007 Retractatori tribuo (alios alii ab Euripide abiud. edd.)
994 ἔξεισιν Porson, Elmsley: ἥξει δι’ L

ὅμως δ' ὅσον γε δυνατὸν αἰδεῖσθαι χρεών.

ΑΧΙΛΛΕΥΣ

σὺ μήτε σὴν παῖδ' ἔξαγ' ὄψιν εἰς ἐμήν,
μήτ' εἰς ὄνειδος ἀμαθὲς ἔλθωμεν, γύναι·
1000 στρατὸς γὰρ ἀθρόος, ἀργὸς ὢν τῶν οἴκοθεν,
λέσχας πονηρὰς καὶ κακοστόμους φιλεῖ.
πάντως δέ μ' ἱκετεύοντέ θ' ἥξετ' εἰς ἴσον,
ἐπ' ἀνικετεύτοις θ'· εἷς ἐμοὶ γάρ ἐστ' ἀγὼν
μέγιστος, ὑμᾶς ἐξαπαλλάξαι κακῶν.
1005 ὡς ἕν γ' ἀκούσασ' ἴσθι, μὴ ψευδῶς μ' ἐρεῖν·
ψευδῆ λέγων δὲ καὶ μάτην ἐγκερτομῶν,
θάνοιμι· μὴ θάνοιμι δ', ἢν σώσω κόρην.]

ΚΛΥΤΑΙΜΗΣΤΡΑ

ὄναιο συνεχῶς δυστυχοῦντας ὠφελῶν.

ΑΧΙΛΛΕΥΣ

ἄκουε δή νυν, ἵνα τὸ πρᾶγμ' ἔχῃ καλῶς.

ΚΛΥΤΑΙΜΗΣΤΡΑ

1010 τί τοῦτ' ἔλεξας; ὡς ἀκουστέον γέ σου.

ΑΧΙΛΛΕΥΣ

πείθωμεν αὖθις πατέρα βέλτιον φρονεῖν.

ΚΛΥΤΑΙΜΗΣΤΡΑ

κακός τίς ἐστι καὶ λίαν ταρβεῖ στρατόν.

ΑΧΙΛΛΕΥΣ

ἀλλ' οἱ λόγοι γε καταπαλαίουσιν φόβους.

ΚΛΥΤΑΙΜΗΣΤΡΑ

ψυχρὰ μὲν ἐλπίς· ὅ τι δὲ χρή με δρᾶν φράσον.

so far as circumstances permit.

ACHILLES

Don't bring your daughter before me, lady, and let us
not lay ourselves open to the reproach of the vulgar. The
massed soldiery, freed from the toils they have at home,
love to engage in malicious gossip. In any case you will
reach the same result whether you supplicate me or not.
My one great struggle is to rescue you from calamity. Be
assured that you have heard this: I shall never speak falsely.
If I ever lie or deceive anyone, may I die! But may I live if I
save your daughter!]

CLYTAEMESTRA

Eternal blessings on you for your help to those in misfor-
tune!

ACHILLES

Listen, then, so that all may be well.

CLYTAEMESTRA

What are your instructions? I must obey you.

ACHILLES

Let us try persuading the father to return to his senses.

CLYTAEMESTRA

He's a coward and fears the army too much.

ACHILLES

But reason can overcome fear.

CLYTAEMESTRA

A cold hope this. But tell me what I must do.

1002 ἱκετεύοντέ θ' Wecklein: -τες L
1003 ἐπ' ἀνικετεύτοις θ' Weil: εἴ τ' ἀνικέτευτος L
1013 φόβους Musgrave: λόγους L

277

ΑΧΙΛΛΕΥΣ

1015 ἱκέτευ᾽ ἐκεῖνον πρῶτα μὴ κτείνειν τέκνον·
ἢν δ᾽ ἀντιβαίνῃ, πρὸς ἐμέ σοι πορευτέον.
[οὐ γάρ, τὸ χρῇζον εἰ πίθοι, τοὐμὸν χρεὼν
χωρεῖν· ἔχει γὰρ τοῦτο τὴν σωτηρίαν.
κἀγώ τ᾽ ἀμείνων πρὸς φίλον γενήσομαι,
1020 στρατός τ᾽ ἂν οὐ μέμψαιτό μ᾽, εἰ τὰ πράγματα
λελογισμένως πράσσοιμι μᾶλλον ἢ σθένει.]
καλῶς δὲ κρανθὲν κἂν ἐμοῦ χωρὶς τόδε
σοί τ᾽ ἂν γένοιτο καὶ φίλοις πρὸς ἡδονήν.

ΚΛΥΤΑΙΜΗΣΤΡΑ

ὡς σῶφρον᾽ εἶπας· δραστέον δ᾽ ἅ σοι δοκεῖ.
1025 ἢν δ᾽ αὖ τι μὴ πράσσωμεν ὧν ἐγὼ θέλω,
ποῦ σ᾽ αὖθις ὀψόμεσθα, ποῖ χρή μ᾽ ἀθλίαν
ἐλθοῦσαν εὑρεῖν σὴν χέρ᾽ ἐπίκουρον κακῶν;

ΑΧΙΛΛΕΥΣ

ἡμεῖς σε, φύλακος οὗ χρέος, φυλάξομεν,
μή τίς σ᾽ ἴδῃ στείχουσαν ἐπτοημένην
1030 Δαναῶν δι᾽ ὄχλου· μηδὲ πατρῷον δόμον
αἴσχυν᾽· ὁ γάρ τοι Τυνδάρεως οὐκ ἄξιος
[κακῶς ἀκούειν· ἐν γὰρ Ἕλλησιν μέγας].

ΚΛΥΤΑΙΜΗΣΤΡΑ

ἔσται τάδ᾽· ἄρχε· σοί με δουλεύειν χρεών.
εἰ δ᾽ εἰσὶ ⟨συνετοὶ⟩ θεοί, δίκαιος ὢν ἀνὴρ
1035 ἐσθλῶν κυρήσεις· εἰ δὲ μή, τί δεῖ πονεῖν;

1015 τέκνον Diggle: -α L
1017–21 Retractatori tribuo (una cum 1022–3 del. Dindorf)

ACHILLES

First beg him not to kill his child. If he resists, you must come to me. [If entreaty prevails on him, no need for me to intervene: entreaty by itself wins her life. That way I will prove to be kindlier to my friend, and the army will not find fault with me if I handle things cleverly and not by might.] If fortune smiles, even without my aid this affair will turn out well for you and your family.

CLYTAEMESTRA

What sensible words! We must do as you think best. But if I fail in my attempt, where can I find you again? Where must I go in my misery to find your hand to rescue me from trouble?

ACHILLES

I will keep an eye out for you (the situation wants watching): no one must see you running distractedly though the Greek army. Do not shame your paternal house: Tyndareus does not deserve it [to be ill spoken of, for he is a great man in Greece].

CLYTAEMESTRA

It shall be so. You be the ruler: I must be your servant. If the gods are ⟨sensible⟩, you, just man that you are, will be rewarded. And if not, why should we toil?

1017 sic Jackson: εἴη γὰρ τὸ χρῇζον ἐπίθετ' οὐ τοὐμὸν L

1022–3 sic Murray: καλῶς δὲ κρανθέντων καὶ πρὸς ἡδονὴν φίλοις / σοί τ' ἂν γένοιτο κἂν ἐμοῦ χωρὶς τάδε L

1025 αὖ τι . . . ὧν Monk: αὐτὰ . . . ἂν L   1026 ποῖ Wecklein: ποῦ L   1028 φύλακος . . . χρέος England: φύλακες . . . χρεὼν L   1032 del. F. W. Schmidt

1033 ἔσται Markland: ἔστιν L   1034 ⟨συνετοὶ⟩ Diggle

279

ΧΟΡΟΣ

στρ.

τίν' ἄρ' ὑμεναίοις διὰ λωτοῦ Λίβυος
μετά τε φιλοχόρου κιθάρας
συρίγγων θ' ὑπὸ καλαμοεσ-
σᾶν ἔστασαν ἰαχάν,
1040 ὅτ' ἀνὰ Πήλιον αἱ καλλιπλόκαμοι
Πιερίδες μετὰ δαῖτα θεῶν
χρυσεοσάνδαλον ἴχνος
ἐν γᾷ κρούουσαι
Πηλέως ἐς γάμον ἦλθον,
1045 μελῳδοῖς Θέτιν ἀχήμασι τόν τ' Αἰακίδαν,
Κενταύρων ἐν ὄρεσι κλέουσαι
Πηλιάδα καθ' ὕλαν;
ὁ δὲ Δαρδανίδας, Διὸς
1050 λέκτρων τρύφημα φίλον,
χρυσέοισιν ἄφυσσε λοι-
βὰν ἐκ κρατήρων γυάλοις,
ὁ Φρύγιος Γανυμήδης.
παρὰ δὲ λευκοφαῆ ψάμαθον
1055 εἱλισσόμεναι κύκλια
πεντήκοντα κόραι
Νηρέως γάμους ἐχόρευσαν.

ἀντ.

ἅμα δ' ἐλάταις σὺν στεφανώδει τε χλόᾳ

1036 τίν' Portus: τίς L   ὑμεναίοις Willink: Ὑμέναιος L, quo
recepto ἔστασεν 1039 Portus

IPHIGENIA AT AULIS

Exit ACHILLES by Eisodos B.

CHORUS

What cry, in their wedding hymns, did they raise
to the Libyan pipe
and the cithara that loves the dance
and to the strains of the reedy syrinx,
when upon Pelion's ridges the fair-tressed
Pierian Muses were coming,
striking their gold-sandaled
feet on the earth,
to a feast of the gods, the marriage of Peleus?
Upon the Centaurs' mountains
on the wooded slopes of Pelion they hymned
with songs melodious Thetis and the son of Aeacus.
And Dardanus' son, the luxurious
darling of Zeus's bed,
the Phrygian Ganymede,
poured the wine
from the mixing bowl into golden cups.
Upon the white-gleaming sand
Nereus' fifty daughters
trod their whirling measures
and danced the nuptials.

Holding fir trunks, their heads wreathed with leaves,

1041 μετὰ δαῖτα Wecklein: ἐν δαιτὶ L
1045–6 μελῳδοῖς . . . ἀχήμασι Elmsley: -δοὶ . . . ἰαχ- L
1047 κλέουσαι Monk: κλυ- L   1058 ἅμα Conington: ἀνὰ
L   ἐλάταις σὺν Weil: ἐλάταισιν L

281

EURIPIDES

θίασος ἔμολεν ἱπποβάτας
1060 Κενταύρων ἐπὶ δαῖτα τὰν
θεῶν κρατῆρά τε Βάκχου.
μέγα δ' ἀνέκλαγον· Ὦ Νηρηὶ κόρα,
παῖδά σε Θεσσαλίᾳ μέγα φῶς
μάντις ὁ φοιβάδα μοῦσαν
1065 εἰδὼς γεννάσειν
Χείρων ἐξονόμαζεν,
ὃς ἥξει χθόνα λογχήρεσι σὺν Μυρμιδόνων
ἀσπισταῖς Πριάμοιο κλεινάν,
1070 †γαῖαν† ἐκπυρώσων,
περὶ σώματι χρυσέων
ὅπλων Ἡφαιστοπόνων
κεκορυθμένος ἐνδύτ', ἐκ
θεᾶς ματρὸς δωρήματ' ἔχων
1075 Θέτιδος, ἅ νιν ἔτικτεν.
μακάριον τότε δαίμονες
τᾶς εὐπάτριδος γάμον
Νηρήδων ἔθεσαν
πρώτας Πηλέως θ' ὑμεναίους.

ἐπῳδ.

1080 σὲ δ', ὦ κόρα, στέψουσι καλλικόμαν
πλόκαμον Ἀργεῖοι, βαλιὰν
ὥστε πετραίων ἀπ' ἄν-
τρων ἔλαφον ὀρείαν
⟨ἢ⟩ μόσχον ἀκήρατον,

1063 παῖδά σε Θεσσαλίᾳ Weil: παῖδες αἱ Θεσσαλαὶ L

came the horse-mounted throng
of Centaurs to the feast of the gods
and the mixing bowl of Bacchus.
Loud was their cry: "O daughter of Nereus,
Chiron, the prophet who well knows
the song of Phoebus
says that you will bear a son
who will be a light to Thessaly!
He will come to the renowned land of Priam
with his lance-bearing Myrmidon hoplites
to burn its towers,
wearing about him as covering
the golden armor
made by Hephaestus' labor,
received as a gift from the goddess Thetis
who bore him."
Blessed on that occasion
did the gods make the marriage
of the eldest of the nobly born Nereids
to Peleus.

But you, maiden, the Greeks
shall garland about your fair tresses
like some dappled hind of the mountain
from a rocky cave
‹or› a spotless heifer

1064 ὁ φοιβάδα Hermann: δ' ὁ φοῖβα L
1065 γεννάσειν Weil: -άσεις L   1070 πέργαμ' Willink
1080 ὦ κόρα Hermann: ἐπὶ κάρα L   1083 ἔλαφον Monk:
ἐλθοῦσαν L   ὀρείαν ‹ἢ› Monk: ὀρέων L

283

[βρότειον αἱμάσσοντες λαιμόν]
1085 οὐ σύριγγι τραφεῖσαν οὐδ᾽
ἐν ῥοιβδήσεσι βουκόλων,
παρὰ δὲ ματέρι νυμφοκόμῳ
⟨κλεινὸν⟩ Ἰναχίδαις γάμον.
1090 ποῦ τὸ τᾶς Αἰδοῦς ἢ τὸ τᾶς Ἀρετᾶς
σθένει τι πρόσωπον,
ὁπότε τὸ μὲν ἄσεπτον ἔχει
δύνασιν, ἁ δ᾽ Ἀρετὰ κατόπι-
σθεν θνατοῖς ἀμελεῖται,
1095 Ἀνομία δὲ νόμων κρατεῖ,
κοὐ κοινὸς ἀγὼν βροτοῖς
μή τις θεῶν φθόνος ἔλθῃ;

ΚΛΥΤΑΙΜΗΣΤΡΑ

ἐξῆλθον οἴκων προσκοπουμένη πόσιν,
χρόνιον ἀπόντα κἀκλελοιπότα στέγας.
1100 ἐν δακρύοισι δ᾽ ἡ τάλαινα παῖς ἐμή,
πολλὰς ἱεῖσα μεταβολὰς ὀδυρμάτων,
θάνατον ἀκούσασ᾽ ὃν πατὴρ βουλεύεται.
    μνήμην δ᾽ ἄρ᾽ εἶχον πλησίον βεβηκότος
Ἀγαμέμνονος τοῦδ᾽, ὃς ἐπὶ τοῖς αὑτοῦ τέκνοις
1105 ἀνόσια πράσσων αὐτίχ᾽ εὑρεθήσεται.

1084 del. Monk
1087 νυμφοκόμῳ Markland: -ον L
1088 ⟨κλεινὸν⟩ Monk
1091 σθένει Bothe: δύνασιν ἔχει σθένειν L
1096 κοὐ Willink: καὶ L

[bloodying your mortal neck].
You were not raised to the whirring
of the shepherd's pipe
but at the side of your bride-conducting mother
to be a <splendid> catch for the sons of Inachus.
Where does Modesty's or Virtue's face
hold any sway?
What is unholy
enjoys power, Virtue is left behind
and ignored by mortals,
Lawlessness controls the laws,
and mortals do not bend common effort
to avert the ill will of heaven.

Enter from the skene CLYTAEMESTRA.

CLYTAEMESTRA

I have come out of the house looking for my husband, for
he has been a long time away from it. My unhappy daugh-
ter is in tears, uttering laments of every sort since she
heard of the death her father is planning for her.

But it seems I have been talking about the man who
approaches, Agamemnon here. His unholy machinations
against his own children will soon be found out.

Enter by Eisodos B AGAMEMNON.

ΑΓΑΜΕΜΝΩΝ

Λήδας γένεθλον, ἐν καλῷ σ' ἔξω δόμων
ηὕρηχ', ἵν' εἴπω παρθένου χωρὶς λόγους
οὓς οὐκ ἀκούειν τὰς γαμουμένας πρέπει.

ΚΛΥΤΑΙΜΗΣΤΡΑ

τί δ' ἔστιν οὗ σοι καιρὸς ἀντιλάζυται;

ΑΓΑΜΕΜΝΩΝ

1110 ἔκπεμπε παῖδα ⟨τῶνδε⟩ δωμάτων πάρος·
ὡς χέρνιβες πάρεισιν ηὐτρεπισμέναι,
προχύται τε, βάλλειν πῦρ καθάρσιον χεροῖν,
μόσχοι τε, πρὸ γάμων ἃς θεᾷ πεσεῖν χρεών
[Ἀρτέμιδι μέλανος αἵματος φυσήματα].

ΚΛΥΤΑΙΜΗΣΤΡΑ

1115 [τοῖς ὀνόμασιν μὲν εὖ λέγεις, τὰ δ' ἔργα σου
οὐκ οἶδ' ὅπως χρή μ' ὀνομάσασαν εὖ λέγειν.
χώρει δέ, θύγατερ, ἐκτός—οἶσθα γὰρ πατρὸς
πάντως ἃ μέλλει—χ̓ὑπὸ τοῖς πέπλοις ἄγε
λαβοῦσ' Ὀρέστην, σὸν κασίγνητον, τέκνον.]
1120 ἰδοὺ πάρεστιν ἥδε πειθαρχοῦσά σοι.
τὰ δ' ἄλλ' ἐγὼ πρὸ τῆσδε κἀμαυτῆς φράσω.

ΑΓΑΜΕΜΝΩΝ

τέκνον, τί κλαίεις οὐδ' ἔθ' ἡδέως ⟨μ'⟩ ὁρᾷς,
ἐς γῆν δ' ἐρείσασ' ὄμμα πρόσθ' ἔχεις πέπλους;

1098–1105 del. Monk (1099–1103) et Conington
    1110 ⟨τῶνδε⟩ England (⟨δεῦρο⟩ Heimsoeth)   πάρος
Heimsoeth: πατρὸς μέτα L

AGAMEMNON

Daughter of Leda, it is timely that I find you outside the house so that I can say to you, away from our daughter, words that do not befit brides to hear.

CLYTAEMESTRA

What is it for which this is an opportune moment for you?

AGAMEMNON

Send the girl out in front of the tent, for the lustral water is ready, as are the sacrificial barley grains for casting into the purifying fire and the heifers, which must be slain before the wedding [for the goddess Artemis with a profusion of black blood].

Enter from the skene *IPHIGENIA.*

CLYTAEMESTRA

[In your words you speak fair, but as for your deeds, I do not know what one can call them and give them a good name. Come out of the house, daughter—for you know in any case all that your father intends—and bring out your brother Orestes under the protection of your garments!] See, she is here in obedience to you. But as for the rest I shall speak on her behalf as well as on my own.

AGAMEMNON

Daughter, why do you weep and no longer look at me with pleasure? Why do you fix your glance on the ground and hold your garments before your face?

1114 del. England
1115–9 del. Kovacs (1117–21 Paley)

[ΚΛΥΤΑΙΜΗΣΤΡΑ

φεῦ·
τίν' ἂν λάβοιμι τῶν ἐμῶν ἀρχὴν κακῶν;
1125 ἅπασι γὰρ πρώτοισι χρήσασθαι πάρα
κἂν ὑστάτοισι κἂν μέσοισι πανταχοῦ.

ΑΓΑΜΕΜΝΩΝ
τί δ' ἔστιν; ὥς μοι πάντες εἰς ἓν ἥκετε,
σύγχυσιν ἔχοντες καὶ ταραγμὸν ὀμμάτων.]

ΚΛΥΤΑΙΜΗΣΤΡΑ
εἴφ' ἂν ἐρωτήσω σε γενναίως, πόσι.

[ΑΓΑΜΕΜΝΩΝ
1130 οὐδὲν κελευσμοῦ δεῖ σ'· ἐρωτᾶσθαι θέλω.

ΚΛΥΤΑΙΜΗΣΤΡΑ
τὴν παῖδα τὴν σὴν τήν τ' ἐμὴν μέλλεις κτανεῖν;

ΑΓΑΜΕΜΝΩΝ
ἔα·
τλήμονά γ' ἔλεξας ὑπονοεῖς θ' ἃ μή σε χρή.

ΚΛΥΤΑΙΜΗΣΤΡΑ
ἔχ' ἥσυχος.
κἀκεῖνό μοι τὸ πρῶτον ἀπόκριναι πάλιν.]

ΑΓΑΜΕΜΝΩΝ
σὺ δ', ἤν γ' ἐρωτᾷς εἰκότ', εἰκότ' ἂν κλύοις.

ΚΛΥΤΑΙΜΗΣΤΡΑ
1135 οὐκ ἀλλ' ἐρωτῶ, καὶ σὺ μὴ λέγ' ἄλλα μοι.

[CLYTAEMESTRA

Oh my! What shall I take as the beginning of my woes?
For everything can serve my speech as its beginning or its
end or its middle.

AGAMEMNON

What is wrong? You are all in the same state and show confusion and distress in your eyes.]

CLYTAEMESTRA

Answer my questions honestly, husband.

[AGAMEMNON

You have no need to bid me. I am willing to be asked.

CLYTAEMESTRA

Do you intend to kill your daughter and mine?

AGAMEMNON

Ah! Your words are dreadful and your suspicions are improper!

CLYTAEMESTRA

Control your agitation! And answer again the first question
I put to you.]

AGAMEMNON

If you ask questions that are reasonable, you will receive
reasonable answers.

CLYTAEMESTRA

I will ask no other kind. And you must give me no other
kind of answers.

1122 ⟨μ'⟩ Markland
1124–8 del. Kovacs (1124–6 Weil)

EURIPIDES

ΑΓΑΜΕΜΝΩΝ

ὦ πότνια μοῖρα καὶ τύχη δαίμων τ' ἐμός.

ΚΛΥΤΑΙΜΗΣΤΡΑ

κἀμός γε καὶ τῆσδ', εἷς τριῶν δυσδαιμόνων.

ΑΓΑΜΕΜΝΩΝ

τί δ' ἠδίκησαι;

ΚΛΥΤΑΙΜΗΣΤΡΑ

τοῦτ' ἐμοῦ πεύθῃ πάρα;
ὁ νοῦς ὅδ' αὐτὸς νοῦν ἔχων οὐ τυγχάνει.

ΑΓΑΜΕΜΝΩΝ

1140   ἀπωλόμεσθα· προδέδοται τὰ κρυπτά μου.

ΚΛΥΤΑΙΜΗΣΤΡΑ

πάντ' οἶδα καὶ πεπύσμεθ' ἃ σὺ μέλλεις με δρᾶν·
αὐτὸ δὲ τὸ σιγᾶν ὁμολογοῦντός ἐστί σου
καὶ τὸ στενάζειν· πολλὰ μὴ κάμῃς λέγων.

ΑΓΑΜΕΜΝΩΝ

ἰδοὺ σιωπῶ· τὸ γὰρ ἀναίσχυντον τί δεῖ
1145 ψευδῆ λέγοντα προσλαβεῖν τῇ συμφορᾷ;

ΚΛΥΤΑΙΜΗΣΤΡΑ

ἄκουε δή νυν· ἀνακαλύψω γὰρ λόγους
κοὐκέτι παρῳδοῖς χρησόμεσθ' αἰνίγμασιν.
[πρῶτον μέν, ἵνα σοι πρῶτα τοῦτ' ὀνειδίσω,
ἔγημας ἄκουσάν με κἄλαβες βίᾳ,

1130–3 del. Günther
1136 μοῖρα καὶ τύχη Musgrave: τ- καὶ μ- L

290

AGAMEMNON

O Lady Dispensation and fate and my guiding spirit!

CLYTAEMESTRA

Yes, and mine and hers, one spirit of three unhappy
people!

AGAMEMNON

What wrong has been done to you?

CLYTAEMESTRA

Can you ask this question of me? This cleverness of yours is
not very clever.

AGAMEMNON

(aside) I am lost! My secret has been betrayed!

CLYTAEMESTRA

I know all: I have learned what you intend to do to me.
Your very silence and your groans are a sign that you admit
it. You need not trouble yourself to make a long reply.

AGAMEMNON

See, I am silent: why should I, by speaking falsely, add
shamelessness to my misfortunes?

CLYTAEMESTRA

Listen, then! I shall speak plainly, no longer in distorting
riddles.

[My first reproach to you is this, that you married me
against my will and took me by force, killing my former

1138 τί δ' ἠδίκησαι Matthiae: τί μ' ἠδίκησε L
1138–9 del. Wilamowitz
1144 τί Elmsley: με L

1150   τὸν πρόσθεν ἄνδρα Τάνταλον κατακτανών·
βρέφος τε τοὐμὸν †σῷ προσουρίσας πάλῳ†,
μαστῶν βιαίως τῶν ἐμῶν ἀποσπάσας.
καὶ τὼ Διός σε παῖδ᾽, ἐμὼ δὲ συγγόνω,
ἵπποισι μαρμαίροντ᾽ ἐπεστρατευσάτην·
1155   πατὴρ δὲ πρέσβυς Τυνδάρεώς σ᾽ ἐρρύσατο
ἱκέτην γενόμενον, τἀμὰ δ᾽ ἔσχες αὖ λέχη.

    οὗ σοι καταλλαχθεῖσα περὶ σὲ καὶ δόμους
συμμαρτυρήσεις ὡς ἄμεμπτος ἦ γυνή,
ἔς τ᾽ Ἀφροδίτην σωφρονοῦσα καὶ τὸ σὸν
1160   μέλαθρον αὔξουσ᾽, ὥστε σ᾽ εἰσιόντα τε
χαίρειν θύραζέ τ᾽ ἐξιόντ᾽ εὐδαιμονεῖν.
σπάνιον δὲ θήρευμ᾽ ἀνδρὶ τοιαύτην λαβεῖν
δάμαρτα· φλαύραν δ᾽ οὐ σπάνις γυναῖκ᾽ ἔχειν.
τίκτω δ᾽ ἐπὶ τρισὶ παρθένοισι παῖδά σοι
1165   τόνδ᾽· ὧν μιᾶς σὺ τλημόνως μ᾽ ἀποστερεῖς.
κἄν τίς σ᾽ ἔρηται τίνος ἕκατί νιν κτενεῖς,
λέξον, τί φήσεις; ἢ ᾽μὲ χρὴ λέγειν τὰ σά;
Μενέλαος Ἑλένην ἵνα λάβῃ. καλὸν †γένος†
κακῆς γυναικὸς μισθὸν ἀποτεῖσαι τέκνα,
1170   τἄχιστα τοῖσι φιλτάτοις ὠνούμενον.

    ἄγ᾽, εἰ στρατεύσῃ καταλιπών μ᾽ ἐν δώμασιν,
κἀκεῖ γενήσῃ διὰ μακρᾶς ἀπουσίας,
τίν᾽ ἐν δόμοις με καρδίαν ἕξειν δοκεῖς,
ὅταν κενοὺς μὲν εἰσίδω παιδὸς θρόνους,
1175   κενοὺς δὲ παρθενῶνας, ἐπὶ δὲ δακρύοις
μόνη κάθωμαι, τήνδε θρηνῳδοῦσ᾽ ἀεί·
Ἀπώλεσέν σ᾽, ὦ τέκνον, ὁ φυτεύσας πατήρ,

husband Tantalus. My baby you hurled to the ground, tearing it violently from my breast. The two Dioscuri, my brothers, made an expedition against you with the flashing of cavalry. My old father Tyndareus rescued you when you supplicated him, and you got me back as a wife.

Once I was reconciled to you, you will be my witness that as a wife I was blameless in regard to you and your house. I was self-controlled where sex was concerned and caused your house to grow great, so that when you came in you felt pleasure, and you went forth a prosperous man. It is a rare find to marry a woman like that: there is no lack of opportunity to have a bad wife. I bore you this son here, in addition to three daughters. And by depriving me of one of these you are making me miserable. And if someone asks you why you will kill her, tell me, what will you say? Or shall I say your words for you? "So that Menelaus may get back Helen." What a fine thing, to pay for a bad woman in the coin of your own children, buying what is most hateful at the cost of what you love best!

Come, if you go on campaign, leaving me in the house, and are there for a long time, what kind of heart do you think I will have in my breast at home when I see the chair of your daughter empty, and her maiden chamber empty, and I sit alone in tears, always bewailing her? "Daughter, the father who begot you has destroyed you, killing you

---

1148–84 Retractatori tribuo (alios alii del. edd.)

1151 σῷ] ζῶν Musgrave   προσούδισας πέδῳ Scaliger

1168 γένος] γ᾽ ἔθος Elmsley, κλέος Hermann

1170 ὠνούμενον Wecklein: ὠνούμεθα L

1174 sic Diggle (παιδὸς iam Rauchenstein): ὅταν θρόνους τῆσδ᾽ εἰσίδω πάντας κένους L

αὐτὸς κτανών, οὐκ ἄλλος οὐδ' ἄλλῃ χερί;
τοιόνδε μῖσος καταλιπὼν ⟨τοῖς φιλτάτοις
νόστου θελήσεις τυγχάνειν⟩ πρὸς τοὺς δόμους;
1180 ἐπεὶ βραχείας προφάσεως ἐνδεῖ μόνον,
ἐφ' ᾗ σ' ἐγὼ καὶ παῖδες αἱ λελειμμέναι
δεξόμεθα δέξιν ἥν σε δέξασθαι χρεών.
μὴ δῆτα πρὸς θεῶν μήτ' ἀναγκάσῃς ἐμὲ
κακὴν γενέσθαι περὶ σέ, μήτ' αὐτὸς γένῃ.]
1185 εἶέν· σὺ θύσεις παῖδα· τίνας εὐχὰς ἐρεῖς;
τί σοι κατεύξῃ τἀγαθόν, σφάζων τέκνον;
νόστον πονηρόν, οἴκοθέν γ' αἰσχρῶς ἰών;
ἀλλ' ἐμὲ δίκαιον ἀγαθὸν εὔχεσθαί τί σοι;
οὔ τἄρα συνέτους τοὺς θεοὺς ἡγοίμεθ' ἄν,
1190 εἰ τοῖσιν αὐθένταισιν εὖ φρονήσομεν.
ἥκων δ' ἐς Ἄργος προσπεσῇ τέκνοισι σοῖς;
ἀλλ' οὐ θέμις σοι. τίς δὲ καὶ προσβλέψεται
παίδων σ', ἵν' αὐτῶν προσέμενος κτάνῃς τινά;
ταῦτ' ἦλθες ἤδη διὰ λόγων, ἢ σκῆπτρά σοι
1195 μόνον διαφέρειν καὶ στρατηλατεῖν μέλει;
ὃν χρῆν δίκαιον λόγον ἐν Ἀργείοις λέγειν·
Βούλεσθ', Ἀχαιοί, πλεῖν Φρυγῶν ἐπὶ χθόνα;
κλῆρον τίθεσθε παῖδ' ὅτου θανεῖν χρεών.
ἐν ἴσῳ γὰρ ἦν τόδ', ἀλλὰ μὴ σ' ἐξαίρετον
1200 σφάγιον παρασχεῖν Δαναΐδαισι παῖδα σήν,
ἢ Μενέλεων πρὸ μητρὸς Ἑρμιόνην κτανεῖν,
οὗπερ τὸ πρᾶγμ' ἦν. νῦν δ' ἐγὼ μὲν ἡ τὸ σὸν
σῴζουσα λέκτρον παιδὸς ἐστερήσομαι,

himself! It is he and no one else nor by any other's hand!"
Having left such cause for hatred <to your kin, will you de-
sire to return> to your own home? It needs but little excuse
for me and your daughters who are left to give you such
reception as you deserve. Do not compel me, I beg you by
the gods, to become wicked toward you! Do not become
wicked yourself!]

Well, then, you are going to sacrifice your daughter:
what prayers will you utter? What blessing will you ask
for yourself as you cut your child's throat? An evil home-
coming to match your shameful departure? Well, is it right
that I should ask some blessing for you? We would be
supposing that the gods are fools if we showed good will
towards the slayers of our own kin.

When you return to Argos, will you embrace your chil-
dren? It will be wrong to do so. And who of your children
will look at you? Will they want you to pull one of them
away for slaughter? Have you considered these things, or is
your only thought to carry the scepter and be general? You
ought to make a just proposal among the Greeks: "Do you
want to sail to the land of the Phrygians, you Achaeans?
Draw lots to see whose child must die." For that would be
just rather than for you alone to offer the Greeks your
daughter as a victim. Alternatively, Menelaus ought to kill
Hermione for her mother's sake: this is his affair. As things
stand, I who am your faithful wife, shall be deprived of my

1176 κάθωμαι Elmsley: -ημαι L

1179 μῖσος Musgrave: μισθὸν L   post καταλιπὼν lac.
indic. Kovacs   1185 sic Nauck: εἶέν· θύσεις δὲ παῖδ' ἔνθα τ-
εὐ- ἐ- L   1193 ἵν' Elmsley: ἐὰν L   προσέμενος Weil:
προθέμ- L   1194 ἦλθες Hermann: ἦλθ' L

ἡ δ' ἐξαμαρτοῦσ', ὑπόροφον νεάνιδα
1205 Σπάρτῃ κομίζουσ', εὐτυχὴς γενήσεται.
τούτων ἄμειψαί μ' εἴ τι μὴ καλῶς λέγω·
εἰ δ' εὖ λέλεκται τἀμά, μὴ κατακτάνῃς
τὴν σήν τε κἀμὴν παῖδα, καὶ σώφρων ἔσῃ.

ΧΟΡΟΣ
πιθοῦ· τὸ γάρ τοι τέκνα συσσῴζειν καλόν,
1210 Ἀγάμεμνον· οὐδεὶς πρὸς τάδ' ἀντερεῖ βροτῶν.

ΙΦΙΓΕΝΕΙΑ
εἰ μὲν τὸν Ὀρφέως εἶχον, ὦ πάτερ, λόγον,
πείθειν ἐπᾴδουσ', ὥσθ' ὁμαρτεῖν μοι πέτρας
κηλεῖν τε τοῖς λόγοισιν οὓς ἐβουλόμην,
ἐνταῦθ' ἂν ἦλθον· νῦν δέ, τἀπ' ἐμοῦ σοφά,
1215 δάκρυα παρέξω· ταῦτα γὰρ δυναίμεθ' ἄν.
ἱκετηρίαν δὲ γόνασιν ἐξάπτω σέθεν
τὸ σῶμα τοὐμόν, ὅπερ ἔτικτεν ἥδε σοι·
μή μ' ἀπολέσῃς ἄωρον· ἡδὺ γὰρ τὸ φῶς
βλέπειν· τὰ δ' ὑπὸ γῆς μή μ' ἰδεῖν ἀναγκάσῃς.
1220 πρώτη σ' ἐκάλεσα πατέρα καὶ σὺ παῖδ' ἐμέ·
πρώτη δὲ γόνασι σοῖσι σῶμα δοῦσ' ἐμὸν
φίλας χάριτας ἔδωκα κἀντεδεξάμην.
λόγος δ' ὁ μὲν σὸς ἦν ὅδ'· Ἆρά σ', ὦ τέκνον,
εὐδαίμον' ἀνδρὸς ἐν δόμοισιν ὄψομαι,
1225 ζῶσάν τε καὶ θάλλουσαν ἀξίως ἐμοῦ;
οὑμὸς δ' ὅδ' ἦν αὖ περὶ σὸν ἐξαρτωμένης
γένειον, οὗ νῦν ἀντιλάζυμαι χερί·
Τί δ' ἄρ' ἐγὼ σέ; πρέσβυν ἆρ' ἐσδέξομαι

child, while the adulterous woman will keep her child safe
under her roof at Sparta and be blessed. Tell me whether
any of what I have said is wrong. If it is right, do not kill
your daughter and mine—and you will show good sense.

CHORUS LEADER

Do as she says! To join in saving children's lives is honor-
able, Agamemnon! No one in the world can deny this!

IPHIGENIA

If I possessed Orpheus' power of speech and could per-
suade by incantation so that rocks would follow me and I
could charm anyone I pleased, I would use that power. But
now all the skill I have is in my tears, and these I will give
you: that is all I can do. (*kneeling before Agamemnon*) As a
suppliant I lay my body at your knees, the body she gave
birth to. Do not kill me before my time: to see the light
of day is sweet. And do not compel me to look upon the
Underworld. I was the first to call you father, and you
called me your daughter first of all. I was the first to be
dandled on your knees and to give and receive that dear
joy. You used to say, "Shall I see you happy in your hus-
band's house, living a flourishing life worthy of me?" And I
used to say as I hung about your chin, the chin I now grasp
with my hand, "And how shall I see you faring, father?

1195 μέλει Musgrave: σε δεῖ L
1207 τἀμά Elmsley: νῶι L   μὴ κατακτάνῃς Jackson: μὴ δή

297

ἐμῶν φίλαισιν ὑποδοχαῖς δόμων, πάτερ,
1230   πόνων τιθηνοὺς ἀποδιδοῦσά σοι τροφάς;
τούτων ἐγὼ μὲν τῶν λόγων μνήμην ἔχω,
σὺ δ᾽ ἐπιλέλησαι, καί μ᾽ ἀποκτεῖναι θέλεις.
μή, πρός σε Πέλοπος καὶ πρὸς Ἀτρέως πατρὸς
καὶ τῆσδε μητρός, ἢ πρὶν ὠδίνουσ᾽ ἐμὲ
1235   νῦν δευτέραν ὠδῖνα τήνδε λαμβάνει.
τί μοι μέτεστι τῶν Ἀλεξάνδρου γάμων
Ἑλένης τε; πόθεν ἦλθ᾽ ἐπ᾽ ὀλέθρῳ τὠμῷ, πάτερ;
βλέψον πρὸς ἡμᾶς, ὄμμα δὸς φίλημά τε,
ἵν᾽ ἀλλὰ τοῦτο κατθανοῦσ᾽ ἔχω σέθεν
1240   μνημεῖον, ἢν μὴ τοῖς ἐμοῖς πεισθῇς λόγοις.
[ἀδελφέ, μικρὸς μὲν σύ γ᾽ ἐπίκουρος φίλοις,
ὅμως δὲ συνδάκρυσον, ἱκέτευσον πατρὸς
τὴν σὴν ἀδελφὴν μὴ θανεῖν· αἴσθημά τοι
κἀν νηπίοις γε τῶν κακῶν ἐγγίγνεται.
1245   ἰδοὺ σιωπῶν λίσσεταί σ᾽ ὅδ᾽, ὦ πάτερ.
ἀλλ᾽ αἴδεσαί με καὶ κατοίκτιρον βίου.
ναί, πρὸς γενείου σ᾽ ἀντόμεσθα δύο φίλω·
ὁ μὲν νεοσσός ἐστιν, ἡ δ᾽ ηὐξημένη.
ἓν συντεμοῦσα πάντα νικήσω λόγον·
1250   τὸ φῶς τόδ᾽ ἀνθρώποισιν ἥδιστον βλέπειν,
τὰ νέρθε δ᾽ οὐδέν· μαίνεται δ᾽ ὃς εὔχεται
θανεῖν. κακῶς ζῆν κρεῖσσον ἢ καλῶς θανεῖν.]

ΧΟΡΟΣ

ὦ τλῆμον Ἑλένη, διὰ σὲ καὶ τοὺς σοὺς γάμους
ἀγὼν Ἀτρείδαις καὶ τέκνοις ἥκει μέγας.

Shall I lovingly receive you into my house as an old man,
father, repaying you for the toil of my nurture?" I remem-
ber these words, but you have forgotten them and wish to
kill me. I beg you by Pelops and Atreus your father, don't
do it! And by my mother, who brought me forth in travail
and now has further travail here. What have I to do with
Alexandros' and Helen's marriage? Why has that come to
destroy me, father? Look at me, give me your glance and
your kiss so that when I have died I may at least have that to
remember you by, if you are not moved by my words!

[Brother, the aid you can give is slight, but weep with
me and supplicate our father that your sister shall not die:
even babes have some perception of trouble. See, father,
he supplicates you by his silence. So have a care for me and
take pity on my life. We two blood kin entreat you by your
beard, one a mere babe, the other grown. I shall say one
thing and overtop all argument: this light is the sweetest
thing to look on, and what is below is nothing. Anyone who
prays for death is a fool: better to live ignobly than to die
nobly.]

CHORUS LEADER

Cruel Helen, because of you and your marriage, a great
struggle has descended on the sons of Atreus and their
children.

γε κτάνῃς L
   1241–52 Retractatori tribuo (in suspic. voc. Diggle, alios alii del.
edd.)

ΑΓΑΜΕΜΝΩΝ

1255 ἐγὼ τά τ' οἰκτρὰ συνετός εἰμι καὶ τὰ μή,
φιλῶ τ' ἐμαυτοῦ τέκνα· μαινοίμην γὰρ ἄν.
δεινῶς δ' ἔχει μοι τοῦτο τολμῆσαι, γύναι,
δεινῶς δὲ καὶ μή· ταὐτὰ γὰρ πρᾶξαί με δεῖ.
ὁρᾶθ' ὅσον στράτευμα ναύφαρκτον τόδε,
1260 χαλκέων θ' ὅπλων ἄνακτες Ἑλλήνων ὅσοι,
οἷς νόστος οὐκ ἔστ' Ἰλίου πύργους ἔπι,
1263 οὐδ' ἔστι Τροίας ἐξελεῖν κλεινὸν βάθρον,
1262 εἰ μή σε θύσω, μάντις ὡς Κάλχας λέγει.
μέμηνε δ' Ἀφροδίτη τις Ἑλλήνων στρατῷ
1265 πλεῖν ὡς τάχιστα βαρβάρων ἐπὶ χθόνα,
παῦσαί τε λέκτρων ἁρπαγὰς Ἑλληνικῶν·
οἳ τὰς ἐν Ἄργει παρθένους κτενοῦσί μου
ὑμᾶς τε κἀμέ, θέσφατ' εἰ λύσω θεᾶς.
οὐ Μενέλεώς με καταδεδούλωται, τέκνον,
1270 οὐδ' ἐπὶ τὸ κείνου βουλόμενον ἐλήλυθα,
ἀλλ' Ἑλλάς, ᾗ δεῖ, κἂν θέλω κἂν μὴ θέλω,
θῦσαί σε· τούτου δ' ἥσσονες καθέσταμεν.
ἐλευθέραν γὰρ δεῖ νιν ὅσον ἐν σοί, τέκνον,
κἀμοὶ γενέσθαι, μηδὲ βαρβάρων ὕπο
1275 Ἕλληνας ὄντας λέκτρα συλᾶσθαι βίᾳ.

[ΚΛΥΤΑΙΜΗΣΤΡΑ

ὦ τέκνον, ὦ ξέναι,
οἲ 'γὼ θανάτου <τοῦ> σοῦ μελέα.
φεύγει σε πατὴρ Ἅιδῃ παραδούς.]

1246 βίου Markland: βίον L

300

AGAMEMNON

I understand what calls for pity and what does not, and I
love my children: I would be mad otherwise. It is a terrible
thing to steel myself to this deed, but a terrible thing like-
wise not to. For my fate will be the same. See how large a
seagoing army is here, how many Greeks with panoplies of
bronze! They cannot go to the towers of Ilium or capture
the glorious plain of Troy unless I kill you: so Calchas says.
A great longing runs riot in the Greek army to sail with all
speed to the land of the barbarians and stop the abduction
of Greek wives. The Greeks will kill my girls in Argos and
the two of you and me if I make void the goddess' oracle. It
is not Menelaus who has enslaved me, nor have I gone over
to his purpose: it is Hellas. To her I must sacrifice you,
whether I will or no: she is my ruler. As far as it depends on
you, my daughter, and on me, she must be free, and we
Greeks must not have our wives forcibly abducted.

Exit AGAMEMNON *by Eisodos B.*

[CLYTAEMESTRA

Oh child, O foreign ladies, ah me, how miserable your
death makes me! Your father has fled, having handed you
over to Hades!]

1257 τοῦτο England: ταῦτα L
1258 ταὐτὰ Kirchhoff: τοῦτο L
1263 ante 1262 trai. Markland
1263 κλεινὸν Reiske: καινὸν L
1270 in suspic. voc. Diggle
1274 βαρβάρων Musgrave: -οις L
1276–82 in suspic. voc. Diggle (alios alii del. edd.)
1277 ⟨τοῦ⟩ Heath

ΙΦΙΓΕΝΕΙΑ

[οἲ 'γώ, μᾶτερ· ταὐτὸν τόδε γὰρ
1280 μέλος εἰς ἄμφω πέπτωκε τύχης,
κοὐκέτι μοι φῶς
οὐδ' ἀελίου τόδε φέγγος.]
ἰὼ ἰώ.
νιφόβολον Φρυγῶν νάπος Ἴδας τ' ὄρεα,
1285 Πρίαμος ὅθι ποτὲ βρέφος ἁπαλὸν ἔβαλεν
ματέρος ἀποπρὸ νοσφίσας ἐπὶ μόρῳ
θανατόεντι Πάριν, ὃς Ἰδαῖος Ἰ-
1290 δαῖος ἐλέγετ' ἐλέγετ' ἐν Φρυγῶν πόλει,
μήποτ' ὤφελες τὸν ἀμφὶ
βουσὶ βουκόλον τραφέντ' Ἀ-
λέξανδρον οἰκίσαι
ἀμφὶ τὸ λευκὸν ὕδωρ, ὅθι κρῆναι
1295 Νυμφᾶν κεῖνται
λειμών τ' ἔρνεσι θάλλων
χλωροῖς καὶ ῥοδόεντ'
ἄνθε' ὑακίνθινά τε θεαῖς δρέπειν· ἔνθα ποτὲ
1300 Παλλάς ἔμολε καὶ δολιόφρων Κύπρις
χἤρα, <σὺν> δ' Ἑρμᾶς, ὁ Διὸς ἄγγελος,
ἁ μὲν ἐπὶ πόθῳ τρυφῶσα
Κύπρις, ἁ δ' <ἐπὶ> δορὶ Παλλάς,
1305 Ἥρα δὲ Διὸς ἄνακτος
εὐναῖσι βασιλίσιν,
κρίσιν ἐπὶ στυγνὰν ἔριν τε
καλλονᾶς, ἐμοὶ δὲ θάνατον,
ὄνομα μὲν φέροντα Δαναΐ-

IPHIGENIA

[Ah me, mother! For the same song fits both of our fates,
and no more do I have the daylight or the sun's beams!]

Ah, ah!
Snow-covered Phrygian glade and peaks of Ida,
where Priam once cast the tender babe,
taking it from his mother to be given to fate
and death, Paris, who was called, was called Idaean,
Idaean in the city of the Phrygians,
how I wish you had never
settled Alexandros,
raised as a cowherd among the cows,
near the bright water, where lie
the springs of the nymphs
and the meadow luxuriant with shoots
of green and roses
and hyacinths for goddesses to pick. To that place
there once came Pallas and Cypris with guile in her
    heart
and Hera, and ⟨with them⟩ Hermes, Zeus's messenger,
the one, Cypris, pluming herself on love,
Pallas on the spear of war,
and Hera on sharing the royal bed
of King Zeus.
They came for a quarrelsome contest
about beauty, but to me it spelled death:
this death brings honor to Danaid girls,

1301 χήρα Kovacs: Ἥρα L   ⟨σὺν⟩ δ' Kovacs: θ' L
1304 ⟨ἐπὶ⟩ Wilamowitz

303

1310 σιν κόραις, πρόθυμα δ' ἔλαβεν
   Ἄρτεμις πρὸς Ἴλιον.
   ὁ δὲ τεκών με τὰν τάλαιναν,
   ὦ μᾶτερ ὦ μᾶτερ,
   οἴχεται προδοὺς ἔρημον.

1315 δυστάλαιν' ἐγώ, πικρὰν
   πικρὰν ἰδοῦσα Δυσελέναν,
   φονεύομαι διόλλυμαι
   σφαγαῖσιν ἀνοσίοισιν ἀνοσίου πατρός.
   μή μοι ναῶν χαλκεμβολάδων

1320 πρύμνας ἅδ' Αὐλὶς δέξασθαι
   τούσδ' εἰς ὅρμους
   ὤφελεν ἐλατᾶν πομπαία,
   μηδ' ἀνταίαν Εὐρίπῳ
   πνεῦσαι πομπὰν Ζεύς, εἱλίσσων

1325 αὔραν ἄλλοις ἄλλαν θνατῶν
   λαίφεσι χαίρειν,
   τοῖσι δὲ λύπαν, τοῖσι δ' ἀνάγκαν,
   τοῖς δ' ἐξορμᾶν, τοῖς δὲ στέλλειν, τοῖσι δὲ μέλλειν.

1330 ἦ πολύμοχθον ἄρ' ἦν γένος, ἦ πολύμοχθον
   ἀμερίων, <τὸ> χρεὼν δέ τι δύσποτμον
   ἀνδράσιν ἀνευρεῖν.
   ἰὼ ἰώ,
   μεγάλα πάθεα, μεγάλα δ' ἄχεα

1335 Δαναΐδαις τιθεῖσα Τυνδαρὶς κόρα.

1309–10 Δαναῖσιν κόραις West: Δαναΐδαισιν ὦ κόραι L
1310 δ' Hennig: σ' L

yet it was as an early sacrifice
for Troy that Artemis took me.
The father who begot me,
O mother, O mother,
has gone off and abandoned me to misery!
Ah woe is me,
to my cost I have looked on Helen-of-woe
and am slain, murdered
in unholy slaughter by an unholy father!
Would that Aulis here had not received
the prows of bronze-beaked ships
into its harbor,
Aulis the sender forth of vessels,
and that Zeus had not blown his escorting breath
against the Euripus current, whirling
a breeze that is different for different mortals,
a joy for the sails of some,
for others grief, for others harsh necessity,
for some a setting forth, for others the furling of sail, for
    others delay.
How vexed, how vexed, it seems, is our race,
we who live but a day! It is fated
that men must have trouble for their lot.
Ah, ah,
great are the sufferings, great the woes
that Tyndareus' daughter laid upon the children of
    Danaus!

1321 ὅρμους Hartung: ὅ- εἰς Τροίαν L
1322 ἐλατᾶν πομπαία Wilamowitz: ἐλάταν πομπαίαν L
1324 εἰλίσσων Tyrwhitt: μειλ- L   1331–2 ⟨τὸ⟩ Hermann
1333 εὑρεῖν Dindorf

EURIPIDES

ΧΟΡΟΣ

ἐγὼ μὲν οἰκτίρω σε συμφορᾶς κακῆς
τυχοῦσαν, οἵας μήποτ' ὤφελες τυχεῖν.

ΙΦΙΓΕΝΕΙΑ

ὦ τεκοῦσα μῆτερ, ἀνδρῶν ὄχλον εἰσορῶ πέλας.

ΚΛΥΤΑΙΜΗΣΤΡΑ

τόν τε τῆς θεᾶς παῖδα, τέκνον, ᾧ <σὺ> δεῦρ'
ἐλήλυθας.

ΙΦΙΓΕΝΕΙΑ

1340 διαχαλᾶτέ μοι μέλαθρα, δμῶες, ὡς κρύψω δέμας.

ΚΛΥΤΑΙΜΗΣΤΡΑ

τί δέ, τέκνον, φεύγεις;

ΙΦΙΓΕΝΕΙΑ

Ἀχιλλέα τόνδ' ἰδεῖν αἰσχύνομαι.

ΚΛΥΤΑΙΜΗΣΤΡΑ

ὡς τί δή;

ΙΦΙΓΕΝΕΙΑ

τὸ δυστυχές μοι τῶν γάμων αἰδῶ φέρει.

ΚΛΥΤΑΙΜΗΣΤΡΑ

οὐκ ἐν ἁβρότητι κεῖσαι πρὸς τὰ νῦν πεπτωκότα.
ἀλλὰ μίμν'· οὐ σεμνότητος ἔργον, ἢν ὀνώμεθα.

ΑΧΙΛΛΕΥΣ

1345 ὦ γύναι τάλαινα, Λήδας θύγατερ ...

1339 παῖδα Heath: Ἀχιλλέα L   <σὺ> Hermann
1344 ὀνώμεθα Wecklein: δυνώ- L

CHORUS LEADER
I for my part pity you for your evil fate: how I wish it had never been yours!

Enter ACHILLES with retinue by Eisodos B.

IPHIGENIA
Mother who bore me, I see a throng of men coming here!

CLYTAEMESTRA
And the goddess' son, my child, for whose sake you came here.

IPHIGENIA
Open the door, slaves, so that I may hide myself indoors!

CLYTAEMESTRA
But why, child, are you running away?

IPHIGENIA
I am ashamed to look at Achilles.

CLYTAEMESTRA
Why is that?

IPHIGENIA
The ill fortune of my marriage makes me ashamed.

CLYTAEMESTRA
In view of the circumstances, that is a luxury you can't afford. Stay: it is no time for standoffishness if there's a chance of benefit.

ACHILLES
Unfortunate woman, Leda's daughter . . .

307

EURIPIDES

ΚΛΥΤΑΙΜΗΣΤΡΑ

οὐ ψευδῆ θροεῖς.

ΑΧΙΛΛΕΥΣ

. . . δείν᾽ ἐν Ἀργείοις βοᾶται . . .

ΚΛΥΤΑΙΜΗΣΤΡΑ

τίς βοή; σήμαινέ μοι.

ΑΧΙΛΛΕΥΣ

. . . ἀμφὶ σῆς παιδός . . .

ΚΛΥΤΑΙΜΗΣΤΡΑ

πονηρῶν εἶπας οἰωνὸν λόγων.

ΑΧΙΛΛΕΥΣ

. . . ὡς χρεὼν σφάξαι νιν.

ΚΛΥΤΑΙΜΗΣΤΡΑ

οὐδεὶς τοῖσδ᾽ ἐναντίον λέγει;

ΑΧΙΛΛΕΥΣ

ἐς θόρυβον ἐγώ τιν᾽ αὐτὸς ἤλυθον . . .

ΚΛΥΤΑΙΜΗΣΤΡΑ

τίν᾽, ὦ ξένε;

ΑΧΙΛΛΕΥΣ

1350   . . . σῶμα λευσθῆναι πέτροισι.

ΚΛΥΤΑΙΜΗΣΤΡΑ

μῶν κόρην σῴζων ἐμήν;

ΑΧΙΛΛΕΥΣ

αὐτὸ τοῦτο.

CLYTAEMESTRA

Your words are all too true.

ACHILLES

. . . the Greeks are shouting terrible things . . .

CLYTAEMESTRA

Shouting what? Tell me!

ACHILLES

. . . concerning your daughter . . .

CLYTAEMESTRA

Your words are an omen of terrible news.

ACHILLES

. . . that she must be killed.

CLYTAEMESTRA

Did no one speak against this?

ACHILLES

At me too they shouted . . .

CLYTAEMESTRA

What did they shout?

ACHILLES

. . . that I should be stoned to death.

CLYTAEMESTRA

For trying to save my daughter?

ACHILLES

Exactly so.

1346 τίς βοή Herwerden: τίνα βοήν L
1347 πονηρῶν Nauck: -ον L   λόγων Markland: -ον L
1349 τιν' αὐτὸς Blomfield: τοι καὐτὸς L

EURIPIDES

ΚΛΥΤΑΙΜΗΣΤΡΑ
τίς δ᾽ ἂν ἔτλη σώματος τοῦ σοῦ θιγεῖν;

ΑΧΙΛΛΕΥΣ
πάντες Ἕλληνες.

ΚΛΥΤΑΙΜΗΣΤΡΑ
στρατὸς δὲ Μυρμιδὼν οὔ σοι παρῆν;

ΑΧΙΛΛΕΥΣ
πρῶτος ἦν ἐκεῖνος ἐχθρός.

ΚΛΥΤΑΙΜΗΣΤΡΑ
δι᾽ ἄρ᾽ ὀλώλαμεν, τέκνον.

ΑΧΙΛΛΕΥΣ
οἵ με τὸν γάμων ἀπεκάλουν ἥσσον᾽.

ΚΛΥΤΑΙΜΗΣΤΡΑ
ἀπεκρίνω δὲ τί;

ΑΧΙΛΛΕΥΣ
1355 τὴν ἐμὴν μέλλουσαν εὐνὴν μὴ κτανεῖν . . .

ΚΛΥΤΑΙΜΗΣΤΡΑ
δίκαια γάρ.

ΑΧΙΛΛΕΥΣ
ἣν ἐφήμισεν πατήρ μοι.

ΚΛΥΤΑΙΜΗΣΤΡΑ
κἀργόθεν γ᾽ ἐπέμψατο.

ΑΧΙΛΛΕΥΣ
ἀλλ᾽ ἐνικώμην κεκραγμοῦ.

CLYTAEMESTRA
Who would have dared to touch you?

ACHILLES
All the Greeks.

CLYTAEMESTRA
But was the army of Myrmidons not with you?

ACHILLES
They were the most hostile of all.

CLYTAEMESTRA
We are done for then, my daughter!

ACHILLES
They said that I was a slave of a marriage.

CLYTAEMESTRA
And what did you reply?

ACHILLES
I begged them not to kill my future wife . . .

CLYTAEMESTRA
As is only fair.

ACHILLES
. . . whom her father promised me.

CLYTAEMESTRA
Yes, and summoned from Argos.

ACHILLES
But I was drowned out by the shouting.

ΚΛΥΤΑΙΜΗΣΤΡΑ

τὸ πολὺ γὰρ δεινὸν κακόν.

ΑΧΙΛΛΕΥΣ

ἀλλ᾽ ὅμως ἀρήξομέν σοι.

ΚΛΥΤΑΙΜΗΣΤΡΑ

καὶ μαχῇ πολλοῖσιν εἷς;

ΑΧΙΛΛΕΥΣ

εἰσορᾷς τεύχη φέροντας τούσδ᾽;

ΚΛΥΤΑΙΜΗΣΤΡΑ

ὄναιο τῶν φρενῶν.

ΑΧΙΛΛΕΥΣ

1360 ἀλλ᾽ ὀνησόμεσθα.

ΚΛΥΤΑΙΜΗΣΤΡΑ

παῖς ἄρ᾽ οὐκέτι σφαγήσεται;

ΑΧΙΛΛΕΥΣ

οὔκ, ἐμοῦ γ᾽ ἑκόντος.

ΚΛΥΤΑΙΜΗΣΤΡΑ

ἥξει δ᾽ ὅστις ἅψεται κόρης;

ΑΧΙΛΛΕΥΣ

μυρίοι γ᾽, ἄξει δ᾽ Ὀδυσσεύς.

ΚΛΥΤΑΙΜΗΣΤΡΑ

ἆρ᾽ ὁ Σισύφου γόνος;

ΑΧΙΛΛΕΥΣ

αὐτὸς οὗτος.

CLYTAEMESTRA

The multitude are a terrible bane.

ACHILLES

Nevertheless I shall come to your aid.

CLYTAEMESTRA

Will you fight all alone against many?

ACHILLES

Do you see these men carrying armor?

CLYTAEMESTRA

Blessings on you for your noble heart!

ACHILLES

Blessings I shall have.

CLYTAEMESTRA

So my daughter will not be killed?

ACHILLES

Not if I can help it!

CLYTAEMESTRA

Will someone come to lay hands on her?

ACHILLES

Yes, countless soldiers, with Odysseus leading them.

CLYTAEMESTRA

You mean the son of Sisyphus?

ACHILLES

That's the man.

1361 γ᾽ ἑκόντος] γε ζῶντος Nauck: γ᾽ ἔτ᾽ ὄντος Stockert

ΚΛΥΤΑΙΜΗΣΤΡΑ
ἴδια πράσσων ἢ στρατοῦ ταχθεὶς ὕπο;

ΑΧΙΛΛΕΥΣ
αἱρεθεὶς ἑκών.

ΚΛΥΤΑΙΜΗΣΤΡΑ
πονηράν γ᾽ αἵρεσιν, μιαιφονεῖν.

ΑΧΙΛΛΕΥΣ
1365 ἀλλ᾽ ἐγὼ σχήσω νιν.

ΚΛΥΤΑΙΜΗΣΤΡΑ
ἄξει δ᾽ οὐχ ἑκοῦσαν ἁρπάσας;

ΑΧΙΛΛΕΥΣ
δηλαδὴ ξανθῆς ἐθείρας.

ΚΛΥΤΑΙΜΗΣΤΡΑ
ἐμὲ δὲ δρᾶν τί χρὴ τότε;

ΑΧΙΛΛΕΥΣ
ἀντέχου θυγατρός.

ΚΛΥΤΑΙΜΗΣΤΡΑ
ὡς τοῦδ᾽ οὕνεκ᾽ οὐ σφαγήσεται.

ΑΧΙΛΛΕΥΣ
ἀλλὰ μὴν ἐς τοῦτό γ᾽ ἥξει.

ΙΦΙΓΕΝΕΙΑ
μῆτερ, εἰσακουστέα
[τῶν ἐμῶν λόγων· μάτην γάρ σ᾽ εἰσορῶ θυμουμένην
1370 σῷ πόσει· τὰ δ᾽ ἀδύναθ᾽ ἡμῖν καρτερεῖν οὐ ῥάδιον].

1366 δρᾶν τί χρὴ Kirchhoff: τί χ- δ- L

314

CLYTAEMESTRA

Acting on his own or chosen by the army?

ACHILLES

Chosen, but with his full consent.

CLYTAEMESTRA

A terrible thing to be elected to, shedding blood!

ACHILLES

But I shall check him.

CLYTAEMESTRA

Will he drag her away against her will?

ACHILLES

Yes, by her blond hair.

CLYTAEMESTRA

What must I do then?

ACHILLES

Hold fast to your daughter.

CLYTAEMESTRA

You may be sure: if that can save her she will not be killed.

ACHILLES

It will come to that.

IPHIGENIA

Mother, you must listen [to what I have to say. For I see that you are angry at your husband to no purpose. It is not easy for us to endure beyond our limits]! It is right to thank

---

1368 εἰσακουστέα Diggle: -ούσατε L
1369–70 del. Kovacs

τὸν μὲν οὖν ξένον δίκαιον αἰνέσαι προθυμίας·
ἀλλὰ καὶ σὲ τοῦθ' ὁρᾶν χρή, μὴ διαβληθῇ στρατῷ,
καὶ πλέον πράξωμεν οὐδέν, ὅδε δὲ συμφορᾶς τύχῃ.
οἷα δ' εἰσῆλθέν μ', ἄκουσον, μῆτερ, ἐννοουμένην·
1375 κατθανεῖν μέν μοι δέδοκται· τοῦτο δ' αὐτὸ βούλομαι
εὐκλεῶς πρᾶξαι, παρεῖσά γ' ἐκποδὼν τὸ δυσγενές.
δεῦρο δὴ σκέψαι μεθ' ἡμῶν, μῆτερ, ὡς καλῶς λέγω·
εἰς ἔμ' Ἑλλὰς ἡ μεγίστη πᾶσα νῦν ἀποβλέπει,
κἂν ἐμοὶ πορθμός τε ναῶν καὶ Φρυγῶν κατασκαφαί,
1380 τάς γε μελλούσας γυναῖκας μή τι δρῶσι βάρβαροι
[μηκέθ' ἁρπάζειν ἐᾶν †τὰς† ὀλβίας ἐξ Ἑλλάδος,
τὸν Ἑλένης τείσαντας ὄλεθρον, ἣν ἀνήρπασεν
  Πάρις].
ταῦτα πάντα κατθανοῦσα ῥύσομαι, καί μου κλέος,
Ἑλλάδ' ὡς ἠλευθέρωσα, μακάριον γενήσεται.
1385 καὶ γὰρ οὐδέ τοί ⟨τι⟩ λίαν ἐμὲ φιλοψυχεῖν χρεών·
πᾶσι γάρ μ' Ἕλλησι κοινὸν ἔτεκες, οὐχὶ σοὶ μόνῃ.
ἀλλὰ μυρίοι μὲν ἄνδρες ἀσπίσιν πεφαργμένοι,
μυρίοι δ' ἐρέτμ' ἔχοντες, πατρίδος ἠδικημένης,
δρᾶν τι τολμήσουσιν ἐχθροὺς χὐπὲρ Ἑλλάδος
  θανεῖν,
1390 ἡ δ' ἐμὴ ψυχὴ μί' οὖσα πάντα κωλύσει τάδε;
τί τὸ δίκαιον ἆρα τούτοις ἔχομεν ἀντειπεῖν ἔπος;
  κἀπ' ἐκεῖν' ἔλθωμεν· οὐ δεῖ τόνδε διὰ μάχης
  μολεῖν
πᾶσιν Ἀργείοις γυναικὸς οὕνεκ' οὐδὲ κατθανεῖν.

---

¹³⁷² διαβληθῇ Hartung: -ῆς L

the stranger for his efforts. But you also must take care: he could well be put in the wrong with the army and suffer misfortune, yet we might be no better off.

Hear, mother, the thoughts that have come to me as I pondered. It is determined that I must die: but to do so gloriously—that is the thing I want to do,[24] clearing myself from all taint of baseness. Consider with me, mother, the truth of what I am saying. Hellas in all its might now looks to me, and upon me depends the power to take their ships over and destroy the Phrygians, so that the barbarians will not do anything to women in the future [and not allow them to abduct women from rich Hellas, since they have paid for the loss of Helen, whom Paris abducted]. All this rescuing is accomplished by my death, and the fame I win for freeing Hellas will make me blessed.

Truly it is not right that I should be too in love with my life: you bore me for all the Greeks in common, not for yourself alone. Countless hoplites and countless rowers will dare, since their country has been wronged, to fight bravely against the enemy and die on behalf of Hellas: shall my single life stand in the way of all this? What just plea can we make to counter this argument?

And there's another thing to be said. This man should not do battle with all the Greeks and be killed for a wom-

---

24 Or "I have decided to die: my one wish is to act nobly."

1375 μὲν ἐμὲ Rauchenstein, μέν μοι πέπρωται Vitelli
1380 γε Günther: τε L   μή Weil: ἤν L
1381–2 del. Wecklein
1385 ⟨τι⟩ Elmsley
1391 ἆρα τούτοις ἔχομεν Weil: τοῦτ᾽ ἄρ᾽ ἔχοιμεν L

317

εἷς γ' ἀνὴρ κρείσσων γυναικῶν μυρίων ὁρᾶν φάος.
1395 εἰ βεβούληται δὲ σῶμα τοὐμὸν Ἄρτεμις λαβεῖν,
ἐμποδὼν γενήσομαι 'γὼ θνητὸς οὖσα τῇ θεῷ;
ἀλλ' ἀμήχανον· δίδωμι σῶμα τοὐμὸν Ἑλλάδι.
θύετ', ἐκπορθεῖτε Τροίαν· ταῦτα γὰρ μνημεῖά μου
διὰ μακροῦ καὶ παῖδες οὗτοι καὶ γάμοι καὶ δόξ'
ἐμή.
1400 βαρβάρων δ' Ἕλληνας ἄρχειν εἰκός, ἀλλ' οὐ
βαρβάρους
μῆτερ, Ἑλλήνων· τὸ μὲν γὰρ δοῦλον, οἱ δ'
ἐλεύθεροι.

ΧΟΡΟΣ
τὸ μὲν σόν, ὦ νεᾶνι, γενναίως ἔχει·
τὸ τῆς τύχης δὲ καὶ τὸ τῆς θεοῦ νοσεῖ.

ΑΧΙΛΛΕΥΣ
Ἀγαμέμνονος παῖ, μακάριόν μέ τις θεῶν
1405 ἔμελλε θήσειν, εἰ τύχοιμι σῶν γάμων.
ζηλῶ δὲ σοῦ μὲν Ἑλλάδ', Ἑλλάδος δὲ σέ.
[εὖ γὰρ τόδ' εἶπας ἀξίως τε πατρίδος·
τὸ θεομαχεῖν γὰρ ἀπολιποῦσ', ὅ σου 'κράτει,
ἐξελογίσω τὰ χρηστὰ τἀναγκαῖά τε.
1410 μᾶλλον δὲ λέκτρων σῶν πόθος μ' ἐσέρχεται
ἐς τὴν φύσιν βλέψαντα· γενναία γὰρ εἶ.
ὅρα δ'· ἐγὼ γὰρ βούλομαί σ' εὐεργετεῖν
λαβεῖν τ' ἐς οἴκους· ἄχθομαί δ', ἴστω Θέτις,

―――――――――――――――――――――――
1395 βεβούληται δὲ Headlam: δ' ἐβουλήθη L

an's sake. Better to save the life of a single man than ten
thousand women! If Artemis has decided to take my body,
shall I, who am mortal, oppose a goddess? That is impossi-
ble: I shall give myself to Greece.

   Make sacrifice, all of you, and sack Troy! That shall be
my long-lived memorial, that for me will be my children,
my marriage, my good name! Greeks, mother, must rule
over barbarians, not barbarians over Greeks: the one sort
are slaves but the others are free men!

CHORUS LEADER

Your conduct, maiden, is noble. Yet ill is the fate the gods
have sent you.[25]

ACHILLES

Daughter of Agamemnon, some god would have made me
a blessed man if I could have won you as my wife. Hellas I
consider enviable because she has you, and you I consider
enviable because you have her. [Your words are splendid,
worthy of your country. You were fighting against heaven,
but you have ceased to do so and have considered carefully
what is beneficial and necessary. The desire to be your hus-
band affects me all the more when I consider your nature:
you are a noble person. But look: I want to be your bene-
factor and take you to my home. Thetis be my witness how

---

[25] It is imperative that Achilles respond to the speech and that
he leave the stage before the end of the scene. But I judge that in
1404–32 nothing except 1404–6 and 1431–2 belongs to the first
performance, the rest being the work of the Reviser.

1407–30 Retractatori tribuo (alios alii del. edd.)
1408 ᾽κράτει G. Dindorf: κρατεῖ L

εἰ μή σε σώσω Δαναΐδαισι διὰ μάχης
1415 ἐλθών. ἄθρησον· ὁ θάνατος δεινὸν κακόν.

ΙΦΙΓΕΝΕΙΑ

λέγω τάδ᾽ ⟨οὐδὲν οὐδέν᾽ εὐλαβουμένη⟩.
ἡ Τυνδαρὶς παῖς διὰ τὸ σῶμ᾽ ἀρκεῖ μάχας
ἀνδρῶν τιθεῖσα καὶ φόνους· σὺ δ᾽, ὦ ξένε,
μὴ θνῆσκε δι᾽ ἐμὲ μηδ᾽ ἀποκτείνῃς τινά,
1420 ἔα δὲ σῶσαί μ᾽ Ἑλλάδ᾽, ἢν δυνώμεθα.

ΑΧΙΛΛΕΥΣ

ὦ λῆμ᾽ ἄριστον, οὐκ ἔχω πρὸς τοῦτ᾽ ἔτι
λέγειν, ἐπεί σοι τάδε δοκεῖ· γενναῖα γὰρ
φρονεῖς· τί γὰρ τἀληθὲς οὐκ εἴποι τις ἄν;
ὅμως δ᾽, ἴσως γὰρ κἂν μεταγνοίης τάδε,
1425 ὡς οὖν ἂν εἰδῇς τἀπ᾽ ἐμοῦ λελεγμένα,
ἐλθὼν τάδ᾽ ὅπλα θήσομαι βωμοῦ πέλας,
ὡς οὐκ ἐάσων σ᾽ ἀλλὰ κωλύσων θανεῖν.
χρήσῃ δὲ καὶ σὺ τοῖς ἐμοῖς λόγοις τάχα,
ὅταν πέλας σῆς φάσγανον δέρης ἴδῃς.
1430 οὔκουν ἐάσω σ᾽ ἀφροσύνῃ τῇ σῇ θανεῖν.]
ἐλθὼν δὲ σὺν ὅπλοις τοῖσδε πρὸς ναὸν θεᾶς
καραδοκήσω σὴν ἐκεῖ παρουσίαν.

ΙΦΙΓΕΝΕΙΑ

μῆτερ, τί σιγῇ δακρύοις τέγγεις κόρας;

ΚΛΥΤΑΙΜΗΣΤΡΑ

ἔχω τάλαινα πρόφασιν ὥστ᾽ ἀλγεῖν φρένα.

pained I am that I shall not save your life by fighting against
the sons of Danaus. Consider: death is a terrible evil.

IPHIGENIA

I say this ⟨without any fear of anyone⟩: it is enough that
the daughter of Tyndareus causes battles and murders be-
cause of her body. As for you, stranger, do not die on my
behalf or kill anyone, but allow me to save Hellas if I can.

ACHILLES

O noble heart, I cannot say anything further in reply to this
since that is your decision. Your thoughts are noble: why
should one not speak the truth? But nevertheless, since
you might have a change of heart, hear my proposal: I shall
go and station my arms near the altar so that I may prevent
and hinder your death. You might adopt my counsel when
you see the sword near your neck. I shall therefore not
allow you to die by your folly.] I shall go with my armor to
the goddess' temple and there await your arrival.

Exit ACHILLES *by Eisodos B.*

IPHIGENIA

Mother, why do you weep and say nothing?

CLYTAEMESTRA

Poor woman that I am, I have cause to grieve in my heart.

1416 ⟨οὐδὲν οὐδέν᾽ εὐλαβουμένη⟩ suppl. Tr3
1424 γὰρ Hermann: γε L
1425 del. Hermann

[ΙΦΙΓΕΝΕΙΑ

1435 †παῦσαί με μὴ κάκιζε†· τάδε δέ μοι πιθοῦ.

ΚΛΥΤΑΙΜΗΣΤΡΑ

λέγ'· ὡς παρ' ἡμῶν οὐδὲν ἀδικήσῃ, τέκνον.

ΙΦΙΓΕΝΕΙΑ

μήτ' οὖν γε τὸν σὸν πλόκαμον ἐκτέμῃς τριχὸς
μήτ' ἀμφὶ σῶμα μέλανας ἀμπίσχῃ πέπλους.

ΚΛΥΤΑΙΜΗΣΤΡΑ

τί δὴ τόδ' εἶπας, τέκνον; ἀπολέσασά σε;]

ΙΦΙΓΕΝΕΙΑ

1440 οὐ σύ γε· σέσωμαι, κατ' ἐμὲ δ' εὐκλεὴς ἔσῃ.

ΚΛΥΤΑΙΜΗΣΤΡΑ

πῶς εἶπας; οὐ πενθεῖν με σὴν ψυχὴν χρεών;

ΙΦΙΓΕΝΕΙΑ

ἥκιστ', ἐπεί μοι τύμβος οὐ χωσθήσεται.

ΚΛΥΤΑΙΜΗΣΤΡΑ

τί δή; τυθεῖσιν οὐ τάφος νομίζεται.

ΙΦΙΓΕΝΕΙΑ

βωμὸς θεᾶς μοι μνῆμα τῆς Διὸς κόρης.

ΚΛΥΤΑΙΜΗΣΤΡΑ

1445 ἀλλ' ὦ τέκνον σοι πείσομαι· λέγεις γὰρ εὖ.

ΙΦΙΓΕΝΕΙΑ

ὡς εὐτυχοῦσά γ' Ἑλλάδος τ' εὐεργέτις.

1435–9 in susp. voc. Diggle   1435 κλαυθμῷ με μὴ κάκιζε
vel παῦσαί με θηλύνουσα England

IPHIGENIA AT AULIS

[IPHIGENIA
Don't make me a coward: rather, do as I say.

CLYTAEMESTRA
Speak: you will receive no injustice at my hands.

IPHIGENIA
Do not cut off a lock of your hair or put black garments about your body.

CLYTAEMESTRA
What is this you have said, daughter? After losing you?]

IPHIGENIA
No, you do not. My life has been saved, and your name will be honored because of me.

CLYTAEMESTRA
What do you mean? Shall I not grieve for your death?

IPHIGENIA
No, for no grave mound will be raised for me.

CLYTAEMESTRA
What? Is it not customary for sacrificial victims to be buried?

IPHIGENIA
The altar of Zeus's daughter will be my memorial.

CLYTAEMESTRA
Well, daughter, I will do as you say: your advice is good.

IPHIGENIA
Yes, for I enjoy good fortune and am Hellas' benefactor.

1443 δή; Gaisford: δὲ L   τυθεῖσιν Vitelli: τὸ θνῄσκειν L

[ΚΛΥΤΑΙΜΗΣΤΡΑ

τί δὴ κασιγνήταισιν ἀγγείλω σέθεν;

ΙΦΙΓΕΝΕΙΑ

μηδ' ἀμφὶ κείναις μέλανας ἐξάψῃ πέπλους.

ΚΛΥΤΑΙΜΗΣΤΡΑ

εἴπω δὲ παρὰ σοῦ φίλον ἔπος τι παρθένοις;

ΙΦΙΓΕΝΕΙΑ

1450   χαίρειν γ'. Ὀρέστην τ' ἔκτρεφ' ἄνδρα τόνδε μοι.

ΚΛΥΤΑΙΜΗΣΤΡΑ

προσέλκυσαί νιν ὕστατον θεωμένη.

ΙΦΙΓΕΝΕΙΑ

ὦ φίλτατ', ἐπεκούρησας ὅσον εἶχες φίλοις.]

ΚΛΥΤΑΙΜΗΣΤΡΑ

ἔσθ' ὅ τι κατ' Ἄργος δρῶσά σοι χάριν φέρω;

ΙΦΙΓΕΝΕΙΑ

πατέρα τὸν ἀμὸν μὴ στύγει πόσιν τε σόν.

ΚΛΥΤΑΙΜΗΣΤΡΑ

1455   δεινοὺς ἀγῶνας διὰ σὲ δεῖ κεῖνον δραμεῖν.

ΙΦΙΓΕΝΕΙΑ

ἄκων μ' ὑπὲρ γῆς Ἑλλάδος διώλεσεν.

ΚΛΥΤΑΙΜΗΣΤΡΑ

δόλῳ δ', ἀγεννῶς Ἀτρέως τ' οὐκ ἀξίως.

1447–52 Retractatori tribuo (1449–52 del. Wecklein, England)
1447 ἀγγείλω Weil: ἀγγελῶ L

[CLYTAEMESTRA

What message shall I carry back to your sisters?

IPHIGENIA

Do not dress them in black either.

CLYTAEMESTRA

But shall I tell the girls some loving word from you?

IPHIGENIA

Tell them farewell. And for my sake raise Orestes here to
manhood.

CLYTAEMESTRA

Embrace him: you are looking at him for the last time.

IPHIGENIA

Dearest brother, you did what you could to help your
sister!]

CLYTAEMESTRA

Is there anything I can do in Argos as a favor to you?

IPHIGENIA

Do not hate my father, your husband.

CLYTAEMESTRA

He must endure a terrible struggle because of you.

IPHIGENIA

He killed me for Hellas' sake against his will.

CLYTAEMESTRA

By a trick: that was ignoble and unworthy of Atreus.

[ΙΦΙΓΕΝΕΙΑ

τίς μ᾽ εἶσιν ἄξων πρὶν σπαράσσεσθαι κόμης;

ΚΛΥΤΑΙΜΗΣΤΡΑ

ἐγώ, μετά γε σοῦ . . .

ΙΦΙΓΕΝΕΙΑ

μὴ σύ γ᾽· οὐ καλῶς λέγεις.

ΚΛΥΤΑΙΜΗΣΤΡΑ

1460   . . . πέπλων ἐχομένη σῶν.]

ΙΦΙΓΕΝΕΙΑ

[ἐμοί, μῆτερ, πιθοῦ·

μέν᾽· ὡς ἐμοί τε σοί τε κάλλιον τόδε.]

πατρὸς δ᾽ ὀπαδῶν τῶνδέ τίς με πεμπέτω

Ἀρτέμιδος ἐς λειμῶν᾽, ὅπου σφαγήσομαι.

ΚΛΥΤΑΙΜΗΣΤΡΑ

ὦ τέκνον, οἴχῃ;

ΙΦΙΓΕΝΕΙΑ

καὶ πάλιν γ᾽ οὐ μὴ μόλω.

ΚΛΥΤΑΙΜΗΣΤΡΑ

1465   λιποῦσα μητέρ᾽;

ΙΦΙΓΕΝΕΙΑ

ὡς ὁρᾷς γ᾽, οὐκ ἀξίως.

ΚΛΥΤΑΙΜΗΣΤΡΑ

σχές, μή με προλίπῃς.

1458–61 in susp. voc. Diggle
1465 εὖ κἀξίως Hermann cl. *Hec.* 990

[IPHIGENIA
Who will go and bring me before I am grabbed by the hair?

CLYTAEMESTRA
I shall, accompanying you . . .

IPHIGENIA
Do not do it: what you suggest is not good.

CLYTAEMESTRA
. . . holding onto your garments.]

IPHIGENIA
[Be ruled by me, mother: stay behind, for it is better that
way for both me and you.] One of my father's servants, con-
duct me to Artemis' meadow, the place of my slaying!

Enter from the skene *one of Agamemnon's servants.*

CLYTAEMESTRA
Daughter, are you on your way?

IPHIGENIA
Yes, never to return again.

CLYTAEMESTRA
Will you leave your mother?

IPHIGENIA
Yes, as you see, all undeserving.

CLYTAEMESTRA
Stop, don't leave me!

ΙΦΙΓΕΝΕΙΑ

οὐκ ἐῶ στάζειν δάκρυ.
ὑμεῖς δ᾽ ἐπευφημήσατ᾽, ὦ νεάνιδες,
παιᾶνα τἠμῇ συμφορᾷ Διὸς κόρην
Ἄρτεμιν· ἴτω δὲ Δαναΐδαις εὐφημία.
1470 κανᾶ δ᾽ ἐναρχέσθω τις, αἰθέσθω δὲ πῦρ
προχύταις καθαρσίοισι, καὶ πατὴρ ἐμὸς
ἐνδεξιούσθω βωμόν· ὡς σωτηρίαν
Ἕλλησι δώσουσ᾽ ἔρχομαι νικηφόρον.

1475 [ἄγετέ με τὰν Ἰλίου
καὶ Φρυγῶν ἑλέπτολιν.
στέφεα περίβολα δίδοτε, φέρε-
τε—πλόκαμος ὅδε καταστέφειν—
χερνίβων τε παγάς.
1480 ἑλίσσετ᾽ ἀμφὶ ναὸν
ἀμφὶ βωμὸν Ἄρτεμιν,
τὰν ἄνασσαν Ἄρτεμιν,
τὰν μάκαιραν· ὡς ἐμοῖσιν, εἰ χρεών,
1485 αἵμασι θύμασί τε
θέσφατ᾽ ἐξαλείψω.
ὦ πότνια πότνια μᾶτερ, οὐ δάκρυά γέ σοι
δώσομεν ἁμέτερα·
1490 παρ᾽ ἱεροῖς γὰρ οὐ πρέπει.
ἰὼ ἰὼ νεάνιδες,
συνεπαείδετ᾽ Ἄρτεμιν
Χαλκίδος ἀντίπορον,
ἵνα τε δόρατα μέμονε νάϊ

328

IPHIGENIA

I forbid you to weep.

You young women, because of what has happened to me raise a paean in honor of Zeus's daughter Artemis! Let the sons of Danaus keep holy silence! Let someone prepare the sacrificial basket, let the purifying barley meal make the fire blaze up! Let my father make his rightward course about the altar! For I am departing to give the Greeks salvation and victory!

[Bring me away, me the sacker
of Ilium and the Phrygians!
Give me a garland to surround my head—
here are my tresses to garland—
and water from the basins!
Dance about the shrine,
about the altar, in honor of Artemis,
our lady Artemis,
the blessed: for if I must,
with blood, with sacrifice,
I shall blot out the oracles!
O lady, lady mother, I shall not tender you
my tears:
tears are not proper at a sacred rite.
Ho there, maidens,
sing with me to Artemis
whose temple stands opposite Chalcis,
where the wooden ships are keen for battle

1475–1509 del. Kovacs   1479 παγάς Reiske: -αῖσι L
1487–8 οὐ Höpfner: ὡς L   1491 ἰὼ ἰὼ Hermann: ὢ Trl:
om. L   1494 ναί᾿ Hartung (-ια): δάϊα L

329

1495 ὄνομα δι' ἐμὸν Αὐλίδος
στενοπόροις ἐν ὅρμοις.
ἰὼ γᾶ μᾶτερ ὦ Πελασγία,
Μυκηναῖαί τ' ἐμαὶ θεράπναι . . .

ΧΟΡΟΣ

1500 καλεῖς πόλισμα Περσέως,
Κυκλωπιᾶν πόνον χερῶν;

ΙΦΙΓΕΝΕΙΑ

. . . ἐθρέψαθ' Ἑλλάδι με φάος·
θανοῦσα δ' οὐκ ἀναίνομαι.

ΧΟΡΟΣ

κλέος γὰρ οὔ σε μὴ λίπῃ.

ΙΦΙΓΕΝΕΙΑ

1505 ἰὼ ἰώ·
λαμπαδοῦχος ἀμέρα
Διός τε φέγγος, ἕτερον αἰ-
ῶνα καὶ μοῖραν οἰκήσομεν.
χαῖρέ μοι, φίλον φάος.]

ΧΟΡΟΣ

1510 ἰὼ ἰώ·
ἴδεσθε τὰν Ἰλίου
καὶ Φρυγῶν ἐλέπτολιν
στείχουσαν, ἐπὶ κάρα στέφη
βαλουμέναν χερνίβων τε παγάς,

1495 ὄνομα δι' ἐμὸν Murray: δι' ἐ- ὄ- L   Αὐλίδος Matthiae: τᾶσδ' Αὐλ- L   1496 στενοπόροις ἐν Burges: -σιν L

because of my name
in the narrow-straited harbors of Aulis!
O land of Pelasgia, mother who bore me,
and Mycenae, place of my dwelling . . .

CHORUS

You call upon the fortress of Perseus,
the work of Cyclopean hands.

IPHIGENIA

. . . you raised me as a light of salvation to Greece.
I do not regret my death.

CHORUS

No, for fame will never leave you.

IPHIGENIA

Ah, ah,
daystar that lights our way,
Zeus's sunlight, I shall take as my dwelling
another life, another lot!
Farewell, dear light!]

Exit IPHIGENIA *by Eisodos B, accompanied by the servant.*

CHORUS

Ah, ah!
See her, the sacker
of Ilium and the Phrygians,
going on her way, destined
to have her head garlanded and sprinkled

1501 Κυκλωπιᾶν Diggle: -ίων L   1502 ἐθρέψαθ’ Elmsley:
ἔθρεψας L   με Elmsley: μέγα L   1507 ἕτερον Dindorf:
ἕ- ἕ- L   1513 βαλουμέναν Bothe: βαλλομ- L

βωμόν τε δαίμονος
1515 ῥανίσιν αἱματορρύτοις
χρανοῦσαν εὐφυοῦς τε σώματος δέραν.
εὔδροσοί ⟨σε⟩ παγαὶ
πατρῷαι μένουσι χέρνιβές τε
στρατός τ' Ἀχαιῶν θέλων
1520 Ἰλίου πόλιν μολεῖν.
ἀλλὰ τὰν Διὸς κόραν
κλήσωμεν Ἄρτεμιν,
θεῶν ἄνασσαν, ὡς ἐπ' εὐτυχεῖ πότμῳ.
ὦ πότνια ⟨πότνια⟩, θύμασιν βροτησίοις
1525 χαρεῖσα, πέμψον ἐς Φρυγῶν
γαῖαν Ἑλλάνων στρατὸν
†καὶ δολόεντα Τροίας ἕδη†
⟨δός⟩ τ' Ἀγαμέμνονα λόγχαις
Ἑλλάδι κλεινότατον στέφανον
1530 [δὸς ἀμφὶ κάρα ἑὸν]
κλέος ⟨τ'⟩ ἀείμνηστον ἀμφιθεῖναι.

[ΑΓΓΕΛΟΣ Β
ὦ Τυνδαρεία παῖ, Κλυταιμήστρα, δόμων
ἔξω πέρασον, ὡς κλύῃς ἐμῶν λόγων.

1514 τε Reiske: γε L   δαίμονος Bothe: δαίμονος θεᾶς L
1516 χρανοῦσαν Monk: θανοῦσαν L   εὐφυοῦς Kovacs:
-φυῇ L   1517 εὔδροσοι Dindorf: σφαγεῖσαν. εὔδροσοι L
⟨σε⟩ Willink   1518 χέρνιβές Willink: σε χ- L
1523 θεὰν Bothe   1524 ⟨πότνια⟩ Hermann
1528 ⟨δός⟩ τ' Ἀγαμέμνονα Monk: Ἀγαμέμνονά τε L
1530 del. Monk   1531 ⟨τ'⟩ Kovacs

and to stain the goddess' altar
and her lovely body's throat
with the drops of her flowing blood!
The fair water of your father's streams
and his lustral vessels await ⟨you⟩,
and the Greek army keen
to make their way to Ilium.
So let us hymn
Zeus's daughter Artemis,
our lady, as if in good fortune.
O lady ⟨lady⟩, who take joy
in human sacrifice, convey
the Hellene army to the Phrygians' land
and to treacherous Troy,
and ⟨grant⟩ that Agamemnon by the spear
may lay upon Hellas' brow a crown most glorious
[grant about their head]
⟨and⟩ fame that is never forgotten!

Exit CHORUS *by Eisodos B,* CLYTAEMESTRA *by Eisodos A.*[26]

[SECOND MESSENGER

Clytaemestra, daughter of Tyndareus, come out of the house so that you can hear my report!

---

26 Here, in all probability, is the end of the play as it was presented at its first performance. The rest is probably a later addition meant to bring the play into mythical agreement with *Iphigenia among the Taurians*.

1532–1629 del. Porson

ΚΛΥΤΑΙΜΗΣΤΡΑ

φθογγῆς κλυοῦσα δεῦρο σῆς ἀφικόμην,
1535 ταρβοῦσα τλήμων κἀκπεπληγμένη φόβῳ.
μή μοί τιν' ἄλλην ξυμφορὰν ἥκεις φέρων
πρὸς τῇ παρούσῃ;

ΑΓΓΕΛΟΣ Β

σῆς μὲν οὖν παιδὸς πέρι
θαυμαστά σοι καὶ δεινὰ σημῆναι θέλω.

ΚΛΥΤΑΙΜΗΣΤΡΑ

μὴ μέλλε τοίνυν, ἀλλὰ φράζ' ὅσον τάχος.

ΑΓΓΕΛΟΣ Β

1540 ἀλλ', ὦ φίλη δέσποινα, πᾶν πεύσῃ σαφῶς.
λέξω δ' ἀπ' ἀρχῆς, ἤν τι μὴ σφαλεῖσά που
γνώμῃ ταράξῃ γλῶσσαν ἐν λόγοις ἐμήν.
ἐπεὶ γὰρ ἱκόμεσθα τῆς Διὸς κόρης
Ἀρτέμιδος ἄλσος λείμακάς τ' ἀνθεσφόρους,
1545 ἵν' ἦν Ἀχαιῶν σύλλογος στρατεύματος,
σὴν παῖδ' ἄγοντες, εὐθὺς Ἀργείων ὄχλος
ἠθροίζεθ'. ὡς δ' ἐσεῖδεν Ἀγαμέμνων ἄναξ
ἐπὶ σφαγὰς στείχουσαν εἰς ἄλσος κόρην,
ἀνεστέναξε κἄμπαλιν στρέψας κάρα
1550 δάκρυα προῆκεν, ὀμμάτων πέπλον προθείς.
ἡ δὲ σταθεῖσα τῷ τεκόντι πλησίον
ἔλεξε τοιάδ'· Ὦ πάτερ, πάρειμί σοι·
τοὐμὸν δὲ σῶμα τῆς ἐμῆς ὑπὲρ πάτρας
καὶ τῆς ἁπάσης Ἑλλάδος γαίας ὕπερ
1555 θῦσαι δίδωμ' ἑκοῦσα πρὸς βωμὸν θεᾶς

Enter CLYTAEMESTRA *from the* skene.

CLYTAEMESTRA
I have heard your voice and come hither, a poor woman frightened and dazed with fear. Are you bringing me news of some other disaster in addition to my present one?

SECOND MESSENGER
No: I want to tell you amazing and dread things about your daughter.

CLYTAEMESTRA
Don't delay, then, but tell me quickly.

SECOND MESSENGER
Well, my dear lady, you shall hear a true account of everything. I will tell my tale from the beginning unless my mind trips up and throws my tongue into confusion in the telling of it.

When we had come, bringing your daughter, to the grove and flowery meadows of Zeus's daughter Artemis, the mustering place of the Achaean army, at once the Greek host assembled. When king Agamemnon saw the girl entering the grove to be sacrificed, he groaned aloud, and bending his head backward he wept, holding his garment before his face. But she stood next to her father and said, "Father, I have come to you. I willingly grant that your men may bring me to the goddess' altar and sacrifice me, if

---

1538 κλεινὰ Murray, κεδνὰ Weil
1541 που Markland: μου L
1550 προῆκεν Dindorf: -ῆγεν L

ἄγοντας, εἴπερ ἐστὶ θέσφατον τόδε.
καὶ τοὐπ’ ἔμ’ εὐτυχοῖτε καὶ νικηφόρου
δορὸς τύχοιτε πατρίδα τ’ ἐξίκοισθε γῆν.
πρὸς ταῦτα μὴ ψαύσῃ τις Ἀργείων ἐμοῦ·
1560 σφαγῇ παρέξω γὰρ δέρην εὐκαρδίως.
τοσαῦτ’ ἔλεξε· πᾶς δ’ ἐθάμβησεν κλυὼν
εὐψυχίαν τε κἀρετὴν τῆς παρθένου.

στὰς δ’ ἐν μέσῳ Ταλθύβιος, ᾧ τόδ’ ἦν μέλον,
εὐφημίαν ἀνεῖπε καὶ σιγὴν στρατῷ·
1565 Κάλχας δ’ ὁ μάντις ἐς κανοῦν χρυσήλατον
ἔθηκεν ὀξὺ χειρὶ φάσγανον σπάσας
κολεῶν ἔσωθεν κρᾶτά τ’ ἔστεψεν κόρης.
ὁ παῖς δ’ ὁ Πηλέως ἐν κύκλῳ βωμοῦ θεᾶς
λαβὼν κανοῦν ἔθρεξε χέρνιβάς θ’ ὁμοῦ,
1570 ἔλεξε δ’· Ὦ παῖ Ζηνός, ὦ θηροκτόνε,
τὸ λαμπρὸν εἰλίσσουσ’ ἐν εὐφρόνῃ φάος,
δέξαι τὸ θῦμα τόδ’ ὅ γέ σοι δωρούμεθα
στρατός τ’ Ἀχαιῶν Ἀγαμέμνων τ’ ἄναξ ὁμοῦ,
ἄχραντον αἷμα καλλιπαρθένου δέρης,
1575 καὶ δὸς γενέσθαι πλοῦν νεῶν ἀπήμονα
Τροίας τε πέργαμ’ ἐξελεῖν ἡμᾶς δορί.
ἐς γῆν δ’ Ἀτρεῖδαι πᾶς στρατός τ’ ἔστη βλέπων.
ἱερεὺς δὲ φάσγανον λαβὼν ἐπεύξατο,
λαιμόν τ’ ἐπεσκόπειθ’, ἵνα πλήξειεν ἄν·
1580 ἐμοὶ δέ τ’ ἄλγος οὐ μικρὸν εἰσῄει φρενί,
κἄστην νενευκώς· θαῦμα δ’ ἦν αἴφνης ὁρᾶν.
πληγῆς κτύπον γὰρ πᾶς τις ᾔσθετ’ ἂν σαφῶς,

that is what the oracle requires. As far as depends on me
may you all have good fortune, win victory in war, and re-
turn to your native land! In view of this, let no Greek take
hold of me: I will bravely submit my neck to the knife."
Those were her words, and everyone heard and felt amaze-
ment at the bravery and goodness of the maiden.

Standing in their midst Talthybius, whose task this was,
called for silence from the army. Then Calchas the seer
took a sharp knife from its sheath and laid it in a golden
basket and garlanded the girl's head. The son of Peleus
took the basket and the lustral basin and sped in a circle
about the altar, saying, "Daughter of Zeus, slayer of beasts,
who send your bright gleam on its circular path in the
night,[27] receive this sacrifice which we tender you, the
Achaean army and lord Agamemnon, the pure blood from
her lovely neck, and grant that our ships may have fair voy-
age and that our spears may destroy the towers of Troy!"

The sons of Atreus and the whole army stood with their
eyes fixed on the ground.[28] A priest took a sword, uttered a
prayer, and began to examine her neck for a place to strike.
I felt a sharp pang in my heart and stood with head down-
cast. But at once something miraculous occurred. Every-
one could have heard clearly the sound of the blow, but no

[27] Artemis is being identified with Selene, the moon goddess.

[28] Hereafter the large number of metrical errors shows that
the text was written long after the classical age. The last page of
the play was probably lost or damaged in some exemplar of our
manuscript, and someone tried to restore the end as best he could.

1558 δορὸς Pierson: δώρου L   1560 σφαγῇ Jacobs: σιγῇ L
1568 βωμοῦ Heath: -ὸν L

τὴν παρθένον δ' οὐκ εἶδεν οὗ γῆς εἰσέδυ.
βοᾷ δ' ἱερεύς, ἅπας δ' ἐπήχησε στρατός,
1585 ἄελπτον εἰσιδόντες ἐκ θεῶν τινος
φάσμ', οὗ γε μηδ' ὁρωμένου πίστις παρῆν·
ἔλαφος γὰρ ἀσπαίρουσ' ἔκειτ' ἐπὶ χθονὶ
ἰδεῖν μεγίστη διαπρεπής τε τὴν θέαν,
ἧς αἵματι βωμὸς ἐραίνετ' ἄρδην τῆς θεοῦ.
1590 κἀν τῷδε Κάλχας πῶς δοκεῖς χαίρων ἔφη·
Ὦ τοῦδ' Ἀχαιῶν κοίρανοι κοινοῦ στρατοῦ,
ὁρᾶτε τήνδε θυσίαν, ἣν ἡ θεὸς
προύθηκε βωμίαν, ἔλαφον ὀρειδρόμον;
ταύτην μάλιστα τῆς κόρης ἀσπάζεται,
1595 ὡς μὴ μιάνῃ βωμὸν εὐγενεῖ φόνῳ.
ἡδέως τε τοῦτ' ἐδέξατο καὶ πλοῦν οὔριον
δίδωσιν ἡμῖν Ἰλίου τ' ἐπιδρομάς.
πρὸς ταῦτα πᾶς τις θάρσος αἶρε ναυβάτης,
χώρει τε πρὸς ναῦν· ὡς ἡμέρᾳ τῇδε δεῖ
1600 λιπόντας ἡμᾶς Αὐλίδος κοίλους μυχοὺς
Αἴγαιον οἶδμα διαπερᾶν.
                              ἐπεὶ δ' ἅπαν
κατηνθρακώθη θῦμ' ἐν Ἡφαίστου φλογί,
τὰ πρόσφορ' ηὔξαθ', ὡς τύχοι νόστου στρατός.
πέμπει δ' Ἀγαμέμνων μ' ὥστε σοι φράσαι τάδε,
1605 λέγειν θ' ὁποίας ἐκ θεῶν μοίρας κυρεῖ
καὶ δόξαν ἔσχεν ἄφθιτον καθ' Ἑλλάδα.
ἐγὼ παρὼν δὲ καὶ τὸ πρᾶγμ' ὁρῶν λέγω·
ἡ παῖς σαφῶς σοι πρὸς θεοὺς ἀφίπτατο.
λύπης δ' ἀφαίρει καὶ πόσει πάρες χόλον·

one could see where in the world the girl had disappeared to. The priest raised a shout, and the whole army roared in answer when an unexpected sight sent by the gods met their eyes, one they could not believe though they had seen it: a doe, large and conspicuous to behold, lay breathing her last upon the ground, and with her blood the goddess' altar was thoroughly drenched. Then Calchas, with a joy you can well imagine, said, "You chieftains of our united army, do you see this sacrifice, this doe that runs on the mountains, that the goddess has laid upon her altar? She accepts this in place of the girl so that she may not stain her altar with noble blood. She receives this gladly and grants us a fair voyage to attack Ilium. Therefore all sailors take heart and make for your ships! For today we must leave the hollow bays of Aulis behind and cross the swelling Aegean!"

When the victim had been completely consumed by Hephaestus' flame, Calchas made the customary prayer that the army might get safely home. Agamemnon sends me to tell you this and to say what kind of portion she[29] has received from the gods and what kind of imperishable glory she has won in Hellas. I was there and saw the thing and I say that your daughter clearly has flown away up to heaven. So put away your grief and do not be angry with

---

29 It is awkward to supply Iphigenia as subject since she has not been mentioned for ten lines, but that is clearly what the author meant.

1594 μάλιστα] γὰρ ἀντὶ Herwerden
1596 ἐδέξατ᾽ οὔριόν τε πλοῦν Semitelos

1610 ἀπροσδόκητα δὲ βροτοῖς τὰ τῶν θεῶν,
σῴζουσί θ' οὓς φιλοῦσιν. ἦμαρ γὰρ τόδε
θανοῦσαν εἶδε καὶ βλέπουσαν παῖδα σήν.

XOPOΣ

ὡς ἥδομαί τοι ταῦτ' ἀκούσασ' ἀγγέλου·
ζῶν δ' ἐν θεοῖσι σὸν μένειν φράζει τέκος.

ΚΛΥΤΑΙΜΗΣΤΡΑ

1615 ὦ παῖ, θεῶν τοῦ κλέμμα γέγονας;
πῶς σε προσείπω; πῶς δ' οὐ φῶ
παραμυθεῖσθαι τούσδε μάτην
μύθους, ὥς σου
πένθους λυγροῦ παυσαίμην;

XOPOΣ

καὶ μὴν Ἀγαμέμνων ἄναξ στείχει,
1620 τούσδ' αὐτοὺς ἔχων σοι φράζειν μύθους.

ΑΓΑΜΕΜΝΩΝ

γύναι, θυγατρὸς ἕνεκ' ὄλβιοι γενοίμεθ' ἄν·
ἔχει γὰρ ὄντως ἐν θεοῖς ὁμιλίαν.
χρὴ δέ σε λαβοῦσαν τόνδε μόσχον νεαγενῆ
στείχειν πρὸς οἴκους· ὡς στρατὸς πρὸς πλοῦν ὁρᾷ.
1625 καὶ χαῖρε· χρόνια τἀμά σοι προσφθέγματα
Τροίηθεν ἔσται. καὶ γένοιτό σοι καλῶς.

XOPOΣ

χαίρων, Ἀτρείδη, γῆν ἵκου
Φρυγίαν, χαίρων δ' ἐπάνηκε,
κάλλιστά μοι σκῦλ' ἀπὸ Τροίας ἑλών.]

340

your husband. Truly what the gods send confounds mortal expectation: they save those whom they love. This day has seen your daughter both dead and alive.

CHORUS LEADER

How delighted I am to hear this from the messenger. He says your daughter is alive and dwells among the gods.

CLYTAEMESTRA

My daughter, which of the gods has stolen you away? How can I speak to you? How shall I not maintain that these are false consoling tales to make me cease from my keen grief for you?

CHORUS LEADER

See, here comes lord Agamemnon, who has the same tale to tell you.

Enter by Eisodos B AGAMEMNON.

AGAMEMNON

My wife, where our daughter is concerned we can be blessed: truly her life is with the gods. And now you must take our young son here and go home: the army is watching for its chance to sail. Farewell: much time will go by before I can greet you on my return from Troy. May all be well with you!

CHORUS LEADER

Go rejoicing, son of Atreus, to the land of the Phrygians and return rejoicing, having taken fair spoils from Troy.]

EURIPIDES, FRAG. 857 NAUCK

Aelian. nat. an. 7.39:

ὅσοι λέγουσι θῆλυν ἔλαφον κέρατα οὐ φύειν, οὐκ
αἰδοῦνται τοὺς τοῦ ἐναντίου μάρτυρας· . . . ὁ δὲ Εὐ-
ριπίδης ἐν τῇ Ἰφιγενείᾳ

 ἔλαφον δ' Ἀχαιῶν χερσὶν ἐνθήσω φίλαις
 κεροῦσσαν, ἣν σφάζοντες αὐχήσουσι σὴν
 σφάζειν θυγατέρα.

A FRAGMENT OF ANOTHER ENDING

Aelian, *On the Nature of Animals* 7.39:

Those who say that the female deer does not grow horns show no respect for those who attest the opposite: . . . And Euripides in his *Iphigenia* says, "And I shall put into the dear hands of the Greeks a horned doe: and when they sacrifice it they will suppose that they are sacrificing your daughter."

RHESUS

INTRODUCTION

Our earliest extant treatment of the myth of Rhesus, king of Thrace and owner of the finest horses in the world after those of Achilles, is Book Ten of the *Iliad*, the so-called "Doloneia." The Greeks have just been worsted by the Trojans since Achilles has withdrawn from battle in anger at Agamemnon. It is now night, and the Trojans, confident of victory, are encamped on the plain against the Greek ships, their watch fires burning in the night as a reminder of their success. The Greeks in panic send an embassy to try to persuade Achilles to return, but he refuses. Early in Book Ten both the Greeks and the Trojans hold assemblies, and both decide to send out men that night to spy on the enemy camp. On the Greek side Diomedes and Odysseus volunteer for this dangerous mission, while Dolon, son of Eumedes, offers to be the Trojan spy provided he receives as his reward, after the defeat of the Greeks, the horses of Achilles. The two Greeks encounter Dolon and overpower him, and he, hoping his life will be spared, answers Odysseus' questions about the whereabouts of Hector and the state of the sentinels, telling him that the Trojans are on alert but their allies are asleep. In response to a further question, he reveals the location of Rhesus, newly arrived from Thrace with snow-white, wind-swift horses. Odysseus cuts Dolon's throat, and the two spies set off, find Rhesus, kill him and his men, and take the horses.

But there is evidence, in the scholia to *Iliad* 10.435, for two other versions of this legend, both of which are likely to have been known to Homer but altered by him to suit his *Iliad*. (For a discussion see Fenik 1964.) In one, used in a lost poem of Pindar, Rhesus arrives in Troy as an ally and defeats the Greeks, whereupon Hera sends Athena to urge Odysseus and Diomedes to go on a night mission and kill him. According to the other it was prophesied that if Rhesus and his horses drank of the River Scamander in the Troad, he would be invincible. But since he arrives at night and is killed before that happens, his fated rout of the Greeks is avoided. (I refer to these below as the Pindar version and the oracle version.) Both these versions contain elements that would tend to diminish the stature and importance of either Hector or Achilles, and it is not surprising that those elements are suppressed by Homer. *Iliad* 10 never mentions Rhesus' invincibility, and Odysseus and Diomedes apparently set out to kill Hector and find out about Rhesus not because Athena sends them to kill him (as in the Pindar version) but because they meet Dolon. His death has no lasting or important consequences.

The play that has come down to us as Euripides' *Rhesus*—the much-disputed question of its attribution will be discussed below—is basically a dramatization of the oracle version in which Rhesus, had he lived, would have been invincible, though there are elements that derive from *Iliad* 10 and the Pindar version. As in Homer the two Greeks seem to have set out to kill Hector, but they are directed to Rhesus by Athena, not by Dolon. Dolon appears, as in Homer, but he knows nothing of Rhesus and is able only to direct the Greeks to Hector's resting place and tell them the Trojan password before being killed. When Athena appears to warn them off killing Hector and direct them to Rhesus, she tells them that if he lives until the morning neither Achilles nor Ajax will be able to keep him from destroying the Greek ships: this is, in effect, the oracle motif. Certain other changes and additions have been made in order to adapt the story to a play set in the Trojan camp.

The play as we have it begins with the entry of the Chorus of Trojan sentinels, who are looking for Hector. (There may originally have been a prologue: see the second Hypothesis, printed at the end of the play.) They bring the news that the Greeks are burning huge watch fires near the ships. (The motif of watch fires is here shifted from the Trojan camp to the Greek. The play never makes it clear why the Greeks have lit them, but this may have been explained in the lost prologue.) Hector comes forth, declares that the Greeks are about to run away, and proposes a night attack on the ships. Aeneas dissuades him from the risky venture of crossing palisaded trenches in the dark, proposing instead that someone be sent to spy on the Greek camp. Hector, who is blustery but changeable, agrees and calls for a volunteer. Dolon answers the call but asks for a reward: Achilles' horses. Hector too had his heart set on them, but he yields. Dolon sets off on his mission and is never seen again.

A shepherd then arrives as messenger. Hector, once more headstrong and once more mistaken, assumes that he is there to tell them about the prosperity of the flocks and directs him to the palace, but the man has news affecting the army: while watching his flocks he heard and saw the Thracian army arrive led by the godlike Rhesus in a

349

golden chariot drawn by snow-white horses. Hector, convinced that Rhesus has deliberately come late to a war that has already been all but won, announces that he will not welcome him, then that he will receive him not as companion-in-arms but as a guest only. Finally he is won over by the Chorus and the messenger to accept him as ally. The Chorus sing an ode in which they welcome Rhesus as their savior.

The meeting of Hector and Rhesus is a dramatic scene. Each is confident that he can end the war the next day. Hector accuses Rhesus of neglecting his duty to his friends by not coming sooner to Troy. Rhesus replies that he has been unavoidably detained by an incursion of Scythians into Thrace and by the difficulties of his journey. He ends by saying that whereas Hector had toiled nine years without success, he himself will conquer the Greeks on the morrow and go home the following day. After a somewhat inconclusive dialogue Hector leads Rhesus off to where he and the Thracian army will spend the night. The Chorus leave the stage in search of their relief on the watch.

Odysseus and Diomedes enter, and from their conversation we learn that they have killed Dolon, first getting from him the Trojan password and the location of Hector's encampment. They are disappointed not to find Hector there, and Diomedes wants to try to kill Aeneas or Paris when Athena appears and tells them that neither Hector nor Paris is fated to die at their hands but that they should go and slay Rhesus, who will be an invincible enemy if he lives through the night and who has horses well worth stealing.

Now Alexandros (Paris) appears looking for Hector. His arrival causes the Greek heroes to depart, and the scene between him and Athena allows stage time for the two to carry out the killing of Rhesus. Alexandros has heard that there are suspicious persons roaming the camp and wants to tell Hector. Athena, pretending to be Aphrodite, assures him that all is well, and tells him in highly ironic terms that his affairs are of the greatest concern to her. He departs. Athena calls offstage to warn the two Greeks, who have despatched Rhesus, that they should make their escape since the Trojans are coming. Odysseus and Diomedes reenter, and Odysseus is accosted by the Chorus, who regard him with suspicion. Since he knows the password he is able to fool them, and the two Greeks make their escape.

The news of Rhesus' death is brought by the driver of his chariot, who enters wounded and tells his vivid story. When Hector arrives the driver accuses him of having killed Rhesus in order to get his horses: how could a Greek have done it since none knew—unless a god told them— that Rhesus had arrived or where his camp lay? They wrangle until the driver is taken away to Hector's house to have his wounds treated.

The play ends with the appearance of Rhesus' mother, one of the Muses, carrying the body of Rhesus. She laments her son's death, reveals that she warned him that he was fated to die if he went to Troy, and accuses Athena, as Rhesus' real killer, of ingratitude: her city of Athens is most blessed by the Muses, yet she killed a Muse's son. Hector is glad to be freed of the charge of murdering Rhesus and offers to bury him richly in Troy. The Muse replies that he will not be buried: her son will not go to the Underworld but "shall lie hidden in the caves of the silver-rich land as a man-god." Day is now dawning, and Hector orders all the

Trojans to prepare for battle, confident that today will bring victory to the Trojans. All depart.

This play is far from being a masterpiece. So many of the characters are monotonously bombastic and overconfident: Dolon promises to bring back Odysseus' head, Hector and Rhesus both claim boastfully that they will finish the war in a day, and even the Chorus are infected in 254–63. Yet this characterization has no bearing on the plot. The language is monotonous, with a far higher number of phrases repeated verbatim (identical phrasing at 150, 155, 203, 222, 471, 502, and 589, and likewise at 395 and 423) than we find in any other play. We know from the second Hypothesis that in antiquity some people thought the play was not by Euripides. We know from the same source that Euripides wrote a *Rhesus*, listed in the *Didascaliae*, and we have reason to think that this play was an early work. So the chief line of defense for those who believe Euripides wrote our *Rhesus* is to say that it is a work of his youth. This cannot be disproved, but I think it more likely that at some point a *Rhesus* by an unknown poet of the fourth century was mistaken for the by then lost *Rhesus* of Euripides.

Some support for this view comes from the discussion of prologues in the second Hypothesis. The author claims that the play came with two prologues (πρόλογοι δὲ διττοὶ φέρονται). In proof of this he cites Dicaearchus for the one prologue and "some of the copies" of the play for the other. It was Dicaearchus' custom to write plot summaries of the plays of Euripides and to prefix these with a verbatim citation of each play's first line, intended to help identify the play. The author of the hypothesis can quote at length from a prologue he considers unworthy of Euripides, which he finds in copies available to him. His claim that there was another prologue in addition to this is an inference (γοῦν, "at any rate") from the citation of Dicaearchus. He concludes that there were two prologues to the same play, but a more natural conclusion is that Dicaearchus' citation comes from a different play entirely. It is at least possible that between Dicaearchus' day (late fourth century) and the Alexandrian edition (early second century) Euripides' play was lost and another play of the same name was included in the collected works. That our *Rhesus* originally began with a dialogue between Hera and Athena in which Hera sends Athena to inspire Odysseus and Diomedes to visit the Trojan camp by night is an attractive idea: the entrance of the two Greeks would then be prepared for, as well as the appearance of Athena. We cannot guess, however, why such a prologue, if it originally existed, should have been removed.

SELECT BIBLIOGRAPHY

Editions

W. H. Porter (2nd ed., Cambridge, 1929).
D. Ebener (Berlin, 1966).
I. Zanetto (Stuttgart and Leipzig, 1993).

Literary Criticism

L. Battezzato, "The Thracian Camp and the Fourth Actor at *Rhesus* 565–691," *CQ* 50 (2000), 367–73.
A. Burlando, *Reso: I Problemi, la Scena* (Genoa, 1997).

EURIPIDES

A. P. Burnett, *"Rhesus*: Are Smiles Allowed?" in P. Burian, ed., *Directions in Euripidean Criticism* (Durham, N. C., 1985), pp. 13–51.

B. Fenik, *"Iliad X" and the "Rhesus": The Myth*, Collection Latomus, vol. 73 (Brussels, 1964).

E. Fraenkel, review of Ritchie, *Gnomon* 37 (1965), 228–41.

H. D. F. Kitto, "The *Rhesus* and Related Matters," *YCS* 25 (1977), 317–50.

G. Murray, *The Rhesus of Euripides* (London, 1913), pp. v-xii.

W. Ritchie, *The Authenticity of the Rhesus of Euripides* (Cambridge, 1964).

H. Strohm, "Beobachtungen zum 'Rhesos'," *Hermes* 87 (1959), 257–74.

ΧΟΡΟΣ   CHORUS of Trojan soldiers on
                     guard duty
ΕΚΤΩΡ   HECTOR, king of Troy
ΑΙΝΕΙΑΣ   AENEAS, a Trojan noble
ΔΟΛΩΝ   DOLON, a Trojan soldier
ΑΓΓΕΛΟΣ   Trojan shepherd as MESSENGER
ΡΗΣΟΣ   RHESUS, son of a Muse, leader of
                     the Thracian army
ΟΔΥΣΣΕΥΣ   ODYSSEUS, a Greek leader
ΔΙΟΜΗΔΗΣ   DIOMEDES, a Greek leader
ΑΘΗΝΑ   ATHENA
ΑΛΕΞΑΝΔΡΟΣ   ALEXANDROS, also called Paris,
                     prince of Troy
ΗΝΙΟΧΟΣ   DRIVER of Rhesus' chariot
ΜΟΥΣΑ   MUSE, mother of Rhesus

A Note on Staging

The *skene* represents the tent of Hector in the camp the
Trojans have made near the Greek ships. Eisodos A leads
to the seashore, the Greek camp, and the main body of
Trojans, Eisodos B inland to the Thracian camp, the pas-
tures of Mount Ida, and the city of Troy.

ΡΗΣΟΣ

ΧΟΡΟΣ

Βῆθι πρὸς εὐνὰς τὰς Ἑκτορέους·
τίς ὑπασπιστῶν ἄγρυπνος βασιλέως
ἢ τευχοφόρων;
δέξαιτο νέων κληδόνα μύθων,
5 οἳ τετράμοιρον νυκτὸς φυλακὴν
πάσης στρατιᾶς προκάθηνται·
ὄρθου κεφαλὴν πῆχυν ἐρείσας,
λῦσον βλεφάρων γοργωπὸν ἕδραν,
λεῖπε χαμεύνας φυλλοστρώτους,
10 Ἕκτορ· καιρὸς γὰρ ἀκοῦσαι.

ΕΚΤΩΡ

τίς ὅδ᾽—ἦ φίλιος φθόγγος;—τίς ἀνήρ;
τί τὸ σῆμα; θρόει.
τίνες ἐκ νυκτῶν τὰς ἡμετέρας
κοίτας πλάθουσ᾽; ἐνέπειν χρή.

ΧΟΡΟΣ

15 φύλακες στρατιᾶς.

ΕΚΤΩΡ

τί φέρῃ θορύβῳ;

RHESUS

Enter by Eisodos A a CHORUS *of Trojan sentinels.*

CHORUS LEADER

Ho, there, any of the prince's squires or armor bearers who are awake, go to where Hector sleeps! Let him receive a message from those who keep the fourth watch of the night and guard the whole army: "Raise your head on your crooked forearm, open your eyes so dreadful to look upon, leave your bed of strewn leaves, Hector! High time to hear our report!"

Enter HECTOR *from the* skene *with retinue.*

HECTOR

What man is this, friend or foe? What is the watchword? Speak! What men by night have come to my resting place? Tell me!

CHORUS LEADER

We are the army's watch.

HECTOR

Why this troubled haste?

---

11 parenthesin indic. Diggle

ΧΟΡΟΣ

θάρσει.

ΕΚΤΩΡ

θαρσῶ.
μῶν τις λόχος ἐκ νυκτῶν;

[ΧΟΡΟΣ

οὐκ ἔστι.

ΕΚΤΩΡ]

τί σὺ γὰρ
φυλακὰς προλιπὼν κινεῖς στρατιάν,
εἰ μή τιν' ἔχων νυκτηγορίαν;
20   οὐκ οἶσθα δορὸς πέλας Ἀργείου
νυχίαν ἡμᾶς
κοίτην πανόπλους κατέχοντας;

ΧΟΡΟΣ

στρ.

ὁπλίζου χέρα· συμμάχων,
Ἕκτορ, βᾶθι πρὸς εὐνάς,
25   ὄτρυνον ἔγχος αἴρειν, ἀφύπνισον.
πέμπε φίλους ἰέναι ποτὶ σὸν λόχον,
ἁρμοσάτω ψαλίοις ἵππους.
τίς εἶσ' ἐπὶ Πανθοΐδαν
ἢ τὸν Εὐρώπας, Λυκίων ἀγὸν ἀνδρῶν;
30   ποῦ σφαγίων ἔφοροι,
ποῦ δὲ γυμνήτων μόναρχοι
τοξοφόροι τε Φρυγῶν;
ζεύγνυτε κερόδετα τόξα νευραῖς.

RHESUS

CHORUS LEADER

Have no fear!

HECTOR

Not I! Is there some night raid?

[CHORUS

No.

HECTOR]

Why have you left your guard post and thrown the army
into confusion if you have nothing to report by night?
Don't you know that we are encamped under arms near
the Argive army?

CHORUS

Take your weapon in your hand, Hector! Go
to where our allies are sleeping,
urge them to take up the spear, wake them up!
Send trusted men to your own companions,
let them fit bridles to their horses!
Who will go to Panthus' son[1]
or to Europa's scion, the leader of the Lycian warriors?[2]
Where are men to oversee the sacrifices,
where are the marshalers of light-armed troops,
and the Phrygian archers?
String your horned bows!

---

1 Either Polydamas or Euphorbus, Trojan nobles.
2 Sarpedon, son of Zeus and Europa.

---

17 [Χο. οὐκ ἔστι. Εκ.] τί Dindorf
19 fort. τιν' ἐρῶν νυκτηγρεσίαν
23 συμμάχων Bothe: σύμμαχον C
27 ἁρμοσάτω Musgrave: -μόσατε C

ΕΚΤΩΡ

τὰ μὲν ἀγγέλλεις δείματ' ἀκούειν,
35 τὰ δὲ θαρσύνεις, κοὐδὲν καθαρῶς.
ἀλλ' ἦ Κρονίου Πανὸς τρομερᾷ
μάστιγι φοβῇ; [φυλακὰς δὲ λιπὼν
κινεῖς στρατιάν.] τί θροεῖς; τί σε φῶ
νέον ἀγγέλλειν; πολλὰ γὰρ εἰπὼν
40 οὐδὲν τρανῶς ἀπέδειξας.

ΧΟΡΟΣ

ἀντ.

πῦρ' αἴθει στρατὸς Ἀργόλας,
Ἕκτορ, πᾶσαν ἀν' ὄρφναν,
διειπετῆ δὲ ναῶν πυρσοῖς σταθμά.
πᾶς δ' Ἀγαμεμνονίαν προσέβα στρατὸς
45 ἐννύχιος θορύβῳ σκηνάν,
νέαν τιν' ἐφιέμενοι
βάξιν. οὐ γάρ πω πάρος ὧδ' ἐφοβήθη
ναυσιπόρος στρατιά.
σοὶ δ', ὑποπτεύων τὸ μέλλον,
50 ἤλυθον ἄγγελος ὡς
μήποτέ τιν' ἐς ἐμὲ μέμψιν εἴπῃς.

ΕΚΤΩΡ

ἐς καιρὸν ἥκεις, καίπερ ἀγγέλλων φόβον·
ἄνδρες γὰρ ἐκ γῆς τῆσδε νυκτέρῳ πλάτῃ
λαθόντες ὄμμα τοὐμὸν ἀρεῖσθαι φυγὴν
55 μέλλουσι· σαίνει μ' ἔννυχος φρυκτωρία.

37b–38a del. Dobree cl. 18

HECTOR

Some of your report is alarming to hear, some is encouraging: nothing is clear. Can it be that the goad of Pan, Cronus' son, has made you afraid?[3] [You have left your guard post and throw the army into confusion.] What are you saying? What strange business must I think you are reporting? You have said nothing clearly for all your many words.

CHORUS

The Greek army is burning watch fires,
Hector, all through the night,
and the ships' mooring places are bright with torch gleam.
The whole army by night comes in tumult
to Agamemnon's tent,
desiring to hear some new
report: never before was this seagoing host
so frightened.
Fearing what may be to come
I have brought word to you:
I do not want you to rebuke me.

HECTOR

Your coming is timely even though your message brought fright: these men are about to give my watchful eye the slip and escape from this land by night voyage—the import of their night fires comes home to me.

---

3 Pan, goat-footed god of Arcadia, was credited with sudden and unexplained "panic" fear.

---

51 τιν᾽ ἐς ἐμὲ μέμψιν Lindemann: τινα μέμψιν εἰς ἔμ᾽ C

ὦ δαῖμον, ὅστις μ' εὐτυχοῦντ' ἐνόσφισας
θοίνης λέοντα, πρὶν τὸν Ἀργείων στρατὸν
σύρδην ἅπαντα τῷδ' ἀναλῶσαι δορί.
εἰ γὰρ φαεννοὶ μὴ 'ξανεῖσαν ἡλίου
60 λαμπτῆρες, οὔτἂν ἔσχον εὐτυχοῦν δόρυ,
πρὶν ναῦς πυρῶσαι καὶ διὰ σκηνῶν μολεῖν
κτείνων Ἀχαιοὺς τῇδε πολυφόνῳ χερί.
κἀγὼ μὲν ἦ πρόθυμος ἰέναι δόρυ
ἐν νυκτὶ χρῆσθαί τ' εὐτυχεῖ ῥύμῃ θεοῦ·
65 ἀλλ' οἱ σοφοί με καὶ τὸ θεῖον εἰδότες
μάντεις ἔπεισαν ἡμέρας μεῖναι φάος
κἄπειτ' Ἀχαιῶν μηδέν' ἐν χέρσῳ λιπεῖν.
οἱ δ' οὐ μένουσι τῶν ἐμῶν θυοσκόων
βουλάς· ἐν ὄρφνῃ δραπέτης μέγα σθένει.
70 ἀλλ' ὡς τάχιστα χρὴ παραγγέλλειν στρατῷ
τεύχη πρόχειρα λαμβάνειν λῆξαί θ' ὕπνου,
ὡς ἄν τις αὐτῶν καὶ νεὼς θρῴσκων ἔπι
νῶτον χαραχθεὶς κλίμακας ῥάνῃ φόνῳ,
οἱ δ' ἐν βρόχοισι δέσμιοι λελημμένοι
75 Φρυγῶν ἀρούρας ἐκμάθωσι γαπονεῖν.

ΧΟΡΟΣ
Ἕκτορ, ταχύνεις πρὶν μαθεῖν τὸ δρώμενον·
ἄνδρες γὰρ εἰ φεύγουσιν οὐκ ἴσμεν τορῶς.

ΕΚΤΩΡ
τίς γὰρ πύρ' αἴθειν πρόφασις Ἀργείων στρατόν;

ΧΟΡΟΣ
οὐκ οἶδ'· ὕποπτον δ' ἐστὶ κάρτ' ἐμῇ φρενί.

362

O fate, you have robbed me of the feast, like a lion of his kill, before I could destroy in one swoop the whole Argive army with this spear of mine! If the bright lamp of day had not failed me, I would not have checked my victorious spear until I had fired their ships and passed through their tents slaying Achaeans with this murderous right hand! I myself was keen to hurl the spear in the night and to make use of the lucky momentum the god had sent, but the seers, wise men who know the gods' will, persuaded me to wait until dawn and only then rid the land of Achaeans. But these men do not stay for the plans of my prophets: a runaway is a mighty man in the dark.

So we must quickly order the army to wake up and put on its ready armor: that way even if someone is leaping onto his ship he will be speared in the back and drench the ladder with his blood, and others will be tied up with ropes and be taught to till the Phrygians' fields!

CHORUS LEADER
Hector, you are acting hastily before learning what is going on: we don't know for sure whether the men are fleeing.

HECTOR
What other reason could there be for the Argive army to burn watchfires?

CHORUS LEADER
I don't know, but it's very troubling to my mind.

---

59 'ξανεῖσαν Heimsoeth: ξυνέσχον C

ΕΚΤΩΡ

80 πάντ᾽ ἂν φοβηθεὶς ἴσθι, δειμαίνων τόδε.

ΧΟΡΟΣ

οὔπω πρὶν ἦψαν πολέμιοι τοσόνδε φῶς.

ΕΚΤΩΡ

οὐδ᾽ ὧδέ γ᾽ αἰσχρῶς ἔπεσον ἐν τροπῇ δορός.

ΧΟΡΟΣ

σὺ ταῦτ᾽ ἔπραξας· καὶ τὰ λοιπὰ νῦν σκόπει.

ΕΚΤΩΡ

ἁπλοῦς ἐπ᾽ ἐχθροῖς μῦθος ὁπλίζειν χέρα.

ΧΟΡΟΣ

85 καὶ μὴν ὅδ᾽ Αἰνέας καὶ μάλα σπουδῇ ποδὸς
στείχει, νέον τι πρᾶγμ᾽ ἔχων φίλοις φράσαι.

ΑΙΝΕΙΑΣ

Ἕκτορ, τί χρῆμα νύκτεροι κατὰ στρατὸν
τὰς σὰς πρὸς εὐνὰς φύλακες ἐλθόντες φόβῳ
νυκτηγοροῦσι καὶ κεκίνηται στρατός;

ΕΚΤΩΡ

90 Αἰνέα, πύκαζε τεύχεσιν δέμας σέθεν.

ΑΙΝΕΙΑΣ

τί δ᾽ ἔστι; μῶν τις πολεμίων ἀγγέλλεται
δόλος κρυφαῖος ἑστάναι κατ᾽ εὐφρόνην;

ΕΚΤΩΡ

φεύγουσιν ἄνδρες κἀπιβαίνουσιν νεῶν.

HECTOR

You'd quake at nothing if you're afraid of that!

CHORUS LEADER

The enemy have never before lit such a big fire.

HECTOR

No, nor have they ever suffered such a reverse in battle.

CHORUS LEADER

That was your doing: now give a thought to what comes next.

HECTOR

Where enemies are concerned my orders are simple: to arms!

Enter by Eisodos A AENEAS *with retinue.*

CHORUS LEADER

But look, here comes Aeneas in great haste! He has something to report to his friends.

AENEAS

Hector, why have the night watch come to your resting place in panic? Why are they deliberating at night, why is the army thrown into confusion?

HECTOR

Aeneas, put on your armor.

AENEAS

What's going on? Have we heard that the enemy are engaged in some nocturnal ploy?

HECTOR

The men are running away, getting on board their ships.

365

EURIPIDES

ΑΙΝΕΙΑΣ

τί τοῦδ᾽ ἂν εἴποις ἀσφαλὲς τεκμήριον;

ΕΚΤΩΡ

95   αἴθουσι πᾶσαν νύκτα λαμπάδας πυρός·
καί μοι δοκοῦσιν οὐ μενεῖν ἐς αὔριον,
ἀλλ᾽ ἐκκέαντες πύρσ᾽ ἐπ᾽ εὐσέλμων νεῶν
φυγῇ πρὸς οἴκους τῆσδ᾽ ἀφορμήσειν χθονός.

ΑΙΝΕΙΑΣ

σὺ δ᾽ ὡς τί δράσων πρὸς τάδ᾽ ὁπλίζῃ χέρα;

ΕΚΤΩΡ

100 φεύγοντας αὐτοὺς κἀπιθρῴσκοντας νεῶν
λόγχῃ καθέξω κἀπικείσομαι βαρύς·
αἰσχρὸν γὰρ ἡμῖν, καὶ πρὸς αἰσχύνῃ κακόν,
θεοῦ διδόντος πολεμίους ἄνευ μάχης
φεύγειν ἐᾶσαι πολλὰ δράσαντας κακά.

ΑΙΝΕΙΑΣ

105 εἴθ᾽ ἦσθ᾽ ἀνὴρ εὔβουλος ὡς δρᾶσαι χερὶ
⟨ἰταμῇ πρόθυμος τοὺς ἐναντίους κακῶς⟩.
ἀλλ᾽ οὐ γὰρ αὐτὸς πάντ᾽ ἐπίστασθαι βροτῶν
πέφυκεν· ἄλλῳ δ᾽ ἄλλο πρόσκειται γέρας,
σὲ μὲν μάχεσθαι, τοὺς δὲ βουλεύειν καλῶς·
ὅστις πυρὸς λαμπτῆρας ἐξήρθης κλυὼν
110 φλέγειν Ἀχαιούς, καὶ στρατὸν μέλλεις ἄγειν
τάφρους ὑπερβὰς νυκτὸς ἐν καταστάσει.
καίτοι περάσας κοῖλον αὐλώνων βάθος,
εἰ μὴ κυρήσεις πολεμίους ἀπὸ χθονὸς
φεύγοντας ἀλλὰ σὸν βλέποντας ἐς δόρυ,

AENEAS

What proof of this can you tell me?

HECTOR

All night they burn fires. I don't think they will stay until tomorrow: having burnt their watch fires they will flee for home on their well-benched ships.

AENEAS

What are you going to do about this? Why are you taking spear in hand?

HECTOR

As they run away leaping onto their ships I shall stop them with my spear, hurling my full weight against them. The god has handed our enemies to us, and it is a disgrace to us, and a mischief as well, to let them run away without giving them battle, considering the great harm they have done us.

AENEAS

How I wish you were as prudent at making plans as ⟨you are eager⟩ to harm ⟨the enemy with bold⟩ hand. But that's the nature of things: the same man cannot do everything. One man has one gift, another a different one: yours is to fight, while it belongs to others to make prudent plans. Your hopes have been roused by hearing that the Achaeans are burning fires, and you intend to cross the moats at night with the army. Yet if you cross the deep ditch, you could find the enemy not fleeing but facing your spears, and if

---

105 post h. v. lac. indicandam suspicatus est Diggle

115 νικώμενος μὲν οὔτι μὴ μόλῃς πάλιν·
πῶς γὰρ περάσει σκόλοπας ἐν τροπῇ στρατός;
πῶς δ' αὖ γεφύρας διαβαλοῦσ' ἱππηλάται,
ἢν ἄρα μὴ θραύσαντες ἀντύγων χνόας;
νικῶν δ' ἔφεδρον παῖδ' ἔχεις τὸν Πηλέως,
120 ὅς σ' οὐκ ἐάσει ναυσὶν ἐμβαλεῖν φλόγα,
οὐδ' ὧδ' Ἀχαιοὺς ὡς δοκεῖς ἀναρπάσαι.
αἴθων γὰρ ἀνὴρ καὶ πεπύργωται θράσει.
ἀλλὰ στρατὸν μὲν ἥσυχον παρ' ἀσπίδας
εὕδειν ἐῶμεν ἐκ κόπων ἀρειφάτων,
125 κατάσκοπον δὲ πολεμίων, ὃς ἂν θέλῃ,
πέμπειν δοκεῖ μοι· κἂν μὲν αἴρωνται φυγήν,
στείχοντες ἐμπέσωμεν Ἀργείων στρατῷ·
εἰ δ' ἐς δόλον τιν' ἤδ' ἄγει φρυκτωρία,
μαθόντες ἐχθρῶν μηχανὰς κατασκόπου
130 βουλευσόμεσθα· τήνδ' ἔχω γνώμην, ἄναξ.

ΧΟΡΟΣ

στρ.

τάδε δοκεῖ, τάδε μεταθέμενος νόει.
σφαλερὰ δ' οὐ φιλῶ στρατηγῶν κράτη.
τί γὰρ ἄμεινον ἢ ταχυβάταν νεῶν
κατόπταν μολεῖν
135 πέλας ὅ τι ποτ' ἄρα δαΐοις
πυρὰ κατ' ἀντίπρω-
ρα ναυστάθμων δαίεται;

ΕΚΤΩΡ

νικᾷς, ἐπειδὴ πᾶσιν ἀνδάνει τάδε.

you are defeated you will never get back again. How will
the army get over the palisade if they are routed? How will
the charioteers cross the embankments without smashing
their chariot axles? Yet if you beat them, you will have to
face Achilles, now waiting to see what happens, and he will
not let you set fire to the ships or plunder the Achaeans, as
you suppose. The man is burning hot, and his courage
makes him tower massively. No, let's let the soldiery, lying
near their shields, rest quietly from their battle fatigue. I
think it best to send a volunteer to spy on the enemy: if the
Argive army is running away, let's go and fall upon them,
but if this fire burning is meant as a trick, we can learn the
enemy's devices from our spy and plan accordingly. That is
my opinion, my lord.

CHORUS

That seems best: change your mind and adopt this view!
I do not like it when generals order unsafe things.
What is better than for a swift-footed man to go
and spy on the ships
from close up, to see why in the world the foe
are burning fires in front of their naval encampment?

HECTOR

Aeneas, you win: everyone thinks your course is best. But

---

115 οὔτι μὴ Cobet: τήνδ᾽ οὐ μὴ fere C
131 δόκει Dawe
137 νικᾷς Bothe: νικᾶτ᾽ C

στείχων δὲ κοίμα συμμάχους· τάχ᾽ ἂν στρατὸς
κινοῖτ᾽ ἀκούσας νυκτέρους ἐκκλησίας.
140 ἐγὼ δὲ πέμψω πολεμίων κατάσκοπον.
κἂν μέν τιν᾽ ἐχθρῶν μηχανὴν πυθώμεθα,
σὺ πάντ᾽ ἀκούσῃ καὶ παρὼν εἴσῃ λόγον·
ἐὰν δ᾽ ἀπαίρωσ᾽ ἐς φυγὴν ὁρμώμενοι,
σάλπιγγος αὐδὴν προσδοκῶν καραδόκει,
145 ὡς οὐ μενοῦντά μ᾽· ἀλλὰ προσμείξω νεῶν
ὁλκοῖσι νυκτὸς τῆσδ᾽ ἐπ᾽ Ἀργείων στρατῷ.

ΑΙΝΕΙΑΣ

πέμφ᾽ ὡς τάχιστα· νῦν γὰρ ἀσφαλῶς φρονεῖς.
σὺν σοὶ δ᾽ ἔμ᾽ ὄψῃ καρτεροῦνθ᾽ ὅταν δέῃ.

ΕΚΤΩΡ

τίς δῆτα Τρώων οἳ πάρεισιν ἐν λόγῳ
150 θέλει κατόπτης ναῦς ἐπ᾽ Ἀργείων μολεῖν;
τίς ἂν γένοιτο τῆσδε γῆς εὐεργέτης;
τίς φησιν; οὔτοι πάντ᾽ ἐγὼ δυνήσομαι
πόλει πατρῴᾳ συμμάχοις θ᾽ ὑπηρετεῖν.

ΔΟΛΩΝ

ἐγὼ πρὸ γαίας τόνδε κίνδυνον θέλω
155 ῥίψας κατόπτης ναῦς ἐπ᾽ Ἀργείων μολεῖν,
καὶ πάντ᾽ Ἀχαιῶν ἐκμαθὼν βουλεύματα
ἥξω· ᾽πὶ τούτοις τόνδ᾽ ὑφίσταμαι πόνον.

ΕΚΤΩΡ

ἐπώνυμος μὲν κάρτα καὶ φιλόπτολις

---

138 κοίμα Pierson: κόσμει vel σκόπει C

go and calm our allies: perhaps the army might be stirred up by hearing of our night meeting. I shall send someone to spy on our foes. If we learn of some enemy trick, you will hear the whole story, being stationed nearby. But if they are starting to run away, you must listen for the trumpet signal since I will not wait around: I will put myself among the beached ships this very night to fight the Argive army.

AENEAS

Yes, send someone at once: now you're being cautious. You will see that when the need arises I shall be as brave as you.

Exit AENEAS *by Eisodos* A.

HECTOR

(*in a loud voice*) Well then, who of the Trojans within hearing of my words is willing to go as a spy to the Argive ships? Who will do this land a good turn? Who agrees? I can't do everything for city and allies.

Enter DOLON *by Eisodos* A.

DOLON

I am willing to run this risk for the country and go as a spy to the Argive ships. I will find out all the Achaeans' plans before returning: those are the terms of my promise.

HECTOR

Dolon by name and Dolon by nature,[4] and a great lover of

---

4 Hector derives Dolon's name from *dolos*, "trick."

---

146 τῆσδε κἀργείων Schumacher

371

Δόλων· πατρὸς δὲ καὶ πρὶν εὐκλεᾶ δόμον
160　νῦν δὶς τόσως ἔθηκας εὐκλεέστερον.

ΔΟΛΩΝ

οὔκουν πονεῖν μὲν χρή, πονοῦντα δ᾽ ἄξιον
μισθὸν φέρεσθαι; παντὶ γὰρ προσκείμενον
κέρδος πρὸς ἔργῳ τὴν χάριν τίκτει διπλῆν.

ΕΚΤΩΡ

ναί, καὶ δίκαια ταῦτα κοὐκ ἄλλως λέγω.
165　τάξαι δὲ μισθόν, πλὴν ἐμῆς τυραννίδος.

ΔΟΛΩΝ

οὐ σῆς ἐρῶμεν πολιόχου τυραννίδος.

ΕΚΤΩΡ

σὺ δ᾽ ἀλλὰ γήμας Πριαμιδῶν γαμβρὸς γενοῦ.

ΔΟΛΩΝ

οὐδ᾽ ἐξ ἐμαυτοῦ μειζόνων γαμεῖν θέλω.

ΕΚΤΩΡ

χρυσὸς πάρεστιν, εἰ τόδ᾽ αἰτήσεις γέρας.

ΔΟΛΩΝ

170　ἀλλ᾽ ἔστ᾽ ἐν οἴκοις· οὐ βίου σπανίζομεν.

ΕΚΤΩΡ

τί δῆτα χρῄζεις ὧν κέκευθεν Ἴλιον;

ΔΟΛΩΝ

ἑλὼν Ἀχαιοὺς δῶρά μοι ξυναίνεσον.

ΕΚΤΩΡ

δώσω· σὺ δ᾽ αἴτει πλὴν στρατηλάτας νεῶν.

his country! Your father's house was glorious before this, but you have made it twice as glorious.

DOLON

Shouldn't a man when he works also win a wage worthy of his work? A reward attached to a task doubles the pleasure of it.

HECTOR

Yes, that is quite right, I can't deny it. Name your reward—anything except my kingship.

DOLON

I have no desire to be the city's protector and king like you.

HECTOR

Well then, marry and become brother-in-law of Priam's sons.

DOLON

I do not want a marriage tie with my betters.

HECTOR

Perhaps you will ask for gold: we have plenty of that.

DOLON

I have money at home and do not lack livelihood.

HECTOR

Well what of Ilium's treasures do you desire?

DOLON

Promise me a gift once we destroy the Greeks.

HECTOR

I will give you anything you ask except the admirals.

ΔΟΛΩΝ

κτεῖν', οὔ σ' ἀπαιτῶ Μενέλεω σχέσθαι χέρα.

ΕΚΤΩΡ

175 οὐ μὴν τὸν Οἰλέως παῖδά μ' ἐξαιτῇ λαβεῖν;

ΔΟΛΩΝ

κακαὶ γεωργεῖν χεῖρες εὖ τεθραμμέναι.

ΕΚΤΩΡ

τίν' οὖν Ἀχαιῶν ζῶντ' ἀποινᾶσθαι θέλεις;

ΔΟΛΩΝ

καὶ πρόσθεν εἶπον· ἔστι χρυσὸς ἐν δόμοις.

ΕΚΤΩΡ

καὶ μὴν λαφύρων γ' αὐτὸς αἱρήσῃ παρών.

ΔΟΛΩΝ

180 θεοῖσιν αὐτὰ πασσάλευε πρὸς δόμοις.

ΕΚΤΩΡ

τί δῆτα μεῖζον τῶνδέ μ' αἰτήσεις γέρας;

ΔΟΛΩΝ

ἵππους Ἀχιλλέως· χρὴ δ' ἐπ' ἀξίοις πονεῖν
ψυχὴν προβάλλοντ' ἐν κύβοισι δαίμονος.

ΕΚΤΩΡ

καὶ μὴν ἐρῶντί γ' ἀντερᾷς ἵππων ἐμοί·
185 ἐξ ἀφθίτων γὰρ ἄφθιτοι πεφυκότες
τὸν Πηλέως φέρουσι θούριον γόνον·
δίδωσι δ' αὐτὸς πωλοδαμνήσας ἄναξ
Πηλεῖ Ποσειδῶν, ὡς λέγουσι, πόντιος.
ἀλλ' οὔ σ' ἐπάρας ψεύσομαι· δώσω δέ σοι,

DOLON

Kill away! I won't beg you to spare Menelaus!

HECTOR

Surely you're not asking to receive the son of Oïleus?[5]

DOLON

The hands of those nobly nurtured are bad at farming.

HECTOR

Which of the Achaeans do you want to hold to ransom?

DOLON

I've said already that I have gold in my house.

HECTOR

You can come yourself and take some of the booty.

DOLON

Nail it to the temples in honor of the gods!

HECTOR

Well, what greater gift than these will you ask me for?

DOLON

The horses of Achilles: it is right for me to work and risk my life in the dice game of fate for a prize that is worthy.

HECTOR

Well, you have me as a rival in your love for the horses: immortal and sired by immortals they carry the swift son of Peleus. Poseidon himself, horse-mastering lord of the sea, gave them to Peleus, men say. But I shall not raise your hopes only to dash them: I will give you the horses and

5 The lesser Ajax.

---

187 αὐτὸς Dobree: -τοὺς vel -τὰς C

190 κάλλιστον οἴκοις κτῆμ’, Ἀχιλλέως ὄχον.

ΔΟΛΩΝ

αἰνῶ· λαβὼν δ’ ἄν φημι κάλλιστον Φρυγῶν
δῶρον δέχεσθαι τῆς ἐμῆς εὐσπλαγχνίας.
σὲ δ’ οὐ φθονεῖν χρή· μυρί’ ἔστιν ἄλλα σοι,
ἐφ’ οἷσι τέρψῃ τῆσδ’ ἀριστεύων χθονός.

ΧΟΡΟΣ

ἀντ.

195 μέγας ἀγών, μεγάλα δ’ ἐπινοεῖς ἑλεῖν·
μακάριός γε μὰν κυρήσας ἔσῃ.
πόνος ὅδ’ εὐκλεής· μέγα δὲ κοιράνοι-
σι γαμβρὸν πέλειν.
τὰ θεόθεν ἐπιδέτω Δίκα,
200 τὰ δὲ παρ’ ἀνδράσιν
τέλειά σοι φαίνεται.

ΔΟΛΩΝ

στείχοιμ’ ἄν· ἐλθὼν δ’ ἐς δόμους ἐφέστιος
σκευῇ πρεπόντως σῶμ’ ἐμὸν καθάψομαι,
κἀκεῖθεν ἤσω ναῦς ἐπ’ Ἀργείων πόδα.

ΧΟΡΟΣ

ἐπεὶ τίν’ ἄλλην ἀντὶ τῆσδ’ ἕξεις στολήν;

ΔΟΛΩΝ

205 πρέπουσαν ἔργῳ κλωπικοῖς τε βήμασιν.

ΧΟΡΟΣ

σοφοῦ παρ’ ἀνδρὸς χρὴ σοφόν τι μανθάνειν·

chariot of Achilles, a most splendid possession for your house.

DOLON

Thank you. I say this: if I get them, I will be receiving from the Trojans a most noble gift in return for my valor. And you should not begrudge me this: as our country's great hero you will have countless other things to delight your heart.

CHORUS

Great is the contest, great the prize you intend to capture:
if you succeed, you will enjoy blessedness.
Glorious is the toil. It is a great thing, though, to marry into the royal house.
What the gods will send must be determined by Lady Justice,
but where men are concerned
it seems your lot is complete.

DOLON

I shall depart now. I'm going home and will clothe myself fittingly and then set out from there to the Argive ships.

CHORUS LEADER

What outfit will you wear instead of the one you are wearing?

DOLON

One that befits the task and my covert journey.

CHORUS LEADER

From a clever man one should learn cleverness: tell us,

---

191 δ' ἀν Verrall: δὲ C   197 ὅδ' Nauck: δ' C
199 τὰ Bothe: τὰ δὲ C

λέξον, τίς ἔσται τοῦδε σώματος σαγή;

ΔΟΛΩΝ

λύκειον ἀμφὶ νῶτ' ἐνάψομαι δορὰν
καὶ χάσμα θηρὸς ἀμφ' ἐμῷ θήσω κάρᾳ,
210 βάσιν τε χερσὶ προσθίαν καθαρμόσας
καὶ κῶλα κώλοις, τετράπουν μιμήσομαι
λύκου κέλευθον πολεμίοις δυσεύρετον,
τάφροις πελάζων καὶ νεῶν προβλήμασιν.
ὅταν δ' ἔρημον χῶρον ἐμβαίνω ποδί,
215 δίβαμος εἰμι· τῇδε σύγκειται δόλος.

ΧΟΡΟΣ

ἀλλ' εὖ σ' ὁ Μαίας παῖς ἐκεῖσε καὶ πάλιν
πέμψειεν Ἑρμῆς, ὅς γε φηλητῶν ἄναξ.
ἔχεις δὲ τοὔργον· εὐτυχεῖν μόνον σε δεῖ.

ΔΟΛΩΝ

σωθήσομαί τοι καὶ κτανὼν Ὀδυσσέως
220 οἴσω κάρα σοι—σύμβολον δ' ἔχων σαφὲς
φήσεις Δόλωνα ναῦς ἐπ' Ἀργείων μολεῖν—
ἢ παῖδα Τυδέως· οὐδ' ἀναιμάκτῳ χερὶ
ἥξω πρὸς οἴκους πρὶν φάος μολεῖν χθόνα.

ΧΟΡΟΣ

στρ. α

Θυμβραῖε καὶ Δάλιε καὶ Λυκίας
225 ναὸν ἐμβατεύων
Ἄπολλον, ὦ Δία κεφαλά, μόλε τοξή-

<hr>

219 τοι Diggle: τε C

how will you clothe yourself?

DOLON
On my back I shall wrap the pelt of a wolf, with the beast's gaping jaws about my head: fitting its forelegs to my arms and its hindlegs to my feet I shall imitate the four-footed gate of a wolf, hard for enemies to detect as I approach the moat and the ships' fortifications. When I reach deserted ground, I will walk on two feet. That is how my deceit is concocted.

CHORUS LEADER
May the son of Maia[6] bring you successfully there and back since he is the lord of deceivers. You know what you must do: now all you need is to succeed.

DOLON
I'll get through safely and when I have killed Odysseus I will bring his head back to you—that way you will have clear proof that Dolon reached the Argive ships—or perhaps I'll kill the son of Tydeus.[7] I shall return before dawn breaks with bloodied hands.

Exit DOLON *by Eisodos A.*

CHORUS
Apollo of Thymbra and Delos and treader
of Lycia's temple,
son of Zeus, come with your bow,

6 Hermes, god of thieves.
7 Diomedes.

ρης, ἱκοῦ ἐννύχιος
καὶ γενοῦ σωτήριος ἀνέρι πομπᾶς
230 ἀγεμὼν καὶ ξύλλαβε Δαρδανίδαις,
ὦ παγκρατές, ὦ Τροίας
τείχη παλαιὰ δείμας.

ἀντ. α

μόλοι δὲ ναυκλήρια καὶ στρατιᾶς
Ἑλλάδος διόπτας
235 ἵκοιτο καὶ κάμψειε πάλιν θυμέλας οἴ-
κων πατρὸς Ἰλιάδας.
Φθιάδων δ' ἵππων ποτ' ἐπ' ἄντυγα βαίη,
δεσπότου πέρσαντος Ἀχαιὸν Ἄρη,
240 τὰς πόντιος Αἰακίδᾳ
Πηλεῖ δίδωσι δαίμων.

στρ. β

ἐπεὶ πρό τ' οἴκων πρό τε γᾶς ἔτλα μόνος
ναύσταθμα βὰς κατιδεῖν· ἄγαμαι
245 λήματος· ἦ σπάνις αἰεὶ
τῶν ἀγαθῶν, ὅταν ἦ δυσάλιον ἐν πελάγει
καὶ σαλεύῃ
πόλις. ἔστι Φρυγῶν τις ἔστιν ἄλκιμος·
250 ἔνι δὲ θράσος ἐν αἰχ-
μᾷ· πόθι Μυσῶν ὃς ἐμὰν
συμμαχίαν ἀτίζει;

ἀντ. β

τίν' ἄνδρ' Ἀχαιῶν ὁ πεδοστιβὴς σφαγεὺς
255 οὐτάσει ἐν κλισίαις, τετράπουν

come by night,
be a saving guide
to a man's journey, and help the sons of Dardanus,
O mighty lord, builder
of Troy's ancient walls!

May he come to the mooring places, arrive
to spy on the army of Greece,
and return once more to the Trojan
altars of his father's house!
And when our king has ravaged the Achaean army,
grant that he may mount chariot and horses of Phthia,
horses that the lord of the sea
gave to Aeacus' son Peleus!

For he alone on behalf of home and country
dared to go and spy on their ships: I am amazed
at his courage. Brave men are always hard to find
when days are dark at sea
and the city is being tossed
on the waves. There are brave men yet among the Phryg-
    ians,
there is boldness among the warriors:
where is the Mysian who scorns
to have me as his ally?

What Achaean in the camp will the earth-treading killer
wound as he imitates on the ground

228–30 καὶ γενοῦ ... ἀγεμὼν Dindorf: ἀγεμὼν ... καὶ γενοῦ C
245 σπάνις αἰεὶ Wilamowitz: σπάνια fere C
251 πόθι Hoffman: ποτὶ C

μῖμον ἔχων ἐπὶ γαίας
θηρός; ἕλοι Μενέλαν, κτανὼν δ᾽ Ἀγαμεμνόνιον
κρᾶτ᾽ ἐνέγκοι
260 Ἑλένᾳ κακόγαμβρον ἐς χέρας γόον,
ὃς ἐπὶ πόλιν, ὃς ἐπὶ
γᾶν Τροΐαν χιλιόναυν
ἤλυθ᾽ ἔχων στρατείαν.

ΑΓΓΕΛΟΣ

ἄναξ, τοιούτων δεσπόταισιν ἄγγελος
265 εἴην τὸ λοιπὸν οἷά σοι φέρω μαθεῖν.

ΕΚΤΩΡ

ἦ πόλλ᾽ ἀγρώσταις σκαιὰ πρόσκειται φρενί·
καὶ γὰρ σὺ ποίμνας δεσπόταις τευχεσφόροις
ἥκειν ἔοικας ἀγγελῶν ἵν᾽ οὐ πρέπει.
οὐκ οἶσθα δῶμα τοὐμὸν ἢ θρόνους πατρός,
270 οἳ χρῆν γεγωνεῖν σ᾽ εὐτυχοῦντα ποίμνια;

ΑΓΓΕΛΟΣ

σκαιοὶ βοτῆρές ἐσμεν· οὐκ ἄλλως λέγω.
ἀλλ᾽ οὐδὲν ἧσσον σοι φέρω κεδνοὺς λόγους.

ΕΚΤΩΡ

παῦσαι λέγων μοι τὰς προσαυλείους τύχας·
μάχας πρὸ χειρῶν καὶ δόρη βαστάζομεν.

ΑΓΓΕΛΟΣ

275 τοιαῦτα κἀγὼ σημανῶν ἐλήλυθα·
ἀνὴρ γὰρ ἀλκῆς μυρίας στρατηλατῶν
στείχει φίλος σοι σύμμαχός τε τῇδε γῇ.

the gait of a four-footed beast?
May he kill Menelaus, slay Agamemnon
and put his head
in Helen's hands to make her lament her evil brother-in-
    law,
who came against the city, against
the land of Troy, bringing
a thousand-ship armada.

Enter by Eisodos B a Trojan shepherd as MESSENGER.

MESSENGER

My lord, I wish that I may always bring such news to my
masters as I am now bringing for you to hear!

HECTOR

How stupid the minds of rustics are! Here you are, it
seems, bringing news of the herds to your masters in their
fighting gear, bringing it to the wrong place! Don't you
know that my house or my father's throne is where you
should report the prosperity of our flocks?

MESSENGER

We herdsmen are stupid—no argument there. But none-
theless I bring you good news.

HECTOR

No more tales of sheepfold fortunes! We have spears and
battles on our hands!

MESSENGER

That's just what I have come to report: a man is approach-
ing, as friend to you and ally to this land, at the head of a
vast force.

ΕΚΤΩΡ

ποίας πατρῴας γῆς ἐρημώσας πέδον;

ΑΓΓΕΛΟΣ

Θρῄκης· πατρὸς δὲ Στρυμόνος κικλήσκεται.

ΕΚΤΩΡ

280 Ῥῆσον τιθέντ' ἔλεξας ἐν Τροίᾳ πόδα;

ΑΓΓΕΛΟΣ

ἔγνως· λόγου δὲ δὶς τόσου μ' ἐκούφισας.

ΕΚΤΩΡ

καὶ πῶς πρὸς Ἴδης ὀργάδας πορεύεται,
πλαγχθεὶς πλατείας πεδιάδος θ' ἁμαξιτοῦ;

ΑΓΓΕΛΟΣ

οὐκ οἶδ' ἀκριβῶς· εἰκάσαι γε μὴν πάρα.
285 νυκτὸς γὰρ οὔτι φαῦλον ἐσβαλεῖν στρατόν,
κλυόντα πλήρη πεδία πολεμίας χερός.
φόβον δ' ἀγρώσταις, οἳ κατ' Ἰδαῖον λέπας
οἰκοῦμεν αὐτόρριζον ἑστίαν χθονός,
παρέσχε δρυμὸν νυκτὸς ἔνθηρον μολών.
290 πολλῇ γὰρ ἠχῇ Θρῄκιος ῥέων στρατὸς
ἔστειχε· θάμβει δ' ἐκπλαγέντες ἵεμεν
ποίμνας πρὸς ἄκρας, μή τις Ἀργείων μόλῃ
λεηλατήσων καὶ σὰ πορθήσων σταθμά,
πρὶν δὴ δι' ὤτων γῆρυν οὐχ Ἑλληνικὴν
295 ἐδεξάμεσθα καὶ μετέστημεν φόβου.
στείχων δ' ἔναντα προυξερευνητὰς ὁδοῦ
ἀνιστόρησα Θρηκίοις προσφθέγμασιν·
Τίς ὁ στρατηγὸς καὶ τίνος κεκλημένος

HECTOR

What country has he come from?

MESSENGER

Thrace: he is called the son of the river Strymon.

HECTOR

Do you mean that Rhesus has come to Troy?

MESSENGER

Exactly. You've made my tale easier by half.

HECTOR

How did he miss the broad carriage road and come to the pastures of Ida?

MESSENGER

I don't know exactly, though it's possible to guess. It's no small thing to bring an army into the country by night when one has heard that the plains are full of enemy soldiers. It frightened us rustics, who make our home on the very rock of Mount Ida, when they came through the game-rich thickets in the night: the Thracian army made a great din as it flowed on. We were struck with amazement and started to move our flocks higher up: that way no Argive would raid and pillage your herds for spoil. But then our ears heard non-Greek speech, and our fears were relieved. Marching right up to the advance scouts of the expedition I asked them in Thracian, "Who is the general—what is his father's name—that comes to the city as

---

285 ἐσβαλεῖν Diggle: ἐμβ- C
296 ἔναντα Morstadt: ἄνακτος C

στείχει πρὸς ἄστυ Πριαμίδαισι σύμμαχος;
300   καὶ πάντ᾽ ἀκούσας ὧν ἐφιέμην μαθεῖν
ἔστην· ὁρῶ δὲ Ῥῆσον ὥστε δαίμονα
ἑστῶτ᾽ ἐν ἵπποις Θρηκίοις τ᾽ ὀχήμασιν.
χρυσῆ δὲ πλάστιγξ αὐχένα ζυγηφόρον
πώλων ἔκλῃε χιόνος ἐξαυγεστέρων.
305   πέλτη δ᾽ ἐπ᾽ ὤμων χρυσοκολλήτοις τύποις
ἔλαμπε· Γοργὼν δ᾽ ὡς ἐπ᾽ αἰγίδος θεᾶς
χαλκῆ μετώποις ἱππικοῖσι πρόσδετος
πολλοῖσι σὺν κώδωσιν ἐκτύπει φόβον.
στρατοῦ δὲ πλῆθος οὐδ᾽ ἂν ἐν ψήφου λόγῳ
310   θέσθαι δύναι᾽ ἄν, ὡς ἄπλατον ἦν ἰδεῖν,
πολλοὶ μὲν ἱππῆς, πολλὰ πελταστῶν τέλη,
πολλοὶ δ᾽ ἀτράκτων τοξόται, πολὺς δ᾽ ὄχλος
γυμνῆς ἁμαρτῇ, Θρηκίαν ἔχων στολήν.
τοιόσδε Τροίᾳ σύμμαχος πάρεστ᾽ ἀνήρ,
315 ὃν οὔτε φεύγων οὔθ᾽ ὑποσταθεὶς δορὶ
ὁ Πηλέως παῖς ἐκφυγεῖν δυνήσεται.

ΧΟΡΟΣ
ὅταν πολίταις εὐσταθῶσι δαίμονες,
ἕρπει κατάντης ξυμφορὰ πρὸς τἀγαθά.

ΕΚΤΩΡ
πολλούς, ἐπειδὴ τοὐμὸν εὐτυχεῖ δόρυ
320 καὶ Ζεὺς πρὸς ἡμῶν ἐστιν, εὑρήσω φίλους.
ἀλλ᾽ οὐδὲν αὐτῶν δεόμεθ᾽, οἵτινες πάλαι
μὴ ξυμπονοῦσιν ἡνίκ᾽ ἐξώστης Ἄρης
ἔθραυε λαίφη τῆσδε γῆς μέγας πνέων.

ally to the sons of Priam?"

When I had heard all I wanted to know, I stood by. And then I saw Rhesus mounted like a god behind his horses in his Thracian chariot. A yoke of gold restrained the necks of his steeds, which gleamed brighter than snow. The light shield on his shoulder flashed with a boss of beaten gold. A Gorgon of bronze, like that on Athena's aegis, glared from its place on the horses' cheekpieces and with its many bells struck a note of fear. You could not count his host even by reckoning with pebbles, so ungraspable was it. Many were the cavalry, many the companies of shield bearers, many the shooters of arrows, and many the light troops in Thracian gear.

Such is the ally who has come to aid Troy: Peleus' son will not be able to escape him either by running away or by facing him with his spear.

CHORUS LEADER

Whenever the gods favor the citizens, adversity turns to blessing.

HECTOR

Now that my spear is successful and Zeus is on our side, I shall find many friends. But I have no need of those who did not work with us from the start, when blustering Ares, blowing at gale force, was ripping up this country's sails.

Ῥῆσος δ' ἔδειξεν οἷος ἦν Τροίᾳ φίλος·
325   ἥκει γὰρ ἐς δαῖτ', οὐ παρὼν κυνηγέταις
αἱροῦσι λείαν οὐδὲ συγκαμὼν δορί.

ΧΟΡΟΣ

ὀρθῶς ἀτίζεις κἀπίμομφος εἶ φίλοις·
δέχου δὲ τοὺς θέλοντας ὠφελεῖν πόλιν.

ΕΚΤΩΡ

ἀρκοῦμεν οἱ σῴζοντες Ἴλιον πάλαι.

ΧΟΡΟΣ

330   πέποιθας ἤδη πολεμίους ᾑρηκέναι;

ΕΚΤΩΡ

πέποιθα· δείξει τοὐπιὸν σέλας θεοῦ.

ΧΟΡΟΣ

ὅρα τὸ μέλλον· πόλλ' ἀναστρέφει θεός.

ΕΚΤΩΡ

333   μισῶ φίλοισιν ὕστερον βοηδρομεῖν.
336   ὁ δ' οὖν, ἐπείπερ ἦλθε, σύμμαχος μὲν οὔ,
ξένος δὲ πρὸς τράπεζαν ἡκέτω ξένων·
338   χάρις γὰρ αὐτῷ Πριαμιδῶν διώλετο.

ΧΟΡΟΣ

334   ἄναξ, ἀπωθεῖν συμμάχους ἐπίφθονον.

ΑΓΓΕΛΟΣ

335   φόβος γένοιτ' ἂν πολεμίοις ὀφθεὶς μόνον.

ΕΚΤΩΡ

339   σύ τ' εὖ παραινεῖς καὶ σὺ καιρίως σκοπεῖς.

333–40 hoc ordine Nauck

388

Rhesus has shown what kind of friend he is to Troy. He has turned up for the feast though he did not help the hunters in the chase or lend us the aid of his spear.

CHORUS LEADER

You are quite right to complain and criticize your friends. But accept those who are willing to help the city.

HECTOR

Those of us who have been rescuing Ilium all along are enough.

CHORUS LEADER

Are you confident that you have destroyed the enemy?

HECTOR

Yes: the god's next dawn will make this plain.

CHORUS LEADER

Look to the future: god often sends reverse.

HECTOR

I hate being late to help friends!
    Well, since he has arrived, let him come, not as an ally but as a guest at my table. He has lost the gratitude of the sons of Priam.

CHORUS LEADER

My lord, rejecting allies leads to hatred.

MESSENGER

Just a glimpse of him will frighten the enemy.

HECTOR

(*to the Chorus Leader*) Your advice is good. (*to the Messenger*) And you have done timely lookout duty. Let gold-

340 ὁ χρυσοτευχὴς δ' οὕνεκ' ἀγγέλου λόγων
Ῥῆσος παρέστω τῇδε σύμμαχος χθονί.

ΧΟΡΟΣ

στρ. α

Ἀδράστεια μὲν ἁ Διὸς
παῖς εἴργοι στομάτων φθόνον·
φράσω γὰρ δὴ ὅσον μοι
345 ψυχᾷ προσφιλές ἐστιν εἰπεῖν.
ἥκεις, ὦ ποταμοῦ παῖ,
ἥκεις ἐπλάθης Φιλίου πρὸς αὐλὰν
ἀσπαστός, ἐπεί σε χρόνῳ
Πιερὶς μάτηρ ὅ τε καλλιγέφυ-
350 ρος ποταμὸς πορεύει

ἀντ. α

Στρυμών, ὅς ποτε τᾶς μελῳ-
δοῦ Μούσας δι' ἀκηράτων
δινηθεὶς ὑδροειδὴς
κόλπων σὰν ἐφύτευσεν ἥβαν.
355 σύ μοι Ζεὺς ὁ φαναῖος
ἥκεις διφρεύων βαλιαῖσι πώλοις.
νῦν, ὦ πατρὶς ὦ Φρυγία,
ξὺν θεῷ νῦν σοι τὸν ἐλευθέριον
Ζῆνα πάρεστιν εἰπεῖν.

---

8 Adrasteia, like Nemesis, is a goddess who punishes boastful
words. The Chorus here invoke her to see that Rhesus receives no
harm from the praise of him they are about to give.

armored Rhesus, thanks to this newsbringer's words, join this land as ally.

Exit MESSENGER *by Eisodos B.*

CHORUS

May Adrasteia, daughter of Zeus,[8]
shield my words from divine hostility!
I shall say all that my heart
longs to utter.
O son of the river god, you have come,
you have come and approached the court of Zeus of the
    Kindred,[9]
and most welcome you are since it has taken long
for your Pierian mother and the river of lovely bridges
to send you here.

The Strymon it was who once eddied
in watery wise through the virginal body
of the Muse, the singer,
and begot your fine manhood.
To me you have come as Zeus the Lightbearer,[10]
riding behind your dappled mares.
Now at last, O Phrygia, my fatherland,
God being your helper, you can call upon
Zeus the Liberator![11]

[9] The expression seems to mean that Rhesus has come to a house to which he is related, Zeus Philios being the god who watches over kindred, the patron of ties of affection.

[10] Or Zeus the Revealer.

[11] Zeus the Liberator was invoked by those freed from enslavement.

στρ. β

360 ἆρά ποτ' αὖθις ἁ παλαιὰ Τροία
τοὺς προπότας παναμερεύ-
σει θιάσους ἐρώτων
ψαλμοῖσι καὶ κυλίκων οἰνοπλανήτοις
ἐπιδεξίοις ἁμίλλαις

365 κατὰ πόντον Ἀτρειδᾶν
Σπάρταν οἰχομένων
Ἰλιάδος παρ' ἀκτᾶς;
ὦ φίλος, εἴθε μοι
σᾷ χερὶ καὶ σῷ δορὶ πρά-
ξας τάδ' ἐς οἶκον ἔλθοις.

ἀντ. β

370 ἐλθὲ φάνηθι, τὰν ζάχρυσον προβαλοῦ
Πηλεΐδα κατ' ὄμμα πέλ-
ταν δοχμίαν πεδαίρων
σχιστὰν παρ' ἄντυγα, πώλους ἐρεθίζων
δίβολόν τ' ἄκοντα πάλλων.

375 σὲ γὰρ οὔτις ὑποστὰς
Ἀργείας ποτ' ἐν Ἥ-
ρας δαπέδοις χορεύσει·
ἀλλά νιν ἅδε γᾶ
καπφθίμενον Θρῃκὶ μόρῳ
φίλτατον ἄχθος οἴσει.

364 ἐπιδεξίοις L. Dindorf: ὑποδ- C
373 πώλους Reiske: κώλοις C

Can it ever again be that ancient Troy
will spend the whole day in reveling,
pledging the health of our lady loves
in songs and drinking contests
that make the wine pass quickly round from left to right,
as over the sea the sons of Atreus
make for Sparta, leaving
Ilium's shore behind?
O friend, how I wish that for me
you might accomplish this with your arm and your spear
before you go home again!

Come, show yourself, brandish your golden
shield in the face of Peleus' son,
lifting it aslant
along the gap in the chariot rail, rousing your horses
and shaking your two-pronged javelin!
No one who stands against you
shall ever again tread the measure
in the plains of Argive Hera:
no, he shall die a Thracian death,
and this soil shall support him
as a burden that gives delight.

Enter RHESUS *by Eisodos B.*[12]

12 Possibly Rhesus enters on a chariot drawn by white horses,
as suggested by O. Taplin, *The Stagecraft of Aeschylus* (Oxford,
1977), p. 77.

380—ἰὼ ἰώ, μέγας ὦ βασιλεῦ.
κᾱλόν, ὦ Θρήκη,
σκύμνον ἔθρεψας πολίαρχον ἰδεῖν.
ἴδε χρυσόδετον σώματος ἀλκήν,
κλύε καὶ κόμπους κωδωνοκρότους
παρὰ πορπάκων κελαδοῦντας.
385   θεός, ὦ Τροία, θεός, αὐτὸς Ἄρης
ὁ Στρυμόνιος πῶλος ἀοιδοῦ
Μούσης ἥκων καταπνεῖ σε.

RΗΣΟΣ

χαῖρ᾽, ἐσθλὸς ἐσθλοῦ παῖς, τύραννε τῆσδε γῆς,
Ἕκτορ· παλαιᾷ σ᾽ ἡμέρᾳ προσεννέπω.
390   χαίρω δέ σ᾽ εὐτυχοῦντα καὶ προσήμενον
πύργοισιν ἐχθρῶν· συγκατασκάψων δ᾽ ἐγὼ
τείχη πάρειμι καὶ νεῶν πρήσων σκάφη.

ΕΚΤΩΡ

παῖ τῆς μελῳδοῦ μητέρος Μουσῶν μιᾶς
Θρῃκός τε ποταμοῦ Στρυμόνος, φιλῶ λέγειν
395   τἀληθὲς αἰεὶ κοὐ διπλοῦς πέφυκ᾽ ἀνήρ.
πάλαι πάλαι χρῆν τῇδε συγκάμνειν χθονὶ
ἐλθόντα, καὶ μὴ τοὐπὶ σ᾽ Ἀργείων ὕπο
Τροίαν ἐᾶσαι πολεμίῳ πεσεῖν δορί.
οὐ γάρ τι λέξεις ὡς ἄκλητος ὢν φίλοις
400   οὐκ ἦλθες οὐδ᾽ ἤμυνας οὐδ᾽ ἐπεστράφης.
τίς γάρ σε κῆρυξ ἢ γερουσία Φρυγῶν
ἐλθοῦσ᾽ ἀμύνειν οὐκ ἐπέσκηψεν πόλει;
ποῖον δὲ δώρων κόσμον οὐκ ἐπέμψαμεν;

CHORUS LEADER

Hail, O great king! Splendid, O Thrace, is the whelp you have raised, so royal of mien! See the gold armor about his body, hear the boast of his clanging bells as they ring on his shield rim! As a god, O Troy, a god, Ares himself, this son of the Strymon and the Muse has come to breathe upon you!

RHESUS

Hail, noble son of a noble sire, Hector, this country's king! It is late that I address you. But I am glad that you are enjoying success and are encamped at the enemy's gates. I have come to help tear up their stockade and set fire to their ships.

HECTOR

Son of one of the singing Muses and the Thracian river Strymon, it is my custom always to speak the truth: I am not double-tongued. You ought to have come long, long ago to share in this land's troubles: you should not, as far as in you lay, have allowed Troy to fall by enemy spear at the hands of the Argives. You can't say that it was for lack of an invitation that you failed to come or defend or visit your friends. What Trojan herald or embassy of elders did not arrive to urge you to protect our city? What gifts did we not

σὺ δ᾽ ἐγγενὴς ὢν βάρβαρός τε βαρβάρους
405 Ἕλλησιν ἡμᾶς προύπιες τὸ σὸν μέρος.
καίτοι σε μικρᾶς ἐκ τυραννίδος μέγαν
Θρῃκῶν ἄνακτα τῇδ᾽ ἔθηκ᾽ ἐγὼ χερί,
ὅτ᾽ ἀμφὶ Πάγγαιόν τε Παιόνων τε γῆν
Θρῃκῶν ἀρίστοις ἐμπεσὼν κατὰ στόμα
410 ἔρρηξα πέλτην, σοὶ δὲ δουλώσας λεὼν
παρέσχον· ὧν σὺ λακτίσας πολλὴν χάριν
φίλων νοσούντων ὕστερος βοηδρομεῖς.
οἱ δ᾽ οὐδὲν ἡμῖν ἐγγενεῖς πεφυκότες,
πάλαι παρόντες, οἱ μὲν ἐν χωστοῖς τάφοις
415 κεῖνται πεσόντες, πίστις οὐ σμικρὰ πόλει,
οἱ δ᾽ ἔν θ᾽ ὅπλοισι καὶ παρ᾽ ἱππείοις ὄχοις
ψυχρὰν ἄησιν δίψιόν τε πῦρ θεοῦ
μένουσι καρτεροῦντες, οὐκ ἐν δεμνίοις
πυκνὴν ἄμυστιν ὡς σὺ δεξιούμενοι.
420 ταῦθ᾽, ὡς ἂν εἰδῇς Ἕκτορ᾽ ὄντ᾽ ἐλεύθερον,
καὶ μέμφομαί σοι καὶ λέγω κατ᾽ ὄμμα σόν.

ΡΗΣΟΣ

τοιοῦτός εἰμι καὐτός, εὐθεῖαν λόγων
τέμνων κέλευθον, κοὐ διπλοῦς πέφυκ᾽ ἀνήρ.
ἐγὼ δὲ μεῖζον ἢ σὺ τῆσδ᾽ ἀπὼν χθονὸς
425 λύπῃ πρὸς ἧπαρ δυσφορῶν ἐτειρόμην.
ἀλλ᾽ ἀγχιτέρμων γαῖά μοι, Σκύθης λεώς,
μέλλοντι νόστον τὸν πρὸς Ἴλιον περᾶν
ξυνῆψε πόλεμον· ἀξένου δ᾽ ἀφικόμην
πόντου πρὸς ἀκτάς, Θρῇκα πορθμεύσων στρατόν.

send to honor you? But though you are an outlander like us, a kinsman, you betrayed us to the Greeks for all you did to the contrary. And yet with this hand I made you the great king of Thrace instead of a petty chieftain when near Mount Pangaeum and the land of the Paeonians I hurled myself straight upon the princes of Thrace and broke their shields. I made the people subject and delivered them to you. The great debt of gratitude you owe for this you have repudiated, and you are late in coming to help when your friends are in trouble. Others, unrelated to us, have been here a long time, and some of them have fallen and lie in funeral mounds, no small pledge of their loyalty to the city, while others, serving in armor or on war chariots, bravely endure the chilly blast of the god or his thirsty heat, not lying in blankets and toasting one another in deep drafts like you.

I have uttered these words of complaint to your face so that you may know that Hector is frank of speech.

RHESUS

I too am the sort of man who cuts a straight path in his speech: I am not double-tongued. My heart was more vexed than yours in grief at being absent from this land. But a neighboring land, the people of Scythia, made war on me as I was about to set off for Ilium. I came to the banks of the Hostile Sea[13] in order to take my Thracians

13 The Black Sea was euphemistically called *Euxeinos*, "friendly to strangers," but tragedy generally calls it *Axeinos*, "hostile to strangers."

428 ἀξένου Markland: εὐξ- C

430 ἔνθ' αἱματηρὸς πέλανος ἐς γαῖαν Σκύθης
    ἠντλεῖτο λόγχῃ Θρῇξ τε συμμιγὴς φόνος.
    τοιάδε τοί μ' ἀπεῖργε συμφορὰ πέδον
    Τροίας ἱκέσθαι σύμμαχόν τέ σοι μολεῖν.
    ἐπεὶ δ' ἔπερσα, τῶνδ' ὁμηρεύσας τέκνα
435 τάξας ⟨τ'⟩ ἔτειον δασμὸν ἐς δόμους φέρειν,
    ἥκω περάσας ναυσὶ πόντιον στόμα,
    τὰ δ' ἄλλα πεζὸς γῆς περῶν ὁρίσματα—
    οὐχ ὡς σὺ κομπεῖς τὰς ἐμὰς ἀμύστιδας
    οὐδ' ἐν ζαχρύσοις δώμασιν κοιμώμενος,
440 ἀλλ' οἷα πόντον Θρήικιον φυσήματα
    κρυσταλλόπηκτα Παίονάς τ' ἐπεζάρει,
    ξὺν τοῖσδ' ἄυπνος οἶδα τλὰς πορπάμασιν.
       ἀλλ' ὕστερος μὲν ἦλθον, ἐν καιρῷ δ' ὅμως·
    σὺ μὲν γὰρ ἤδη δέκατον αἰχμάζεις ἔτος
445 κοὐδὲν περαίνεις, ἡμέραν δ' ἐξ ἡμέρας
    ῥίπτεις κυβεύων τὸν πρὸς Ἀργείους Ἄρη·
    ἐμοὶ δὲ φῶς ἓν ἡλίου καταρκέσει
    πέρσαντι πύργους ναυστάθμοις ἐπεσπεσεῖν
    κτεῖναί τ' Ἀχαιούς· θατέρᾳ δ' ἀπ' Ἰλίου
450 πρὸς οἶκον εἶμι, συντεμὼν τοὺς σοὺς πόνους,
    ὑμῶν δὲ μή τις ἀσπίδ' ἄρηται χερί·
    ἐγὼ γὰρ ἥξω τοὺς μέγ' αὐχοῦντας δορὶ
    πέρσας Ἀχαιούς, καίπερ ὕστερος μολών.

ΧΟΡΟΣ

στρ.

    ἰὼ ἰώ.

across to the other side. There the lance made both the Scythians and the Thracians shed much blood together into the soil. This prevented me from coming to the plain of Troy and being your ally. Once I had sacked them, taken their children as hostages, ⟨and⟩ fixed a yearly tribute for them to pay me, I came here: I passed by ship over the sea and through the other territories on foot—not drinking those deep drafts of wine you loudly proclaim I did or sleeping in a golden house. Rather such blasts as vex the frozen Thracian Pontus and the Paeonians I have sleeplessly endured wrapped in this cloak here: I remember it well.

Although I have come late, my coming is timely. This is already the tenth year you have been waging war without effect, and day after day you cast your dice in war against the Argives. But for me a single day's light will suffice to pillage the Achaeans' towers, fall upon their ships, and kill them. On the following day I shall leave Ilium for home, having shortened your labors. None of you need take shield in hand: I shall come back having plundered the boastful Achaeans with my spear, latecomer though I am.

CHORUS

Hurrah!

---

435 ⟨τ᾽⟩ Lenting
446 ῥίπτεις Sallier: πίπτεις C
452 ἥξω Kovacs: ἕξω C

455 φίλα θροεῖς, φίλος Διόθεν εἶ· μόνον
φθόνον ἄμαχον ὕπατος
Ζεὺς θέλοι ἀμφὶ σοῖς λόγοισιν εἴργειν.
τὸ δὲ νάιον Ἀργόθεν δόρυ
οὔτε πρίν τιν᾽ οὔτε νῦν
460 ἀνδρῶν ἐπόρευσε σέθεν κρείσσω. πῶς μοι
Ἀχιλεὺς τὸ σὸν ἔγχος ἂν δύναιτο,
πῶς δ᾽ Αἴας ὑπομεῖναι;
εἰ γὰρ ἐγὼ τόδε γ᾽ ἦμαρ
465 εἰσίδοιμ᾽, ἄναξ, ὅτῳ πολυφόνου
χειρὸς ἄποιν᾽ ἄροιο σᾷ λόγχᾳ.

ΡΗΣΟΣ

τοιαῦτα μέν σοι τῆς μακρᾶς ἀπουσίας
⟨ἢ δυσχεραίνεις, ἄξι᾽ ὠφελήματα⟩
πρᾶξαι παρέξω· σὺν δ᾽ Ἀδραστείᾳ λέγω·
ἐπειδὰν ἐχθρῶν τήνδ᾽ ἐλευθέραν πόλιν
470 θῶμεν θεοῖσί τ᾽ ἀκροθίνι᾽ ἐξέλῃς,
ξὺν σοὶ στρατεύειν γῆν ἐπ᾽ Ἀργείων θέλω
καὶ πᾶσαν ἐλθὼν Ἑλλάδ᾽ ἐκπέρσαι δορί,
ὡς ἂν μάθωσιν ἐν μέρει πάσχειν κακῶς.

ΕΚΤΩΡ

εἰ τοῦ παρόντος τοῦδ᾽ ἀπαλλαχθεὶς κακοῦ
475 πόλιν νεμοίμην ὡς τὸ πρίν ποτ᾽ ἀσφαλῆ,
ἦ κάρτα πολλὴν θεοῖς ἂν εἰδείην χάριν.
τὰ δ᾽ ἀμφί τ᾽ Ἄργος καὶ νομὸν τὸν Ἑλλάδος
οὐχ ὧδε πορθεῖν ῥᾴδι᾽ ὡς λέγεις δορί.

Welcome are your words, and you are a welcome arrival
  sent by Zeus!
Only may Zeus on high grant
that the gods not take offense at your words!
Neither before this nor now
has a ship from Argos
brought a man superior to you. Tell me,
how can Achilles withstand your spear,
how can Ajax?
O that I might see
that day, my lord, when by your spear
you exact retribution for their murderous deeds.

RHESUS

I shall allow you to exact from me ⟨a benefit that befits⟩ my
absence, ⟨at which you take offense,⟩ and it is this (may
Adrasteia not resent my words): when we have freed this
city from its enemies and you have set aside the first fruits
for the gods, I am willing to sail to the land of the Argives
and sack all Greece with my spear so that they in their turn
will know what it is to suffer.

HECTOR

If I can escape our present misfortune and rule the city
securely, as I did before, I will be extremely grateful to the
gods. It is not as easy as you claim to ravage the Argive
territory and the land of Hellas.

---

459 τιν' οὔτε νῦν Nauck: οὔτε νῦν τιν' C
464 τόδε γ' Hermann: τόδ' C
465 ὅτῳ Musgrave: ὅπως C
466 ἄποιν' ἄροιο σᾷ Diggle: ἀποινάσαιο fere C
467 post h. v. lac. indic. Kovacs

401

ΡΗΣΟΣ

οὐ τούσδ᾽ ἀριστέας φασὶν Ἑλλήνων μολεῖν;

ΕΚΤΩΡ

480 κοὐ μεμφόμεσθά γ᾽, ἀλλ᾽ ἄδην ἐλαύνομεν.

ΡΗΣΟΣ

οὔκουν κτανόντες τούσδε πάντ᾽ εἰργάσμεθα;

ΕΚΤΩΡ

μή νυν τὰ πόρσω τἀγγύθεν μεθεὶς σκόπει.

ΡΗΣΟΣ

ἀρκεῖν ἔοικέ σοι παθεῖν, δρᾶσαι δὲ μή.

ΕΚΤΩΡ

πολλῆς γὰρ ἄρχω κἀνθάδ᾽ ὢν τυραννίδος.
485 ἀλλ᾽ εἴτε λαιὸν εἴτε δεξιὸν κέρας
εἴτ᾽ ἐν μέσοισι συμμάχοις πάρεστί σοι
πέλτην ἐρεῖσαι καὶ καταστῆσαι στρατόν.

ΡΗΣΟΣ

μόνος μάχεσθαι πολεμίοις, Ἕκτορ, θέλω.
εἰ δ᾽ αἰσχρὸν ἡγῇ μὴ συνεμπρῆσαι νεῶν
490 πρύμνας, πονήσας τὸν πάρος πολὺν χρόνον,
τάξον μ᾽ Ἀχιλλέως καὶ στρατοῦ κατὰ στόμα.

ΕΚΤΩΡ

οὐκ ἔστ᾽ ἐκείνῳ θοῦρον ἀντᾶραι δόρυ.

ΡΗΣΟΣ

καὶ μὴν λόγος γ᾽ ἦν ὡς ἔπλευσ᾽ ἐπ᾽ Ἴλιον.

480 ἐλαύνομαι Hartung
492 ἀντᾶραι Reiske: ἐντάξαι C

RHESUS

Don't they say that these men who have come are the Greeks' finest heroes?

HECTOR

I find no fault with them: driving them off has been enough work for me.

RHESUS

Then if we kill them, haven't we finished the job?

HECTOR

Don't set your sights on what's distant and neglect what's near at hand.

RHESUS

I think you are content to suffer rather than to act.

HECTOR

I rule over a large kingdom even here. But you may lean your shields and station your army on the left or right wing or in the middle of the allies.

RHESUS

Hector, I want to fight alone against the enemy. But if you consider it a disgrace not to burn the ships' prows since you have toiled so long up to now, station me to face Achilles and his contingent.

HECTOR

Against him you cannot range your furious spear.

RHESUS

But it is said that he sailed to Ilium.

ΕΚΤΩΡ

ἔπλευσε καὶ πάρεστιν· ἀλλὰ μηνίων
495 στρατηλάταισιν οὐ συναίρεται δόρυ.

ΡΗΣΟΣ

τίς δὴ μετ' αὐτὸν ἄλλος εὐδοξεῖ στρατοῦ;

ΕΚΤΩΡ

Αἴας ἐμοὶ μὲν οὐδὲν ἡσσᾶσθαι δοκεῖ
χὠ Τυδέως παῖς· ἔστι δ' αἰμυλώτατον
κρότημ' Ὀδυσσεὺς λῆμά τ' ἀρκούντως θρασὺς
500 καὶ πλεῖστα χώραν τήνδ' ἀνὴρ καθυβρίσας·
ὃς εἰς Ἀθάνας σηκὸν ἔννυχος μολὼν
κλέψας ἄγαλμα ναῦς ἐπ' Ἀργείων φέρει.
ἤδη δ' ἀγύρτης πτωχικὴν ἔχων στολὴν
ἐσῆλθε πύργους, πολλὰ δ' Ἀργείοις κακὰ
505 ἠρᾶτο, πεμφθεὶς Ἰλίου κατάσκοπος·
κτανὼν δὲ φρουροὺς καὶ παραστάτας πυλῶν
ἐξῆλθεν· αἰεὶ δ' ἐν λόχοις εὑρίσκεται
Θυμβραῖον ἀμφὶ βωμὸν ἄστεως πέλας
θάσσων· κακῷ δὲ μερμέρῳ παλαίομεν.

ΡΗΣΟΣ

510 οὐδεὶς ἀνὴρ εὔψυχος ἀξιοῖ λάθρᾳ
κτεῖναι τὸν ἐχθρόν, ἀλλ' ἰὼν κατὰ στόμα.
τοῦτον δ' ὃν ἵζειν φῂς σὺ κλωπικὰς ἕδρας
καὶ μηχανᾶσθαι, ζῶντα συλλαβὼν ἐγὼ
πυλῶν ἐπ' ἐξόδοισιν ἀμπείρας ῥάχιν
515 στήσω πετεινοῖς γυψὶ θοινατήριον.
λῃστὴν γὰρ ὄντα καὶ θεῶν ἀνάκτορα

HECTOR

He sailed and is here. But he is angry with the generals and does not join in the fighting.

RHESUS

Who is thought to be the best fighter after him?

HECTOR

In my judgment Ajax is in no way his inferior, nor is Tydeus' son. Odysseus is a clever rogue: he is plenty bold of heart and has done more harm to this land than any other. He went by night to Athena's shrine, stole the statue, and carried it off to the Argive ships. And then he was sent to spy on Troy: he came within the walls dressed as a beggar in rags and uttering curses on the Argives. But he killed the sentries and gate guards before going out. He is always to be seen about the altars of Thymbraean Apollo near the city, lurking in ambush. He's trouble to wrestle with.

RHESUS

No brave man deigns to kill the enemy by stealth but fights face to face. This man you say lurks in thievish hiding-places and plots—him I shall capture alive, impale him through the spine by the city gate, and set him as a feast before the winged vultures. That's the proper death for a

---

500 τήνδ'] εἰς Boissonade

συλῶντα δεῖ νιν τῷδε κατθανεῖν μόρῳ.

ΕΚΤΩΡ

νῦν μὲν καταυλίσθητε· καὶ γὰρ εὐφρόνη.
δείξω δ' ἐγώ σοι χῶρον, ἔνθα χρὴ στρατὸν
520 τὸν σὸν νυχεῦσαι τοῦ τεταγμένου δίχα.
ξύνθημα δ' ἡμῖν Φοῖβος, ἤν τι καὶ δέῃ·
μέμνησ' ἀκούσας Θρῃκί τ' ἄγγειλον στρατῷ.
    ὑμᾶς δὲ βάντας χρὴ προταινὶ τάξεων
φρουρεῖν ἐγερτὶ καὶ νεῶν κατάσκοπον
525 δέχθαι Δόλωνα· καὶ γάρ, εἴπερ ἐστὶ σῶς,
ἤδη πελάζει στρατοπέδοισι Τρωικοῖς.

ΧΟΡΟΣ

στρ.

τίνος ἁ φυλακά; τίς ἀμείβει τὰν ἐμάν; πρῶτα
δύεται σημεῖα καὶ ἑπτάποροι
530 Πλειάδες αἰθέριαι·
μέσα δ' αἰετὸς οὐρανοῦ ποτᾶται.
ἔγρεσθε, τί μέλλετε; κοιτᾶν
ἔξιτε πρὸς φυλακάν.
οὐ λεύσσετε μηνάδος αἴγλαν;
535 ἀὼς δὴ πέλας ἀὼς
γίγνεται καί τις προδρόμων ὅδε γ' ἐστὶν ἀστήρ.

—τίς ἐκηρύχθη πρώτην φυλακήν;
—Μυγδόνος υἱόν φασι Κόροιβον.

533 ἔξιτε Hartung: ἔγρεσθε C

thief and a temple robber.

HECTOR

Now it is night: time for you to make camp. I will show you
a place where your army may spend the night, separate
from where the rest are stationed. If need arises, the
watchword is "Phoebus": hear and remember and tell your
Thracian army.

(*to the Chorus*) You must go and keep watch in front of
the ranks and receive Dolon, who's spying on the ships. If
he is safe, he must now be approaching the Trojan camp.

Exit HECTOR *and* RHESUS *by Eisodos B.*

CHORUS

Who's on guard duty? Who will relieve me? The early
constellations are setting and the seven-starred
Pleiades are aloft.
The Eagle flies in mid heaven.
Look lively there! What's the delay? Out of your beds
and to the watch!
Don't you see how the moon shines?
Dawn, I tell you, dawn
is near, and this star is her harbinger.

CHORUS LEADER

Who was announced for the first watch?

CHORUS MEMBER

Mygdon's son, they tell me, Coroebus.

540—τίς γὰρ ἐπ' αὐτῷ; —Κίλικας Παίων
στρατὸς ἤγειρεν, Μυσοὶ δ' ἡμᾶς.
—οὔκουν Λυκίους πέμπτην φυλακὴν
βάντας ἐγείρειν
545 καιρὸς κλήρου κατὰ μοῖραν;
ἀντ.

καὶ μὰν ἀίω· Σιμόεντος ἡμένα κοίτας
φοινίας ὑμνεῖ πολυχορδοτάτᾳ
γήρυϊ παιδολέτωρ
550 μελοποιὸν ἀηδονὶς μέριμναν.
ἤδη δὲ νέμουσι κατ' Ἴδαν
ποίμνια· νυκτιβρόμου
σύριγγος ἰὰν κατακούω.
θέλγει δ' ὄμματος ἕδραν
555 ὕπνος· ἅδιστος γὰρ ἔβα βλεφάροις πρὸς ἀῶ.

—τί ποτ' οὐ πελάθει σκοπός, ὃν ναῶν
Ἕκτωρ ὤτρυνε κατόπτην;
—ταρβῶ· χρόνιος γὰρ ἄπεστιν.
560—ἀλλ' ἦ κρυπτὸν λόχον ἐσπαίσας
διόλωλε; τάχ' ἂν ⟨δ'⟩ εἴη ⟨φανερόν.
—καὶ μὴν τόδε γ' ἦν⟩ φοβερόν μοι.

---

556 ἀῶ Blaydes, Headlam: ἀοῦς C
561 ⟨δ'⟩ Diggle   post εἴη lac. indic. et suppl. Diggle

---

[14] I.e. Coroebus' soldiers.
[15] Procne, who killed her son Itys to spite her unfaithful husband, was turned into a nightingale.

CHORUS LEADER

And who followed him?

CHORUS MEMBER

The Paeonian contingent[14] woke the Cilicians, and the Mysians woke us.

CHORUS LEADER

Should we not then go and wake the Lycians, the fifth watch in the lot's apportionment?

CHORUS

Listen! I hear the nightingale! She sits on her bloodstained nest by the Simois, child-slayer she,[15] and
in melodious strain
sings her musical woe.
Already on Ida they are tending
the flocks: I hear the buzz
of the night-murmuring shepherd's pipe.
Sleep puts its spell on my eyes:
most sweetly does it come upon the lids toward dawn.

CHORUS LEADER

Why is he not coming, the man
Hector sent to spy on the ships?

CHORUS MEMBER

I'm worried: he has been gone a long time.

CHORUS LEADER

Has he blundered into a hidden ambush and been killed?
Perhaps this will become <clear>.

<CHORUS MEMBER

Yes, that was what> I was afraid of.

—αὐδῶ Λυκίους πέμπτην φυλακὴν
βάντας ἐγείρειν
ἡμᾶς κλήρου κατὰ μοῖραν.

ΟΔΥΣΣΕΥΣ

565 Διόμηδες, οὐκ ἤκουσας—ἢ κενὸς ψόφος
στάζει δι᾽ ὤτων; —τευχέων τινὰ κτύπον;

ΔΙΟΜΗΔΗΣ

οὔκ, ἀλλὰ δεσμὰ πωλικῶν ἐξ ἀντύγων
κλάζει σίδηρον· κἀμέ τοι, πρὶν ᾐσθόμην
δεσμῶν ἀραγμὸν ἱππικῶν, ἔδυ φόβος.

ΟΔΥΣΣΕΥΣ

570 ὅρα κατ᾽ ὄρφνην μὴ φύλαξιν ἐντύχῃς.

ΔΙΟΜΗΔΗΣ

φυλάξομαί τοι κἂν σκότῳ τιθεὶς πόδα.

ΟΔΥΣΣΕΥΣ

ἢν δ᾽ οὖν ἐγείρῃς, οἶσθα σύνθημα στρατοῦ;

ΔΙΟΜΗΔΗΣ

Φοῖβον Δόλωνος οἶδα σύμβολον κλυών.

ΟΔΥΣΣΕΥΣ

ἔα·
εὐνὰς ἐρήμους τάσδε πολεμίων ὁρῶ.

568 τοι πρὶν] fort. πρὶν γάρ

16 Exit by eisodos followed by entrance by the same eisodos,
causing a delay, is rare in tragedy. Perhaps Odysseus and Dio-
medes enter stealthily during the choral ode and hide behind the

CHORUS LEADER

I say: go and wake the Lycians, the fifth watch in the lot's appointment!

Exit CHORUS *by Eisodos A. After an interval enter to the empty stage by Eisodos A* ODYSSEUS *and* DIOMEDES.[16] *The former carries either Dolon's wolfskin or his weapons.*

ODYSSEUS

Diomedes, did you hear a clash of weapons? Or was it some meaningless sound that my ears caught?

DIOMEDES

It was nothing, an iron clash made by a harness striking a chariot rail. At first I too was frightened, until I realized it was the crash of the harness.

ODYSSEUS

Take care that you don't run into guards in the dark.

DIOMEDES

I will be careful where I tread in darkness.

ODYSSEUS

Supposing you wake someone, do you know the watchword?

DIOMEDES

"Phoebus": I have this watchword from Dolon.

ODYSSEUS

Careful! I see empty beds of the enemy here.

stage altar, as suggested by D. Wiles, *Tragedy in Athens* (Cambridge, 1997).

411

ΔΙΟΜΗΔΗΣ

575 καὶ μὴν Δόλων γε τάσδ' ἔφραζεν Ἕκτορος
κοίτας, ἐφ' ᾧπερ ἔγχος εἵλκυσται τόδε.

ΟΔΥΣΣΕΥΣ

τί δῆτ' ἂν εἴη; μῶν λόχος βέβηκέ ποι;

ΔΙΟΜΗΔΗΣ

ἴσως ἐφ' ἡμῖν μηχανὴν στήσων τινά.

ΟΔΥΣΣΕΥΣ

θρασὺς γὰρ Ἕκτωρ νῦν, ἐπεὶ κρατεῖ, θρασύς.

ΔΙΟΜΗΔΗΣ

580 τί δῆτ', Ὀδυσσεῦ, δρῶμεν; οὐ γὰρ ηὕρομεν
τὸν ἄνδρ' ἐν εὐναῖς, ἐλπίδων δ' ἡμάρτομεν.

ΟΔΥΣΣΕΥΣ

στείχωμεν ὡς τάχιστα ναυστάθμων πέλας.
σῴζει γὰρ αὐτὸν ὅστις εὐτυχῆ θεῶν
τίθησιν· ἡμῖν δ' οὐ βιαστέον τύχην.

ΔΙΟΜΗΔΗΣ

585 οὔκουν ἐπ' Αἰνέαν ἢ τὸν ἔχθιστον Φρυγῶν
Πάριν μολόντε χρὴ καρατομεῖν ξίφει;

ΟΔΥΣΣΕΥΣ

πῶς οὖν ἐν ὄρφνῃ πολεμίων ἀνὰ στρατὸν
ζητῶν δυνήσῃ τούσδ' ἀκινδύνως κτανεῖν;

ΔΙΟΜΗΔΗΣ

αἰσχρόν γε μέντοι ναῦς ἐπ' Ἀργείων μολεῖν
590 δράσαντε μηδὲν πολεμίους νεώτερον.

DIOMEDES

Yes: Dolon said that here Hector was sleeping. My sword is drawn against him.

ODYSSEUS

What could this mean? Has the company gone off somewhere?

DIOMEDES

Perhaps to set some trap for us.

ODYSSEUS

Hector is brash from his victory, brash.

DIOMEDES

What shall we do then, Odysseus? We have not found the man in his bed, and our hopes are dashed.

ODYSSEUS

Let's go as quickly as we can back to our beached ships. Whatever god gave this man victory is now protecting him. We must not fight against fate.

DIOMEDES

Shouldn't we attack Aeneas or Paris, the Phrygian I hate most, and cut off their heads with the sword?

ODYSSEUS

How can you look for them in the dark in the enemy camp and kill them without great risk?

DIOMEDES

But it is a disgrace to go back to the Argive ships without harming the enemy.

ΟΔΥΣΣΕΥΣ

πῶς δ' οὐ δέδρακας; οὐ κτανόντε ναυστάθμων
κατάσκοπον Δόλωνα σῴζομεν τάδε
σκυλεύματ'; ἢ πᾶν στρατόπεδον πέρσειν δοκεῖς;

ΔΙΟΜΗΔΗΣ

πείθεις· πάλιν στείχωμεν· εὖ δοίη τύχη.

ΑΘΗΝΑ

595 ποῖ δὴ λιπόντε Τρωικῶν ἐκ τάξεων
χωρεῖτε, λύπῃ καρδίαν δεδηγμένω,
εἰ μὴ κτανεῖν σφῷν Ἕκτορ' ἢ Πάριν θεὸς
δίδωσιν; ἄνδρα δ' οὐ πέπυσθε σύμμαχον
Τροίᾳ μολόντα Ῥῆσον οὐ φαύλῳ τρόπῳ;
600 ὃς εἰ διοίσει νύκτα τήνδ' ἐς αὔριον,
οὔτ' ἂν σφ' Ἀχιλλεὺς οὔτ' ἂν Αἴαντος δόρυ
μὴ πάντα πέρσαι ναύσταθμ' Ἀργείων σχέθοι,
τείχη κατασκάψαντα καὶ πυλῶν ἔσω
λόγχῃ πλατεῖαν ἐσδρομὴν ποιούμενον.
605 τοῦτον κατακτὰς πάντ' ἔχεις. τὰς δ' Ἕκτορος
εὐνὰς ἔασον καὶ καρατόμους σφαγάς·
ἔσται γὰρ αὐτῷ θάνατος ἐξ ἄλλης χερός.

ΟΔΥΣΣΕΥΣ

δέσποιν' Ἀθάνα, φθέγματος γὰρ ᾐσθόμην
τοῦ σοῦ συνήθη γῆρυν· ἐν πόνοισι γὰρ
610 παροῦσ' ἀμύνεις τοῖς ἐμοῖς ἀεί ποτε·
τὸν ἄνδρα δ' ἡμῖν ποῦ κατηύνασται φράσον·
πόθεν τέτακται βαρβάρου στρατεύματος;

RHESUS

ODYSSEUS

Without harming them? What can you mean? Didn't we
kill Dolon, the ship spy, and aren't we carrying back these
spoils? Did you expect to ravage the entire camp?

DIOMEDES

You win: let's go back. May good luck attend us!

Enter ATHENA *above the* skene.

ATHENA

Where are you going, departing from the Trojan ranks,
heartsick that the god did not permit you to kill Hector or
Paris? Don't you know that in no mean style Rhesus has ar-
rived as an ally to Troy? If he passes the night here until
morning, neither Achilles nor the spear of Ajax will pre-
vent him from destroying all the Argives' beached ships,
breaking down the palisades and cutting a wide swath with
his spear within the gates. If you kill him, all is yours. So
leave Hector's encampment and your plan of beheading
him: death will come to him from another hand.

ODYSSEUS

My lady Athena, your voice is familiar to me, and I recog-
nize its sound: you always stand by me and help me in my
toils. Tell me where the man has bedded down? Where in
the enemy camp is he stationed?

---

594 δοίη Nauck: δ' εἴη C
596 δεδηγμένῳ Wecklein: -οι vel -ον C

ΑΘΗΝΑ

ὅδ' ἐγγὺς ἧσται κοὐ συνήθροισται στρατῷ,
ἀλλ' ἐκτὸς αὐτὸν τάξεων κατήνασεν

615 Ἕκτωρ, ἕως ἂν νύκτ' ἀμείψηται φάος.
πέλας δὲ πῶλοι Θρηκίων ἐξ ἁρμάτων
λευκαὶ δέδενται, διαπρεπεῖς ἐν εὐφρόνῃ·
στίλβουσι δ' ὥστε ποταμίου κύκνου πτερόν.
ταύτας, κτανόντες δεσπότην, κομίζετε,

620 κάλλιστον οἴκοις σκῦλον· οὐ γὰρ ἔσθ' ὅπου
τοιόνδ' ὄχημα χθὼν κέκευθε πωλικόν.

ΟΔΥΣΣΕΥΣ

Διόμηδες, ἢ σὺ κτεῖνε Θρήκιον λεών,
ἢ 'μοὶ πάρες γε, σοὶ δὲ χρὴ πώλους μέλειν.

ΔΙΟΜΗΔΗΣ

ἐγὼ φονεύσω, πωλοδαμνήσεις δὲ σύ·
625 τρίβων γὰρ εἶ τὰ κομψὰ καὶ νοεῖν σοφός.
χρὴ δ' ἄνδρα τάσσειν οὗ μάλιστ' ἂν ὠφελοῖ.

ΑΘΗΝΑ

καὶ μὴν καθ' ἡμᾶς τόνδ' Ἀλέξανδρον βλέπω
στείχοντα, φυλάκων ἔκ τινος πεπυσμένον
δόξας ἀσήμους πολεμίων μεμβλωκότων.

ΔΙΟΜΗΔΗΣ

630 πότερα σὺν ἄλλοις ἢ μόνος πορεύεται;

ΑΘΗΝΑ

μόνος· πρὸς εὐνὰς δ', ὡς ἔοικεν, Ἕκτορος
χωρεῖ, κατόπτας σημανῶν ἥκειν στρατοῦ.

ATHENA

His place is nearby but separate from the army: Hector settled him outside the ranks until day should supplant night. Near him white horses are harnessed to Thracian chariots, clear to see in the dark: they gleam like a swan's wing. Kill their owner and take these horses as splendid spoil for your house: no place on earth contains a team of horses like these.

ODYSSEUS

Diomedes, you must either kill the Thracian soldiery or allow me to while taking care of the horses yourself.

DIOMEDES

I'll do the killing, and you get control of the horses: you are good at clever deeds and have a sharp eye. A man should be put where he can do the most good.

Enter ALEXANDROS by Eisodos A.[17]

ATHENA

Look: I see Alexandros coming toward you. He has heard from one of the watch a confused rumor that enemy soldiers have arrived.

DIOMEDES

Is he coming with others or alone?

ATHENA

Alone: he's coming, it seems, to where Hector sleeps to report the arrival of spies.

17 In all probability Alexandros is played by a fourth actor: see Battezzato 2000.

---

615 νύκτ᾽ Lenting: νὺξ C

ΔΙΟΜΗΔΗΣ

οὔκουν ὑπάρχειν τόνδε κατθανόντα χρή;

ΑΘΗΝΑ

οὐκ ἂν δύναιο τοῦ πεπρωμένου πλέον·
635 τοῦτον δὲ πρὸς σῆς χειρὸς οὐ θέμις θανεῖν.
ἀλλ᾽ οἷπερ ἥξεις μορσίμους φέρων σφαγὰς
τάχυν· ἐγὼ δέ, τῷδε σύμμαχος Κύπρις
δοκοῦσ᾽ ἀρωγὸς ἐν πόνοις παραστατεῖν,
σαθροῖς λόγοισιν ἐχθρὸν ἄνδρ᾽ ἀμείψομαι.
640 καὶ ταῦτ᾽ ἐγὼ μὲν εἶπον· ὃν δὲ χρὴ παθεῖν
οὐκ οἶδεν οὐδ᾽ ἤκουσεν ἐγγὺς ὢν λόγου.

ΑΛΕΞΑΝΔΡΟΣ

σὲ τὸν στρατηγὸν καὶ κασίγνητον λέγω,
Ἕκτορ, καθεύδεις; οὐκ ἐγείρεσθαί σ᾽ ἐχρῆν;
ἐχθρῶν τις ἡμῖν χρίμπτεται στρατεύματι,
645 ἢ κλῶπες ἄνδρες ἢ κατάσκοποί τινες.

ΑΘΗΝΑ

θάρσει· φυλάσσει σ᾽ ἥδε πρευμενὴς Κύπρις.
μέλει δ᾽ ὁ σός μοι πόλεμος, οὐδ᾽ ἀμνημονῶ
τιμῆς, ἐπαινῶ δ᾽ εὖ παθοῦσα πρὸς σέθεν.
καὶ νῦν ἐπ᾽ εὐτυχοῦντι Τρωικῷ στρατῷ
650 ἥκω πορεύουσ᾽ ἄνδρα σοι μέγαν φίλον,
τῆς ὑμνοποιοῦ παῖδα Θρήκιον θεᾶς
[Μούσης· πατρὸς δὲ Στρυμόνος κικλήσκεται].

ΑΛΕΞΑΝΔΡΟΣ

ἀεί ποτ᾽ εὖ φρονοῦσα τυγχάνεις πόλει
κἀμοί, μέγιστον δ᾽ ἐν βίῳ κειμήλιον

DIOMEDES

Well should he not be our first victim?

ATHENA

That would be against destiny, and you can't do it: he is not
fated to die by your hand. But go quickly on your way to
where you will slaughter somone you are fated to. As for
me, I will pretend to be this man's ally Aphrodite and to be
standing by him in trouble and will pay him back by giving
my enemy deceitful advice. I have said this, but my in-
tended victim, though nearby, does not hear or understand
what I said.

Exit by Eisodos B ODYSSEUS *and* DIOMEDES.

ALEXANDROS

Hector, my commander and brother, are you sleeping?
Should you not wake up? Some of the enemy are ap-
proaching our camp: it may be thieves or spies!

ATHENA

Fear not! In good will I, Cypris, am keeping watch over
you! I care about your war: I do not forget your honor to
me and thank you for your good treatment. And now I have
come to bring to the successful Trojan army a great ally, the
Thracian son of the singer [, the Muse: the Strymon, they
say, is his father].

ALEXANDROS

You have always been well disposed to me and my city, and
I claim that the greatest treasure I have won for the city

---

636 οἷπερ ἥξεις Kovacs: ᾧπερ (vel ὥσπερ) ἥκεις C
652 del. Lachmann: cf. 279

655 κρίνας σέ φημι τῇδε προσθέσθαι πόλει.
ἥκω δ' ἀκούσας οὐ τορῶς—φήμη δέ τις
φύλαξιν ἐμπέπτωκεν—ὡς κατάσκοποι
ἥκουσ' Ἀχαιῶν. χὠ μὲν οὐκ ἰδὼν λέγει,
ὁ δ' εἰσιδὼν μολόντας οὐκ ἔχει φράσαι·
660 ὧν οὕνεκ' εὐνὰς ἤλυθον πρὸς Ἕκτορος.

ΑΘΗΝΑ

μηδὲν φοβηθῇς· οὐδὲν ἐν στρατῷ νέον·
Ἕκτωρ δὲ φροῦδος Θρῇκα κοιμήσων στρατόν.

ΑΛΕΞΑΝΔΡΟΣ

σύ τοί με πείθεις, σοῖς δὲ πιστεύων λόγοις
τάξιν φυλάξων εἶμ' ἐλεύθερος φόβου.

ΑΘΗΝΑ

665 χώρει· μέλειν γὰρ πάντ' ἐμοὶ δόκει τὰ σά,
ὥστ' εὐτυχοῦντας συμμάχους ἐμοὺς ὁρᾶν.
γνώσῃ δὲ καὶ σὺ τὴν ἐμὴν προθυμίαν.
ὑμᾶς δ' αὐτῶ τοὺς ἄγαν ἐρρωμένους,
Λαερτίου παῖ, θηκτὰ κοιμίσαι ξίφη.
670 κεῖται γὰρ ἡμῖν Θρήκιος στρατηλάτης,
ἵπποι τ' ἔχονται, πολέμιοι δ' ᾐσθημένοι
χωροῦσ' ἐφ' ὑμᾶς· ἀλλ' ὅσον τάχιστα χρὴ
φεύγειν πρὸς ὁλκοὺς ναυστάθμων. τί μέλλετε
σκηπτοῦ 'πιόντος πολεμίων σῶσαι βίον;

670 ὑμῖν Valcknaer

420

was when I judged you the winner.[18] But I have come here because I heard indistinctly (rumor flies about the sentries) that Achaean spies have come. One man tells the tale without seeing them, another has seen them arrive but can't say anything more. That is why I have come to Hector's bed.

ATHENA

Have no fear: nothing is amiss in the camp. Hector has gone off to take the Thracian army to its encampment.

ALEXANDROS

I take your guidance: trusting in your words I will go off free from fear to guard my station.

ATHENA

Go! You must remember that all that happens to you concerns me, and I will make sure that my allies prosper. You too shall learn the extent of my good will.

Exit ALEXANDROS *by Eisodos* A.

(*calling offstage toward Eisodos* B) I call on you overly brave men: son of Laertes, put your whetted sword to sleep! We've killed the Thracian general, and his horses are yours, but the enemy have got wind of you and are approaching! Quick, flee back to the ships! Hurry and save your lives! A hurricane of enemies is approaching!

Exit ATHENA. *Enter by Eisodos* A *the* CHORUS *and by Eisodos* B ODYSSEUS *and* DIOMEDES.[19]

18 In the beauty contest on Ida.
19 Possibly they have Rhesus' horses with them: see Battezzato, p. 371.

ΧΟΡΟΣ

675 ἔα ἔα·

βάλε βάλε βάλε· θένε θένε ⟨θένε⟩.

τίς ἀνήρ;

677 λεῦσσε· τοῦτον αὐδῶ.

680 δεῦρο δεῦρο πᾶς.

681 τούσδ᾽ ἔχω, τούσδ᾽ ἔμαρψα

678–9 κλῶπας οἵτινες κατ᾽ ὄρφνην τόνδε κινοῦσι στρατόν.

682 τίς ὁ λόχος; πόθεν ἔβας; ποδαπὸς εἶ;

ΟΔΥΣΣΕΥΣ

οὔ σε χρὴ εἰδέναι· θανῇ γὰρ σήμερον δράσας

κακῶς.

ΧΟΡΟΣ

οὐκ ἐρεῖς ξύνθημα, λόγχην πρὶν διὰ στέρνων

μολεῖν;

ΟΔΥΣΣΕΥΣ

685 †ἴστω. θάρσει.

ΧΟΡΟΣ

πέλας ἴθι παῖε πᾶς.†

ΟΔΥΣΣΕΥΣ

ἦ σὺ δὴ Ῥῆσον κατέκτας;

ΧΟΡΟΣ

⟨μὴ⟩ ἀλλὰ τὸν κτενοῦντά σέ.

675b ⟨θένε⟩ Diggle   680–1 post 677 trai. Diggle
678 κλῶπας Diggle: -ες C   685 nec numeris nec sensu
idoneus: fort. Οδ. ἴστ⟨ασ᾽⟩ ὦ θάρσει πελάζων. Χο. παῖε ⟨παῖε⟩
πᾶς ⟨ἀνήρ⟩   686 ⟨μὴ⟩ Dindorf

422

CHORUS

Ho, what's this?
Shoot, shoot, shoot: smite, smite, ⟨smite⟩!
Who is the man?
Look, here's the one I mean.
Over here, everyone!
I've got them, I've caught them,
these robbers, who have disturbed the army by night.
What is your company, where have you come from, what
    nation?

ODYSSEUS

None of your business. It's death for you for your foul deed
of today.

CHORUS LEADER

Tell me the watchword—before you get a spear through
your chest!

The Chorus advance menacingly.

ODYSSEUS

Stop, you that brashly advance!

CHORUS LEADER

Strike, strike him, every man!

ODYSSEUS

Aren't you the slayer of Rhesus?

CHORUS LEADER

No, of you, his intended killer.

ΟΔΥΣΣΕΥΣ

ἴσχε πᾶς τις.

ΧΟΡΟΣ

οὐ μὲν οὖν.

ΟΔΥΣΣΕΥΣ

ἆ· φίλιον ἄνδρα μὴ θένῃς.

ΧΟΡΟΣ

καὶ τί δὴ τὸ σῆμα;

ΟΔΥΣΣΕΥΣ

Φοῖβος.

ΧΟΡΟΣ

ἔμαθον· ἴσχε πᾶς δόρυ.

οἶσθ᾽ ὅποι βεβᾶσιν ἄνδρες;

ΟΔΥΣΣΕΥΣ

τῇδέ πῃ κατείδομεν.

ΧΟΡΟΣ

690 ἕρπε πᾶς κατ᾽ ἴχνος αὐτῶν· ἢ βοὴν ἐγερτέον;
ἀλλὰ συμμάχους ταράσσειν δεινὸν ἐκ νυκτῶν
      φόβῳ.

στρ.

τίς ἀνδρῶν ὁ βάς;
τίς ὁ μέγα θρασὺς ἐπεύξεται
χέρα φυγὼν ἐμάν;
695 πόθεν νιν κυρήσω;
τίνι προσεικάσω,

ODYSSEUS

Hold up!

CHORUS LEADER

We won't.

ODYSSEUS

Stop, don't strike an ally!

CHORUS LEADER

Well what is the password?

ODYSSEUS

"Phoebus."

CHORUS LEADER

I hear you. Hold your spears, everyone! Do you know
where the men have gone?

ODYSSEUS

(*pointing toward Eisodos B*) We saw them go somewhere
along this path.

CHORUS LEADER

Everyone track them down! Shall we raise a shout? No, it's
a terrible thing to alarm our allies at night.

While the CHORUS *go down Eisodos B,* ODYSSEUS *and*
DIOMEDES *slip out by Eisodos A. Reenter* CHORUS *by*
Eisodos B.

CHORUS

Who was the man who left?
What name does this brash fellow boastfully claim
who escaped my grasp?
How can I find him?
What can I guess him to be,

425

ὅστις δι' ὄρφνας ἦλθ' ἀδειμάντῳ ποδὶ
διά τε τάξεων καὶ φυλάκων ἕδρας;
Θεσσαλὸς ἢ
700 παραλίαν Λοκρῶν νεμόμενος πόλιν;
ἢ νησιώταν σποράδα κέκτηται βίον;
τίς ἦν; πόθεν; ποίας πάτρας;
ποῖον ἐπεύχεται τὸν ὕπατον θεῶν;

—ἆρ' ἔστ' Ὀδυσσέως τοὔργον ἢ τίνος τόδε;
705 εἰ τοῖς πάροιθε χρὴ τεκμαίρεσθαι· τί μήν;
—δοκεῖς γάρ;—τί μὴν οὔ;
—θρασὺς γοῦν ἐς ἡμᾶς.
—τίν' ἀλκὴν τίν' αἰνεῖς; —Ὀδυσσῆ.
—μὴ κλωπὸς αἴνει φωτὸς αἱμύλον δόρυ.

ΧΟΡΟΣ

ἀντ.

710 ἔβα καὶ πάρος
κατὰ πόλιν ὕπαφρον ὄμμ' ἔχων,
ῥακοδύτῳ στολᾷ
πυκασθείς, ξιφήρης
κρύφιος ἐν πέπλοις·
715 βίον δ' ἐπαιτῶν εἷρπ' ἀγύρτης τις λάτρις,

703 ἐπεύχεται Hermann: εὔχ- C

this man who came through the dark on fearless foot
passing through our ranks and our sentinel posts?
Is he a Thessalian,
or does he dwell in some Locrian coastal town?
Or does he live the lonely life of an islander?
Who was he? Whence come? What was his nation?
What god does he pray to as highest?

CHORUS LEADER

Isn't this Odysseus' doing? If we can judge by his earlier
exploits, it certainly is.

CHORUS MEMBER

Do you think so?

CHORUS LEADER

How can it be otherwise?

CHORUS MEMBER

Well, he *was* bold against us.

CHORUS LEADER

Whose bravery are you praising?

CHORUS MEMBER

Odysseus'.

CHORUS LEADER

Never praise the deceitful warcraft of that robber!

CHORUS

He came once before
to the city, his face disguised,
his body wrapped in a ragged cloak,
holding a sword
hid beneath his garments.
He came begging his bread, a wretched vagrant,

427

ψαφαρόχρουν κάρα πολυπινές τ' ἔχων·
πολλὰ δὲ τὰν
βασιλίδ' ἑστίαν Ἀτρειδᾶν κακῶς
ἔβαζε δῆθεν ἐχθρὸς ὢν στρατηλάταις.
720 ὄλοιτ' ὄλοιτο πανδίκως,
πρὶν ἐπὶ γᾶν Φρυγῶν ποδὸς ἴχνος βαλεῖν.

—εἴτ' οὖν Ὀδυσσέως εἴτε μή, φόβος μ' ἔχει·
Ἕκτωρ γὰρ ἡμῖν τοῖς φύλαξι μέμψεται.
—τί λάσκων;—δυσοίζων . . .
725—τί δράσας; τί ταρβεῖς;
—. . . καθ' ἡμᾶς περᾶσαι . . .—τίν' ἀνδρῶν;
—. . . οἳ τῆσδε νυκτὸς ἦλθον ἐς Φρυγῶν στρατόν.

ΗΝΙΟΧΟΣ
ἰὼ ἰώ·
δαίμονος τύχα βαρεῖα. φεῦ φεῦ.

ΧΟΡΟΣ
ἔα, ἔα·
730 σῖγα πᾶς ὕφιζ'· ἴσως γὰρ ἐς βόλον τις ἔρχεται.

725 δράσας Wilamowitz: δρᾷς C

428

his face squalid and foul,
and loudly he reviled
the royal house of the sons of Atreus,
pretending to be the generals' enemy.
How I wish he had perished as he deserves
before he set foot on the land of the Phrygians!

CHORUS LEADER

Whether it was Odysseus or not, I am afraid: Hector will
find fault with us sentries.

CHORUS MEMBER

What will he say?

CHORUS LEADER

He will complain . . .

CHORUS MEMBER

At what ill fortune? What are you afraid of?

CHORUS LEADER

. . . that it was by way of us here that they came . . .

CHORUS MEMBER

Who?

CHORUS LEADER

. . . the men who visited the Phrygian army by night.

Enter by Eisodos B the DRIVER *of Rhesus' chariot.*

DRIVER

Ah, ah!
What a heavy blow of fate: ah me!

CHORUS LEADER

But wait! Silence, everyone, hold your places! Perhaps
someone is entering our net.

ΗΝΙΟΧΟΣ

ἰὼ ἰώ·
συμφορὰ βαρεῖα Θρῃκῶν.

ΧΟΡΟΣ

συμμάχων τις ὁ στένων.

ΗΝΙΟΧΟΣ

ἰὼ ἰώ·
δύστηνος ἐγὼ σύ τ᾽, ἄναξ Θρῃκῶν·
ὦ στυγνοτάτην Τροίαν ἐσιδών,
735 οἷόν σε βίου τέλος εἷλεν.

ΧΟΡΟΣ

τίς εἶ ποτ᾽ ἀνδρῶν συμμάχων; κατ᾽ εὐφρόνην
ἀμβλῶπες αὐγαὶ κού σε γιγνώσκω τορῶς.

ΗΝΙΟΧΟΣ

ποῦ τιν᾽ ἀνάκτων Τρώων εὕρω;
ποῦ δῆθ᾽ Ἕκτωρ
740 τὸν ὑπασπίδιον κοῖτον ἰαύει;
τίνι σημήνω διόπων στρατιᾶς
οἷα πεπόνθαμεν, οἷά τις ἡμᾶς
δράσας ἀφανὴ φροῦδος, φανερὸν
Θρῃξὶν πένθος τολυπεύσας;

ΧΟΡΟΣ

745 κακὸν κυρεῖν τι Θρηκίῳ στρατεύματι
ἔοικεν, οἷα τοῦδε γιγνώσκω κλύων.

ΗΝΙΟΧΟΣ

ἔρρει στρατιά, πέπτωκεν ἄναξ
δολίῳ πληγῇ. ἆ ἆ ἆ ἆ,

RHESUS

DRIVER

Ah, ah! Heavy is the Thracians' woe!

CHORUS LEADER

The lamenter is one of our allies.

DRIVER

Ah, ah! How ill-fated am I, how ill-fated are you, king of the Thracians! How hateful the day when you looked on Troy! What a death has taken you away!

CHORUS LEADER

Which of the allies are you? My eyes cannot see well in the dark and I can't make you out clearly.

DRIVER

Where can I find one of the Trojan chiefs? Where does Hector sleep beneath his shield? To which of the army's commanders can I report what has befallen us, the stealthy hurt some man did us and escaped unseen, a man who caused the Thracians a grief all too plain to see?

CHORUS LEADER

It seems some mischief has befallen the Thracian army, to judge from this man's words.

DRIVER

Ruined is the army, fallen our lord, by a crafty blow! Ah, ah,

---

738 Τρώων Diggle: Τρωικῶν C

750 οἷα μ' ὀδύνη τείρει φονίου
τραύματος εἴσω. πῶς ἂν ὀλοίμην;
χρῆν γάρ μ' ἀκλεῶς Ῥῆσόν τε θανεῖν,
Τροίᾳ κέλσαντ' ἐπίκουρον;

ΧΟΡΟΣ

τάδ' οὐκ ἐν αἰνιγμοῖσι σημαίνει κακά·
755 σαφῶς γὰρ αὐδᾷ συμμάχους ὀλωλότας.

ΗΝΙΟΧΟΣ

κακῶς πέπρακται κἀπὶ τοῖς κακοῖσι πρὸς
αἴσχιστα· καίτοι δὶς τόσον κακὸν τόδε·
θανεῖν γὰρ εὐκλεῶς μέν, εἰ θανεῖν χρεών,
λυπρὸν μὲν οἶμαι τῷ θανόντι—πῶς γὰρ οὔ; —
760 τοῖς ζῶσι δ' ὄγκος καὶ δόμων εὐδοξία.
ἡμεῖς δ' ἀβούλως κἀκλεῶς ὀλώλαμεν.
ἐπεὶ γὰρ ἡμᾶς ηὔνασ' Ἑκτόρεια χείρ,
ξύνθημα λέξας, ηὕδομεν πεδοστιβεῖ
κόπῳ δαμέντες, οὐδ' ἐφρουρεῖτο στρατὸς
765 φυλακαῖσι νυκτέροισιν οὐδ' ἐν τάξεσιν
ἔκειτο τεύχη πλῆκτρά τ' οὐκ ἐπὶ ζυγοῖς
ἵππων καθήρμοσθ', ὡς ἄναξ ἐπεύθετο
κρατοῦντας ὑμᾶς κἀφεδρεύοντας νεῶν
πρύμναισι· φαύλως δ' ηὕδομεν πεπτωκότες.
770 κἀγὼ μελούσῃ καρδίᾳ λήξας ὕπνου
πώλοισι χόρτον, προσδοκῶν ἑωθινὴν
ζεύξειν ἐς ἀλκήν, ἀφθόνῳ μετρῶ χερί.
λεύσσω δὲ φῶτε περιπολοῦνθ' ἡμῶν στρατὸν
πυκνῆς δι' ὄρφνης· ὡς δ' ἐκινήθην ἐγώ,

ah, ah, how the pain of the wound deep within afflicts me!
Death take me! Was it fated that Rhesus and I must perish
in disgrace when we came to the aid of Troy?

CHORUS LEADER

It is in no riddling speech that he reports this disaster: he
says plainly that our allies are destroyed.

DRIVER

Disaster has struck, and over and above disaster disgrace:
that makes disaster twice as bad. To die gloriously, if die
one must, though it is of course painful for him who dies, is
a source of magnificence for the survivors and a glory to
their houses. But we perished foolishly and ingloriously.

As soon as Hector had told us the watchword and his
guiding hand found us a place to sleep, we slept, overcome
by weariness from our long march. The army did not stand
guard duty in nightly watches, nor was our armor laid out
in order or the goads set in place next to the horses' yokes,
since our king had been told that your side was victorious
and were lying in wait to attack the ship prows. So we fell
down in no order and slept. My worrying heart woke me
up, and with generous hand I laid out provender for the
horses, expecting to yoke them for tomorrow's fight. I saw
two men moving about our contingent in the deep dark. As

775 ἐπτηξάτην τε κἀνεχωρείτην πάλιν·
ἤπυσα δ' αὐτοῖς μὴ πελάζεσθαι στρατῷ,
κλῶπας δοκήσας συμμάχων πλάθειν τινάς.
οἱ δ' οὐδέν· οὐ μὴν οὐδ' ἐγὼ τὰ πλείονα.
ηὗδον δ' ἀπελθὼν αὖθις ἐς κοίτην πάλιν.

780 καί μοι καθ' ὕπνον δόξα τις παρίσταται·
ἵππους γὰρ ἃς ἔθρεψα κἀδιφρηλάτουν
Ῥήσῳ παρεστὼς εἶδον, ὡς ὄναρ δοκῶν,
λύκους ἐπεμβεβῶτας ἑδραίαν ῥάχιν·
θείνοντε δ' οὐρᾷ πωλικῆς ῥινοῦ τρίχα

785 ἤλαυνον, αἱ δ' ἔρρεγκον ἐξ ἀντηρίδων
θυμὸν πνέουσαι κἀνεχαίτιζον φόβῳ.
ἐγὼ δ' ἀμύνων θῆρας ἐξεγείρομαι
πώλοισιν· ἔννυχος γὰρ ἐξώρμα φόβος.
κλύω δ' ἐπάρας κρᾶτα μυχθισμὸν νεκρῶν.

790 θερμὸς δὲ κρουνὸς δεσπότου παρὰ σφαγῆς
βάλλει με δυσθνῄσκοντος αἵματος νέου.
ὀρθὸς δ' ἀνᾴσσω χειρὶ σὺν κενῇ δορός·
καί μ' ἔγχος αὐγάζοντα καὶ θηρώμενον
παίει παραστὰς νείραν ἐς πλευρὰν ξίφει

795 ἀνὴρ ἀκμάζων· φασγάνου γὰρ ᾐσθόμην
πληγῆς, βαθεῖαν ἄλοκα τραύματος λαβών.
πίπτω δὲ πρηνής· οἱ δ' ὄχημα πωλικὸν
λαβόντες ἵππων ἵεσαν φυγῇ πόδα.
ἆ ἆ.
ὀδύνη με τείρει, κοὐκέτ' ὀρθοῦμαι τάλας.

800 καὶ ξυμφορὰν μὲν οἶδ' ὁρῶν, τρόπῳ δ' ὅτῳ
τεθνᾶσιν οἱ θανόντες οὐκ ἔχω φράσαι,

soon as I stirred, they took fright and retreated. I shouted to them not to come near our army, supposing that some of our allies had come to rob us. They made no reply, and I said nothing further. I went back to bed and slept.

In my sleep I had a dream: I saw, as one does in a dream, the horses I reared and drove at Rhesus' side, but wolves had mounted them and were sitting on their backs, and with their tails as goads they were whipping the horses' furry hides and driving them forward. The horses snorted violently through their nostrils and reared back in terror. I roused myself to defend the horses from the wild beasts: night terror made me stir from my bed. When I raised my head I heard the moaning of men dying. A warm stream of fresh blood struck me from the slaughter of my master, who was in death's throes. I leapt up, no spear in my hand. And as I was peering around looking for my sword, a strapping fellow came at me and struck me right in the side with his sword. I felt the blow of his weapon and took a deep gash. I fell on my face, and the men took the horses and chariot and ran off.

Ah, ah! Pain wears me down and I can no longer stand upright! I know that I have seen a disaster, but how the

---

785 ἀρτηριῶν Musgrave
790 σφαγῆς Musgrave: -αῖς C
794 νεῖραν Bothe: νείαιραν C

οὐδ' ἐξ ὁποίας χειρός. εἰκάσαι δέ μοι
πάρεστι λυπρὰ πρὸς φίλων πεπονθέναι.

ΧΟΡΟΣ

ἡνίοχε Θρῃκὸς τοῦ κακῶς πεπραγότος,
805 μηδὲν δυσοίζου· πολέμιοι 'δρασαν τάδε.
Ἕκτωρ δὲ καὐτὸς συμφορᾶς πεπυσμένος
χωρεῖ· συναλγεῖ δ', ὡς ἔοικε, σοῖς κακοῖς.

ΕΚΤΩΡ

πῶς, ὦ μέγιστα πήματ' ἐξειργασμένοι,
μολόντες ὑμᾶς πολεμίων κατάσκοποι
810 λήθουσιν αἰσχρῶς καὶ κατεσφάγη στρατός,
κοὔτ' εἰσιόντας στρατόπεδ' ἐξηπύσατε
οὔτ' ἐξιόντας; τῶνδε τίς τείσει δίκην
πλὴν σοῦ; σὲ γὰρ δὴ φύλακά φημ' εἶναι στρατοῦ.
φροῦδοι δ' ἄπληκτοι, τῇ Φρυγῶν κακανδρίᾳ
815 πόλλ' ἐγγελῶντες τῷ στρατηλάτῃ τ' ἐμοί.
εὖ νυν τόδ' ἴστε—Ζεὺς ὀμώμοται πατήρ—
ἤτοι μάραγνά γ' ἢ καρανιστὴς μόρος
μένει σε δρῶντα τοιάδ', ἢ τὸν Ἕκτορα
τὸ μηδὲν εἶναι καὶ κακὸν νομίζετε.

ΧΟΡΟΣ

ἀντ.

820 ἰὼ ἰώ,
†μέγας ἐμοὶ μέγας ὦ πολίοχον κράτος,
τότ' ἄρ' ἔμολον ὅτε σοι†
ἄγγελος ἦλθον ἀμφὶ ναῦς πύρ' αἴθειν·

436

slain perished and by whose hand I cannot say. Yet I can guess that this injury was done to us by friends.

CHORUS LEADER

Driver of the unfortunate Thracian, do not distress yourself. It was the enemy who did this.

Enter HECTOR *with retinue by Eisodos B.*

And now Hector is coming, having likewise heard of this disaster. He feels pain, it would appear, at your misfortune.

HECTOR

Workers of great ruin, how could enemy spies have slipped past you to your disgrace, and the army have been put to the sword, and you raised no cry either when they entered the camp or left it? Who is going to be punished for this but you? For you, I maintain, are the men guarding the army. They have got away without a scratch, laughing loudly at the Phrygians' cowardice and at me as general. You may be quite sure—Father Zeus be my witness—that the lash or the headsman's ax awaits you for doing this, or you may consider Hector a cipher and a coward.

CHORUS

Ah, ah!
O great Hector, the city's sustaining power,
they must have come at the time when to you I came
bearing the news that they were burning watch fires near
     the ships:

---

805 πολέμιοι 'δρασαν Murray: πολεμίους δρᾶσαι C
811 ἐξηπύσατε Naber: -απώσατε C
821 μέγα σύ μοι μέγ' ὦ Nauck

ἐπεὶ ἄγρυπνον ὄμμ' ἐν εὐφρόνᾳ
825   οὔτ' ἐκοίμισ' οὔτ' ἔβριξ',
οὐ τὰς Σιμοεντιάδας παγάς· μή μοι
κότον, ὦ ἄνα, θῇς· ἀναίτιος γὰρ
πάντων πάντᾳ ἔγωγε.
εἰ δὲ χρόνῳ παρὰ καιρὸν
830   ἔργον ἢ λόγον πύθῃ, κατά με γᾶς
ζῶντα πόρευσον· οὐ παραιτοῦμαι.

ΗΝΙΟΧΟΣ
τί τοῖσδ' ἀπειλεῖς βάρβαρός τε βαρβάρου
γνώμην ὑφαιρῇ τὴν ἐμήν, πλέκων λόγους;
835   σὺ ταῦτ' ἔδρασας· οὐδέν' ἂν δεξαίμεθα
οὔθ' οἱ θανόντες οὔτ' ἂν οἱ τετρωμένοι
ἄλλον· μακροῦ γε δεῖ σε καὶ σοφοῦ λόγου,
ὅτῳ με πείσεις μὴ φίλους κατακτανεῖν,
ἵππων ἐρασθείς, ὧν ἕκατι συμμάχους
840   τοὺς σοὺς φονεύεις, πόλλ' ἐπισκήπτων μολεῖν.
ἦλθον, τεθνᾶσιν· εὐπρεπέστερον Πάρις
ξενίαν κατῄσχυν' ἢ σὺ συμμάχους κτανών.
   μὴ γάρ τι λέξῃς ὥς τις Ἀργείων μολὼν
διώλεσ' ἡμᾶς· τίς ἂν ὑπερβαλὼν λόχους
845   Τρώων ἐφ' ἡμᾶς ἦλθεν, ὥστε καὶ λαθεῖν;
σὺ πρόσθεν ἡμῶν ἦσο καὶ Φρυγῶν στρατός.
τίς οὖν τέτρωται, τίς τέθνηκε συμμάχων
τῶν σῶν, μολόντων ὧν σὺ πολεμίων λέγεις;
ἡμεῖς δὲ καὶ τετρώμεθ', οἱ δὲ μειζόνως
850   παθόντες οὐχ ὁρῶσιν ἡλίου φάος.

my wakeful eye in the night
has neither slept nor slumbered,
I swear by the springs of the Simois: do not
be angry with me, my lord, I
am guiltless in all these matters.
If in time you find anything amiss
that I have said or done,
bury me alive! I make no protest.

DRIVER

You are no more Greek than I am: why then do you deceitfully weave words, trying to weaken my accusation by threatening these men? It was you who did this: neither the dead nor the wounded will accept anyone else as the culprit. You will need a long and clever speech to persuade me that you have not slain your friends from a desire for the horses: that is why you earnestly begged your allies to come and then murdered them. They have come, and now they are dead. You have shamed the hearth of friendship more discreditably than Paris, you killer of allies!

Don't tell me that some Argive came and killed us. Who could have come through the Trojan companies to us without being seen? You and the Phrygian army were in front of us. Which of your companions in arms was wounded or killed when your so-called enemy soldiers arrived? I in fact was wounded, and others who suffered worse no longer

---

828 πάντων πάντα ἔγωγε Nauck: ἔγωγε πάντων C
844 ἂν Nauck: δ᾽ C
847 συγγενῶν Murray
849 δὲ καὶ] δ᾽ ἑκὰς Murray

ἁπλῶς δ᾽ Ἀχαιῶν οὐδέν᾽ αἰτιώμεθα.
τίς δ᾽ ἂν χαμεύνας πολεμίων κατ᾽ εὐφρόνην
Ῥῆσον μολὼν ἐξηῦρεν, εἰ μή τις θεῶν
ἔφραζε τοῖς κτανοῦσιν; οὐδ᾽ ἀφιγμένον
855 τὸ πάμπαν ᾖσαν· ἀλλὰ μηχαναὶ τάδε.

ΕΚΤΩΡ

χρόνον μὲν ἤδη συμμάχοισι χρώμεθα
ὅσονπερ ἐν γῇ τῇδ᾽ Ἀχαϊκὸς λεώς,
κοὐδὲν πρὸς αὐτῶν οἶδα πλημμελὲς κλυών·
ἐν σοὶ δ᾽ ἂν ἀρχοίμεσθα. μή μ᾽ ἔρως ἕλοι
860 τοιοῦτος ἵππων ὥστ᾽ ἀποκτείνειν φίλους.
καὶ ταῦτ᾽ Ὀδυσσεύς· τίς γὰρ ἄλλος ἄν ποτε
ἔδρασεν ἢ ᾽βούλευσεν Ἀργείων ἀνήρ;
δέδοικα δ᾽ αὐτὸν καί τί μου θράσσει φρένας,
μὴ καὶ Δόλωνα συντυχὼν κατέκτανεν·
865 χρόνον γὰρ ἤδη φροῦδος ὢν οὐ φαίνεται.

ΗΝΙΟΧΟΣ

οὐκ οἶδα τοὺς σοὺς οὓς λέγεις Ὀδυσσέας·
ἡμεῖς δ᾽ ὑπ᾽ ἐχθρῶν οὐδενὸς πεπλήγμεθα.

ΕΚΤΩΡ

σὺ δ᾽ οὖν νόμιζε ταῦτ᾽, ἐπείπερ σοι δοκεῖ.

ΗΝΙΟΧΟΣ

ὦ γαῖα πατρίς, πῶς ἂν ἐνθάνοιμί σοι;

ΕΚΤΩΡ

870 μὴ θνῇσχ᾽· ἅλις γὰρ τῶν τεθνηκότων ὄχλος.

ΗΝΙΟΧΟΣ

ποῖ δὴ τράπωμαι δεσποτῶν μονούμενος;

see the light of day. I tell you bluntly: we blame no Greek.
What enemy in the night could have come and found the
bed of Rhesus unless we suppose some god told the killers
where to look? They did not even know that he had
arrived. This is just your machination.

HECTOR

I have had allies the whole time the Achaean army has
been in this land, and I am sure none of them has accused
me of any wrongdoing: your accusation is the first. May I
never have such a strong desire for horses that I kill my
friends! This is Odysseus' doing: what other Greek could
have planned or done this deed? And I am very worried
and upset that he may have run into Dolon and killed him.
He has been gone a long time, and there is no sign of him.

DRIVER

I know nothing of these "Odysseuses" you speak of. We
were not struck by an enemy hand.

HECTOR

Go on thinking that if you like.

DRIVER

O native land, how I wish I could die in you!

HECTOR

Don't die: enough are dead already.

DRIVER

Where can I turn, deprived of my master?

---

864 κατέκτανεν Matthiae: κατακτάνῃ C

ΕΚΤΩΡ

οἶκός σε κεύθων οὑμὸς ἐξιάσεται.

ΗΝΙΟΧΟΣ

καὶ πῶς με κηδεύσουσιν αὐθεντῶν χέρες;

ΕΚΤΩΡ

ὅδ᾽ αὖ τὸν αὐτὸν μῦθον οὐ λήξει λέγων;

ΗΝΙΟΧΟΣ

875 ὄλοιθ᾽ ὁ δράσας. οὐ γὰρ ἐς σὲ τείνεται
γλῶσσ᾽, ὡς σὺ κομπεῖς· ἡ Δίκη δ᾽ ἐπίσταται.

ΕΚΤΩΡ

λάζυσθ᾽· ἄγοντες ⟨δ᾽⟩ αὐτὸν ἐς δόμους ἐμούς,
οὕτως ὅπως ἂν μὴ ᾽γκαλῇ πορσύνετε·
ὑμᾶς δ᾽ ἰόντας τοῖσιν ἐν τείχει χρεὼν
880 Πριάμῳ τε καὶ γέρουσι σημῆναι νεκροὺς
θάπτειν κελεύθου λεωφόρου πρὸς ἐκτροπάς.

ΧΟΡΟΣ

τί ποτ᾽ εὐτυχίας ἐκ τῆς μεγάλης
Τροίαν ἀνάγει πάλιν ἐς πένθη
δαίμων ἄλλος, τί φυτεύων;
885 ἔα ἔα.
τίς ὑπὲρ κεφαλῆς θεός, ὦ βασιλεῦ,
τὸν νεόκμητον νεκρὸν ἐν χειροῖν
φοράδην πέμπει;
ταρβῶ λεύσσων τόδε πῆμα.

877 ⟨δ᾽⟩ Morstadt
881 κελεύθου Dobree: κελεύειν C

442

RHESUS

HECTOR

My house shall take you in and heal you.

DRIVER

How can the hands of those who have killed my kin take care of me?

HECTOR

Won't this man stop saying the same thing?

DRIVER

A curse on the slayer! It is no mere word I have launched against you, as you disdainfully suppose: Justice knows who is responsible.

HECTOR

(*to his retinue*) Seize him! Bring him to my house and there give him such treatment as he shall not find fault with!

Exit DRIVER, *supported by some of Hector's retinue, by Eisodos B.*

(*to the Chorus*) You must go and tell those on the wall, Priam and the elders, to bury the dead where the highway leaves the city.

CHORUS LEADER

Why does some divinity bring Troy from great success back to grief? What is he bringing to pass?

The Chorus, starting to go down Eisodos B, are checked by the entrance of the MUSE *on the* mechane. *She holds the body of Rhesus in her arms.*

My lord, what goddess above our heads is carrying in her arms a newly slain corpse? As I look at this woe I feel fear.

ΜΟΥΣΑ

890 ὁρᾶν πάρεστι, Τρῶες· ἡ γὰρ ἐν σοφοῖς
τιμὰς ἔχουσα Μοῦσα συγγόνων μία
πάρειμι, παῖδα τόνδ᾽ ὁρῶσ᾽ οἰκτρῶς φίλον
θανόνθ᾽ ὑπ᾽ ἐχθρῶν· ὅν ποθ᾽ ὁ κτείνας χρόνῳ
δόλιος Ὀδυσσεὺς ἀξίαν τείσει δίκην.

στρ.

895 ἰαλέμῳ αὐθιγενεῖ,
τέκνον, σ᾽ ὀλοφύρομαι, ὦ
ματρὸς ἄλγος, οἵαν
ἔκελσας ὁδὸν ποτὶ Τροίαν·
ἦ δυσδαίμονα καὶ μελέαν,
900 ἀπὸ μὲν φαμένας ἐμοῦ πορευθείς,
ἀπὸ δ᾽ ἀντομένου πατρὸς βιαίως.
ὤμοι ἐγὼ σέθεν, ὦ φιλία
φιλία κεφαλά, τέκνον, ὤμοι.

ΧΟΡΟΣ

ὅση προσήκει μὴ γένους κοινωνίαν
905 ἔχοντι λύπῃ τὸν σὸν οἰκτίρω γόνον.

ΜΟΥΣΑ

ἀντ.

ὄλοιτο μὲν Οἰνείδας,
ὄλοιτο δὲ Λαρτιάδας,
ὅς μ᾽ ἄπαιδα γέννας
ἔθηκεν ἀριστοτόκοιο·
910 ἅ θ᾽ Ἕλλανα λιποῦσα δόμον
Φρυγίων λεχέων πλεοῦσ᾽ ἐπλάθη,

MUSE

Do not be afraid to look, Trojans: I am she whom bards
honor, the Muse, one of the sisters, and I have come since I
saw my dear son here pitiably slain by his enemies. And
his killer, the crafty Odysseus, will one day be fittingly
punished.

With lamentation of native strain
I weep for you, my child,
cause of a mother's grief:
what a journey it was you took to Troy!
Ah, a luckless and miserable one it was
as you set out with me dissuading you
and your father pleading with every constraint for you to
    stay.
Ah, I grieve for you,
dear, dear child, ah ah!

CHORUS LEADER

With such grief as befits one unrelated by blood, I lament
for your son.

MUSE

A curse on the son of Oeneus,
and on the son of Laertes,
who made me childless and killed
my noble son!
A curse on her too who left her home in Greece
and sailed off to lie in a Phrygian bed,

---

900 ἀπὸ μὲν φαμένας Dindorf: ἀπομεμφομένας vel -μεμ-
ψαμένας vel -πεμψαμένας C   904 ὅσῃ Wecklein: ὅσον C
910 Ἕλλανα Badham: Ἐλένα C
911 πλέουσ᾽ ἐπλάθη Kovacs: ἔπλευσα πλαθεῖσ᾽ C

ὅπου ὤλεσε μὲν σ' ἕκατι Τροίας,
φίλτατε, μυριάδας τε πόλεις
ἀνδρῶν ἀγαθῶν ἐκένωσεν.

915 ἦ πολλὰ μὲν ζῶν, πολλὰ δ' εἰς Ἅιδου μολών,
Φιλάμμονος παῖ, τῆς ἐμῆς ἥψω φρενός·
ὕβρις γάρ, ἥ σ' ἔσφηλε, καὶ Μουσῶν ἔρις
τεκεῖν μ' ἔθηκε τόνδε δύστηνον γόνον.
περῶσα γὰρ δὴ ποταμίους διὰ ῥοὰς
920 λέκτροις ἐπλάθην Στρυμόνος φυταλμίοις,
ὅτ' ἤλθομεν γῆς χρυσόβωλον ἐς λέπας
Πάγγαιον ὀργάνοισιν ἐξησκημέναι
Μοῦσαι μεγίστην εἰς ἔριν μελῳδίας
κλεινῷ σοφιστῇ Θρῃκὶ κἀκτυφλώσαμεν
925 Θάμυριν, ὃς ἡμῶν πόλλ' ἐδέννασεν τέχνην.
    κἀπεὶ σὲ τίκτω, συγγόνους αἰδουμένη
καὶ παρθενείαν, ἧκ' ἐς εὐύδρου πατρὸς
δίνας· τρέφειν δέ σ' οὐ βρότειον ἐς χέρα
Στρυμὼν δίδωσιν ἀλλὰ πηγαίαις κόραις.
930 ἔνθ' ἐκτραφεὶς κάλλιστα παρθένων ὕπο,
Θρῄκης ἀνάσσων πρῶτος ἦσθ' ἀνδρῶν, τέκνον.
καί σ' ἀμφὶ γῆν μὲν πατρίαν φιλαιμάτους
ἀλκὰς κορύσσοντ' οὐκ ἐδείμαινον θανεῖν·
Τροίας δ' ἀπηύδων ἄστυ μὴ κέλσαι ποτέ,
935 εἰδυῖα τὸν σὸν πότμον· ἀλλά σ' Ἕκτορος
πρεσβεύμαθ' αἵ τε μυρίαι γερουσίαι
ἔπεισαν ἐλθεῖν κἀπικουρῆσαι φίλοις.

where for Troy's sake she destroyed you,
dearest son, and bereft countless cities
of brave warriors.

O son of Philammon,[20] both while you lived and when you
had died you have wounded my heart deeply! The inso-
lence that was your undoing and your challenging of the
Muses caused me to give birth to this poor son of mine. For
as I passed through the streams of the Strymon, I found
myself in the god's bed of love: this was when we Muses
came to Mount Pangaeon, rich in gold, equipped with our
instruments to join in high contest of minstrelsy with the
famous Thracian singer Thamyris. Him we blinded in re-
quital for his many insults against our artistry.

When I had given birth to you, I felt shame before my
sisters because I was unwed and cast you, my son, into the
eddies of your watery father. And the Strymon gave you to
no mortal hand to raise but to the nymphs of the spring.
When you had been well brought up by these maidens, you
were the first of men, my son, as king over the Thracians. I
had no fear for your death when you were marshaling
bloody battles in defense of your country. Yet I warned you
never to go to the city of Troy since I knew your fate. But
messages from Hector and repeated visits of ambassadors
persuaded you to come to the aid of your friends.

20 Thamyris, a singer who challenged the Muses and was pun-
ished.

---

912 ὅπου Wilamowitz: ὑπ᾽ Ἰλίῳ C
924 κλεινῷ Dobree: κείνῳ C: δεινῷ Valckenaer

καὶ τοῦτ', Ἀθάνα, παντὸς αἰτία μόρου—
οὐδὲν δ' Ὀδυσσεὺς οὐδ' ὁ Τυδέως τόκος
940 ἔδρασ'—ἔδρασας· μὴ δόκει λεληθέναι.
καίτοι πόλιν σὴν σύγγονοι πρεσβεύομεν
Μοῦσαι μάλιστα κἀπιχρώμεθα χθονί,
μυστηρίων τε τῶν ἀπορρήτων φανὰς
ἔδειξεν Ὀρφεύς, αὐτανέψιος νεκροῦ
945 τοῦδ' ὃν κατέκτεινας σύ· Μουσαῖόν τε, σὸν
σεμνὸν πολίτην κἀπὶ πλεῖστον ἄνδρ' ἕνα
ἐλθόντα, Φοῖβος σύγγονοί τ' ἠσκήσαμεν.
καὶ τῶνδε μισθὸν παῖδ' ἔχουσ' ἐν ἀγκάλαις
θρηνῶ· σοφιστὴν δ' ἄλλον οὐκ ἐπάξομαι.

ΧΟΡΟΣ

950 μάτην ἄρ' ἡμᾶς Θρήκιος τροχηλάτης
ἐδέννασ', Ἕκτορ, τῷδε βουλεῦσαι φόνον.

ΕΚΤΩΡ

ἤδη τάδ'· οὐδὲν μάντεων ἔδει φράσαι
Ὀδυσσέως τέχναισι τόνδ' ὀλωλότα.
ἐγὼ δὲ γῆς ἔφεδρον Ἑλλήνων στρατὸν
955 λεύσσων, τί μὴν ἔμελλον οὐ πέμψειν φίλοις
κήρυκας, ἐλθεῖν κἀπικουρῆσαι χθονί;
ἔπεμψ'· ὀφείλων δ' ἦλθε συμπονεῖν ἐμοί.
οὐ μὴν θανόντι γ' οὐδαμῶς συνήδομαι.
καὶ νῦν ἕτοιμος τῷδε καὶ τεῦξαι τάφον
960 καὶ ξυμπυρῶσαι μυρίαν πέπλων χλιδήν·
φίλος γὰρ ἐλθὼν δυστυχῶς ἀπέρχεται.

And you, Athena, cause of this whole disaster, this is your doing (for neither Odysseus nor the son of Tydeus are the doers): do not suppose you can escape detection. And yet my sister Muses and I honor and visit your city beyond all others, and it was Orpheus who revealed to it your unutterable mysteries, Orpheus, full cousin to the dead man here, the one you murdered. And Musaeus, your august fellow citizen,[21] the world's supreme artist, was trained by Phoebus and us. As thanks for this I sing a dirge with my son in my arms: I need call in no other singer for this.

CHORUS LEADER

Hector, the Thracian chariot driver's charges that we plotted this man's death are, it seems, groundless.

HECTOR

I knew this: it needed no seer to tell us that this man was killed by the devices of Odysseus.

As for me, when I saw the Greek army encamped against the land, how could I keep from sending heralds to my friends, asking them come help the country? I sent them, and he, being obliged to help me, came. But I do not take any pleasure in his death. And now I am ready to bury him and to make a vast and luxurious burnt offering of garments. For he came in friendship and leaves in disaster.

---

21 Musaeus, pupil of Orpheus, was regarded in some sources as an Athenian.

---

938 τοῦτ᾽ Paley: τοῦδ᾽ C
950 τροχηλάτης Valckenaer: στρατηλάτης C
960 μυρίαν Wecklein: -ίων C

ΜΟΥΣΑ

οὐκ εἰσι γαίας ἐς μελάγχιμον πέδον·
τοσόνδε νύμφην τὴν ἔνερθ' αἰτήσομαι,
τῆς καρποποιοῦ παῖδα Δήμητρος θεᾶς,
965 ψυχὴν ἀνεῖναι τοῦδ'· ὀφειλέτις δέ μοι
τοὺς Ὀρφέως τιμῶσα φαίνεσθαι φίλους.
κἀμοὶ μὲν ὡς θανών τε κοὐ λεύσσων φάος
ἔσται τὸ λοιπόν· οὐ γὰρ ἐς ταὐτόν ποτε
ἔτ' εἶσιν οὐδὲ μητρὸς ὄψεται δέμας·
970 κρυπτὸς δ' ἐν ἄντροις τῆς ὑπαργύρου χθονὸς
ἀνθρωποδαίμων κείσεται βλέπων φάος,
Βάκχου προφήτης, ὅς γε Παγγαίου πέτραν
ᾤκησε, σεμνὸς τοῖσιν εἰδόσιν θεός.

ῥᾷον δὲ πένθος τῆς θαλασσίας θεοῦ
975 οἴσω· θανεῖν γὰρ καὶ τὸν ἐκ κείνης χρεών.
θρήνοις δ' ἀδελφαὶ πρῶτα μὲν σ' ὑμνήσομεν,
ἔπειτ' Ἀχιλλέα Θέτιδος ἐν πένθει ποτέ.
οὐ ῥύσεταί νιν Παλλάς, ἤ σ' ἀπέκτανεν·
τοῖον φαρέτρα Λοξίου σῴζει βέλος.
980 ὦ παιδοποιοὶ συμφοραί, πόνοι βροτῶν·
ὡς ὅστις ὑμᾶς μὴ κακῶς λογίζεται,
ἄπαις διοίσει κοὐ τεκὼν θάψει τέκνα.

ΧΟΡΟΣ

οὗτος μὲν ἤδη μητρὶ κηδεύειν μέλει·

969 ἔτ' . . . οὐδὲ Kirchhoff: οὔτ' . . . οὔτε C
972 ὅς γε Matthiae: ὅς τε vel ὥστε C

MUSE

He will not go down into the black earth: I will make this request of the maid below, the daughter of fruitful Demeter,[22] that she send up his soul. She is under obligation to me to show that she honors the kinsmen of Orpheus. For me, he will be henceforth as one who has died and looks no more on the light: we shall never meet and he will never see his mother. But he shall lie hidden in the caves of the silver-rich land as a man-god, looking on the light, a spokesman of Bacchus, who came to dwell in the cliff of Pangaeon as a god revered by those who have understanding.

I shall bear my grief more easily than will the sea goddess:[23] for it is fated that *her* son too must die. My sisters and I shall first hymn you with lamentations and afterwards will hymn Achilles on Thetis' day of sorrow. Pallas, who killed you, will not be able to save him, such is the arrow Loxias' quiver contains.

What troubles, what disasters mortals have in bearing children! Anyone who calculates them properly will spend his life childless, not beget them only to bury them!

Exit MUSE *by the* mechane.

CHORUS LEADER

It is his mother's duty to mourn for this man. But you, Hec-

---

22 Persephone, wife of Hades and queen of the Underworld.
23 Thetis, the mother of Achilles.

σὺ δ' εἴ τι πράσσειν τῶν προκειμένων θέλεις,
985 Ἕκτορ, πάρεστι· φῶς γὰρ ἡμέρας τόδε.

ΕΚΤΩΡ

χωρεῖτε, συμμάχους δ' ὁπλίζεσθαι τάχος
ἄνωχθε πληροῦν τ' αὐχένας ξυνωρίδων.
πανοὺς δ' ἔχοντας χρὴ μένειν Τυρσηνικῆς
σάλπιγγος αὐδήν· ὡς ὑπερβαλὼν τάφρον
990 τείχη τ' Ἀχαιῶν ναυσὶν αἶθον ἐμβαλεῖν
πέποιθα Τρωσί θ' ἡμέραν ἐλευθέραν
ἀκτῖνα τὴν στείχουσαν ἡλίου φέρειν.

ΧΟΡΟΣ

πείθου βασιλεῖ· στείχωμεν ὅπλοις
κοσμησάμενοι καὶ ξυμμαχίᾳ
995 τάδε φράζωμεν· τάχα δ' ἂν νίκην
δοίη δαίμων ὁ μεθ' ἡμῶν.

HYPOTHESIS II

τοῦτο τὸ δρᾶμα ἔνιοι νόθον ὑπενόησαν, Εὐριπίδου δὲ
μὴ εἶναι· τὸν γὰρ Σοφόκλειον μᾶλλον ὑποφαίνειν
χαρακτῆρα. ἐν μέντοι ταῖς διδασκαλίαις ὡς γνήσιον
ἀναγέγραπται, καὶ ἡ περὶ τὰ μετάρσια δὲ ἐν αὐτῷ
πολυπραγμοσύνη τὸν Εὐριπίδην ὁμολογεῖ. πρόλογοι
δὲ διττοὶ φέρονται. ὁ γοῦν Δικαίαρχος [fr. 81 Wehrli]

988 πανοὺς Reiske: πόνους C
989 τάφρον Jacobs: στρατὸν C

tor, if you desire to accomplish anything that must be done, we are at your service: day is now dawning.

HECTOR

Go, order the allies to quickly arm themselves and harness their horses. They must wait, torches in hand, for the blowing of the Etruscan trumpet. I am confident that when I have crossed the ditch and the Achaean stockades I will set fire to their ships, and that this day's dawn will bring to the Trojans a day of liberty.

Exit HECTOR by Eisodos A.

CHORUS LEADER

Do as our king says! Let us arm ourselves and set off to carry this order to our allies. Perhaps the god who is on our side will grant us victory.

Exit CHORUS by Eisodos A.

HYPOTHESIS II[24]

Some have supposed that this play is spurious and not a work of Euripides since it shows more the stamp of Sophocles. But it is listed as a genuine work of his in the *Didascaliai*, and furthermore the preoccupation with celestial phenomena betrays his hand. Two prologues are

---

[24] This is one of three "hypotheses" or plot summaries prefixed to the play in our medieval manuscripts.

ἐκτιθεὶς τὴν ὑπόθεσιν τοῦ ῾Ρήσου γράφει κατὰ λέξιν
οὕτως [fr. 1108 Nauck]·

Νῦν εὐσέληνον φέγγος ἡ διφρήλατος.

καὶ ἐν ἐνίοις δὲ τῶν ἀντιγράφων ἕτερός τις φέρεται
πρόλογος, πεζὸς πάνυ καὶ οὐ πρέπων Εὐριπίδῃ· καὶ
τάχα ἄν τινες τῶν ὑποκριτῶν διεσκευακότες εἶεν
αὐτόν. ἔχει δὲ οὕτως [fr. 1109 Nauck=TrGF adesp. F 81]:

<ΗΡΑ>

᾿Ω τοῦ μεγίστου Ζηνὸς ἄλκιμον τέκος
Παλλάς, τί δρῶμεν; οὐκ ἐχρῆν ἡμᾶς ἔτι
μέλλειν Ἀχαιῶν ὠφελεῖν στρατεύματα.
νῦν γὰρ κακῶς πράσσουσιν ἐν μάχῃ δορός,
λόγχῃ βιαίως ῞Εκτορος στροβούμενοι.
ἐμοὶ γὰρ οὐδέν ἐστιν ἄλγιον βάρος,
ἐξ οὗ γ᾿ ἔκρινε Κύπριν Ἀλέξανδρος θεὰν
κάλλει προήκειν τῆς ἐμῆς εὐμορφίας
καὶ σῆς, Ἀθάνα, φιλτάτης ἐμοὶ θεῶν,
εἰ μὴ κατασκαφεῖσαν ὄψομαι πόλιν
Πριάμου, βίᾳ πρόρριζον ἐκτετριμμένην.

6 ἀλγέων ἄκος Kirchhoff: sed fort. praestat lac. ante 10
indicare, e.g. <κἀγὼ τὸ μηδὲν κοὐ θεὸς κεκλήσομαι>

current. At any rate Dicaearchus in setting forth the plot of *Rhesus* cites as follows:

> Now the chariot-driven <Dawn is about to banish
> . . . > the moon's fair light.[25]

And in some copies another prologue is current, very prosy and unworthy of Euripides; perhaps some actors created it. It runs as follows:

<HERA>

Pallas, mighty daughter of great Zeus, what are we doing?[26] We ought not to be slow any longer to help the Achaean army. For they are now faring badly in the battle, being violently distressed by Hector's spear. There will be no heavier grief that has befallen me—ever since Alexandros judged that Aphrodite was superior in beauty to me and to you, dearest of gods to me—than if I fail to see Priam's city smashed utterly to pieces by force and its foundations dug up.

25 The content of the second line, which would have corresponded to the words in angle brackets, is purely conjectural, but the feminine noun going with $\delta\iota\phi\rho\eta\lambda\alpha\tau\sigma$ cannot be $\sigma\epsilon\lambda\eta\nu\eta$ with $\epsilon\upsilon\sigma\epsilon\lambda\eta\nu\sigma\nu$ in line 1 and is probably Ἡώς (Dawn). The only action Dawn can perform on the fair light of the moon is to banish it, but since the action of the play is at night, we cannot have the banishing occurring "now," hence my "is about to."

26 Or "what shall we do?"